Arctic Ocean

YO-CXH-111

ASIA

Pacific Ocean

EUROPE

⑧ Petrograd

• Warsaw

Mediterranean S.

CHINA

INDIA

Arabian Sea

• Bombay

⑨

④

Congo R.

⑤

Sumatra

Madagascar

Mauritius I.

Indian

Ocean

⑯ Formosa I.

China Sea

Bangkok

Philippine Is.

⑫ G. of Siam

⑪ ⑬ Borneo ⑭

⑮ Celebes

EAST INDIES

⑰

New Guinea

⑱

+ Java

AUSTRALIA

Adelaide

Melbourne

Tasmania

③ ➔ Sydney

New Zealand

Cape of Good Hope

AN INTRODUCTION TO CONRAD

THE *TORRENS*

AN INTRODUCTION TO

CONRAD

By FRANK W. CUSHWA

Late Odlin Professor of English
Phillips Exeter Academy

THE ODYSSEY PRESS

NEW YORK

PREFACE

"I am sufficient of a democrat to detest the idea of being a writer to any 'coterie' of some small self-appointed aristocracy in the vast domain of art or letters. As a matter of feeling—not as a matter of business—I want to be read by many eyes and by all kinds of them at that."—This book is intended to forward this high ambition of Conrad.

But Conrad is not a writer who can be read at random by all kinds of readers. It is no injustice to him to say that some of his books would puzzle or chill the uninitiated; when, for example, he seems intent on telling everything but the story. Conrad, then, if he is to be read "by many eyes and by all kinds of them," must be judiciously introduced.

This *Introduction* aims to present those parts of Conrad's writings in which the appeal is fairly sure and universal. One part is fiction; the other part, which is the larger, is made up of his own account and interpretation of various incidents in his amazing career. Without a knowledge—even an understanding—of the man, it is impossible to read his works aright. But once knowing the man—his career and character—one is impelled to read on and on.

This book is, in a way, a joint product. In the choice of what had best go into it, I freely consulted my colleagues, who for some years had used Conrad in their classes at Exeter. Mr. Myron R. Williams, Mr. G. L. Richardson, Jr., Dr. Chilson H. Leonard, and Mr. George E. Bennett have given me valuable assistance, Mr. Bennett supplying me with much of the introduction to Conrad's fiction. The students themselves have also had a part in the making of the book.

To Conrad's literary agents, James B. Pinker and Son, and to Doubleday, Doran & Company, Inc., Conrad's American publishers, I am grateful not only for permission to make selections from all the Conrad material, but also for much helpful constructive criticism.

Without the scholarly biography of M. Jean-Aubry, *Joseph Conrad: Life and Letters,* I should have been greatly handicapped; in the preparation of the chronological table and elsewhere, I felt that I could rely completely on this painstaking book. The table of references and the editor's notes will show how much I have drawn from the works of George B. Keating, Gustav Morf, Richard Curle, Edward Garnett, R. L. Mégroz, and others. To all I am grateful.

F. W. C.

Exeter, New Hampshire
March, 1933

CONTENTS

Chronological Table of Conrad's Life and Works   ix

Part I—Autobiography

                                                            PAGE

Introduction to Autobiography   1

The Polish Heritage and Boyhood   3

   The Father   4

   The Mother   10

   Eating a Dog—Pro Patria   13

   Prince Roman's Visit: an Early Disillusionment . .   16

   Militant Geography   20

   Summary of Education   24

   The Desire and the Decision to Go to Sea   25

The Seaman   31

   First Experiences on Salt Water   31

   The *Tremolino*   34

   Signing On   61

   Ships and Shipmasters   64

      Initiation   64

      Meretricious Glory   74

      A Deaf Man vs. an Angry One   77

      The Ship We Serve   79

      A Ship Is Not a Slave   83

   Youth   87

   The Era of Examinations   124

   First Command (from *The Shadow Line*) . . .   133

   Torres Strait   183

                                                          PAGE
The Congo 187
The *Torrens:* Experiences with Passengers . . . 201
The Writer 206
  "English—The Speech of My Secret Choice" . . 207
  The First Book (*Almayer's Folly*) 210
    The Man Almayer 211
    The First Reader of *Almayer's Folly* 217
  "Why Not Write Another?" 220
  Henceforth to Be a Writer 222
  The Artist's Creed (Being the Preface to *The Nigger
    of the "Narcissus"*) 223
  The Writer at Work 227
  The Writer Caught in the Exercise of His Craft . 230
  The Origin of a Heroine 236
  Verdicts and Rebuttals 238
    The Romantic Feeling of Reality 240
    Sea Stuff 242
    The Artist and Mankind 243

Part II—Conrad's Fiction

Introduction to Conrad's Fiction 249
The Lagoon 255
The Secret Sharer 271
Typhoon 320

Appendix

  For Further Study 411
  Suggestions for Further Reading 421
  Table of References 425
  Glossary 429

CHRONOLOGICAL TABLE OF CONRAD'S LIFE AND WORKS

(All references are to pages in this volume.)

1856   Apollo Nalecz Korzeniowski, aged 36 (from a good family on his father's side and of good Lithuanian stock, the Dyakewicz, on his mother's side), marries Evelina Bobrowska, aged 25 (of a family of landowners), at Oratow, in Podolia, one of the southern provinces of Poland under Russian rule. (See pp. 3–4.)

1857   Their only child, Joseph Theodor Konrad Nalecz Korzeniowski, born December 3 at Berdiczew.

1862   Failing in managing an estate in Podolia, parents move to Warsaw. Father is condemned to exile for helping to organize the secret Polish National Committee. (See pp. 4–6.) Mother allowed, at her request, to accompany husband in exile. (See p. 11.)

1863   Insurrection of Poles crushed. Conrad's uncle Robert killed fighting; his uncle Hilary sent to Siberia. His mother allowed three months' leave, with her son, at her brother's estate at Nowofastow. (See pp. 11–13.)

1865   Joseph's mother dies. Father and son dependent on mother's brother, Thaddeus Bobrowski.

1866   Conrad sent to his uncle in Nowofastow in Polish Ukraine for health and companionship.

1867   At Kiev; later again at Nowofastow.

1868   Father allowed to live in Lemberg, Galicia; Conrad sent to Polish high school.

1869   Both move to Cracow; Conrad sent to preparatory school. (See pp. 8–9.) Father dies, May 23. (See pp. 9–10.) At St. Anne High School, Cracow. (See pp. 24–25; 209.)

1870   Grandmother Bobrowska and Count Ladislas Mniszek appointed Conrad's guardians. For four years his studies supervised by a tutor, Mr. Pulman, a student in the University of Cracow.

1872   To honor the memory of his father, Cracow gives Conrad freedom of the city, exempt from tax. He confides to his uncle Thaddeus his desire to be a sailor. (See pp. 25–27.)

1873   While on vacation with Mr. Pulman in Switzerland, becomes more determined to go to sea. (See pp. 27–30.)

1874   "Polish days" are over; enters French marine service. First whole day on salt water. Impressions used in *The Mirror of the Sea*. (See pp. 31–34.)

1875   Apprenticeship on the *Mont-Blanc,* a three-masted vessel of 394 tons bound for Martinique. Impressions used in *The Arrow of Gold*.

1876   From January to July at Marseilles; lives a free life in the company of pilots, in the cafés and at the operas.

1876–7   From July on, on schooner *Saint-Antoine* on West Indies voyage. Among the crew is Dominic Cervoni, used directly in *The Mirror of the Sea* and in *The Arrow of Gold;* indirectly as Jean Peyrol, "an old Dominic" (*The Rover*); as Nostromo (*Nostromo*); as Attilio (*Suspense*); and more subtly as Tom Lingard (*Almayer's Folly, An Outcast of the Islands, The Rescue*). Expedition furnishes substance of plot of *Nostromo*. (See pp. 229–230.)

1877   Buys, with three other young men, a sixty-ton *tartane,* the *Tremolino*—Dominic as *padrone*—plying between Marseilles and the Spanish coast, carrying arms illegally for the Carlists. To escape Spanish coast guards they destroy the vessel by driving it against the rocks. Basis of "The *Tremolino*" in *The Mirror of the Sea* (see pp. 34–61) and *The Arrow of Gold*.

1878   After an unhappy ending to a love affair and after a duel with J. M. K. Blunt, leaves Marseilles on English steamer *Mavis,* bound for Constantinople, and arrives at Lowestoft, June 18, for the first time touching English soil. On coaster *The Skimmer of the Seas,* where he begins to learn English. (See pp. 208–209.)

1878–9   Ordinary seaman on "wool clipper" *Duke of Sutherland,* London to Australia. A negro called James Wait, a member of the crew, provides the name for the "Nigger" in *The Nigger of the "Narcissus."* (See p. 222.)

1879–80 On *Europa,* a London steamship bound for Mediterranean.

1880   In June passed examination as third mate. (See pp. 124–127.) Experience is used in *Chance*.

1880–1   Third mate on sailing ship *Loch-Etive,* London to Sydney. Experience used in *The Mirror of the Sea*. (See pp. 77–79.)

1881–3   On *Anna Frost*. On September 21, 1881, sails as second mate on the *Palestine,* a London barque of 425 tons. Crew and incidents used in *Youth* wherein the ship, however, is called the *Judea*. (See pp. 87–124.)

1883   July 4, passes mate's examination. (See pp. 127–130.) At Marienbad with uncle, not having seen him for five years. September 10, embarks as mate on sailing ship *Riversdale,* bound for Madras—a voyage suggesting some scenes in *Ferndale* episodes in *Chance*.

1884   After dispute with captain of the *Riversdale,* leaves the ship at Madras, and, on April 28, becomes second mate on the graceful sailing ship *Narcissus,* from Bombay to Dunkirk. Most of the characters in *The Nigger of the "Narcissus"* belong to the crew.

1885–6   After passing the winter at London, leaves Hull as second mate on the *Tilkhurst,* a London sailing ship, Hull to Cardiff, Cardiff to Singapore. The captain is "poor Captain B——" in *The Mirror of the Sea*. August 19, 1886, obtains British certificate of naturalization; November 11, passes his examination and obtains his "Certificate of Competency as Master" (see pp. 130–133); submits a story called "The Black Mate" in a prize competition by *Tït-Bits*—his first attempt at writing a story in English.

1887   First mate on *Highland Forest,* a Glasgow sailing vessel, for Java. The captain is the prototype of Captain John MacWhirr of *Typhoon*. Is injured and leaves the ship at Singapore.

1887–8   Second mate on steamship *Vidar,* Singapore to Borneo. From these voyages up the rivers and on the wild coasts of Borneo, Celebes, and Sumatra, carries away into his writing life the greatest number of suggestions: sees there Almayer (see pp. 210–216); sees also Willems, Abdulla, Babalatchi, Lakamba, and Tom and Jim Lingard, characters who figure in *Almayer's Folly, An Outcast of the Islands, The Rescue, Lord Jim*; absorbs Malayan local color for such stories as *Karain* and *The Lagoon*. On *Vidar* serves in his spare minutes his first apprenticeship as a writer.

1888 Leaves *Vidar* at Singapore, January 5 (see pp. 133–137); goes on *Melita* to Bangkok (see pp. 141–149); unexpectedly appointed to command the barque *Otago*, Bangkok to Sydney to Mauritius. *The Shadow Line* is "an exact autobiography" of Conrad's "first command." (See "First Command," pp. 133–183.) At Bangkok meets hotelkeeper Schomberg, who appears in *Falk* and *Victory*. Torres Strait episode (see pp. 183–187) in "Geography and Some Explorers," *Last Essays*. Other experiences used in *The Secret Sharer, A Smile of Fortune,* and *The Mirror of the Sea*.

1889 Resigns command of the *Otago* at Port Adelaide, ending his connection with the East, and returns to England. While at leisure in London begins writing *Almayer's Folly*. Events of this period related in *A Personal Record*.

1890 Visits Poland first time since 1874. Passenger to the Congo. Second in command, and finally in command, of a small river steamer, *Roi des Belges*, on the uncharted banks of the Congo near Stanley Falls. Experiences form basis of *The Heart of Darkness* (see pp. 187–201) and *An Outpost of Progress*.

1891 Returns to Europe with health much impaired, necessitating a year of leisure. After nearly two years' absence from the sea, signs on as second in command of the *Torrens*—used in *Last Essays*. (See pp. 201–205.)

1892–3 On *Torrens*, London to Adelaide. Shows first nine chapters of *Almayer's Folly* to a passenger. (See pp. 217–220.) John Galsworthy also a passenger.

1893–4 Mate on steamer *Adowa*, London to Rouen to London. On January 14, 1894, ends his marine service. (See p. 205.) Finishes *Almayer's Folly* some months afterwards. His uncle, Thaddeus Bobrowski, dies, leaving him a small legacy.

1894–5 Writes *An Outcast of the Islands*. (See pp. 220–222.)

1896   March 24 marries Miss Jessie George; they live in Essex. Begins *The Rescue*, and writes *The Idiots* (based on impressions received during honeymoon in Brittany) and *An Outpost of Progress*; begins *The Nigger of the "Narcissus."* H. G. Wells calls attention to the new writer in *Saturday Review*. Literary friendships increase.

1897   Finishes *The Nigger of the "Narcissus."* Finally decides to give up all thought of a seafaring life for that of a man of letters—"a transition that had been accomplished insensibly." (See p. 222.)

1898   *Tales of Unrest* (including *Karain: A Memory* and *The Lagoon*) appears. Writes *Youth* and *Heart of Darkness*; begins *Lord Jim*. His son Borys born. Moves to Pent Farm in Kent.

1899   Receives one-third of *The Academy* 150-guinea prize for *Tales of Unrest*.

1900   *Lord Jim* finished.

1901   Writes *Typhoon, Falk, Amy Foster,* and begins *Romance* in collaboration with Ford Madox Hueffer.

1902   Finishes *Romance*; writes *The End of the Tether*.

1903–4 For twenty months at Pent Farm, writing *Nostromo*. (See pp. 231–232.)

1905   Travels on the continent for four months. Writes "Autocracy and War" (*Notes on Life and Letters*) on European situation. *One Day More* (dramatization of *Tomorrow*) performed in London. Writes "Initiation" (see pp. 64–74) and "The *Tremolino*" (see pp. 34–61)—two chapters of *The Mirror of the Sea*—and *The Informer*. Begins *The Secret Agent*. Through Edmond Gosse and William Rothenstein is granted a Civil List pension.

1906   At Montpellier, France, for two months. Café life used in *Victory*. (See pp. 236–238.) Conceives the idea there of *Suspense*. Finishes correcting *The Mirror of the Sea* and writes most of *The Secret Agent*. Second son, John Alexander, born August 2 in London in house lent Conrad by John Galsworthy.

1907 Severe illness of children on his return to Montpellier. Writes much of *Chance*. Writes *The Duel* and *Il Conde*.

1908 Begins *Razumov*, afterwards called *Under Western Eyes*.

1909 In Kent. Writes *The Secret Sharer* and corrects proofs of French translation of *The Nigger of the "Narcissus."* Writing *Under Western Eyes*.

1910 Moves to Capel House, Orlestone, near Ashford, Kent, his home for ten years. Writes *A Smile of Fortune*, *The Partner*, and *Freya of the Seven Isles*.

1911–12 Concludes *Chance*. Writes *The Inn of the Two Witches* and *Because of the Dollars*.

1913–14 For nineteen months devotes himself to composition of *Victory*. Writes *The Planter of Malata*. In Cracow, on his native soil, with his family when European war breaks out. Begins *The Shadow Line*. (See pp. 133–183.)

1915 "Poland Revisited" (*Notes on Life and Letters*) written first as four articles for the *Daily Mail*.

1916 Writes *The Warrior's Soul* and *The Tale*. Begins, on the advice of J. B. Pinker, revising and rewriting *The Rescue*, which he had put aside twenty years before. On the Admiralty's invitation visits naval stations in North Sea.

1917–18 Writes prefaces for a new edition of his works. Writes *The Arrow of Gold*.

1919 Finishes *The Rescue* twenty-three years after he had begun it. Moves to Oswalds, Bishopsbourne, near Canterbury, where he spends the remaining years of his life. Continues writing prefaces for his Complete Edition. Arranges *Gaspar Ruiz* as a film play. Begins *Suspense*.

1920 Finishes the dramatization of *The Secret Agent*, begun in 1919. Continues writing prefaces.

1921 In Corsica in preparation for continuing *Suspense*, the Napoleonic romance. Begins *The Rover* first as a story, but it grows into a novel.

1922 *The Rover* completed. *The Secret Agent* first performed November 3. Play soon withdrawn. *Suspense* resumed.

1923 Visits New York, his last voyage at sea.

1924 Offered a knighthood, which he declines to accept. Works on *Suspense*. Dies suddenly August 3 of a heart attack. Buried in Canterbury Cemetery.

PART I

AUTOBIOGRAPHY

The history of men on this earth since the beginning of ages may be "résuméd" in one phrase of infinite poignancy: They were born, they suffered, they died . . . Yet it is a great tale!

INTRODUCTION TO AUTOBIOGRAPHY

On account of his temperament, Conrad would not—and probably could not—have imposed upon himself a complete, consecutive autobiography. The nearest approach to a Conrad autobiography is found in his book entitled *A Personal Record*. But of this Gustav Morf says, in *The Polish Heritage of Joseph Conrad*, "One might be tempted to say that the work was written by fits, without the faintest hint of a directing idea, in that nonchalant, haphazard way which Poles are prone to mistake for a sign of elegance, if not of high art"; and Conrad himself admits that these memories were "put down without any regard for established conventions."

But Conrad's writings abound in autobiographical material. In his letters, in essays, in short stories, and in complete novels, interesting bits of personal experience come most surprisingly to the surface, at any time, in any place. As his art and craft in the writing of novels developed and his powers of character interpretation and portrayal increased, he returned from time to time to his earlier interest in self-interpretation and self-portrayal. Like Shakespeare, he was self-schooled and self-disciplined; but unlike Shakespeare, he often included himself as the subject of his own art.

It has seemed no irreverence to attempt to disengage the authentic autobiographical passages from the whole body of Conrad's writing and to assemble them into a logical and consistent whole, and thus, as it were, have Conrad do what he never consciously attempted—write his own biography.

No liberty beyond that of selection and arrangement has been taken with Conrad's words. There will be found no single addition or alteration; nor, it is believed, will any passage included possess a fundamentally different meaning by reason of separation from its context. The order and arrangement have been made both chronological and topical, with the result that the gradual evolution of Conrad's mind and character may be traced; and—what is very important —each incident or selection is found in its chronological and logical environment. Thus we have allowed Conrad to tell his own story exclusively, with no connecting links except those necessary for clearness.

Here, then, is Conrad's own story of his life—that life which has been called his greatest tale. "Happy he who, like Ulysses, has made an adventurous voyage." Closing behind him "the little gate of mere boyishness," he "enters an enchanted garden" of early youth. He follows "the inexplicable impulse," "the voice from inside," "in the very footprints of geographical discovery"; "goes on recognizing the landmarks of the predecessors, excited, amused, taking the hard luck and the good luck together"; till, perceiving "the twilight region between youth and maturity," he experiences "moments of boredom, of weariness, of dissatisfaction, moments when the still young are inclined to commit rash actions"; attains "his first command"—becomes "a British master mariner" and "vindicates himself from what had been cried upon as a stupid obstinacy or a fantastic caprice." Again following an "inexplicable impulse," obeying "a hidden obscure necessity," he writes his first book "line by line." "Never had Rubicon been more blindly forded, without invocation to the gods, without fear of men." Book after book arrests "the hands busy about the work of the earth"; compels men "to glance for a moment at the surrounding vision of form and color, of sunshine and show"; makes them "pause for a look, for a sigh, for a smile." "And when it is accomplished—behold—all the truth of life is there: a moment of vision, a sigh, a smile— and the return to an eternal rest."

THE POLISH HERITAGE AND BOYHOOD

[Conrad "would have become a good Pole if it had been at all possible in that time to be a good Pole," says Dr. Morf in *The Polish Heritage of Joseph Conrad*. "It was his fate to be born into circumstances, political and social, which admitted only of a degrading opportunism or of a flight into the lands of fantasy, of fairy tales, of sea-stories, of visions of discoverers and discoveries. . . . A few years after the death of his father, Conrad spread his wings and flew away, in search of a freer, fuller life, of glory, and of fortune." Yet even when he had carved a career of eminence and honor in a strange land, there remained, as he said, an "unconscious response to the still voice of that inexorable past." In the following passages, written with a long perspective, Conrad reveals the permanent influence of his Polish heritage.]

My full name being Joseph Theodor Konrad <u>Nalecz</u> Korzeniowski, the underlined word being the appellation of our trade mark . . . . without which none are genuine. . . .

Racially I belong to a group which has historically a political past, with a Western Roman culture derived at first from Italy and then from France; and a rather Southern temperament; an outpost of Westernism with a Roman tradition, situated between Slavo-Tartar Byzantine barbarism on one side and the German tribes on the other; resisting both influences desperately and still remaining true to itself to this very day. . . .

My maternal uncle advised me that if I wanted to know something about my descent I would find it in the archives of the Province of Podolia, relating mainly to the 18th century

3

. . . . He had had researches made already, which showed that during that century my paternal ancestors were men of substance, and what may be called "prominent citizens," frequently elected to provincial offices of trust, and forming alliances in their own modest sphere after the usual several years' service in the army of the Republic. My paternal grandfather served in the Polish army from 1817 to 1820, when he sold his land in Podolia and came to live on his wife's estate in Volhynia. Their fortune, which descended to my father, his brother, and his sister, was confiscated by the Russian Government in consequence of the rebellion of 1863.

THE FATHER

My father Apollonius N. Korzeniowski. Educated in the University of St. Petersburg. Department of Oriental Studies and Philology. No degree. Debts. Social successes and any amount of *bonnes fortunes*. Poet. Married in 1855. [Really in 1856.] Came to Warsaw in 1860. Arrested in 1862 and after ten months' detention in the Citadel condemned to deportation into Russia. First in Archangel, then in Tsherisgow. My mother died in exile. My father liberated in '67 on the representation of Prince Gallitzin that he was no longer dangerous. He was dying.

One of the most sympathetic of my critics tried to account for certain characteristics of my work by the fact of my being, in his own words, "the son of a Revolutionist." No epithet could be more inapplicable to a man with such a strong sense of responsibility in the region of ideas and action and so indifferent to the promptings of personal ambition as my father. Why the description "revolutionary" should have been applied all through Europe to the Polish risings of 1831 and 1863 I really cannot understand. These risings were purely revolts against foreign domination. The Russians themselves called them "rebellions," which, from their point of view, was the exact truth. Amongst the men concerned in the preliminaries of the 1863 movement my father was no more revolutionary than the others, in the sense of working for the subversion of any social or political scheme of existence. He was simply a patriot in the sense of a man who, believing in the spirituality of a national existence, could not bear to see that spirit enslaved . . .

What had impressed me . . . . was the burning of his manuscripts a fortnight or so before his death. It was done under his own superintendence. I happened to go into his room a little earlier than usual that evening, and remaining unnoticed stayed to watch the nursing-sister feeding the blaze in the fireplace. My father sat in a deep armchair, propped up with pillows. This was the last time I saw him out of bed. His aspect was to me not so much that of a man desperately ill, as mortally weary—a vanquished man. That act of destruction affected me profoundly by its air of surrender. Not before death, however. To a man of such strong faith death could not have been an enemy. . . .

I had also imagined him to be completely forgotten forty-five years after his death. But this was not the case. Some young men of letters had discovered him, mostly as a remarkable translator of Shakespeare, Victor Hugo, and Alfred de Vigny, to whose drama *Chatterton*, translated by himself, he had written an eloquent preface defending the poet's deep humanity and his ideal of noble stoicism. The political side of his life was being recalled too; for some men of his time, his co-workers in the task of keeping the national spirit firm in the hope of an independent future, had been in their old age publishing their memoirs, where the part he played was for the first time publicly disclosed to the world. I learned then of things in his life I never knew before, things which outside the group of the initiated could have been known to no living being except my mother. It was thus that from a volume of posthumous memoirs dealing with those bitter years I learned the fact that the first inception of the secret National Committee intended primarily to organize moral resistance to the augmented pressure of Russianism arose on my father's initiative, and that its first meetings were held in our Warsaw house, of which all I remember distinctly is one room, white and crimson, probably the drawing-room. In one of its walls there was the loftiest of all archways. Where it led to remains a mystery; but to this day I cannot get rid of the belief that all this was of enormous proportions, and that the people appearing and disappearing in that immense space were beyond the usual stature of mankind as I got to know it in later life.

Since the age of five I have been a great reader, as is not perhaps wonderful in a child who was never aware of learning to read. At ten years of age I had read much of Victor Hugo and other romantics. I had read, in Polish and in French, history, voyages, novels; I knew *Gil Blas* and *Don Quixote* in abridged editions; I had read in early boyhood Polish poets and some French poets. . . .

My first introduction to English imaginative literature was *Nicholas Nickleby*. It is extraordinary how well Mrs. Nickleby could chatter disconnectedly in Polish and the sinister Ralph rage in that language. As to the Crummles family and the family of the learned Squeers, it seemed as natural to them as their native speech. It was, I have no doubt, an excellent translation. This must have been in the year '70. But I really believe that I am wrong. That book was not my first introduction to English literature. My first acquaintance was (or were) the *Two Gentlemen of Verona,* and that in the very manuscript of my father's translation. It was during our exile in Russia, and it must have been less than a year after my mother's death, because I remember myself in the black blouse with a white border of my heavy mourning. We were living together, quite alone, in a small house on the outskirts of the town of T——. That afternoon, instead of going out to play in the large yard which we shared with our landlord, I had lingered in the room in which my father generally wrote. What emboldened me to clamber into his chair I am sure I don't know, but a couple of hours afterwards he discovered me kneeling in it with my elbows on the table and my head held in both hands over the manuscript of loose pages. I was greatly confused, expecting to get into trouble. He stood in the doorway looking at me with some surprise, but the only thing he said after a moment of silence was:

"Read the page aloud."

Luckily the page lying before me was not over blotted with erasures and corrections, and my father's handwriting was otherwise extremely legible. When I got to the end he nodded and I flew out of doors thinking myself lucky to have escaped reproof for that piece of impulsive audacity. I have tried to discover since the reason of this mildness, and I imagine that all unknown to myself I had earned, in my father's mind, the right to some latitude in my relations with his writing table. It was only a month before, or perhaps it was only a week before, that I had read to him aloud from beginning to end, and to his perfect satisfaction, as he lay on his bed, not being very well at the time, the proofs of his translation of Victor Hugo's *Toilers of the Sea*. Such was my title to consideration, I believe, and also my first introduction to the sea in literature. If I do not remember where, how, and when I learned to read, I am not likely to forget the process of being trained in the art of reading aloud. My poor father, an admirable reader himself, was the most exacting of masters. I reflect proudly that I must have read that page of *Two Gentlemen of Verona* tolerably well at the age of eight. . . .

Books are an integral part of one's life, and my Shakespearean associations are with that first year of our bereavement, the last I spent with my father in exile (he sent me away to Poland to my mother's brother directly he could brace himself up for the separation).

Into this coldly illuminated and dumb emptiness there issued out of my aroused memory a small boy of eleven, wending his way, not very fast, to a preparatory school for day-pupils on the second floor of the third house down from the Florian Gate. It was in the winter months of 1868. At eight o'clock of every morning that God made, sleet or shine, I walked up Florian Street. But of that, my first school, I remember very little. I believe that one of my co-sufferers there has become a much appreciated editor of historical documents. But I didn't suffer much from the various imperfections of my first school. I was rather indifferent to school troubles. I had a private gnawing worm of my own. This was the time of my father's last illness. Every evening at seven, turning my back on the Florian Gate, I walked all the way to a big old house in a quiet narrow street a good distance beyond the Great Square. There, in a large drawing-room, paneled and bare, with heavy cornices and a lofty ceiling, in a little oasis of light made by two candles in a desert of dusk I sat at a little table to worry and ink myself all over till the task of my preparation was done. The table of my toil faced a tall white door, which was kept closed; now and then it would come ajar and a nun in a white coif would squeeze herself through the crack, glide across the room, and disappear. There were two of these noiseless nursing nuns. Their voices were seldom heard. For, indeed, what could they have had to say? When they did speak to me it was with their lips hardly moving, in a claustral clear whisper. Our domestic matters were ordered by the elderly housekeeper of our neighbor on the second floor, a Canon of the Cathedral, lent for the emergency. She, too, spoke but seldom.   She wore a black dress with a cross hanging by a chain on her ample bosom.   And though when she spoke she moved her lips more than the nuns, she never let her voice rise above a peacefully murmuring note.   The air around me was all piety, resignation, and silence.

I don't know what would have become of me if I had not been a reading boy.   My prep finished, I would have had nothing to do but sit and watch the awful stillness of the sick room flow out through the closed door and coldly enfold my scared heart.   I suppose that in a futile childish way I would have gone crazy.   But I was a reading boy.   There were many books about, lying on consoles, on tables, and even on the floor, for we had not had time to settle down. I read!   What did I not read!   Sometimes the elder nun, gliding up and casting a mistrustful look on the open pages, would lay her hand lightly on my head and suggest in a doubtful whisper, "Perhaps it is not very good for you to read these books."   I would raise my eyes to her face mutely, and with a vague gesture of giving it up she would glide away.

Later in the evening, but not always, I would be permitted to tiptoe into the sick room to say good-night to the figure prone on the bed, which often could not acknowledge my presence but by a slow movement of the eyes, put my lips dutifully to the nerveless hand lying on the coverlet, and tiptoe out again.   Then I would go to bed, in a room at the end of the corridor, and often, not always, cry myself into a good sound sleep.

I looked forward to what was coming with an incredulous terror.   I turned my eyes from it sometimes with success, and yet all the time I had an awful sensation of the inevitable. I had also moments of revolt which stripped off me some of my simple trust in the government of the universe.   But when the inevitable entered the sick room and the white door was thrown wide open, I don't think I found a single tear to shed. I have a suspicion that the Canon's house-keeper looked on me as the most callous little wretch on earth.

The day of the funeral came in due course and all the generous "Youth of the Schools," the grave Senate of the University, the delegations of the trade guilds, might have obtained (if they cared) *de visu* evidence of the callousness of the little wretch. There was nothing in my aching head but a few words, some such stupid sentences as, "It's done," or, "It's accomplished" (in Polish it is much shorter), or something of the sort, repeating itself endlessly. The long procession moved out of the narrow street, down a long street, past the Gothic front of St. Mary's under its unequal towers, towards the Florian Gate.

In the moonlight-flooded silence of the old town of glorious tombs and tragic memories, I could see again the small boy of that day following a hearse; a space kept clear in which I walked alone, conscious of an enormous following, the clumsy swaying of the tall black machine, the chanting of the surpliced clergy at the head, the flames of tapers passing under the low archway of the gate, the rows of bared heads on the pavements with fixed, serious eyes. Half the population had turned out on that fine May afternoon. They had not come to honor a great achievement, or even some splendid failure. The dead and they were victims alike of an unrelenting destiny which cut them off from every path of merit and glory. They had come only to render homage to the ardent fidelity of the man whose life had been a fearless confession in word and deed of a creed which the simplest heart in that crowd could feel and understand.

THE MOTHER

I remember my mother, ... dressed in the black of the national mourning worn in defiance of ferocious police regulations. I have also preserved from that particular time the awe of her mysterious gravity, which, indeed, was by no means smileless. For I remember her smiles, too. Perhaps for me she could always find a smile. She was young then, certainly not yet thirty. She died four years later in exile.

I remember in my early years, . . . the man who first put me on horseback, and his four-horse bachelor turn-out; his perfect horsemanship and general skill in manly exercises was one of my earliest admirations. I seem to remember my mother looking on from a colonnade in front of the dining-room windows as I was lifted upon the pony, held, for all I know, by the very Joseph—the groom attached specially to my grandmother's service—who died of cholera. It was certainly a young man in a dark blue, tailless coat and huge Cossack trousers, that being the livery of the men about the stables. It must have been in 1864 [it was in 1863], but reckoning by another mode of calculating time, it was certainly in the year in which my mother obtained permission to travel south and visit her family, from the exile into which she had followed my father. For that, too, she had had to ask permission, and I know that one of the conditions of that favor was that she should be treated exactly as a condemned exile herself. Yet a couple of years later, in memory of her eldest brother who had served in the Guards and dying early left hosts of friends and a loved memory in the great world of St. Petersburg, some influential personages procured for her this permission—it was officially called the "Highest Grace"—of a three months' leave from exile.

This is also the year in which I first began to remember my mother with more distinctness than a mere loving, wide-browed, silent, protecting presence, whose eyes had a sort of commanding sweetness; and I also remember the great gathering of all the relations from near and far, and the gray heads of the family friends paying her the homage of respect and love in the house of her favorite brother who, a few years later, was to take the place for me of both my parents.

I did not understand the tragic significance of it all at the time, though indeed I remember that doctors also came. There were no signs of invalidism about her—but I think that already they had pronounced her doom unless perhaps the change to a southern climate could reëstablish her declining strength. For me it seems the very happiest period of my existence. There was my cousin, a delightful, quicktempered little girl, some months younger than myself, whose life, lovingly watched over, as if she were a royal princess, came to an end with her fifteenth year. There were other children, too, many of whom are dead now, and not a few whose very names I have forgotten. Over all this hung the oppressive shadow of the great Russian Empire —the shadow lowering with the darkness of a new-born national hatred fostered by the Moscow school of journalists against the Poles after the ill-omened rising of 1863.

. . . . I remember well the day of our departure back to exile. The elongated, bizarre, shabby traveling carriage with four post-horses, standing before the long front of the house with its eight columns, four on each side of the broad flight of stairs. On the steps, groups of servants, a few relations, one or two friends from the nearest neighborhood, a perfect silence, on all the faces an air of sober concentration; my grandmother all in black gazing stoically, my uncle giving his arm to my mother down to the carriage in which I had been placed already; at the top of the flight my little cousin in a short skirt of a tartan pattern with a deal of red in it, and like a small princess attended by the women of her own household: the head *gouvernante*, our dear, corpulent Francesca (who had been for thirty years in the service of the B. family), the former nurse, now outdoor attendant, a handsome peasant face wearing a compassionate expression, and the good, ugly Mlle. Durand, the governess, with her black eyebrows meeting over a short thick nose, and a complexion like pale brown paper. Of all the eyes turned towards the carriage, her good-natured eyes only were dropping tears, and it was her sobbing voice alone that broke the silence with an appeal to me: *"N'oublie pas ton français, mon chéri."* In three months, simply by playing with us, she had taught me not only to speak French but to read it as well. She was indeed an excellent playmate. In the distance, halfway down to the great gates, a light, open trap, harnessed with three horses in Russian fashion, stood drawn up on one side with the police captain of the district sitting in it, the vizor of his flat cap with a red band pulled down over his eyes.

Meeting with calm fortitude the cruel trials of a life reflecting all the national and social misfortunes of the community, she realized the highest conceptions of duty as a wife, a mother and a patriot, sharing the exile of her husband and representing nobly the ideal of Polish womanhood.

EATING A DOG—PRO PATRIA

I knew, at a very early age, that my grand-uncle Nicholas B. was a Knight of the Legion of Honor and that he had also the Polish Cross for valor, *Virtuti Militari.* The knowledge of these glorious facts inspired in me an admiring veneration; yet it is not that sentiment, strong as it was, which resumes for me the force and the significance of his personality. It is overborne by another and complex impression of awe, compassion, and horror. Mr. Nicholas B. remains for me the unfortunate and miserable (but heroic) being who once upon a time had eaten a dog.

It is a good forty years since I heard the tale, and the effect has not worn off yet. I believe this is the very first, say, realistic, story I heard in my life; but all the same, I don't know why I should have been so frightfully impressed. Of course I know what our village dogs look like—but still . . . . No! At this very day, recalling the horror and compassion of my childhood, I ask myself whether I am right in disclosing to a cold and fastidious world that awful episode in the family history. I ask myself—is it right?— especially as the B. family had always been honorably known in a wide countryside for the delicacy of their tastes in the matter of eating and drinking. But upon the whole, and considering that this gastronomical degradation overtaking a gallant young officer lies really at the door of the Great Napoleon, I think that to cover it up by silence would be an exaggeration of literary restraint. Let the truth stand here. The responsibility rests with the Man of St. Helena in view of his deplorable levity in the conduct of the Russian campaign. It was during the memorable retreat from Moscow that Mr. Nicholas B., in company of two brother officers— as to whose morality and natural refinement I know nothing —bagged a dog on the outskirts of a village and subsequently devoured him. As far as I can remember, the weapon used was a cavalry saber, and the issue of the sporting episode was rather more of a matter of life and death than if it had been an encounter with a tiger. A picket of Cossacks was sleeping in that village lost in the depths of the great Lithuanian forest. The three sportsmen had observed them from a hiding-place making themselves very much at home amongst the huts just before the early winter darkness set in at four o'clock. They had observed them with disgust, and perhaps with despair. Late in the night the rash counsels of hunger overcame the dictates of prudence. Crawling through the snow, they crept up to the fence of dry branches which generally encloses a village in that part of Lithuania. What they expected to get, and in what manner, and whether this expectation was worth the risk, goodness only knows. However, these Cossack parties in most cases wandering without an officer, were known to guard themselves badly and often not at all. In addition, the village lying at a great distance from the line of French retreat, they could not suspect the presence of stragglers from the Grand Army. The three officers had strayed away in a blizzard from the main column and had been lost for days in the woods, which explains sufficiently the terrible straits to which they were reduced. Their plan was to try and attract the attention of the peasants in that one of the huts which was nearest to the enclosure; but as they were preparing to venture into the very jaws of the lion, so to speak, a dog (it is mighty strange that there was but one), a creature quite as formidable under the circumstances as a lion, began to bark on the other side of the fence . . .

At this stage of the narrative, which I heard many times (by request) from the lips of Captain Nicholas B.'s sister-in-law, my grandmother, I used to tremble with excitement.

The dog barked. And if he had done no more than bark, three officers of the Great Napoleon's army would have perished honorably on the points of Cossacks' lances, or perchance escaping the chase, would have died decently of starvation. But before they had time to think of running away, that fatal and revolting dog, being carried away by the excess of his zeal, dashed out through a gap in the fence. He dashed out and died. His head, I understand, was severed at one blow from his body. I understand also that, later on, within the gloomy solitudes of the snow-laden woods, when, in a sheltering hollow, a fire had been lit by the party, the condition of the quarry was discovered to be distinctly unsatisfactory. It was not thin—on the contrary, it seemed unhealthily obese; its skin showed bare patches of an unpleasant character. However, they had not killed that dog for the sake of the pelt. He was large. . . . He was eaten. . . . The rest is silence. . . . A silence in which a small boy shudders and says firmly:

"I could not have eaten that dog."

And his grandmother remarks with a smile:

"Perhaps you don't know what it is to be hungry."

I have learned something of it since. Not that I have been reduced to eat dog. I have fed on the emblematical animal, which, in the language of the volatile Gauls, is called *la vache enragée;* I have lived on ancient salt junk, I know the taste of shark, of trepang, of snake, of nondescript dishes containing things without a name—but of the Lithuanian village dog, never! I wish it to be distinctly understood that it is not I, but my grand-uncle Nicholas, of the Polish landed gentry, *Chevalier de la Légion d'Honneur,* etc., etc., who, in his young days, had eaten the Lithuanian dog.

I wish he had not. The childish horror of the deed clings absurdly to the grizzled man. I am perfectly helpless against it. Still, if he really had to, let us charitably remember that he had eaten him on active service, while bearing up bravely against the greatest military disaster of modern history, and, in a manner, for the sake of his country. He had eaten him to appease his hunger, no doubt, but also for the sake of an unappeasable and patriotic desire, in the glow of a great faith that lives still, and in the pursuit of a great illusion kindled like a false beacon by a great man to lead astray the effort of a brave nation.

Pro patria!

Looked at in that light it appears a sweet and decorous meal.

PRINCE ROMAN'S VISIT: AN EARLY DISILLUSIONMENT

I was staying in the country house of my mother's brother in our southern provinces.

It was the dead of winter. The great lawn in front was as pure and smooth as an alpine snowfield, a white and feathery level sparkling under the sun as if sprinkled with diamond-dust, declining gently to the lake—a long, sinuous piece of frozen water looking bluish and more solid than the earth. A cold brilliant sun glided low above an undulating horizon of great folds of snow in which the villages of Ukrainian peasants remained out of sight, like clusters of boats hidden in the hollows of a running sea. And every-thing was very still.

I don't know now how I had managed to escape at eleven o'clock in the morning from the schoolroom. I was a boy of eight; the little girl, my cousin, a few months younger than myself, though hereditarily more quick-tempered, was less adventurous. So I had escaped alone; and presently I found myself in the great stone-paved hall, warmed by a monumental stove of white tiles, a much more pleasant locality than the schoolroom, which, for some reason or other, perhaps hygienic, was always kept at a low tempera-ture.

We children were aware that there was a guest staying in the house. He had arrived the night before just as we were being driven off to bed. We broke back through the line of beaters to rush and flatten our noses against the dark window panes; but we were too late to see him alight. We had only watched in a ruddy glare the big traveling carriage on sleigh-runners harnessed with six horses, a black mass against the snow, going off to the stables, preceded by a horseman carry-ing a blazing ball of tow and resin in an iron basket at the end of a long stick swung from his saddle bow. Two stable boys had been sent out early in the afternoon along the snow-tracks to meet the expected guest at dusk and light his way with these road torches. At that time, you must re-member, there was not a single mile of railways in our southern provinces. My little cousin and I had no knowl-edge of trains and engines, except from picture-books, as of things rather vague, extremely remote, and not particularly interesting unless to grown-ups who traveled abroad.

Our notion of princes, perhaps a little more precise, was mainly literary and had a glamour reflected from the light of fairy tales, in which princes always appear young, charming, heroic, and fortunate. Yet, as well as any other children, we could draw a firm line between the real and the ideal. We knew that princes were historical personages. And there was some glamour in that fact, too. But what had driven me to roam cautiously over the house like an escaped prisoner was the hope of snatching an interview with a special friend of mine, the head forester, who generally came to make his report at that time of the day. I yearned for news of a certain wolf. You know, in a country where wolves are to be found, every winter almost brings forward an individual eminent by the audacity of his misdeeds, by his more perfect wolfishness—so to speak. I wanted to hear some new thrilling tale of that wolf—perhaps the dramatic story of his death. . . .

But there was no one in the hall.

Deceived in my hopes, I became suddenly very much depressed. Unable to slip back in triumph to my studies I elected to stroll spiritlessly into the billiard room where certainly I had no business. There was no one there either, and I felt very lost and desolate under its high ceiling, all alone with the massive English billiard table, which seemed, in heavy, rectilinear silence, to disapprove of that small boy's intrusion.

As I began to think of retreat I heard footsteps in the adjoining drawing room; and, before I could turn tail and flee, my uncle and his guest appeared in the doorway. To run away after having been seen would have been highly improper, so I stood my ground. My uncle looked surprised to see me; the guest by his side was a spare man, of average stature, buttoned up in a black frock coat and holding himself very erect with a stiffly soldier-like carriage. From the folds of a soft white cambric neck-cloth peeped the points of a collar close against each shaven cheek. A few wisps of thin gray hair were brushed smoothly across the top of his bald head. His face, which must have been beautiful in its day, had preserved in age the harmonious simplicity of its lines. What amazed me was its even, almost deathlike pallor. He seemed to me to be prodigiously old. A faint smile, a mere momentary alteration in the set of his thin lips acknowledged my blushing confusion; and I became greatly interested to see him reach into the inside breastpocket of his coat. He extracted therefrom a lead pencil and a block of detachable pages, which he handed to my uncle with an almost imperceptible bow.

I was very much astonished, but my uncle received it as a matter of course. He wrote something at which the other glanced and nodded slightly. A thin wrinkled hand—the hand was older than the face—patted my cheek and then rested on my head lightly. An unringing voice, a voice as colorless as the face itself, issued from his sunken lips, while the eyes, dark and still, looked down at me kindly.

"And how old is this shy little boy?"

Before I could answer my uncle wrote down my age on the pad. I was deeply impressed. What was this ceremony? Was this personage too great to be spoken to? Again he glanced at the pad, and again gave a nod, and again that impersonal, mechanical voice was heard: "He resembles his grandfather."

I remembered my paternal grandfather. He had died not long before. He, too, was prodigiously old. And to me it seemed perfectly natural that two such ancient and venerable persons should have known each other in the dim ages of creation before my birth. But my uncle obviously had not been aware of the fact. So obviously that the mechanical voice explained: "Yes, yes. Comrades in '31. He was one of those who knew. Old times, my dear sir, old times. . . ."

He made a gesture as if to put aside an importunate ghost.

And now they were both looking down at me. I wondered whether anything was expected from me. To my round, questioning eyes my uncle remarked: "He's completely deaf." And the unrelated, inexpressive voice said: "Give me your hand."

Acutely conscious of inky fingers, I put it out timidly. I had never seen a deaf person before and was rather startled. He pressed it firmly and then gave me a final pat on the head.

My uncle addressed me weightily: "You have shaken hands with Prince Roman S——. It's something for you to remember when you grow up."

I was impressed by his tone. I had enough historical information to know vaguely that the Princes S—— counted amongst the sovereign Princes of Ruthenia till the union of all Ruthenian lands to the kingdom of Poland, when they became great Polish magnates, sometime at the beginning of the fifteenth century. But what concerned me most was the failure of the fairy-tale glamour. It was shocking to discover a prince who was deaf, bald, meagre, and so prodigiously old. It never occurred to me that this imposing and disappointing man had been young, rich, beautiful; I could not know that he had been happy in the felicity of an ideal marriage uniting two young hearts, two great names, and two great fortunes; happy with a happiness which, as in fairy tales, seemed destined to last forever. . . .

But it did not last forever. It is only found in the conclusion of fairy tales.

MILITANT GEOGRAPHY

The last words unveiling the mystery of the *Erebus* and *Terror* expedition were brought home and disclosed to the world by Sir Leopold McClintock, in his book, *The Voyage of the "Fox" in the Arctic Seas.* It is a little book, but it

records with manly simplicity the tragic ending of a great
tale.   It so happened that I was born in the year of its
publication.   Therefore, I may be excused for not getting
hold of it till ten years afterwards. . . .

There could hardly have been imagined a better book for
letting in the breath of the stern romance of polar exploration into the existence of a boy whose knowledge of the
poles of the earth had been till then of an abstract formal
kind as mere imaginary ends of the imaginary axis upon
which the earth turns.   The great spirit of the realities of the
story sent me off on the romantic explorations of my inner
self; to the discovery of the taste of poring over maps; and
revealed to me the existence of a latent devotion (such as it
was) to my other schoolwork.

Unfortunately, the marks awarded for that subject were
almost as few as the hours apportioned to it in the school
curriculum by persons of no romantic sense for the real,
ignorant of the great possibilities of active life; with no desire
for struggle, no notion of the wide spaces of the world—
mere bored professors, in fact, who were not only middle-
aged but looked to me as if they had never been young.   And
their geography was very much like themselves, a bloodless
thing with a dry skin covering a repulsive armature of uninteresting bones.

I would be ashamed of my warmth in digging up a hatchet
which has been buried now for nearly fifty years if those
fellows had not tried so often to take my scalp at the yearly
examinations.   There are things that one does not forget.
And besides, the geography which I had discovered for myself
was the geography of open spaces and wide horizons built up
on men's devoted work in the open air, the geography still
militant but already conscious of its approaching end with
the death of the last great explorer.   The antagonism was
radical.

Thus it happened that I got no marks at all for my first

and only paper on Arctic geography, which I wrote at the age of thirteen.   I still think that for my tender years it was an erudite performance.   I certainly did know something of Arctic geography, but what I was after really, I suppose, was the history of Arctic exploration.   My knowledge had considerable gaps, but I managed to compress my enthusiasm into just two pages, which in itself was a sort of merit.   Yet I got no marks.   For one thing it was not a set subject.   I believe the only comment made about it to my private tutor was that I seemed to have been wasting my time in reading books of travel instead of attending to my studies.   I tell you, those fellows were always trying to take my scalp.   On another occasion I just saved it by proficiency in map-drawing. It must have been good, I suppose; but all I remember about it is that it was done in a loving spirit.

I have no doubt that star-gazing is a fine occupation, for it leads you within the borders of the unattainable.   But map-gazing, to which I became addicted so early, brings the problems of the great spaces of the earth into stimulating and directing contact with sane curiosity and gives an honest precision to one's imaginative faculty.   And the honest maps of the nineteenth century nourished in me a passionate interest in the truth of geographical facts and a desire for precise knowledge which was extended later to other subjects.

Not the least interesting part in the study of geographical discovery lies in the insight it gives one into the characters of that special kind of men who devoted the best part of their lives to the exploration of land and sea.   In the world of mentality and imagination which I was entering it was they and not the characters of famous fiction who were my first friends.   Of some of them I had soon formed for myself an image indissolubly connected with certain parts of the world.   For instance, western Sudan, of which I could draw the rivers and principal features from memory even now, means for me an episode in Mungo Park's life.

It means for me the vision of a young, emaciated, fair-haired man, clad simply in a tattered shirt and worn-out breeches, gasping painfully for breath and lying on the ground in the shade of an enormous African tree (species unknown), while from a neighboring village of grass huts a charitable black-skinned woman is approaching him with a calabash full of pure cold water, a simple draught which, according to himself, seems to have effected a miraculous cure. The central Sudan, on the other hand, is represented to me by a very different picture, that of a self-confident and keen-eyed person in a long cloak and wearing a turban on his head, riding slowly towards a gate in the mud walls of an African city, from which an excited population is streaming out to behold the wonder—Doctor Barth, the protégé of Lord Palmerston, and subsidized by the British Foreign Office, approaching Kano, which no European eye had seen till then, but where forty years later my friend Sir Hugh Clifford, the Governor of Nigeria, traveled in state in order to open a college.

I must confess that I read that bit of news and inspected the many pictures in the illustrated papers without any particular elation. Education is a great thing, but Doctor Barth gets in the way. Neither will the monuments left by all sorts of empire builders suppress for me the memory of David Livingstone. The words "Central Africa" bring before my eyes an old man with a rugged, kind face and a clipped, gray mustache, pacing wearily at the head of a few black followers along the reed-fringed lakes towards the dark native hut on the Congo headwaters in which he died, clinging in his very last hour to his heart's unappeased desire for the sources of the Nile.

That passion had changed him in his last days from a great

explorer into a restless wanderer refusing to go home any more. From his exalted place among the blessed of militant geography and with his memory enshrined in Westminster Abbey, he can well afford to smile without bitterness at the fatal delusion of his exploring days, a notable European figure and the most venerated perhaps of all the objects of my early geographical enthusiasm.

Once only did that enthusiasm expose me to the derision of my schoolboy chums. One day, putting my finger on a spot in the very middle of the then white heart of Africa, I declared that some day I would go there. My chums' chaffing was perfectly justifiable. I myself was ashamed of having been betrayed into mere vaporing. Nothing was further from my wildest hopes. Yet it is a fact that, about eighteen years afterwards, a wretched little stern-wheel steamboat I commanded lay moored to the bank of an African river.

Everything was dark under the stars. Every other white man on board was asleep. I was glad to be alone on deck, smoking the pipe of peace after an anxious day. The subdued thundering mutter of the Stanley Falls hung in the heavy night air of the last navigable reach of the Upper Congo, while no more than ten miles away, in Reshid's camp just above the Falls, the yet unbroken power of the Congo Arabs slumbered wearily. Their day was over. Away in the middle of the stream, on a little island nestling all black in the foam of the broken water, a solitary little light glimmered feebly, and I said to myself with awe, "This is the very spot of my boyish boast."

SUMMARY OF EDUCATION

I went out into the world before I was seventeen, to France and England . . . Apart from Polish my youth has been fed on French and English literature. While I was a boy in a great public school we were steeped in classicism to the lips, and, though our historical studies were naturally tinted with Germanism, I know that all we boys, the six hundred of us, resisted that influence with all our might, while accepting the results of German research and thoroughness. And that was only natural. I am a child, not of a savage but of a chivalrous tradition, and if my mind took a tinge from anything it was from French romanticism perhaps. It was fed on ideas, not of revolt but of liberalism of a perfectly disinterested kind, and on severe moral lessons of national misfortune. Of course I broke away early. Excess of individualism, perhaps? . . . I admit that I was never an average, able boy. As a matter of fact, I was not able at all.

THE DESIRE AND THE DECISION TO GO TO SEA

[From about the age of fourteen, Conrad had secretly longed to be a sailor. At the age of sixteen, in 1872, he confided this ambition to his uncle. The following account, assembled from *A Personal Record,* shows the strength of Conrad's desire, the extremity of opposition, and the almost mystical influence of a stranger. It should be noted that the "unforgettable Englishman" spoke no word to Conrad, or Conrad to him; that it was the stranger's "striving-forward" appearance at a critical moment which emboldened the youth at the top of the Alpine pass not to capitulate. A little more than a year later, Conrad was on the docks at Marseilles. Thirteen years later—not eleven, as Conrad states in the last sentence of this section—he was a master in the British Merchant Service, November 11, 1886. His visit to Switzerland was in the early summer of 1873.]

. . . It was the year in which I had first spoken aloud of my desire to go to sea. At first, like those sounds that, ranging outside the scale to which men's ears are attuned, remain inaudible to our sense of hearing, this declaration passed unperceived. It was as if it had not been. Later on,

by trying various tones, I managed to arouse here and there
a surprised momentary attention—the "What was that funny
noise?" sort of inquiry.   Later on it was—"Did you hear
what that boy said?   What an extraordinary outbreak!"
Presently a wave of scandalized astonishment (it could not
have been greater if I had announced the intention of entering a Carthusian monastery) ebbing out of the educational
and academical town of Cracow spread itself over several
provinces.   It spread itself shallow but far-reaching.   It
stirred up a mass of remonstrance, indignation, pitying wonder, bitter irony, and downright chaff.   I could hardly
breathe under its weight, and certainly had no words for an
answer. . . .

. . . I don't mean to say that a whole country had been
convulsed by my desire to go to sea.   But for a boy between
fifteen and sixteen, sensitive enough, in all conscience, the
commotion of his little world had seemed a very considerable
thing indeed.   So considerable that, absurdly enough, the
echoes of it linger to this day.   I catch myself in hours of
solitude and retrospect meeting arguments and charges made
thirty-five years ago by voices now for ever still; finding
things to say that an assailed boy could not have found,
simply because of the mysteriousness of his impulses to himself.   I understood no more than the people who called upon
me to explain myself.   There was no precedent.   I verily
believe mine was the only case of a boy of my nationality and
antecedents taking a, so to speak, standing jump out of his
racial surrounding and associations.

. . . People wondered what Mr. T. B. would do now with
his worrying nephew and, I dare say, hoped kindly that he
would make short work of my nonsense.
What he did was to come down all the way from Ukraine
to have it out with me and to judge by himself, unprejudiced,

impartial, and just, taking his stand on the ground of wisdom and affection.   As far as is possible for a boy whose power of expression is still unformed, I opened the secret of my thoughts to him and he in return allowed me a glimpse into his mind and heart; the first glimpse of an inexhaustible and noble treasure of clear thought and warm feeling, which through life was to be mine to draw upon with a never-deceived love and confidence.   Practically, after several exhaustive conversations, he concluded that he would not have me later on reproach him for having spoiled my life by an unconditional opposition.   But I must take time for serious reflection.   And I must not only think of myself but of others; weigh the claims of affection and conscience against my own sincerity of purpose.   "Think well what it all means in the larger issues, my boy," he exhorted me finally with special friendliness.   "And meantime try to get the best place you can at the yearly examinations."

The scholastic year came to an end.   I took a fairly good place at the exams, which for me (for certain reasons) happened to be a more difficult task than for other boys.   In that respect I could enter with a good conscience upon that holiday which was like a long visit *pour prendre congé* of the mainland of old Europe I was to see so little of for the next four-and-twenty years.   Such, however, was not the avowed purpose of that tour.   It was rather, I suspect, planned in order to distract and occupy my thoughts in other directions.   Nothing had been said for months of my going to sea.   But my attachment to my young tutor and his influence over me were so well known that he must have received a confidential mission to talk me out of my romantic folly.   It was an excellently appropriate arrangement, as neither he nor I had ever had a single glimpse of the sea in our lives.   That was to come by-and-by for both of us in Venice, from the outer shore of Lido.   Meantime he had taken his mission to heart so well that I began to feel crushed

before we reached Zurich.   He argued in railway trains, in
lake steamboats, he had argued away for me the obligatory
sunrise on the Rigi, by Jove!   Of his devotion to his unworthy pupil there can be no doubt.   He had proved it
already by two years of unremitting and arduous care.   I
could not hate him.   But he had been crushing me slowly,
and when he started to argue on the top of the Furca Pass he
was perhaps nearer a success than either he or I imagined.   I
listened to him in despairing silence, feeling that ghostly,
unrealized, and desired sea of my dreams escape from the
unnerved grip of my will.

We sat down by the side of the road to continue the argument begun half a mile or so before.   I am certain it was an
argument because I remember perfectly how my tutor
argued and how without the power of reply I listened with
my eyes fixed obstinately on the ground.   A stir on the road
made me look up—and then I saw my unforgettable Englishman.   There are acquaintances of later years, familiars,
shipmates, whom I remember less clearly.   He marched
rapidly towards the east (attended by a hangdog Swiss guide)
with the mien of an ardent and fearless traveler.   He was
clad in a knickerbocker suit, but as at the same time he wore
short socks under his laced boots, for reasons which, whether
hygienic or conscientious, were surely imaginative, his calves,
exposed to the public gaze and to the tonic air of high
altitudes, dazzled the beholder by the splendor of their
marble-like condition and their rich tone of young ivory.   He
was the leader of a small caravan.   The light of a headlong,
exalted satisfaction with the world of men and the scenery
of mountains illumined his clean-cut, very red face, his short,
silver-white whiskers, his innocently eager and triumphant
eyes.   In passing he cast a glance of kindly curiosity and a
friendly gleam of big, sound, shiny teeth towards the man
and the boy sitting like dusty tramps by the roadside, with a

modest knapsack lying at their feet. His white calves twinkled sturdily, the uncouth Swiss guide with a surly mouth stalked like an unwilling bear at his elbow; a small train of three mules followed in single file the lead of this inspiring enthusiast. . . .

I tell you it was a memorable year! One does not meet such an Englishman twice in a lifetime. Was he in the mystic ordering of common events the ambassador of my future, sent out to turn the scale at a critical moment on the top of an Alpine pass, with the peaks of the Bernese Oberland for mute and solemn witnesses? His glance, his smile, the inextinguishable and comic ardor of his striving-forward appearance helped me to pull myself together. . . .

The enthusiastic old Englishman had passed—and the argument went on. What reward could I expect from such a life at the end of my years, either in ambition, honor, or conscience? An unanswerable question. But I felt no longer crushed. Then our eyes met and a genuine emotion was visible in his as well as in mine. The end came all at once. He picked up the knapsack suddenly and got on to his feet.

"You are an incorrigible, hopeless Don Quixote. That's what you are."

I was surprised. I was only fifteen and did not know what he meant exactly. But I felt vaguely flattered at the name of the immortal knight turning up in connection with my own folly, as some people would call it to my face. Alas! I don't think there was anything to be proud of. Mine was not the stuff the protectors of forlorn damsels, the redressers of this world's wrongs are made of; and my tutor was the man to know that best. Therein, in his indignation, he was superior to the barber and the priest when he flung at me an honored name like a reproach.

I walked behind him for full five minutes; then without looking back he stopped.   The shadows of distant peaks were lengthening over the Furca Pass.   When I came up to him he turned to me and in full view of the Finster-Aarhorn, with his band of giant brothers rearing their monstrous heads against a brilliant sky, put his hand on my shoulder affectionately.

"Well!   That's enough.   We will have no more of it."

And indeed there was no more question of my mysterious vocation between us.   There was to be no more question of it at all, nowhere or with any one.   We began the descent of the Furca Pass conversing merrily.   Eleven years later, month for month, I stood on Tower Hill on the steps of the St. Katherine's Dockhouse, a master in the British Merchant Service.

THE SEAMAN

[Marseilles, on the Mediterranean coast of France, was "the place," Conrad wrote to John Galsworthy, "where the puppy opened his eyes." There he had his first experiences of the sea; and from there he made his first long voyages,—to Spain, to the West Indies, and to the north coast of South America.]

WHAT I had in view was not a naval career, but the sea. There seemed no way open to it but through France. I had the language at any rate, and of all the countries in Europe it is with France that Poland has most connection. There were some facilities for having me a little looked after, at first. Letters were being written, answers were being received, arrangements were being made for my departure for Marseilles, where an excellent fellow called Solary, got at in a roundabout fashion through various French channels, had promised good-naturedly to put *le jeune homme* in the way of getting a decent ship for his first start if he really wanted a taste of *ce métier de chien*.

I watched all these preparations gratefully, and kept my own counsel.

FIRST EXPERIENCES ON SALT WATER

The very first whole day I ever spent on salt water was by invitation, in a big half-decked pilot boat, cruising under close reefs, on the look-out, in misty, blowing weather, for the sails of ships and the smoke of steamers rising out there, beyond the slim and tall Planier lighthouse cutting the line of the wind-swept horizon with a white perpendicular stroke. They were hospitable souls, these sturdy Provençal seamen. Under the general designation of *le petit ami de Baptistin* I was made the guest of the Corporation of Pilots, and had the freedom of their boats night or day. And many a day and a night, too, did I spend cruising with these rough, kindly men, under whose auspices my intimacy with the sea began. Many a time "the little friend of Baptistin" had the hooded cloak of the Mediterranean sailor thrown over him by their honest hands while dodging at night under the lee of Château d'If on the watch for the lights of ships. Their sea-tanned faces, whiskered or shaved, lean or full, with the intent wrinkled sea-eyes of the pilot-breed, and here and there a thin gold loop at the lobe of a hairy ear, bent over my sea-infancy. The first operation of seamanship I had an opportunity of observing was the boarding of ships at sea, at all times, in all states of the weather. They gave it to me to the full. And I have been invited to sit in more than one tall, dark house of the old town at their hospitable board, had the *bouillabaisse* ladled out into a thick plate by their high-voiced, broad-browed wives, talked to their daughters—thick-set girls, with pure profiles, glorious masses of black hair arranged with complicated art, dark eyes, and dazzlingly white teeth.

I had also other acquaintances of quite a different sort. One of them, Madame Delestang, an imperious, handsome lady in a statuesque style, would carry me off now and then on the front seat of her carriage to the Prado, at the hour of fashionable airing. She belonged to one of the old aristocratic families in the south. In her haughty weariness she used to make me think of Lady Dedlock in Dickens' *Bleak House,* a work of the master for which I have such an admiration, or rather such an intense and unreasoning affection, dating from the days of my childhood, that its very weaknesses are more precious to me than the strength of other men's work. I have read it innumerable times, both in Polish and in English. . . .

One day, after putting me down at the corner of a street, she offered me her hand, and detained me by a slight pressure, for a moment. While the husband sat motionless and looking straight before him, she leaned forward in the carriage to say, with just a shade of warning in her leisurely tone: "*Il faut, cependant, faire attention à ne pas gâter sa vie.*" I had never seen her face so close to mine before. She made my heart beat, and caused me to remain thoughtful for a whole evening. Certainly one must, after all, take care not to spoil one's life. But she did not know—nobody could know—how impossible that danger seemed to me.

Can the transports of first love be calmed, checked, turned to a cold suspicion of the future by a grave quotation from a work on Political Economy? I ask—Is it conceivable? Is it possible? Would it be right? With my feet on the very shores of the sea and about to embrace my blue-eyed dream, what could a good-natured warning as to spoiling one's life mean to my youthful passion? It was the most unexpected and the last, too, of the many warnings I had received. It sounded to me very bizarre—and, uttered as it was in the very presence of my enchantress, like the voice of folly, the voice of ignorance. But I was not so callous or so stupid as not to recognize there also the voice of kindness. And then the vagueness of the warning—because what can be the meaning of the phrase: to spoil one's life?—arrested one's attention by its air of wise profundity. At any rate, as I have said before, the words of *la belle Madame Delestang* made me thoughtful for a whole evening. I tried to understand and tried in vain, not having any notion of life as an enterprise that could be mismanaged. But I left off being thoughtful shortly before midnight, at which hour, haunted by no ghosts of the past and by no visions of the future, I walked down the quay of the *Vieux Port* to join the pilot-boat of my friends.

I may well remember that last night spent with the pilots of the Third Company. I have known the spell of moonlight since, on various seas and coasts—coasts of forests, of rocks, of sand dunes—but no magic so perfect in its revelation of unsuspected character, as though one were allowed to look upon the mystic nature of material things. For hours I suppose no word was spoken in that boat. The pilots, seated in two rows facing each other, dozed with their arms folded and their chins resting upon their breasts. They displayed a great variety of caps: cloth, wool, leather, ear-flaps, tassels, with a picturesque round *béret* or two pulled down over the brows; and one grandfather, with a shaved, bony face and a great beak of a nose, had a cloak with a hood which made him look in our midst like a cowled monk being carried off goodness knows where by that silent company of seamen— quiet enough to be dead.

My fingers itched for the tiller, and in due course my friend, the *patron,* surrendered it to me in the same spirit in which the family coachman lets a boy hold the reins on an easy bit of road. There was a great solitude around us; the islets ahead, Monte Cristo and the Château d'If in full light, seemed to float towards us—so steady, so imperceptible was the progress of our boat. "Keep her in the furrow of the moon," the *patron* directed me in a quiet murmur, sitting down ponderously in the stern-sheets and reaching for his pipe.

THE *TREMOLINO*

(From *The Mirror of the Sea*)

[—"the subject of the paper being the *Tremolino* and her fate. *That* is literally true"—so Conrad wrote to Sir Sidney Colvin. This enterprise, which Conrad pursued with so much romantic adventure, had to do with the Carlists' ill-fated efforts to place the claimant and pretender, Don Carlos, on the throne of Spain. Marseilles was the base for sending provisions and ammunition to

[the revolutionists in Spain. Conrad was about twenty-one at the time.]

IT WAS written that there, in the nursery of our navigating ancestors, I should learn to walk in the ways of my craft and grow in the love of the sea, blind as young love often is, but absorbing and unselfish as all true love must be. I demanded nothing from it—not even adventure. In this I showed, perhaps, more intuitive wisdom than high self-denial. No adventure ever came to one for the asking. He who starts on a deliberate quest of adventure goes forth but to gather dead-sea fruit, unless, indeed, he be beloved of the gods and great amongst heroes, like that most excellent cavalier Don Quixote de la Mancha. By us ordinary mortals of a mediocre animus that is only too anxious to pass by wicked giants for so many honest windmills, adventures are entertained like visiting angels. They come upon our complacency unawares. As unbidden guests are apt to do, they often come at inconvenient times. And we are glad to let them go unrecognized, without any acknowledgment of so high a favor. After many years, on looking back from the middle turn of life's way at the events of the past, which, like a friendly crowd, seem to gaze sadly after us hastening towards the Cimmerian shore, we may see here and there, in the gray throng, some figure glowing with a faint radiance, as though it had caught all the light of our already crepuscular sky. And by this glow we may recognize the faces of our true adventures, of the once unbidden guests entertained unawares in our young days.

The charm of the Mediterranean dwells in the unforgettable flavor of my early days, and to this hour this sea, upon which the Romans alone ruled without dispute, has kept for me the fascination of youthful romance.

If the Mediterranean, the venerable (and sometimes atrociously ill-tempered) nurse of all navigators, was to rock my

youth, the providing of the cradle necessary for that operation was entrusted by Fate to the most casual assemblage of
irresponsible young men (all, however, older than myself)
who, as if drunk with Provençal sunshine, frittered life away
in joyous levity on the model of Balzac's *Histoire des Treize*
qualified by a dash of romance *de cape et d'épée*.

She who was my cradle in those years had been built on
the River of Savona by a famous builder of boats, was rigged
in Corsica by another good man, and was described on her
papers as a "tartane" of sixty tons. In reality, she was a true
balancelle, with two short masts raking forward and two
curved yards, each as long as her hull; a true child of the
Latin Lake, with a spread of two enormous sails resembling
the pointed wings on a sea-bird's slender body, and herself,
like a bird indeed, skimming rather than sailing the seas.

Her name was the *Tremolino*. How is this to be translated? The *Quiverer*? What a name to give the pluckiest
little craft that ever dipped her sides in angry foam! I had
felt her, it is true, trembling for nights and days together
under my feet, but it was with the high-strung tenseness of
her faithful courage. In her short but brilliant career she
has taught me nothing, but she has given me everything. I
owe to her the awakened love for the sea that, with the
quivering of her swift little body and the humming of the
wind under the foot of her lateen sails, stole into my heart
with a sort of gentle violence, and brought my imagination
under its despotic sway. The *Tremolino*! To this day I
cannot utter or even write that name without a strange tightening of the breast and the gasp of mingled delight and
dread of one's first passionate experience.

*　　　*　　　*

We four formed (to use a term well understood nowadays
in every social sphere) a "syndicate" owning the *Tremolino*:
an international and astonishing syndicate. And we were

all ardent Royalists of the snow-white Legitimist complexion
—Heaven only knows why! In all associations of men there
is generally one who, by the authority of age and of a more
experienced wisdom, imparts a collective character to the
whole set. If I mention that the oldest of us was very old,
extremely old—nearly thirty years old—and that he used
to declare with gallant carelessness, "I live by my sword," I
think I have given enough information on the score of our
collective wisdom. He was a North Carolinian gentleman;
J. M. K. B. were the initials of his name, and he really did
live by the sword, as far as I know. He died by it, too, later
on, in a Balkanian squabble, in the cause of some Serbs or
else Bulgarians, who were neither Catholics nor gentlemen
—at least, not in the exalted but narrow sense he attached
to that last word.

Poor J. M. K. B., *Américain, Catholique, et gentilhomme,*
as he was disposed to describe himself in moments of lofty
expansion! Are there still to be found in Europe gentlemen keen of face and elegantly slight of body, of distinguished aspect, with a fascinating drawing-room manner
and with a dark, fatal glance, who live by their swords, I
wonder? His family had been ruined in the Civil War, I
fancy, and seems for a decade or so to have led a wandering
life in the Old World. As to Henry C——, the next in age
and wisdom of our band, he had broken loose from the unyielding rigidity of his family, solidly rooted, if I remember
rightly, in a well-to-do London suburb. On their respectable
authority he introduced himself meekly to strangers as a
"black sheep." I have never seen a more guileless specimen
of an outcast. Never.

However, his people had the grace to send him a little
money now and then. Enamored of the South, of Provence,
of its people, its life, its sunshine, and its poetry, narrow-
chested, tall and short-sighted, he strode along the streets
and the lanes, his long feet projecting far in advance of his

body, and his white nose and gingery mustache buried in an open book: for he had the habit of reading as he walked. How he avoided falling into precipices, off the quays, or down staircases is a great mystery. The sides of his overcoat bulged out with pocket editions of various poets. When not engaged in reading Virgil, Homer, or Mistral, in parks, restaurants, streets, and such-like public places, he indited sonnets (in French) to the eyes, ears, chin, hair, and other visible perfections of a nymph called Thérèse, the daughter, honesty compels me to state, of a certain Madame Leonore who kept a small café for sailors in one of the narrowest streets of the old town.

No more charming face, clear-cut like an antique gem, and delicate in coloring like the petal of a flower, had ever been set on, alas! a somewhat squat body. He read his verses aloud to her in the very café with the innocence of a little child and the vanity of a poet. We followed him there willingly enough, if only to watch the divine Thérèse laugh, under the vigilant black eyes of Madame Leonore, her mother. She laughed very prettily, not so much at the sonnets, which she could not but esteem, as at poor Henry's French accent, which was unique, resembling the warbling of birds, if birds ever warbled with a stuttering, nasal intonation.

Our third partner was Roger P. de la S——, the most Scandinavian-looking of Provençal squires, fair, and six feet high, as became a descendant of sea-roving Northmen, authoritative, incisive, wittily scornful, with a comedy in three acts in his pocket, and in his breast a heart blighted by a hopeless passion for his beautiful cousin, married to a wealthy hide-and-tallow merchant. He used to take us to lunch at their house without ceremony. I admired the good lady's sweet patience. The husband was a conciliatory soul, with a great fund of resignation, which he expended on "Roger's friends." I suspect he was secretly horrified at these invasions. But it was a Carlist salon, and as such we

THE *TREMOLINO*   39

were made welcome. The possibility of raising Catalonia in
the interest of the *Rey netto,* who had just then crossed the
Pyrenees, was much discussed there.

Don Carlos, no doubt, must have had many queer friends
(it is the common lot of all Pretenders), but amongst them
none more extravagantly fantastic than the *Tremolino* Syndicate, which used to meet in a tavern on the quays of the
old port. The antique city of Massilia had surely never,
since the days of the earliest Phœnicians, known an odder
set of shipowners. We met to discuss and settle the plan
of operations for each voyage of the *Tremolino.* In these
operations a banking-house, too, was concerned—a very
respectable banking-house. But I am afraid I shall end by
saying too much. Ladies, too, were concerned (I am really
afraid I am saying too much)—all sorts of ladies, some old
enough to know better than to put their trust in princes,
others young and full of illusions.

One of these last was extremely amusing in the imitations
she gave us in confidence of various highly placed personages she was perpetually rushing off to Paris to interview in
the interests of the cause—*Por el Rey!* For she was a Carlist,
and of Basque blood at that, with something of a lioness in
the expression of her courageous face (especially when she let
her hair down), and with the volatile little soul of a spar-
row dressed in fine Parisian feathers, which had the trick of
coming off disconcertingly at unexpected moments.

But her imitations of a Parisian personage, very highly
placed indeed, as she represented him standing in the corner
of a room with his face to the wall, rubbing the back of his
head and moaning helplessly, "Rita, you are the death of
me!" were enough to make one (if young and free from
cares) split one's sides laughing. She had an uncle still living, a very effective Carlist, too, the priest of a little mountain parish in Guipuzcoa. As the sea-going member of the
syndicate (whose plans depended greatly on Doña Rita's

information), I used to be charged with humbly affectionate messages for the old man. These messages I was supposed to deliver to the Arragonese muleteers (who were sure to await at certain times the *Tremolino* in the neighborhood of the Gulf of Rosas), for faithful transportation inland, together with the various unlawful goods landed secretly from under the *Tremolino's* hatches.

Well, now, I have really let out too much (as I feared I should in the end) as to the usual contents of my sea-cradle. But let it stand. And if anybody remarks cynically that I must have been a promising infant in those days, let that stand, too. I am concerned but for the good name of the *Tremolino*, and I affirm that a ship is ever guiltless of the sins, transgressions, and follies of her men.

*   *   *

It was not the *Tremolino's* fault that the syndicate depended so much on the wit and wisdom and the information of Doña Rita. She had taken a little furnished house on the Prado for the good of the cause—*Por el Rey!* She was always taking little houses for somebody's good, for the sick or the sorry, for broken-down artists, cleaned-out gamblers, temporarily unlucky speculators—*vieux amis*—old friends, as she used to explain apologetically, with a shrug of her fine shoulders.

Whether Don Carlos was one of the "old friends," too, it's hard to say. More unlikely things have been heard of in smoking-rooms. All I know is that one evening, entering incautiously the salon of the little house just after the news of a considerable Carlist success had reached the faithful, I was seized round the neck and waist and whirled recklessly three times round the room, to the crash of upsetting furniture and the humming of a valse tune in a warm contralto voice.

When released from the dizzy embrace, I sat down on the

carpet—suddenly, without affectation. In this unpretentious attitude I became aware that J. M. K. B. had followed me into the room, elegant, fatal, correct, and severe in a white tie and large shirt-front. In answer to his politely sinister, prolonged glance of inquiry, I overheard Doña Rita murmuring, with some confusion and annoyance, *"Vous êtes bête, mon cher. Voyons! Ça n'a aucune conséquence."* Well content in this case to be of no particular consequence, I had already about me the elements of some worldly sense.

Rearranging my collar, which, truth to say, ought to have been a round one above a short jacket, but was not, I observed felicitously that I had come to say good-bye, being ready to go off to sea that very night with the *Tremolino*. Our hostess, slightly panting yet, and just a shade disheveled, turned tartly upon J. M. K. B., desiring to know when *he* would be ready to go off by the *Tremolino*, or in any other way, in order to join the royal headquarters. Did he intend, she asked ironically, to wait for the very eve of the entry into Madrid? Thus by a judicious exercise of tact and asperity we re-established the atmospheric equilibrium of the room long before I left them a little before midnight, now tenderly reconciled, to walk down to the harbor and hail the *Tremolino* by the usual soft whistle from the edge of the quay. It was our signal, invariably heard by the ever-watchful Dominic, the *padrone*.

He would raise a lantern silently to light my steps along the narrow, spring plank of our primitive gangway. "And so we are going off," he would murmur directly my foot touched the deck. I was the harbinger of sudden departures, but there was nothing in the world sudden enough to take Dominic unawares. His thick black mustaches, curled every morning with hot tongs by the barber at the corner of the quay, seemed to hide a perpetual smile. But nobody, I believe, had ever seen the true shape of his lips. From the slow imperturbable gravity of that broad-chested man you

would think he had never smiled in his life. In his eyes
lurked a look of perfectly remorseless irony, as though he
had been provided with an extremely experienced soul; and
the slightest distension of his nostrils would give to his
bronzed face a look of extraordinary boldness. This was the
only play of feature of which he seemed capable, being a
Southerner of a concentrated, deliberate type. His ebony
hair curled slightly on the temples. He may have been forty
years old, and he was a great voyager on the inland sea.

Astute and ruthless, he could have rivalled in resource the
unfortunate son of Laertes and Anticlea. If he did not pit
his craft and audacity against the very gods, it is only because
the Olympian gods are dead. Certainly no woman could
frighten him. A one-eyed giant would not have had the
ghost of a chance against Dominic Cervoni, of Corsica, not
Ithaca; and no king, son of kings, but of very respectable
family—authentic Caporali, he affirmed. But that is as it
may be. The Caporali families date back to the twelfth
century.

For want of more exalted adversaries Dominic turned his
audacity, fertile in impious stratagems, against the powers of
the earth, as represented by the institution of customhouses
and every mortal belonging thereto—scribes, officers, and
guardacostas afloat and ashore. He was the very man for
us, this modern and unlawful wanderer with his own legend
of loves, dangers, and bloodshed. He told us bits of it sometimes in measured, ironic tones. He spoke Catalonian, the
Italian of Corsica, and the French of Provence, with the
same easy naturalness. Dressed in shore-togs, a white
starched shirt, black jacket, and round hat, as I took him
once to see Doña Rita, he was extremely presentable. He
could make himself interesting by a tactful and rugged reserve set off by a grim, almost imperceptible, playfulness of
tone and manner.

He had the physical assurance of strong-hearted men.

It was for this venomous performance rather than for his lies, impudence, and laziness that his uncle used to knock him down. It must not be imagined that it was anything in the nature of a brutal assault. Dominic's brawny arm would be seen describing deliberately an ample horizontal gesture, a dignified sweep, and Cesar would go over suddenly like a ninepin—which was funny to see. But, once down, he would writhe on the deck, gnashing his teeth in impotent rage—which was pretty horrible to behold. And it also happened more than once that he would disappear completely—which was startling to observe. This is the exact truth. Before some of these majestic cuffs Cesar would go down and vanish. He would vanish heels overhead into open hatchways, into scuttles, behind up-ended casks, according to the place where he happened to come into contact with his uncle's mighty arm.

Once—it was in the old harbor, just before the *Tremolino's* last voyage—he vanished thus overboard to my infinite consternation. Dominic and I had been talking business together aft, and Cesar had sneaked up behind us to listen, for, amongst his other perfections, he was a consummate eavesdropper and spy. At the sound of the heavy plop alongside, horror held me rooted to the spot; but Dominic stepped quietly to the rail and leaned over waiting for his nephew's miserable head to bob up for the first time.

"Ohé, Cesar!" he yelled, contemptuously, to the spluttering wretch. "Catch hold of that mooring hawser—*charogne!*"

He approached me to resume the interrupted conversation. "What about Cesar?" I asked, anxiously.

"*Canallia!* Let him hang there," was his answer. And he went on talking over the business in hand calmly, while I tried vainly to dismiss from my mind the picture of Cesar steeped to the chin in the water of the old harbor, a decoction of centuries of marine refuse. I tried to dismiss it, because the mere notion of that liquid made me feel very sick.

Presently Dominic, hailing an idle boatman, directed him to
go and fish his nephew out; and by and by Cesar appeared
walking on board from the quay, shivering, streaming with
filthy water, with bits of rotten straws in his hair and a
piece of dirty orange-peel stranded on his shoulder. His
teeth chattered; his yellow eyes squinted balefully at us as
he passed forward. I thought it my duty to remonstrate.

"Why are you always knocking him about, Dominic?" I
asked. Indeed, I felt convinced it was no earthly good—
a sheer waste of muscular force.

"I must try to make a man of him," Dominic answered,
hopelessly.

I restrained the obvious retort that in this way he ran the
risk of making, in the words of the immortal Mr. Mantalini,
"a demnition damp, unpleasant corpse of him."

"He wants to be a locksmith!" burst out Cervoni. "To
learn how to pick locks, I suppose," he added with sardonic
bitterness.

"Why not let him be a locksmith?" I ventured.

"Who would teach him?" he cried. "Where could I
leave him?" he asked, with a drop in his voice; and I had my
first glimpse of genuine despair. "He steals, you know, alas!
Par la Madonne! I believe he would put poison in your food
and mine—the viper!"

He raised his face and both his clenched fists slowly to
heaven. However, Cesar never dropped poison into our
cups. One cannot be sure, but I fancy he went to work in
another way.

This voyage, of which the details need not be given, we
had to range far afield for sufficient reasons. Coming up
from the South to end it with the important and really dangerous part of the scheme in hand, we found it necessary to
look into Barcelona for certain definite information. This
appears like running one's head into the very jaws of the
lion, but in reality it was not so. We had one or two high,

influential friends there, and many others humble but valuable because bought for good hard cash. We were in no danger of being molested; indeed, the important information reached us promptly by the hands of a Custom-house officer, who came on board full of showy zeal to poke an iron rod into the layer of oranges which made the visible part of our cargo in the hatchway.

I forgot to mention before that the *Tremolino* was officially known as a fruit and cork-wood trader. The zealous officer managed to slip a useful piece of paper into Dominic's hand as he went ashore, and a few hours afterwards, being off duty, he returned on board again athirst for drinks and gratitude. He got both as a matter of course. While he sat sipping his liqueur in the tiny cabin, Dominic plied him with questions as to the whereabouts of the guardacostas. The preventive service afloat was really the one for us to reckon with, and it was material for our success and safety to know the exact position of the patrol craft in the neighborhood. The news could not have been more favorable. The officer mentioned a small place on the coast some twelve miles off, where, unsuspicious and unready, she was lying at anchor, with her sails unbent, painting yards and scraping spars. Then he left us after the usual compliments, smirking reassuringly over his shoulder.

I had kept below pretty close all day from excess of prudence. The stake played on that trip was big.

"We are ready to go at once, but for Cesar, who has been missing ever since breakfast," announced Dominic to me in his slow, grim way.

Where the fellow had gone, and why, we could not imagine. The usual surmises in the case of a missing seaman did not apply to Cesar's absence. He was too odious for love, friendship, gambling, or even casual intercourse. But once or twice he had wandered away like this before.

Dominic went ashore to look for him, but returned at

the end of two hours alone and very angry, as I could see by the token of the invisible smile under his mustache being intensified. We wondered what had become of the wretch, and made a hurried investigation amongst our portable property. He had stolen nothing.

"He will be back before long," I said, confidently.

Ten minutes afterwards one of the men on deck called out loudly:

"I can see him coming."

Cesar had only his shirt and trousers on. He had sold his coat, apparently for pocket-money.

"You knave!" was all Dominic said, with a terrible softness of voice. He restrained his choler for a time. "Where have you been, vagabond?" he asked, menacingly.

Nothing would induce Cesar to answer that question. It was as if he even disdained to lie. He faced us, drawing back his lips and gnashing his teeth, and did not shrink an inch before the sweep of Dominic's arm. He went down as if shot, of course. But this time I noticed that, when picking himself up, he remained longer than usual on all fours, baring his big teeth over his shoulder and glaring upwards at his uncle with a new sort of hate in his round, yellow eyes. That permanent sentiment seemed pointed at that moment by especial malice and curiosity. I became quite interested. If he ever manages to put poison in the dishes, I thought to myself, this is how he will look at us as we sit at our meal. But I did not, of course, believe for a moment that he would ever put poison in our food. He ate the same things himself. Moreover, he had no poison. And I could not imagine a human being so blinded by cupidity as to sell poison to such an atrocious creature.

*   *   *

We slipped out to sea quietly at dusk, and all through the night everything went well. The breeze was gusty; a southerly blow was making up. It was fair wind for our course. Now and then Dominic slowly and rhythmically struck his hands together a few times, as if applauding the performance of the *Tremolino*. The balancelle hummed and quivered as she flew along, dancing lightly under our feet.

At daybreak I pointed out to Dominic, amongst the several sail in view running before the gathering storm, one particular vessel. The press of canvas she carried made her loom up high, end on, like a gray column standing motionless directly in our wake.

"Look at this fellow, Dominic," I said. "He seems to be in a hurry."

The padrone made no remark, but wrapping his black cloak about him stood up to look. His weather-tanned face, framed in the hood, had an aspect of authority and challenging force, with the deep-set eyes gazing far away fixedly, without a wink, like the intent, merciless, steady eyes of a sea-bird.

"*Chi va piano va sano,*" he remarked at last, with a derisive glance over the side, in ironic allusion to our own tremendous speed.

The *Tremolino* was doing her best, and seemed hardly to touch the great bursts of foam over which she darted. I crouched down again to get some shelter from the low bulwark. After more than half an hour of swaying immobility expressing a concentrated, breathless watchfulness, Dominic sank on the deck by my side. Within the monkish cowl his eyes gleamed with a fierce expression which surprised me. All he said was:

"He has come out here to wash the new paint off his yards, I suppose."

"What?" I shouted, getting up on my knees. "Is she the guardacosta?"

The perpetual suggestion of a smile under Dominic's

piratical mustaches seemed to become more accentuated—
quite real, grim, actually almost visible through the wet and
uncurled hair. Judging by that symptom, he must have
been in a towering rage.   But I could also see that he was
puzzled, and that discovery affected me disagreeably.   Dominic puzzled!   For a long time, leaning against the bulwark,
I gazed over the stern at the gray column that seemed to
stand swaying slightly in our wake always at the same distance.

Meanwhile Dominic, black and cowled, sat cross-legged on
the deck, with his back to the wind, recalling vaguely an
Arab chief in his *burnous* sitting on the sand.   Above his
motionless figure the little cord and tassel on the stiff point
of the hood swung about inanely in the gale.   At last I gave
up facing the wind and rain, and crouched down by his
side.   I was satisfied that the sail was a patrol craft. Her
presence was not a thing to talk about, but soon, between
two clouds charged with hail-showers, a gleam of sunshine
fell upon her sails, and our men discovered her character for
themselves.   From that moment I noticed that they seemed
to take no heed of each other or of anything else.   They
could spare no eyes and no thought but for the slight column-
shape astern of us.   Its swaying had become perceptible.
For a moment she remained dazzlingly white, then faded
away slowly to nothing in a squall, only to reappear again,
nearly black, resembling a post stuck upright against the
slaty background of solid cloud.   Since first noticed she had
not gained on us a foot.

"She will never catch the *Tremolino*," I said, exultingly.

Dominic did not look at me.   He remarked absently, but
justly, that the heavy weather was in our pursuer's favor.
She was three times our size. What we had to do was to keep
our distance till dark, which we could manage easily, and
then haul off to seaward and consider the situation.   But his
thoughts seemed to stumble in the darkness of some not-

solved enigma, and soon he fell silent. We ran steadily, wing-and-wing. Cape San Sebastian nearly ahead seemed to recede from us in the squalls of rain, and come out again to meet our rush, every time more distinct between the showers.

For my part I was by no means certain that this *gabelou* (as our men alluded to her opprobriously) was after us at all. There were nautical difficulties in such a view which made me express the sanguine opinion that she was in all innocence simply changing her station. At this Dominic condescended to turn his head.

"I tell you she is in chase," he affirmed, moodily, after one short glance astern.

I never doubted his opinion. But with all the ardor of a neophyte and the pride of an apt learner I was at that time a great nautical casuist.

"What I can't understand," I insisted, subtly, "is how on earth, with this wind, she has managed to be just where she was when we first made her out. It is clear that she could not and did not gain twelve miles on us during the night. And there are other impossibilities. . . ."

Dominic had been sitting motionless, like an inanimate black cone posed on the stern deck, near the rudder-head, with a small tassel fluttering on its sharp point, and for a time he preserved the immobility of his meditation. Then, bending over with a short laugh, he gave my ear the bitter fruit of it. He understood everything now perfectly. She was where we had seen her first, not because she had caught us up, but because we had passed her during the night while she was already waiting for us, hove-to, most likely, on our very track.

"Do you understand—already?" Dominic muttered in a fierce undertone. "Already! You know we left a good eight hours before we were expected to leave, otherwise she would have been in time to lie in wait for us on the other side of the Cape, and"—he snapped his teeth like a wolf close to my face—"and she would have had us like—that."

I saw it all plainly enough now. They had eyes in their heads and all their wits about them in that craft. We had passed them in the dark as they jogged on easily towards their ambush with the idea that we were yet far behind. At daylight, however, sighting a balancelle ahead under a press of canvas, they had made sail in chase. But if that was so, then——

Dominic seized my arm.

"Yes, yes! She came out on an information—do you see it?—on information. . . . We have been sold—betrayed. Why? How? What for? We always paid them all so well on shore. . . . No! But it is my head that is going to burst."

He seemed to choke, tugged at the throat button of the cloak, jumped up open-mouthed as if to hurl curses and denunciation, but instantly mastered himself, and, wrapping up the cloak closer about him, sat down on the deck again as quiet as ever.

"Yes, it must be the work of some scoundrel ashore," I observed.

He pulled the edge of the hood well forward over his brow before he muttered:

"A scoundrel . . . Yes. . . . It's evident."

"Well," I said, "they can't get us, that's clear."

"No," he assented, quietly, "they cannot."

We shaved the Cape very close to avoid an adverse current. On the other side, by the effect of the land, the wind failed us so completely for a moment that the *Tremolino's* two great lofty sails hung idle to the masts in the thundering uproar of the seas breaking upon the shore we had left behind. And when the returning gust filled them again, we saw with amazement half of the new mainsail, which we thought fit to drive the boat under before giving way, absolutely fly out of the bolt-ropes. We lowered the yard at once, and saved it all, but it was no longer a sail; it was only a heap of soaked strips of canvas cumbering the deck and weighting the craft. Dominic gave the order to throw the whole lot overboard.

"I would have had the yard thrown overboard, too," he said, leading me aft again, "if it had not been for the trouble. Let no sign escape you," he continued, lowering his voice, "but I am going to tell you something terrible. Listen: I have observed that the roping stitches on that sail have been cut! You hear? Cut with a knife in many places. And yet it stood all that time. Not enough cut. That flap did it at last. What matters it? But look! there's treachery seated on this very deck. By the horns of the devil! seated here at our very backs. Do not turn, signorino."

We were facing aft then.

"What's to be done?" I asked, appalled.

"Nothing. Silence! Be a man, signorino."

"What else?" I said.

To show I could be a man, I resolved to utter no sound as long as Dominic himself had the force to keep his lips closed. Nothing but silence becomes certain situations. Moreover, the experience of treachery seemed to spread a hopeless drowsiness over my thoughts and senses. For an hour or more we watched our pursuer surging out nearer and nearer from amongst the squalls that sometimes hid her altogether. But even when not seen, we felt her there like a knife at our throats. She gained on us frightfully. And the *Tremolino*, in a fierce breeze and in much smoother water, swung on easily under her one sail, with something appallingly careless in the joyous freedom of her motion. Another half-hour went by. I could not stand it any longer.

"They will get the poor barky," I stammered out, suddenly, almost on the verge of tears.

Dominic stirred no more than a carving. A sense of catastrophic loneliness overcame my inexperienced soul. The

vision of my companions passed before me. The whole
Royalist gang was in Monte Carlo now, I reckoned. And
they appeared to me clear-cut and very small, with affected
voices and stiff gestures, like a procession of rigid marionettes
upon a toy stage. I gave a start. What was this? A mysterious, remorseless whisper came from within the motionless
black hood at my side.

"*Il faut la tuer.*"

I heard it very well.

"What do you say, Dominic?" I asked, moving nothing
but my lips.

And the whisper within the hood repeated mysteriously.
"She must be killed."

My heart began to beat violently.

"That's it," I faltered out. "But how?"

"You love her well?"

"I do."

"Then you must find the heart for that work, too. You
must steer her yourself, and I shall see to it that she dies
quickly, without leaving as much as a chip behind."

"Can you?" I murmured, fascinated by the black hood
turned immovably over the stern, as if in unlawful communion with that old sea of magicians, slave-dealers, exiles,
and warriors, the sea of legends and terrors, where the
mariners of remote antiquity used to hear the restless shade
of an old wanderer weep aloud in the dark.

"I know a rock," whispered the initiated voice within the
hood secretly. "But—caution! It must be done before our
men perceive what we are about. Whom can we trust now?
A knife drawn across the fore halyards would bring the foresail down, and put an end to our liberty in twenty minutes.
And the best of our men may be afraid of drowning. There
is our little boat, but in an affair like this no one can be sure
of being saved."

The voice ceased. We had started from Barcelona with our dinghy in tow; afterwards it was too risky to try to get her in, so we let her take her chance of the seas at the end of a comfortable scope of rope. Many times she had seemed to us completely overwhelmed, but soon we would see her bob up again on a wave, apparently as buoyant and whole as ever.

"I understand," I said softly. "Very well, Dominic. When?"

"Not yet. We must get a little more in first," answered the voice from the hood in a ghostly murmur.

*　　　*　　　*

It was settled. I had now the courage to turn about. Our men crouched about the decks here and there with anxious, crestfallen faces, all turned one way to watch the chaser. For the first time that morning I perceived Cesar stretched out full length on the deck near the foremast and wondered where he had been skulking till then. But he might in truth have been at my elbow all the time for all I knew. We had been too absorbed in watching our fate to pay attention to each other. Nobody had eaten anything that morning, but the men had been coming constantly to drink at the water-butt.

I ran down to the cabin. I had there, put away in a locker, ten thousand francs in gold, of whose presence on board, so far as I was aware, not a soul except Dominic had the slightest inkling. When I emerged on deck again Dominic had turned about and was peering from under his cowl at the coast. Cape Creux closed the view ahead. To the left a wide bay, its waters torn and swept by fierce squalls, seemed full of smoke. Astern the sky had a menacing look.

Directly he saw me, Dominic, in a placid tone, wanted to know what was the matter. I came close to him and, looking as unconcerned as I could, told him in an undertone that I had found the locker broken open and the money-belt gone. Last evening it was still there.

"What did you want to do with it?" he asked me, trembling violently.

"Put it round my waist, of course," I answered, amazed to hear his teeth chattering.

"Cursed gold!" he muttered. "The weight of the money might have cost you your life, perhaps." He shuddered. "There is no time to talk about that now."

"I am ready."

"Not yet. I am waiting for that squall to come over," he muttered. And a few leaden minutes passed.

The squall came over at last. Our pursuer, overtaken by a sort of murky whirlwind, disappeared from our sight. The *Tremolino* quivered and bounded forward. The land ahead vanished, too, and we seemed to be left alone in a world of water and wind.

"*Prenez la barre, monsieur,*" Dominic broke the silence suddenly in an austere voice. "Take hold of the tiller." He bent his hood to my ear. "The balancelle is yours. Your own hands must deal the blow. I—I have yet another piece of work to do." He spoke up loudly to the man who steered. "Let the signorino take the tiller, and you with the others stand by to haul the boat alongside quickly at the word."

The man obeyed, surprised, but silent. The others stirred, and pricked up their ears at this. I heard their murmurs: "What now? Are we going to run in somewhere and take to our heels? The Padrone knows what he is doing."

Dominic went forward. He paused to look down at Cesar, who, as I have said before, was lying full length face down by the foremast, then stepped over him, and dived out of my sight under the foresail. I saw nothing ahead. It was impossible for me to see anything except the foresail open and still, like a great shadowy wing. But Dominic had his bearings. His voice came to me from forward, in a just audible cry:

"Now, signorino!"

I bore on the tiller, as instructed before. Again I heard him faintly, and then I had only to hold her straight. No ship ran so joyously to her death before. She rose and fell, as if floating in space, and darted forward, whizzing like an arrow. Dominic, stooping under the foot of the foresail, reappeared, and stood steadying himself against the mast, with a raised forefinger in an attitude of expectant attention. A second before the shock his arm fell down by his side. At that I set my teeth. And then——

Talk of splintered planks and smashed timbers! This shipwreck lies upon my soul with the dread and horror of a homicide, with the unforgettable remorse of having crushed a living, faithful heart at a single blow. At one moment the rush and the soaring swing of speed; the next a crash, and death, stillness—a moment of horrible immobility, with the song of the wind changed to a strident wail, and the heavy waters boiling up menacing and sluggish around the corpse. I saw in a distracting minute the foreyard fly fore and aft with a brutal swing, the men all in a heap, cursing with fear, and hauling frantically at the line of the boat. With a strange welcoming of the familiar I saw also Cesar amongst them, and recognized Dominic's old, well-known, effective gesture, the horizontal sweep of his powerful arm. I recollect distinctly saying to myself, "Cesar must go down, of course," and then, as I was scrambling on all fours, the swinging tiller I had let go caught me a crack under the ear, and knocked me over senseless.

I don't think I was actually unconscious for more than a few minutes, but when I came to myself the dinghy was driving before the wind into a sheltered cove, two men just keeping her straight with their oars. Dominic, with his arm around my shoulders, supported me in the stern sheets.

We landed in a familiar part of the country. Dominic took one of the boat's oars with him. I suppose he was thinking of the stream we would have presently to cross, on which there was a miserable specimen of a punt, often robbed of its pole. But first of all we had to ascend the ridge of land at the back of the Cape. He helped me up. I was dizzy. My head felt very large and heavy. At the top of the ascent I clung to him, and we stopped to rest.

To the right, below us, the wide, smoky bay was empty. Dominic had kept his word. There was not a chip to be seen around the black rock from which the *Tremolino*, with her plucky heart crushed at one blow, had slipped off into deep water to her eternal rest. The vastness of the open sea was smothered in driving mists, and in the center of the thinning squall, phantomlike, under a frightful press of canvas, the unconscious guardacosta dashed on, still chasing to the northward. Our men were already descending the reverse slope to look for that punt, which, we knew from experience, was not always to be found easily. I looked after them with dazed, misty eyes. One, two, three, four.

"Dominic, where's Cesar?" I cried.

As if repulsing the very sound of the name, the Padrone made that ample, sweeping, knocking-down gesture. I stepped back a pace and stared at him fearfully. His open shirt uncovered his muscular neck and the thick hair on his chest. He planted the oar upright in the soft soil, and rolling up slowly his right sleeve, extended the bare arm before my face.

"This," he began, with an extreme deliberation, whose superhuman restraint vibrated with the suppressed violence of his feelings, "is the arm which delivered the blow. I am afraid it is your own gold that did the rest. I forgot all about your money." He clasped his hands together in sudden distress. "I forgot, I forgot," he repeated, disconsolately.

"Cesar stole the belt?" I stammered out, bewildered.

"And who else? *Canallia!* He must have been spying on you for days. And he did the whole thing. Absent all day in Barcelona. *Traditore!* Sold his jacket—to hire a horse. Ha! ha! A good affair! I tell you it was he who set him at us. . . ."

Dominic pointed at the sea, where the guardacosta was a mere dark speck. His chin dropped on his breast.

". . . On information," he murmured, in a gloomy voice. "A Cervoni! Oh! my poor brother! . . ."

"And you drowned him," I said, feebly.

"I struck once, and the wretch went down like a stone —with the gold. Yes. But he had time to read in my eyes that nothing could save him while I was alive. And had I not the right—I, Dominic Cervoni, Padrone, who brought him aboard your felucca—my nephew, a traitor?"

He pulled the oar out of the ground and helped me carefully down the slope. All the time he never once looked me in the face. He punted us over, then shouldered the oar again and waited till our men were at some distance before he offered me his arm. After we had gone a little way, the fishing hamlet we were making for came into view. Dominic stopped.

"Do you think you can make your way as far as the houses by yourself?" he asked me, quietly.

"Yes, I think so. But why? Where are you going, Dominic?"

"Anywhere. What a question! Signorino, you are but little more than a boy to ask such a question of a man having this tale in his family. Ah! *Traditore!* What made me ever own that spawn of a hungry devil for our own blood! Thief, cheat, coward, liar—other men can deal with that. But I was his uncle, and so . . . I wish he had poisoned me

—*charogne!* But this: that I, a confidential man and a Corsican, should have to ask your pardon for bringing on board your vessel, of which I was Padrone, a Cervoni, who has betrayed you—a traitor!—that is too much. It is too much. Well, I beg your pardon; and you may spit in Dominic's face because a traitor of our blood taints us all. A theft may be made good between men, a lie may be set right, a death avenged, but what can one do to atone for a treachery like this? . . . Nothing."

He turned and walked away from me along the bank of the stream, flourishing a vengeful arm and repeating to himself slowly, with savage emphasis: "Ah! *Canaille! Canaille! Canaille!* . . ." He left me there trembling with weakness and mute with awe. Unable to make a sound, I gazed after the strangely desolate figure of that seaman carrying an oar on his shoulder up a barren, rock-strewn ravine under the dreary leaden sky of *Tremolino's* last day. Thus, walking deliberately, with his back to the sea, Dominic vanished from my sight.

With the quality of our desires, thoughts, and wonder proportioned to our infinite littleness we measure even time itself by our own stature. Imprisoned in the house of personal illusions thirty centuries in mankind's history seem less to look back upon than thirty years of our own life. And Dominic Cervoni takes his place in my memory by the side of the legendary wanderer on the sea of marvels and terrors, by the side of the fatal and impious adventurer, to whom the evoked shade of the soothsayer predicted a journey inland with an oar on his shoulder, till he met men who had never set eyes on ships and oars. It seems to me I can see them side by side in the twilight of an arid land, the unfortunate possessors of the secret lore of the sea, bearing the emblem of their hard calling on their shoulders, surrounded by silent and curious men: even as I, too, having turned my back upon the sea, am bearing these few pages in the twilight, with the

hope of finding in an inland valley the silent welcome of
some patient listener.

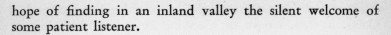

SIGNING ON

[The *Tremolino* adventure left this impression on Conrad: it was
"conducted with inconceivable stupidity and a foredoomed failure
from the first.   There was indeed nothing great there worthy of
anybody's passionate devotion."   On his return to Marseilles, a
brief love affair with Rita ended also in "a foredoomed failure."
When Rita learned that Conrad had recovered from a bullet wound
which he had received in a duel with J. M. K. Blunt, she disappeared.   Marseilles became intolerable to him, and he left there on
April 24, 1878, on board an English steamer for Constantinople.
Finally he arrived at Lowestoft, England, on June 18, 1878.   After
a brief apprenticeship on coasters, he set out for London.   As is
revealed in the following passages, he meant to be "a seaman worthy
of the service."]

The North Sea was my finishing school of seamanship before I launched myself on the wider oceans . . . . My class-
room was the region of the English East Coast . . . . It was
a peaceful coast, agricultural, industrial, the home of fishermen.   At night the lights of its many towns played on the
clouds, or in clear weather lay still, here and there, in brilliant
pools above the ink-black outline of the land.   On many a
night I have hauled at the braces under the shadow of that
coast, envying, as sailors will, the people on the shore sleeping
quietly in their beds within sound of the sea . . .
After a period of probation and training I had imposed
upon myself as ordinary seaman on board a North Sea
coaster, I had come up from Lowestoft—my first long railway journey in England—to "sign on" for an Antipodean
voyage in a deep-water ship.   Straight from a railway carriage I had walked into the great city with something of the

feeling of a traveler penetrating into a vast and unexplored wilderness. No explorer could have been more lonely. I did not know a single soul of all these millions that all around me peopled the mysterious distances of the streets. I cannot say I was free from a little youthful awe, but at that age one's feelings are simple. I was elated. I was pursuing a clear aim, I was carrying out a deliberate plan of making out of myself, in the first place, a seaman worthy of the service, good enough to work by the side of the men with whom I was to live; and in the second place, I had to justify my existence to myself, to redeem a tacit moral pledge. Both these aims were to be attained by the same effort. How simple seemed the problem of life then, on that hazy day of early September in the year 1878, when I entered London for the first time.

From that point of view—youth and a straightforward scheme of conduct—it was certainly a year of grace. All the help I had to get in touch with the world I was invading was a piece of paper not much bigger than the palm of my hand—in which I held it—torn out of a larger plan of London for the greater facility of reference. It had been the object of careful study for some days past. The fact that I could take a conveyance at the station never occurred to my mind, no, not even when I got out into the street, and stood, taking my anxious bearings, in the midst, so to speak, of twenty thousand hansoms. A strange absence of mind or unconscious conviction that one cannot approach an important moment of one's life by means of a hired carriage? Yes, it would have been a preposterous proceeding. And indeed I was to make an Australian voyage and encircle the globe before ever entering a London hansom.

Another document, a cutting from a newspaper, containing the address of an obscure shipping agent, was in my pocket. And I needed not to take it out. That address was as if graven deep in my brain. I muttered its words to myself as I walked on, navigating the sea of London by the chart concealed in the palm of my hand; for I had vowed to myself not to inquire my way from any one. Youth is the time of rash pledges. Had I taken a wrong turning I would have been lost; and if faithful to my pledge I might have remained lost for days, for weeks, have left perhaps my bones to be discovered bleaching in some blind alley of the Whitechapel district, as it has happened to lonely travelers lost in the bush. But I walked on to my destination without hesitation or mistake, showing there, for the first time, some of that faculty to absorb and make my own the imagined topography of a chart, which in later years was to help me in regions of intricate navigation to keep the ships entrusted to me off the ground. The place I was bound to was not easy to find. It was one of those courts hidden away from the charted and navigable streets, lost among the thick growth of houses like a dark pool in the depths of a forest, approached by an inconspicuous archway as if by a secret path; a Dickensian nook of London, that wonder city, the growth of which bears no sign of intelligent design, but many traces of freakishly somber fantasy the Great Master knew so well how to bring out by the magic of his understanding love. And the office I entered was Dickensian too. The dust of the Waterloo year lay on the panes and frames of its windows; early Georgian grime clung to its somber wainscoting.

It was one o'clock in the afternoon, but the day was gloomy. By the light of a single gas jet depending from the smoked ceiling I saw an elderly man, in a long coat of black broadcloth. He had a gray beard, a big nose, thick lips, and heavy shoulders. His curly white hair and the general character of his head recalled vaguely a burly apostle in the *barocco* style of Italian art. Standing up at a tall, shabby, slanting desk, his silver-rimmed spectacles pushed up high on his forehead, he was eating a mutton-chop, which had been just brought to him from some Dickensian eating-house round the corner.

Without ceasing to eat he turned to me his florid *barocco* apostle's face with an expression of inquiry.

I produced elaborately a series of vocal sounds which must have borne sufficient resemblance to the phonetics of English speech, for his face broke into a smile of comprehension almost at once. "Oh it's you who wrote a letter to me the other day from Lowestoft about getting a ship."

I had written to him from Lowestoft. I can't remember a single word of that letter now. It was my very first composition in the English language. And he had understood it, evidently, for he spoke to the point at once, explaining that his business, mainly, was to find good ships for young gentlemen who wanted to go to sea as premium apprentices with a view of being trained for officers. But he gathered that this was not my object. I did not desire to be apprenticed. Was that the case?

It was. He was good enough to say then, "Of course I see that you are a gentleman. But your wish is to get a berth before the mast as an Able Seaman if possible. Is that it?"

It was certainly my wish. . . .

SHIPS AND SHIPMASTERS

[The following group of selections, arranged topically rather than chronologically, is Conrad's own interpretation of his development during his exacting life on the sea. From 1874, at the age of seventeen, to 1888, he served on various ships under a large variety of shipmasters. Each experience left its mark.]

INITIATION

The most amazing wonder of the deep is its unfathomable cruelty. I felt its dread for the first time in mid-Atlantic one day, many years ago, when we took off the crew of a Danish brig homeward bound from the West Indies. A thin, silvery mist softened the calm and majestic splendor of light without shadows—seemed to render the sky less remote and the ocean less immense. It was one of the days when the might of the sea appears indeed lovable, like the nature of a strong man in moments of quiet intimacy. At sunrise we had made out a black speck to the westward, apparently suspended high up in the void behind a stirring, shimmering veil of silvery blue gauze that seemed at times to stir and float in the breeze which fanned us slowly along. The peace of that enchanting forenoon was so profound, so untroubled, that it seemed that every word pronounced loudly on our deck would penetrate to the very heart of that infinite mystery born from the conjunction of water and sky. We did not raise our voices. "A water-logged derelict, I think, sir," said the second officer, quietly, coming down from aloft with the binoculars in their case slung across his shoulders; and our captain, without a word, signed to the helmsman to steer for the black speck. Presently we made out a low, jagged stump sticking up forward—all that remained of her departed masts.

The captain was expatiating in a low conversational tone to the chief mate upon the danger of these derelicts, and upon his dread of coming upon them at night, when suddenly a man forward screamed out, "There's people on board of her, sir! I see them!" in a most extraordinary voice—a voice never heard before in our ship; the amazing voice of a stranger. It gave the signal for a sudden tumult of shouts. The watch below ran up the forecastle head in a body, the cook dashed out of the galley. Everybody saw the poor fellows now. They were there! And all at once our ship, which had the well-earned name of being without a rival for speed in light winds, seemed to us to have lost the power of motion, as if the sea, becoming viscous, had clung to her sides.   And yet she moved.   Immensity, the inseparable companion of a ship's life, chose that day to breathe upon her as gently as a sleeping child.   The clamor of our excitement had died out, and our living ship, famous for never losing steerage way as long as there was air enough to float a feather, stole, without a ripple, silent and white as a ghost, towards her mutilated and wounded sister, come upon at the point of death in the sunlit haze of a calm day at sea.

With the binoculars glued to his eyes, the captain said in a quavering tone: "They are waving to us with something aft there." He put down the glasses on the skylight brusquely, and began to walk about the poop. "A shirt or flag," he ejaculated, irritably. "Can't make it out. . . . Some damn rag or other!" He took a few more turns on the poop, glancing down over the rail now and then to see how fast we were moving. His nervous footsteps rang sharply in the quiet of the ship, where the other men, all looking the same way, had forgotten themselves in a staring immobility. "This will never do!" he cried out, suddenly. "Lower the boats at once!   Down with them!"

Before I jumped into mine he took me aside, as being an inexperienced junior, for a word of warning:

"You look out as you come alongside that she doesn't take you down with her.   You understand?"

He murmured this confidentially, so that none of the men at the falls should overhear, and I was shocked. "Heavens! as if in such an emergency one stopped to think of danger!" I exclaimed to myself mentally, in scorn of such cold-blooded caution.

It takes many lessons to make a real seaman, and I got my rebuke at once.   My experienced commander seemed in one searching glance to read my thoughts on my ingenuous face.

"What you're going for is to save life, not to drown your boat's crew for nothing," he growled, severely, in my ear. But as we shoved off he leaned over and cried out: "It all rests on the power of your arms, men. Give way for life!"

We made a race of it, and I would never have believed that a common boat's crew of a merchantman could keep up so much determined fierceness in the regular swing of their stroke. What our captain had clearly perceived before we left had become plain to all of us since. The issue of our enterprise hung on a hair above that abyss of waters which will not give up its dead till the Day of Judgment. It was a race of two ship's boats matched against Death for a prize of nine men's lives, and Death had a long start. We saw the crew of the brig from afar working at the pumps—still pumping on that wreck, which already had settled so far down that the gentle, low swell, over which our boats rose and fell easily without a check to their speed, welling up almost level with her head-rails, plucked at the ends of broken gear swinging desolately under her naked bowsprit.

We could not, in all conscience, have picked out a better day for our regatta had we had the free choice of all the days that ever dawned upon the lonely struggles and solitary agonies of ships since the Norse rovers first steered to the westward against the run of Atlantic waves. It was a very good race. At the finish there was not an oar's length between the first and second boat, with Death coming in a good third on the top of the very next smooth swell, for all one knew to the contrary. The scuppers of the brig gurgled softly all together when the water rising against her sides subsided sleepily with a low wash, as if playing about an immovable rock. Her bulwarks were gone fore and aft, and one saw her bare deck low-lying like a raft and swept clean of boats, spars, houses—of everything except the ringbolts and the heads of the pumps. I had one dismal glimpse of it as I braced myself up to receive upon my breast the last man to leave her, the captain, who literally let himself fall into my arms.

It had been a weirdly silent rescue—a rescue without a

hail, without a single uttered word, without a gesture or a sign, without a conscious exchange of glances. Up to the very last moment those on board stuck to their pumps, which spouted two clear streams of water upon their bare feet. Their brown skin showed through the rents of their shirts; and the two small bunches of half-naked, tattered men went on bowing from the waist to each other in their back-breaking labor, up and down, absorbed, with no time for a glance over the shoulder at the help that was coming to them. As we dashed, unregarded, alongside, a voice let out one, only one hoarse howl of command, and then, just as they stood, without caps, with the salt drying gray in the wrinkles and folds of their hairy, haggard faces, blinking stupidly at us their red eyelids, they made a bolt away from the handles, tottering and jostling against each other, and positively flung themselves over upon our very heads. The clatter they made tumbling into the boats had an extraordinarily destructive effect upon the illusion of tragic dignity our self-esteem had thrown over the contests of mankind with the sea. On that exquisite day of gentle breathing peace and veiled sunshine perished my romantic love to what men's imagination had proclaimed the most august aspect of Nature. The cynical indifference of the sea to the merits of human suffering and courage, laid bare in this ridiculous, panic-tainted perform-ance extorted from the dire extremity of nine good and honorable seamen, revolted me. I saw the duplicity of the sea's most tender mood. It was so because it could not help itself, but the awed respect of the early days was gone. I felt ready to smile bitterly at its enchanting charm and glare viciously at its furies. In a moment, before we shoved off, I had looked coolly at the life of my choice. Its illusions were gone, but its fascination remained. I had become a seaman at last.

We pulled hard for a quarter of an hour, then laid on our oars waiting for our ship. She was coming down on us with swelling sails, looking delicately tall and exquisitely noble through the mist. The captain of the brig, who sat in the stern sheets by my side with his face in his hands, raised his head and began to speak with a sort of somber volubility. They had lost their masts and sprung a leak in a hurricane; drifted for weeks, always at the pumps, met more bad weather; the ships they sighted failed to make them out, the leak gained upon them slowly, and the seas had left them nothing to make a raft of. It was very hard to see ship after ship pass by at a distance, "as if everybody had agreed that we must be left to drown," he added. But they went on trying to keep the brig afloat as long as possible, and working the pumps constantly on insufficient food, mostly raw, till "yesterday evening," he continued, monotonously, "just as the sun went down, the men's hearts broke."

He made an almost imperceptible pause here, and went on again with exactly the same intonation:

"They told me the brig could not be saved, and they thought they had done enough for themselves. I said nothing to that. It was true. It was no mutiny. I had nothing to say to them. They lay about aft all night as still as so many dead men. I did not lie down. I kept a look-out. When the first light came I saw your ship at once. I waited for more light; the breeze began to fail on my face. Then I shouted out as loud as I was able, 'Look at that ship!' but only two men got up very slowly and came to me. At first only we three stood alone, for a long time, watching you coming down to us, and feeling the breeze drop to a calm almost; but afterwards others, too, rose, one after another, and by and by I had all my crew behind me. I turned round and said to them that they could see the ship was coming our way, but in this small breeze she might come too late after all, unless we turned to and tried to keep the brig afloat long enough to give you time to save us all. I spoke like that to them, and then I gave the command to man the pumps.

He gave the command, and gave the example too, by going himself to the handles, but it seems that these men did actually hang back for a moment, looking at each other dubiously before they followed him. "He! he! he!" He broke out into a most unexpected, imbecile, pathetic, nervous little giggle. "Their hearts were broken so! They had been played with too long," he explained, apologetically, lowering his eyes, and became silent.

Twenty-five years is a long time—a quarter of a century is a dim and distant past; but to this day I remember the dark-brown feet, hands, and faces of two of these men whose hearts had been broken by the sea. They were lying very still on their sides on the bottom boards between the thwarts, curled up like dogs. My boat's crew, leaning over the looms of their oars, stared and listened as if at the play. The master of the brig looked up suddenly to ask me what day it was.

They had lost the date. When I told him it was Sunday, the 22nd, he frowned, making some mental calculation, then nodded twice sadly to himself, staring at nothing.

His aspect was miserably unkempt and wildly sorrowful. Had it not been for the unquenchable candor of his blue eyes, whose unhappy, tired glance every moment sought his abandoned, sinking brig, as if it could find rest nowhere else, he would have appeared mad. But he was too simple to go mad, too simple with that manly simplicity which alone can bear men unscathed in mind and body through an encounter with the deadly playfulness of the sea or with its less abominable fury.

Neither angry, nor playful, nor smiling, it enveloped our distant ship growing bigger as she neared us, our boats with the rescued men and the dismantled hull of the brig we were leaving behind, in the large and placid embrace of its quietness, half lost in the fair haze, as if in a dream of infinite and tender clemency. There was no frown, no wrinkle on its face, not a ripple. And the run of the slight swell was so

After half an hour's interview in the dining-room, during which they got in touch with each other in an amazing way, Rita told us in her best *grande dame* manner: *"Mais il est parfait, cet homme."* He was perfect. On board the *Tremolino,* wrapped up in a black *caban,* the picturesque cloak of Mediterranean seamen, with those massive mustaches and his remorseless eyes set off by the shadow of the deep hood, he looked piratical and monkish and darkly initiated into the most awful mysteries of the sea.

*　　*　　*

Anyway, he was perfect, as Doña Rita had declared. The only thing unsatisfactory (and even inexplicable) about our Dominic was his nephew, Cesar. It was startling to see a desolate expression of shame veil the remorseless audacity in the eyes of that man superior to all scruples and terrors.

"I would never have dared to bring him on board your balancelle," he once apologized to me. "But what am I to do? His mother is dead, and my brother has gone into the bush."

In this way, I learned that our Dominic had a brother. As to "going into the bush," this only means that a man has done his duty successfully in the pursuit of an hereditary vendetta. The feud which had existed for ages between the families of Cervoni and Brunaschi was so old that it seemed to have smouldered out at last. One evening Pietro Brunaschi, after a laborious day amongst his olive-trees, sat on a chair against the wall of his house with a bowl of broth on his knees and a piece of bread in his hand. Dominic's brother, going home with a gun on his shoulder, found a sudden offence in this picture of content and rest so obviously calculated to awaken the feelings of hatred and revenge. He and Pietro had never had any personal quarrel; but, as Dominic explained, "all our dead cried out to him." He shouted from behind a wall of stones, "O Pietro! Behold

what is coming!" And as the other looked up innocently
he took aim at the forehead and squared the old vendetta
account so neatly that, according to Dominic, the dead
man continued to sit with the bowl of broth on his knees and
the piece of bread in his hand.

This is why—because in Corsica your dead will not leave
you alone—Dominic's brother had to go into the *maquis,*
into the bush on the wild mountain-side, to dodge the gen-
darmes for the insignificant remainder of his life, and
Dominic had charge of his nephew with a mission to make
a man of him.

No more unpromising undertaking could be imagined.
The very material for the task seemed wanting. The
Cervonis, if not handsome men, were good sturdy flesh and
blood. But his extraordinarily lean and livid youth seemed
to have no more blood in him than a snail.

"Some cursed witch must have stolen my brother's child
from the cradle and put that spawn of a starved devil in its
place," Dominic would say to me. "Look at him! Just
look at him!"

To look at Cesar was not pleasant. His parchment skin,
showing dead white on his cranium through the thin wisps
of dirty brown hair, seemed to be glued directly and tightly
upon his big bones. Without being in any way deformed,
he was the nearest approach which I have ever seen or could
imagine to what is commonly understood by the word
"monster." That the source of the effect produced was
really moral I have no doubt. An utterly, hopelessly de-
praved nature was expressed in physical terms, that taken
each separately had nothing positively startling. You
imagined him clammily cold to the touch, like a snake. The
slightest reproof, the most mild and justifiable remonstrance,
would be met by a resentful glare and an evil shrinking of
his thin dry upper lip, a snarl of hate to which he generally
added the agreeable sound of grinding teeth.

smooth that it resembled the graceful undulation of a piece
of shimmering gray silk shot with gleams of green. We
pulled an easy stroke; but when the master of the brig, after
a glance over his shoulder, stood up with a low exclamation,
my men feathered their oars instinctively, without an order,
and the boat lost her way.

He was steadying himself on my shoulder with a strong
grip, while his other arm, flung up rigidly, pointed a de-
nunciatory finger at the immense tranquillity of the ocean.
After his first exclamation, which stopped the swing of our
oars, he made no sound, but his whole attitude seemed to cry
out an indignant "Behold!" . . . I could not imagine what
vision of evil had come to him. I was startled, and the
amazing energy of his immobilized gesture made my heart
beat faster with the anticipation of something monstrous and
unsuspected. The stillness around us became crushing.

For a moment the succession of silky undulations ran on
innocently. I saw each of them swell up the misty line of the
horizon, far, far away beyond the derelict brig, and the next
moment, with a slight friendly toss of our boat, it had passed
under us and was gone. The lulling cadence of the rise and
fall, the invariable gentleness of this irresistible force, the
great charm of the deep waters, warmed my breast de-
liciously, like the subtle poison of a love-potion. But all
this lasted only a few soothing seconds before I jumped up,
too, making the boat roll like the veriest land-lubber.

Something startling, mysterious, hastily confused was taking place. I watched it with incredulous and fascinated
awe, as one watches the confused, swift movements of some
deed of violence done in the dark. As if at a given signal,
the run of the smooth undulations seemed checked suddenly
around the brig. By a strange optical delusion the whole
sea appeared to rise upon her in one overwhelming heave of
its silky surface where in one spot a smother of foam broke
out ferociously. And then the effort subsided. It was all

over, and the smooth swell ran on as before from the horizon in uninterrupted cadence of motion, passing under us with a slight friendly toss of our boat. Far away, where the brig had been, an angry white stain undulating on the surface of steely-gray waters, shot with gleams of green, diminished swiftly without a hiss, like a patch of pure snow melting in the sun. And the great stillness after this initiation into the sea's implacable hate seemed full of dread thoughts and shadows of disaster.

"Gone!" ejaculated from the depths of his chest my bowman in a final tone. He spat in his hands, and took a better grip on his oar. The captain of the brig lowered his rigid arm slowly, and looked at our faces in a solemnly conscious silence, which called upon us to share in his simple-minded, marveling awe. All at once he sat down by my side, and leaned forward earnestly at my boat's crew, who, swinging together in a long, easy stroke, kept their eyes fixed upon him faithfully.

"No ship could have done so well," he addressed them, firmly, after a moment of strained silence, during which he seemed with trembling lips to seek for words fit to bear such high testimony. "She was small, but she was good. I had no anxiety. She was strong. Last voyage I had my wife and two children in her. No other ship could have stood so long the weather she had to live through for days and days before we got dismasted a fortnight ago. She was fairly worn out, and that's all. You may believe me. She lasted under us for days and days, but she could not last forever. It was long enough. I am glad it is over. No better ship was ever left to sink at sea on such a day as this."

He was competent to pronounce the funeral oration of a ship, this son of ancient sea-folk, whose national existence, so little stained by the excesses of manly virtues, had demanded nothing but the merest foothold from the earth. By the merits of his sea-wise forefathers and by the artlessness of his heart, he was made fit to deliver this excellent discourse. There was nothing wanting in its orderly arrangement—neither piety nor faith, nor the tribute of praise due to the worthy dead, with the edifying recital of their achievement. She had lived, he had loved her; she had suffered, and he was glad she was at rest. It was an excellent discourse. And it was orthodox, too, in its fidelity to the cardinal article of a seaman's faith, of which it was a single-minded confession. "Ships are all right." They are. They who live with the sea have got to hold by that creed first and last; and it came to me, as I glanced at him sideways, that some men were not altogether unworthy in honor and conscience to pronounce the funeral eulogium of a ship's constancy in life and death.

After this, sitting by my side with his loosely clasped hands hanging between his knees, he uttered no word, made no movement till the shadow of our ship's sails fell on the boat, when, at the loud cheer greeting the return of the victors with their prize, he lifted up his troubled face with a faint smile of pathetic indulgence. This smile of the worthy descendant of the most ancient sea-folk whose audacity and hardihood had left no trace of greatness and glory upon the waters, completed the cycle of my initiation. There was an infinite depth of hereditary wisdom in its pitying sadness. It made the hearty bursts of cheering sound like a childish noise of triumph. Our crew shouted with immense confidence—honest souls! As if anybody could ever make sure of having prevailed against the sea, which has betrayed so many ships of great "name," so many proud men, so many towering ambitions of fame, power, wealth, greatness!

As I brought the boat under the falls my captain, in high good-humor, leaned over, spreading his red and freckled elbows on the rail, and called down to me sarcastically out of the depths of his cynic philosopher's beard:

"So you have brought the boat back after all, have you?"

Sarcasm was "his way," and the most that can be said for it is that it was natural. This did not make it lovable. But it is decorous and expedient to fall in with one's commander's way. "Yes. I brought the boat back all right, sir," I answered. And the good man believed me. It was not for him to discern upon me the marks of my recent initiation. And yet I was not exactly the same youngster who had taken the boat away—all impatience for a race against Death, with the prize of nine men's lives at the end.

Already I looked with other eyes upon the sea. I knew it capable of betraying the generous ardor of youth as implacably as, indifferent to evil and good, it would have betrayed the basest greed or the noblest heroism. My conception of its magnanimous greatness was gone. And I looked upon the true sea—the sea that plays with men till their hearts are broken, and wears stout ships to death. Nothing can touch the brooding bitterness of its soul. Open to all and faithful to none, it exercises its fascination for the undoing of the best. To love it is not well. It knows no bond of plighted troth, no fidelity to misfortune, to long companionship, to long devotion. The promise it holds out perpetually is very great; but the only secret of its possession is strength, strength—the jealous, sleepless strength of a man guarding a coveted treasure within his gates.

MERETRICIOUS GLORY

There was an infinite diversity of temperament amongst the masters of the fine art I have known. Some were great impressionists. They impressed upon you the fear of God and Immensity—or, in other words, the fear of being drowned with every circumstance of terrific grandeur. One may think that the locality of your passing away by means of suffocation in water does not really matter very much. I am not so sure of that. I am, perhaps, unduly sensitive, but

I confess that the idea of being suddenly spilt into an in-furiated ocean in the midst of darkness and uproar affected me always with a sensation of shrinking distaste. To be drowned in a pond, though it might be called an ignominious fate by the ignorant, is yet a bright and peaceful ending in comparison with some other endings to one's earthly career which I have mentally quaked at in the intervals, or even in the midst, of violent exertions.

But let that pass. Some of the masters whose influence left a trace upon my character to this very day, combined a fierceness of conception with a certitude of execution upon the basis of just appreciation of means and ends which is the highest quality of the man of action. And an artist is a man of action, whether he creates a personality, invents an ex-pedient, or finds the issue of a complicated situation.

There were masters, too, I have known, whose very art consisted in avoiding every conceivable situation. It is need-less to say that they never did great things in their craft; but they were not to be despised for that. They were modest; they understood their limitations. Their own masters had not handed the sacred fire into the keeping of their cold and skilful hands. One of those last I remember specially, now gone to his rest from that sea which his tem-perament must have made a scene of little more than a peace-ful pursuit. Once only did he attempt a stroke of audacity, one early morning, with a steady breeze, entering a crowded roadstead. But he was not genuine in this display which might have been art. He was thinking of his own self; he hankered after the meretricious glory of a showy per-formance.

As, rounding a dark, wooded point, bathed in fresh air and sunshine, we opened to view a crowd of shipping at anchor lying half a mile ahead of us perhaps, he called me aft from my station on the forecastle head, and, turning over and over his binoculars in his brown hands, said: "Do you see that big, heavy ship with white lower masts? I am going to take up a berth between her and the shore. Now do you see to it that the men jump smartly at the first order."

I answered, "Ay, ay, sir," and verily believed that this would be a fine performance. We dashed on through the fleet in magnificent style. There must have been many open mouths and following eyes on board those ships—Dutch, English, with a sprinkling of Americans and a German or two—who had all hoisted their flags at eight o'clock as if in honor of our arrival. It would have been a fine performance if it had come off, but it did not. Through a touch of self-seeking that modest artist of solid merit became untrue to his temperament. It was not with him art for art's sake: it was art for his own sake; and a dismal failure was the penalty he paid for that greatest of sins. It might have been even heavier, but, as it happened, we did not run our ship ashore, nor did we knock a large hole in the big ship whose lower masts were painted white. But it is a wonder that we did not carry away the cables of both our anchors, for, as may be imagined, I did not stand upon the order to "Let go!" that came to me in a quavering, quite unknown voice from his trembling lips. I let them both go with a celerity which to this day astonishes my memory. No average merchantman's anchors have ever been let go with such miraculous smartness. And they both held. I could have kissed their rough, cold iron palms in gratitude if they had not been buried in slimy mud under ten fathoms of water. Ultimately they brought us up with the jib boom of a Dutch brig poking through our spanker—nothing worse. And a miss is as good as a mile.

But not in art. Afterwards the master said to me in a shy mumble, "She wouldn't luff up in time, somehow. What's the matter with her?" And I made no answer.

Yet the answer was clear. The ship had found out the momentary weakness of her man. Of all the living creatures upon land and sea, it is ships alone that cannot be taken in by barren pretences, that will not put up with bad art from their masters.

A DEAF MAN VS. AN ANGRY ONE

I had been some time at sea before I became aware of the fact that hearing plays a perceptible part in gauging the force of the wind. It was at night. The ship was one of those iron wool-clippers that the Clyde had floated out in swarms upon the world during the seventh decade of the last century. It was a fine period in ship-building, and also, I might say, a period of overmasting. The spars rigged up on the narrow hulls were indeed tall then, and the ship of which I think, with her colored-glass skylight ends bearing the motto, "Let Glasgow Flourish," was certainly one of the most heavily-sparred specimens. She was built for hard driving, and unquestionably she got all the driving she could stand. Our captain was a man famous for the quick passages he had been used to make in the old *Tweed*, a ship famous the world over for her speed. The *Tweed* had been a wooden vessel, and he brought the tradition of quick passages with him into the iron clipper. I was the junior in her, a third mate, keeping watch with the chief officer; and it was just during one of the night watches in a strong, freshening breeze that I overheard two men in a sheltered nook of the main deck exchanging these informing remarks. Said one:

"Should think 'twas time some of them light sails were coming off her."

And the other, an older man, uttered grumpily:

"No fear! not while the chief mate's on deck. He's that deaf he can't tell how much wind there is."

And, indeed, poor P——, quite young, and a smart seaman, was very hard of hearing. At the same time, he had the name of being the very devil of a fellow for carrying on sail on a ship. He was wonderfully clever at concealing his deafness, and, as to carrying on heavily, though he was a fearless man, I don't think that he ever meant to take undue risks.   I can never forget his naïve sort of astonishment when remonstrated with for what appeared a most dare-devil performance.   The only person, of course, that could remonstrate with telling effect was our captain, himself a man of dare-devil tradition, and really, for me, who knew under whom I was serving, those were impressive scenes.   Captain S—— had a great name for sailorlike qualities—the sort of name that compelled my youthful admiration.   To this day I preserve his memory, for, indeed, it was he in a sense who completed my training.   It was often a stormy process, but let that pass.   I am sure he meant well, and I am certain that never, not even at the time, could I bear him malice for his extraordinary gift of incisive criticism.   And to hear *him* make a fuss about too much sail on the ship seemed one of those incredible experiences that take place only in one's dreams.

It generally happened in this way: Night clouds racing overhead, wind howling, royals set, and the ship rushing on in the dark, an immense white sheet of foam level with the lee rail.   Mr. P——, in charge of the deck, hooked on to the windward mizzen rigging in a state of perfect serenity; myself, the third mate, also hooked on somewhere to windward of the slanting poop, in a state of the utmost preparedness to jump at the very first hint of some sort of order, but otherwise in a perfectly acquiescent state of mind.   Suddenly, out of the companion would appear a tall, dark figure, bareheaded, with a short white beard of a perpendicular cut, very visible in the dark—Captain S——, disturbed in his reading down below by the frightful bounding and lurching of the ship.   Leaning very much against the precipitous incline of the deck, he would take a turn or two, perfectly silent, hang on by the compass for a while, take another couple of turns, and suddenly burst out:

"What are you trying to do with the ship?"

And Mr. P——, who was not good at catching what was shouted in the wind, would say interrogatively:

"Yes, sir?"

Then in the increasing gale of the sea there would be a little private ship's storm going on in which you could detect strong language, pronounced in a tone of passion, and exculpatory protestations uttered with every possible inflection of injured innocence.

"By Heavens, Mr. P——! I used to carry on sail in my time, but——"

And the rest would be lost to me in a stormy gust of wind.

Then, in a lull, P——'s protesting innocence would become audible:

"She seems to stand it very well."

And then another burst of an indignant voice:

"Any fool can carry sail on a ship——"

And so on and so on, the ship meanwhile rushing on her way with a heavier list, a noisier splutter, a more threatening hiss of the white, almost blinding, sheet of foam to leeward. For the best of it was that Captain S—— seemed constitutionally incapable of giving his officers a definite order to shorten sail; and so that extraordinarily vague row would go on till at last it dawned upon them both, in some particularly alarming gust, that it was time to do something. There is nothing like the fearful inclination of your tall spars overloaded with canvas to bring a deaf man and an angry one to their senses.

THE SHIP WE SERVE

I have even had a downright thief in my experience. One. This is indeed a minute proportion, but it might have been my luck; and since I am writing in eulogy of seamen I feel irresistibly tempted to talk about this unique specimen; not indeed to offer him as an example of morality, but to bring

out certain characteristics and set out a certain point of view.
He was a large, strong man with a guileless countenance, not
very communicative with his shipmates; but when drawn
into any sort of conversation displaying a very painstaking
earnestness. He was fair and candid-eyed, of a very satisfactory smartness, and, from the officer-of-the-watch point
of view, altogether dependable. Then, suddenly, he went
and stole. And he didn't go away from his honorable kind
to do that thing to somebody on shore; he stole right there
on the spot, in proximity to his shipmates, on board his own
ship, with complete disregard for old Brown, our night
watchman (whose fame for trustworthiness was utterly
blasted for the rest of the voyage) and in such a way as to
bring the profoundest possible trouble to all the blameless
souls animating that ship. He stole eleven golden sovereigns,
and a gold pocket chronometer and chain. I am really in
doubt whether the crime should not be entered under the
category of sacrilege rather than theft. Those things belonged to the captain! There was certainly something in
the nature of the violation of a sanctuary, and of a particularly impudent kind, too, because he got his plunder out
of the captain's stateroom while the captain was asleep there.
But look, now, at the fantasy of the man! After going
through the pockets of the clothes, he did not hasten to retreat. No. He went deliberately into the saloon and removed from the sideboard two big, heavy, silver-plated
lamps, which he carried to the fore-end of the ship and stood
symmetrically on the knightheads. This, I must explain,
means that he took them away as far as possible from the
place where they belonged. These were the deeds of darkness. In the morning the bos'n came along dragging after
him a hose to wash the foc's'le head, and, beholding the shiny
cabin lamps, resplendent in the morning light, one on each
side of the bowsprit, he was paralyzed with awe. He dropped

the nozzle from his nerveless hands—and such hands, too!
I happened along, and he said to me in a distracted whisper,
"Look at that, sir, look." "Take them back aft at once
yourself," I said, very amazed, too. As we approached the
quarterdeck we perceived the steward, a prey to a sort of
sacred horror, holding up before us the captain's trousers.

Bronzed men with brooms and buckets in their hands stood
about with open mouths. "I have found them lying in the
passage outside the captain's door," the steward declared
faintly. The additional statement that the captain's watch
was gone from its hook by the bedside raised the painful
sensation to the highest pitch. We knew then we had a
thief amongst us. Our thief! Behold the solidarity of a
ship's company. He couldn't be to us like any other thief.
We all had to live under the shadow of his crime for days;
but the police kept on investigating, and one morning a
young woman appeared on board swinging a parasol, attended
by two policemen, and identified the culprit. She was a
barmaid of some bar near the Circular Quay, and knew
really nothing of our man except that he looked like a respectable sailor. She had seen him only twice in her life.
On the second occasion he begged her nicely as a great favor
to take care for him of a small solidly tied-up paper parcel
for a day or two. But he never came near her again. At
the end of three weeks she opened it, and, of course, seeing
the contents, was much alarmed, and went to the nearest
police-station for advice. The police took her at once on
board our ship, where all hands were mustered on the
quarterdeck. She stared wildly at all our faces, pointed suddenly a finger with a shriek, "That's the man," and incontinently went off into a fit of hysterics in front of thirty-six
seamen. I must say that never in my life did I see a ship's
company look so frightened. Yes, in this tale of guilt, there
was a curious absence of mere criminality, and a touch of

that fantasy which is often a part of a seaman's character. It wasn't greed that moved him, I think. It was something much less simple: boredom, perhaps, or a bet, or the pleasure of defiance.

And now for the point of view. It was given to me by a short, black-bearded A. B. of the crew, who on sea passages washed my flannel shirts, mended my clothes and generally looked after my room. He was an excellent needleman and washerman, and a very good sailor. Standing in this peculiar relation to me, he considered himself privileged to open his mind on the matter one evening when he brought back to my cabin three clean and neatly folded shirts. He was profoundly pained. He said: "What a ship's company! Never seen such a crowd! Liars, cheats, thieves . . ."

It was a needlessly jaundiced view. There were in that ship's company three or four fellows who dealt in tall yarns, and I knew that on the passage out there had been a dispute over a game in the foc'sle once or twice of a rather acute kind, so that all card-playing had to be abandoned. In regard to thieves, as we know, there was only one, and he, I am convinced, came out of his reserve to perform an exploit rather than to commit a crime. But my black-bearded friend's indignation had its special morality, for he added, with a burst of passion: "And on board our ship, too—a ship like this. . . ."

Therein lies the secret of the seamen's special character as a body. The ship, this ship, our ship, the ship we serve, is the moral symbol of our life. A ship has to be respected, actually and ideally; her merit, her innocence, are sacred things. Of all the creations of man she is the closest partner of his toil and courage. From every point of view it is imperative that you should do well by her. And, as always in the case of true love, all you can do for her adds only to the tale of her merits in your heart. Mute and compelling, she claims not only your fidelity, but your respect.

A SHIP IS NOT A SLAVE

Your ship is a tender creature, whose idiosyncrasies must be attended to if you mean her to come with credit to herself and you through the rough-and-tumble of her life.

So seemed to think the new captain, who arrived the day after we had finished loading, on the very eve of the day of sailing. I first beheld him on the quay, a complete stranger to me, obviously not a Hollander, in a black bowler and a short drab overcoat, ridiculously out of tone with the winter aspect of the waste lands, bordered by the brown fronts of houses with their roofs dripping with melting snow.

This stranger was walking up and down absorbed in the marked contemplation of the ship's fore and aft trim; but when I saw him squat on his heels in the slush at the very edge of the quay to peer at the draught of water under her counter, I said to myself, "This is the captain." And presently I descried his luggage coming along—a real sailor's chest, carried by means of rope-beckets between two men, with a couple of leather portmanteaus and a roll of charts sheeted in canvas piled upon the lid. The sudden, spontaneous agility with which he bounded aboard right off the rail afforded me the first glimpse of his real character. Without further preliminaries than a friendly nod, he addressed me: "You have got her pretty well in her fore and aft trim. Now, what about your weights?"

I told him I had managed to keep the weight sufficiently well up, as I thought, one-third of the whole being in the upper part "above the beams," as the technical expression has it. He whistled "Phew!" scrutinizing me from head to foot. A sort of smiling vexation was visible on his ruddy face.

"Well, we shall have a lively time of it this passage, I bet," he said.

He knew. It turned out he had been chief mate of her for

the two preceding voyages; and I was already familiar with his handwriting in the old log books I had been perusing in my cabin with a natural curiosity, looking up the records of my new ship's luck, of her behavior, of the good times she had had, and of the troubles she had escaped.

He was right in his prophecy. On our passage from Amsterdam to Samarang with a general cargo, of which, alas! only one-third in weight was stowed "above the beams," we had a lively time of it. It was lively, but not joyful. There was not even a single moment of comfort in it, because no seaman can feel comfortable in body or mind when he has made his ship uneasy.

To travel along with a cranky ship for ninety days or so is no doubt a nerve-trying experience; but in this case what was wrong with our craft was this: that by my system of loading she had been made much too stable.

Neither before nor since have I felt a ship roll so abruptly, so violently, so heavily. Once she began, you felt that she would never stop, and this hopeless sensation, characterizing the motion of ships whose center of gravity is brought down too low in loading, made everyone on board weary of keeping on his feet. I remember once overhearing one of the hands say: "By Heavens, Jack! I feel as if I didn't mind how soon I let myself go, and let the blamed hooker knock my brains out if she likes." The captain used to remark frequently: "Ah, yes; I dare say one-third weight above beams would have been quite enough for most ships. But then, you see, there's no two of them alike on the seas, and she's an uncommonly ticklish jade to load."

Down south, running before the gales of high latitudes, she made our life a burden to us. There were days when nothing would keep even on the swing-tables, when there was no position where you could fix yourself so as not to feel a constant strain upon all the muscles of your body. She rolled and rolled with an awful dislodging jerk and that dizzily fast sweep of her masts on every swing. It was a wonder that the men sent aloft were not flung off the yards, the yards not flung off the masts, the masts not flung overboard. The captain in his armchair, holding on grimly at the head of the table, with the soup tureen rolling on one side of the cabin and the steward sprawling on the other, would observe, looking at me: "That's your one-third above the beams. The only thing that surprises me is that the sticks have stuck to her all this time."

Ultimately some of the minor spars did go—nothing important: spanker and booms and such like—because at times the frightful impetus of her rolling would part a fourfold tackle of new three-inch Manilla line as if it were weaker than pack-thread.

It was only poetic justice that the chief mate who had made a mistake—perhaps a half-excusable one—about the distribution of his ship's cargo should pay the penalty. A piece of one of the minor spars that did carry away flew against the chief mate's back, and sent him sliding on his face for quite a considerable distance along the main deck. Thereupon followed various and unpleasant consequences of a physical order—"queer symptoms," as the captain, who treated them, used to say; inexplicable periods of powerlessness, sudden accesses of mysterious pain; and the patient agreed fully with the regretful mutters of his very attentive captain wishing that it had been a straightforward broken leg. Even the Dutch doctor who took the case up in Samarang offered no scientific explanation. All he said was: "Ah, friend, you are young yet; it may be very serious for your whole life. You must leave your ship; you must quite silent be for three months—quite silent."

Of course, he meant the chief mate to keep quiet—to lay up, as a matter of fact. His manner was impressive enough, if his English was childishly imperfect when compared with the fluency of Mr. Hudig, the figure at the other end of that passage, and memorable enough in its way. In a great airy ward of a Far Eastern hospital, lying on my back, I had plenty of leisure to remember the dreadful cold and snow of Amsterdam, while looking at the fronds of the palm trees tossing and rustling at the height of the window. I could remember the elated feeling and the soul-gripping cold of those tramway journeys taken into town to put what in diplomatic language is called pressure upon the good Hudig, with his warm fire, his armchair, his big cigar, and the never-failing suggestion in his good-natured voice: "I suppose in the end it is you they will appoint captain before the ship sails?" It may have been his extreme good-nature, the serious, unsmiling good-nature of a fat, swarthy man with coal-black mustache and steady eyes; but he might have been a bit of a diplomatist, too. His enticing suggestions I used to repel modestly by the assurance that it was extremely unlikely, as I had not enough experience. "You know very well how to go about business matters," he used to say, with a sort of affected moodiness clouding his serene round face. I wonder whether he ever laughed to himself after I had left the office. I dare say he never did, because I understand that diplomatists, in and out of the career, take themselves and their tricks with an exemplary seriousness.

But he had nearly persuaded me that I was fit in every way to be trusted with a command. There came three months of mental worry, hard rolling, remorse, and physical pain to drive home the lesson of insufficient experience.

Yes, your ship wants to be humored with knowledge. You must treat with an understanding consideration the mysteries of her feminine nature, and then she will stand by you faithfully in the unceasing struggle with forces wherein defeat is no shame. It is a serious relation, that in which a man stands to his ship. She has her rights as though she could breathe and speak; and, indeed, there are ships that, for the right man, will do anything but speak, as the saying goes.

A ship is not a slave. You must make her easy in a seaway, you must never forget that you owe her the fullest share of your thought, of your skill, of your self-love. If you remember that obligation, naturally and without effort, as if it were an instinctive feeling of your inner life, she will sail, stay, run for you as long as she is able, or, like a sea-bird going to rest upon the angry waves, she will lay out the heaviest gale that ever made you doubt living long enough to see another sunrise.

YOUTH

[Perhaps Conrad's most important interpretation of his development is contained in *Youth*. It is, he said, "a piece of autobiography—'emotions remembered [recollected] in tranquillity'"; "a record of experience." "I cannot help thinking what a lucky day it was for me when in 1880 [it was really 1881, September 21] I shipped in the *Palestine*."

It should be remembered that the *Judea* of *Youth* is an obvious pseudonym for *Palestine*, and that Marlow is really Conrad. As Professor Wilbur L. Cross says in his *Four Contemporary Novelists*, "Marlow was created because Conrad felt the need of a character through whom he could speak in various moods. . . . In *Youth*, where he first appeared, as the chronicler of Conrad's initial voyage to the East, he was hardly more than the author himself under another name."]

THIS could have occurred nowhere but in England, where men and sea interpenetrate, so to speak—the sea entering into the life of most men, and the men knowing something or everything about the sea, in the way of amusement, of travel, or of bread-winning.

We were sitting round a mahogany table that reflected the bottle, the claret-glasses, and our faces as we leaned on our elbows. There was a director of companies, an accountant, a lawyer, Marlow, and myself. The director had been a *Conway* boy, the accountant had served four years at sea, the lawyer—a fine crusted Tory, High Churchman, the best of old fellows, the soul of honor—had been chief officer in the P. & O. service in the good old days when mail and boats were square-rigged at least on two masts, and used to come down the China Sea before a fair monsoon with stun'-sails set alow and aloft. We all began life in the merchant service. Between the five of us there was the strong bond of the sea, and also the fellowship of the craft, which no amount of enthusiasm for yachting, cruising, and so on can give, since one is only the amusement of life and the other is life itself.

Marlow (at least I think that is how he spelled his name) told the story, or rather the chronicle, of a voyage:—

"Yes, I have seen a little of the Eastern seas; but what I remember best is my first voyage there. You fellows know there are those voyages that seem ordered for the illustration of life, that might stand for a symbol of existence. You fight, work, sweat, nearly kill yourself, sometimes do kill yourself, trying to accomplish something—and you can't. Not from any fault of yours. You simply can do nothing, neither great nor little—not a thing in the world—not even marry an old maid, or get a wretched 600-ton cargo of coal to its port of destination.

"It was altogether a memorable affair. It was my first voyage to the East, and my first voyage as second mate; it was also my skipper's first command. You'll admit it was time. He was sixty if a day; a little man, with a broad, not very straight back, with bowed shoulders and one leg more bandy than the other, he had that queer twisted-about appearance you see so often in men who work in the fields. He had a nutcracker face—chin and nose trying to come together over a sunken mouth—and it was framed in iron-gray fluffy hair, that looked like a chin-strap of cotton-wool sprinkled with coal-dust. And he had blue eyes in that old face of his, which were amazingly like a boy's, with that candid expression some quite common men preserve to the end of their days by a rare internal gift of simplicity of heart and rectitude of soul. What induced him to accept me was a wonder. I had come out of a crack Australian clipper, where I had been third officer, and he seemed to have a prejudice against crack clippers as aristocratic and high-toned. He said to me, 'You know, in this ship you will have to work.' I said I had to work in every ship I had ever been in. 'Ah, but this is different, and you gentlemen out of them big ships; . . . but there! I dare say you will do. Join tomorrow.'

"I joined tomorrow. It was twenty-two years ago; and I was just twenty. How time passes! It was one of the happiest days of my life. Fancy! Second mate for the first time—a really responsible officer! I wouldn't have thrown up my new billet for a fortune. The mate looked me over carefully. He was also an old chap, but of another stamp. He had a Roman nose, a snow-white, long beard, and his name was Mahon, but he insisted that it should be pro-nounced Mann. He was well connected; yet there was some-thing wrong with his luck, and he had never got on.

"As to the captain, he had been for years in coasters, then in the Mediterranean, and last in the West Indian trade. He had never been round the Capes. He could just write a kind of sketchy hand, and didn't care for writing at all. Both were thorough good seamen, of course, and between those two old chaps I felt like a small boy between two grandfathers.

"The ship also was old. Her name was the *Judea*. Queer name, isn't it? She belonged to a man Wilmer, Wilcox— some name like that; but he has been bankrupt and dead these twenty years or more, and his name don't matter. She had been laid up in Shadwell basin for ever so long. You may imagine her state. She was all rust, dust, grime—soot aloft, dirt on deck. To me it was like coming out of a palace into a ruined cottage. She was about 400 tons, had a primitive windlass, wooden latches to the doors, not a bit of brass about her, and a big square stern. There was on it, below her name in big letters, a lot of scrollwork, with the gilt off, and some sort of a coat of arms, with the motto 'Do or Die' underneath. I remember it took my fancy immensely. There was a touch of romance in it, something that made me love the old thing—something that appealed to my youth!

"We left London in ballast—sand ballast—to load a cargo of coal in a northern port for Bangkok. Bangkok! I thrilled. I had been six years at sea, but had only seen Melbourne and Sydney, very good places, charming places in their way—but Bangkok!

"We worked out of the Thames under canvas, with a North Sea pilot on board. His name was Jermyn, and he dodged all day long about the galley drying his handkerchief before the stove. Apparently he never slept. He was a dismal man, with a perpetual tear sparkling at the end of his nose, who either had been in trouble, or was in trouble, or expected to be in trouble—couldn't be happy unless something went wrong. He mistrusted my youth, my commonsense, and my seamanship, and made a point of showing it in a hundred little ways. I dare say he was right. It seems to me I knew very little then, and I know not much more now; but I cherish a hate for that Jermyn to this day.

"We were a week working up as far as Yarmouth Roads, and then we got into a gale—the famous October gale of twenty-two years ago. It was wind, lightning, sleet, snow, and a terrific sea. We were flying light, and you may imagine how bad it was when I tell you we had smashed bulwarks and a flooded deck. On the second night she shifted her ballast into the lee bow, and by that time we had been blown off somewhere on the Dogger Bank. There was nothing for it but go below with shovels and try to right her, and there we were in that vast hold, gloomy like a cavern, the tallow dips stuck and flickering on the beams, the gale nowling above, the ship tossing about like mad on her side; there we all were, Jermyn, the captain, every one, hardly able to keep our feet, engaged on that gravedigger's work, and trying to toss shovelfuls of wet sand up to windward. At every tumble of the ship you could see vaguely in the dim light men falling down with a great flourish of shovels. One of the ship's boys (we had two), impressed by the weirdness of the scene, wept as if his heart would break. We could hear him blubbering somewhere in the shadows.

"On the third day the gale died out, and by and by a north-country tug picked us up. We took sixteen days in all to get from London to the Tyne! When we got into dock we had lost our turn for loading, and they hauled us off to a tier where we remained for a month. Mrs. Beard (the captain's name was Beard) came from Colchester to see the old man. She lived on board. The crew of runners had left, and there remained only the officers, one boy and the steward, a mulatto who answered to the name of Abraham. Mrs. Beard was an old woman, with a face all wrinkled and ruddy like a winter apple, and the figure of a young girl. She caught sight of me once, sewing on a button, and insisted on having my shirts to repair. This was something different from the captains' wives I had known on board crack clippers. When I brought her the shirts, she said: 'And the socks? They want mending, I am sure, and John's—Captain Beard's—things are all in order now. I would be glad of something to do.' Bless the old woman. She overhauled my outfit for me, and meantime I read for the first time *Sartor Resartus* and Burnaby's *Ride to Khiva*. I didn't understand much of the first then; but I remember I preferred the soldier to the philosopher at the time; a preference which life has only confirmed. One was a man, and the other was either more—or less. However, they are both dead and Mrs. Beard is dead, and youth, strength, genius, thoughts, achievements, simple hearts—all die. . . . No matter.

"They loaded us at last. We shipped a crew. Eight able seamen and two boys. We hauled off one evening to the buoys at the dock-gates, ready to go out, and with a fair prospect of beginning the voyage next day. Mrs. Beard was to start for home by a late train. When the ship was fast we went to tea. We sat rather silent through the meal— Mahon, the old couple, and I. I finished first, and slipped away for a smoke, my cabin being in a deck-house just against the poop. It was high water, blowing fresh with a drizzle; the double dock-gates were opened, and the steam-colliers were going in and out in the darkness with their lights burning bright, a great plashing of propellers, rattling of winches, and a lot of hailing on the pierheads. I watched the procession of headlights gliding high and of green lights gliding low in the night, when suddenly a red gleam flashed at me, vanished, came into view again, and remained. The fore-end of a steamer loomed up close. I shouted down the cabin, 'Come up, quick!' and then heard a startled voice saying afar in the dark, 'Stop her, sir.' A bell jingled. An-other voice cried warningly, 'We are going right into that barque, sir.' The answer to this was a gruff 'All right,' and the next thing was a heavy crash as the steamer struck a glancing blow with the bluff of her bow about our fore-rigging. There was a moment of confusion, yelling, and running about. Steam roared. Then somebody was heard saying, 'All clear, sir.' . . . 'Are you all right?' asked the gruff voice. I had jumped forward to see the damage, and hailed back, 'I think so.' 'Easy astern,' said the gruff voice. A bell jingled. 'What steamer is that?' screamed Mahon. By that time she was no more to us than a bulky shadow maneuvering a little way off. They shouted at us some name—a woman's name, Miranda or Melissa—or some such thing. 'This means another month in this beastly hole,' said Mahon to me, as we peered with lamps about the splintered bulwarks and broken braces. 'But where's the captain?'

"We had not heard or seen anything of him all that time. We went aft to look. A doleful voice arose hailing somewhere in the middle of the dock, '*Judea* ahoy!' . . . How the devil did he get there? . . . 'Hallo!' we shouted. 'I am adrift in our boat without oars,' he cried. A belated waterman offered his services, and Mahon struck a bargain with him for half-a-crown to tow our skipper alongside; but it was Mrs. Beard that came up the ladder first. They had been floating about the dock in that mizzly cold rain for nearly an hour. I was never so surprised in my life.

"It appears that when he heard my shout 'Come up' he understood at once what was the matter, caught up his wife, ran on deck, and across, and down into our boat, which was fast to the ladder. Not bad for a sixty-year-old. Just imagine that old fellow saving heroically in his arms that old woman—the woman of his life. He set her down on a thwart, and was ready to climb back on board when the painter came adrift somehow, and away they went together. Of course in the confusion we did not hear him shouting. He looked abashed. She said cheerfully, 'I suppose it does not matter my losing the train now?' 'No, Jenny—you go below and get warm,' he growled. Then to us: 'A sailor has no business with a wife—I say. There I was, out of the ship. Well, no harm done this time. Let's go and look at what that fool of a steamer smashed.'

"It wasn't much, but it delayed us three weeks. At the end of that time, the captain being engaged with his agents, I carried Mrs. Beard's bag to the railway-station and put her all comfy into a third-class carriage. She lowered the window to say, 'You are a good young man. If you see John —Captain Beard—without his muffler at night, just remind him from me to keep his throat well wrapped up.' 'Certainly, Mrs. Beard,' I said. 'You are a good young man; I noticed how attentive you are to John—to Captain——' The train pulled out suddenly; I took my cap off to the old woman: I never saw her again. . . . Pass the bottle.

"We went to sea next day. When we made that start for Bangkok we had been already three months out of London. We had expected to be a fortnight or so—at the outside.

"It was January, and the weather was beautiful—the beautiful sunny winter weather that has more charm than in the summer-time, because it is unexpected, and crisp, and you know it won't, it can't, last long. It's like a windfall, like a godsend, like an unexpected piece of luck.

"It lasted all down the North Sea, all down Channel; and it lasted till we were three hundred miles or so to the westward of the Lizards: then the wind went round to the sou'west and began to pipe up. In two days it blew a gale. The *Judea*, hove to, wallowed on the Atlantic like an old candle-box. It blew day after day: it blew with spite, without interval, without mercy, without rest. The world was nothing but an immensity of great foaming waves rushing at us, under a sky low enough to touch with the hand and dirty like a smoked ceiling. In the stormy space surrounding us there was as much flying spray as air. Day after day and night after night there was nothing round the ship but the howl of the wind, the tumult of the sea, the noise of water pouring over her deck. There was no rest for her and no rest for us. She tossed, she pitched, she stood on her head, she sat on her tail, she rolled, she groaned, and we had to hold on while on deck and cling to our bunks when below, in a constant effort of body and worry of mind.

"One night Mahon spoke through the small window of my berth. It opened right into my very bed, and I was lying there sleepless, in my boots, feeling as though I had not slept for years, and could not if I tried. He said excitedly—

"'You got the sounding-rod in here, Marlow? I can't get the pumps to suck. By God! it's no child's play.'

"I gave him the sounding-rod and lay down again, trying to think of various things—but I thought only of the pumps. When I came on deck they were still at it, and my watch relieved at the pumps. By the light of the lantern brought on deck to examine the sounding-rod I caught a glimpse of their weary, serious faces. We pumped all the four hours. We pumped all night, all day, all the week—watch and watch. She was working herself loose, and leaked badly—not enough to drown us at once, but enough to kill us with the work at the pumps. And while we pumped the ship was going from us piecemeal: the bulwarks went, the stanchions were torn out, the ventilators smashed, the cabin-door burst in. There was not a dry spot in the ship. She was being gutted bit by bit. The long-boat changed, as if by magic, into matchwood where she stood in her gripes. I had lashed her myself, and was rather proud of my handiwork, which had withstood so long the malice of the sea. And we pumped. And there was no break in the weather. The sea was white like a sheet of foam, like a caldron of boiling milk; there was not a break in the clouds—no, not the size of a man's hand—no, not for so much as ten seconds. There was for us no sky, there were for us no stars, no sun, no universe—nothing but angry clouds and an infuriated sea. We pumped watch and watch, for dear life; and it seemed to last for months, for years, for all eternity, as though we had been dead and gone to a hell for sailors. We forgot the day of the week, the name of the month, what year it was, and whether we had ever been ashore. The sails blew away, she lay broadside on under a weather-cloth, the ocean poured over her, and we did not care. We turned those handles, and had the eyes of idiots. As soon as we had crawled on deck I used to take a round turn with a rope about the men, the pumps, and the mainmast, and we turned, we turned incessantly, with the water to our waists, to our necks, over our heads. It was all one. We had forgotten how it felt to be dry.

"And there was somewhere in me the thought: By Jove! this is the deuce of an adventure—something you read about; and it is my first voyage as second mate—and I am only twenty—and here I am lasting it out as well as any of these men, and keeping my chaps up to the mark. I was pleased. I would not have given up the experience for worlds. I had moments of exultation. Whenever the old dismantled craft pitched heavily with her counter high in the air, she seemed to me to throw up, like an appeal, like a defiance, like a cry to the clouds without mercy, the words written on her stern: '*Judea*, London. Do or Die.'

"O youth! The strength of it, the faith of it, the imagination of it! To me she was not an old rattletrap carting about the world a lot of coal for a freight—to me she was the endeavor, the test, the trial of life. I think of her with pleasure, with affection, with regret—as you would think of someone dead you have loved. I shall never forget her. . . . Pass the bottle.

"One night, when tied to the mast, as I explained, we were pumping on, deafened with the wind, and without spirit enough in us to wish ourselves dead, a heavy sea crashed aboard and swept clean over us. As soon as I got my breath I shouted, as in duty bound, 'Keep on, boys!' when suddenly I felt something hard floating on deck strike the calf of my leg. I made a grab at it and missed. It was so dark we could not see each other's faces within a foot—you understand.

"After that thump the ship kept quiet for a while, and the thing, whatever it was, struck my leg again. This time I caught it—and it was a saucepan. At first, being stupid with fatigue and thinking of nothing but the pumps, I did not understand what I had in my hand. Suddenly it dawned upon me, and I shouted, 'Boys, the house on deck is gone. Leave this, and let's look for the cook.'

"There was a deck-house forward, which contained the galley, the cook's berth, and the quarters of the crew. As we had expected for days to see it swept away, the hands had been ordered to sleep in the cabin—the only safe place in the ship. The steward, Abraham, however, persisted in clinging to his berth, stupidly, like a mule—from sheer fright I believe, like an animal that won't leave a stable falling in an earthquake. So we went to look for him. It was chancing death, since once out of our lashings we were as exposed as if on a raft. But we went. The house was shattered as if a shell had exploded inside. Most of it had gone overboard —stove, men's quarters, and their property, all was gone; but two posts, holding a portion of the bulkhead to which Abraham's bunk was attached, remained as if by a miracle. We groped in the ruins and came upon this, and there he was, sitting in his bunk, surrounded by foam and wreckage, jabbering cheerfully to himself. He was out of his mind; completely and forever mad, with this sudden shock coming upon the fag-end of his endurance. We snatched him up, lugged him aft, and pitched him head-first down the cabin companion. You understand there was no time to carry him down with infinite precautions and wait to see how he got on. Those below would pick him up at the bottom of the stairs all right. We were in a hurry to go back to the pumps. That business could not wait. A bad leak is an inhuman thing.

"One would think that the sole purpose of that fiendish gale had been to make a lunatic of that poor devil of a mulatto. It eased before morning, and next day the sky cleared, and as the sea went down the leak took up. When it came to bending a fresh set of sails the crew demanded to put back—and really there was nothing else to do. Boats gone, decks swept clean, cabin gutted, men without a stitch but what they stood in, stores spoiled, ship strained. We put her head for home, and—would you believe it? The wind came east right in our teeth. It blew fresh, it blew continuously. We had to beat up every inch of the way, but she did not leak so badly, the water keeping comparatively smooth. Two hours' pumping in every four is no joke—but it kept her afloat as far as Falmouth.

"The good people there live on casualties of the sea, and no doubt were glad to see us. A hungry crowd of shipwrights sharpened their chisels at the sight of that carcass of a ship. And, by Jove! they had pretty pickings off us before they were done. I fancy the owner was already in a tight place. There were delays. Then it was decided to take part of the cargo out and calk her topsides. This was done, the repairs finished, cargo reshipped; a new crew came on board, and we went out—for Bangkok. At the end of a week we were back again. The crew said they weren't going to Bangkok—a hundred and fifty days' passage—in a something hooker that wanted pumping eight hours out of the twenty-four; and the nautical papers inserted again the little paragraph: '*Judea*. Barque. Tyne to Bangkok; coals; put back to Falmouth leaky and with crew refusing duty.'

"There were more delays—more tinkering. The owner came down for a day, and said she was as right as a little fiddle. Poor old Captain Beard looked like the ghost of a Geordie skipper—through the worry and humiliation of it. Remember he was sixty, and it was his first command. Mahon said it was a foolish business, and would end badly. I loved the ship more than ever, and wanted awfully to get to Bangkok. To Bangkok! Magic name, blessed name. Mesopotamia wasn't a patch on it. Remember I was twenty, and it was my first second-mate's billet, and the East was waiting for me.

YOUTH   99

"We went out and anchored in the outer roads with a fresh crew—the third. She leaked worse than ever. It was as if those confounded shipwrights had actually made a hole in her. This time we did not even go outside. The crew simply refused to man the windlass.

"They towed us back to the inner harbor, and we became a fixture, a feature, an institution of the place. People pointed us out to visitors as 'That 'ere barque that's going to Bangkok—has been here six months—put back three times.' On holidays the small boys pulling about in boats would hail, '*Judea*, ahoy!' and if a head showed above the rail shouted, 'Where you bound to?—Bangkok?' and jeered. We were only three on board. The poor old skipper mooned in the cabin. Mahon undertook the cooking, and unexpectedly developed all a Frenchman's genius for preparing nice little messes. I looked languidly after the rigging. We became citizens of Falmouth. Every shopkeeper knew us. At the barber's or tobacconist's they asked familiarly, 'Do you think you will ever get to Bangkok?' Meantime the owner, the underwriters, and the charterers squabbled amongst themselves in London, and our pay went on. . . . Pass the bottle.

"It was horrid. Morally it was worse than pumping for life. It seemed as though we had been forgotten by the world, belonged to nobody, would get nowhere; it seemed that, as if bewitched, we would have to live forever and ever in that inner harbor, a derision and a byword to generations of long-shore loafers and dishonest boatmen. I obtained three months' pay and a five days' leave, and made a rush for London. It took me a day to get there and pretty well another to come back—but three months' pay went all the same. I don't know what I did with it. I went to a music-hall, I believe, lunched, dined, and supped in a swell place in Regent Street, and was back to time, with nothing but a complete set of Byron's works and a new railway rug

to show for three months' work.   The boat-man who pulled
me off to the ship said: 'Hallo! I thought you had left the
old thing.   *She* will never get to Bangkok.'   'That's all *you*
know about it,' I said scornfully—but I didn't like that
prophecy at all.

"Suddenly a man, some kind of agent to somebody,
appeared with full powers.   He had grog-blossoms all over
his face, an indomitable energy, and was a jolly soul.   We
leaped into life again.   A hulk came alongside, took our
cargo, and then we went into dry dock to get our copper
stripped.   No wonder she leaked.   The poor thing, strained
beyond endurance by the gale, had, as if in disgust, spat out
all the oakum of her lower seams.   She was recalked, new
coppered, and made as tight as a bottle.   We went back to
the hulk and reshipped our cargo.

"Then, on a fine moonlight night, all the rats left the ship.

"We had been infested with them.   They had destroyed
our sails, consumed more stores than the crew, affably shared
our beds and our dangers, and now, when the ship was made
seaworthy, concluded to clear out.   I called Mahon to enjoy
the spectacle.   Rat after rat appeared on our rail, took a last
look over his shoulder, and leaped with a hollow thud into
the empty hulk.   We tried to count them, but soon lost the
tale.   Mahon said: 'Well, well! don't talk to me about the
intelligence of rats.   They ought to have left before, when we
had that narrow squeak from foundering.   There you have
the proof how silly is the superstition about them.   They leave
a good ship for an old rotten hulk, where there is nothing to
eat, too, the fools! . . . I don't believe they know what is
safe or what is good for them, any more than you or I.'

"And after some more talk we agreed that the wisdom of
rats had been grossly overrated, being in fact no greater than
that of men.

"The story of the ship was known, by this, all up the
Channel from Land's End to the Forelands, and we could get

no crew on the south coast. They sent us one all complete from Liverpool, and we left once more—for Bangkok.

"We had fair breezes, smooth water right into the tropics, and the old *Judea* lumbered along in the sunshine. When she went eight knots everything cracked aloft, and we tied our caps to our heads; but mostly she strolled on at the rate of three miles an hour. What could you expect? She was tired—that old ship. Her youth was where mine is—where yours is—you fellows who listen to this yarn; and what friend would throw your years and your weariness in your face? We didn't grumble at her. To us aft, at least, it seemed as though we had been born in her, reared in her, had lived in her for ages, had never known any other ship. I would just as soon have abused the old village church at home for not being a cathedral.

"And for me there was also my youth to make me patient. There was all the East before me, and all life, and the thought that I had been tried in that ship and had come out pretty well. And I thought of men of old who, centuries ago, went that road in ships that sailed no better, to the land of palms, and spices, and yellow sands, and of brown nations ruled by kings more cruel than Nero the Roman, and more splendid than Solomon the Jew. The old barque lumbered on, heavy with her age and the burden of her cargo, while I lived the life of youth in ignorance and hope. She lumbered on through an interminable procession of days; and the fresh gilding flashed back at the setting sun, seemed to cry out over the darkening sea the words painted on her stern, '*Judea*, London. Do or Die.'

"Then we entered the Indian Ocean and steered northerly for Java Head. The winds were light. Weeks slipped by. She crawled on, do or die, and people at home began to think of posting us as overdue.

"One Saturday evening, I being off duty, the men asked me to give them an extra bucket of water or so—for washing clothes.　As I did not wish to screw on the fresh-water pump so late, I went forward whistling, and with a key in my hand to unlock the forepeak scuttle, intending to serve the water out of a spare tank we kept there.

"The smell down below was as unexpected as it was frightful.　One would have thought hundreds of paraffin-lamps had been flaring and smoking in that hole for days.　I was glad to get out.　The man with me coughed and said, 'Funny smell, sir.'　I answered negligently, 'It's good for the health, they say,' and walked aft.

"The first thing I did was to put my head down the square of the midship ventilator.　As I lifted the lid a visible breath, something like a thin fog, a puff of faint haze, rose from the opening.　The ascending air was hot, and had a heavy, sooty, paraffiny smell.　I gave one sniff, and put down the lid gently.　It was no use choking myself.　The cargo was on fire.

"Next day she began to smoke in earnest.　You see it was to be expected, for though the coal was of a safe kind, that cargo had been so handled, so broken up with handling, that it looked more like smithy coal than anything else.　Then it had been wetted—more than once.　It rained all the time we were taking it back from the hulk, and now with this long passage it got heated, and there was another case of spontaneous combustion.

"The captain called us into the cabin.　He had a chart spread on the table, and looked unhappy.　He said, 'The coast of West Australia is near, but I mean to proceed to our destination.　It is the hurricane month, too; but we will just keep her head for Bangkok, and fight the fire.　No more putting back anywhere, if we all get roasted.　We will try first to stifle this 'ere damned combustion by want of air.'

"We tried.　We battened down everything, and still she smoked.　The smoke kept coming out through imperceptible crevices; it forced itself through bulkheads and covers; it oozed here and there and everywhere in slender threads, in an invisible film, in an incomprehensible manner. It made its way into the cabin, into the forecastle; it poisoned the sheltered places on the deck, it could be sniffed as high as the mainyard. It was clear that if the smoke came out the air came in. This was disheartening. This combustion refused to be stifled.

"We resolved to try water, and took the hatches off. Enormous volumes of smoke, whitish, yellowish, thick, greasy, misty, choking, ascended as high as the trucks. All hands cleared out aft. Then the poisonous cloud blew away, and we went back to work in a smoke that was no thicker now than that of an ordinary factory chimney.

"We rigged the force-pump, got the hose along, and by and by it burst. Well, it was as old as the ship—a prehistoric hose, and past repair. Then we pumped with the feeble head-pump, drew water with buckets, and in this way managed in time to pour lots of Indian Ocean into the main hatch. The bright stream flashed in sunshine, fell into a layer of white crawling smoke, and vanished on the black surface of coal. Steam ascended mingling with the smoke. We poured salt water as into a barrel without a bottom. It was our fate to pump in that ship, to pump out of her, to pump into her; and after keeping water out of her to save ourselves from being drowned, we frantically poured water into her to save ourselves from being burned.

"And she crawled on, do or die, in the serene weather. The sky was a miracle of purity, a miracle of azure. The sea was polished, was blue, was pellucid, was sparkling like a precious stone, extending on all sides, all round to the horizon—as if the whole terrestrial globe had been one jewel, one colossal sapphire, a single gem fashioned into a planet. And on the luster of the great calm waters the *Judea* glided imperceptibly, enveloped in languid and unclean vapors, in a

lazy cloud that drifted to leeward, light and slow; a pestiferous cloud defiling the splendor of sea and sky.

"All this time, of course, we saw no fire. The cargo smol-
dered at the bottom somewhere. Once Mahon, as we were
working side by side, said to me with a queer smile: 'Now,
if she only would spring a tidy leak—like that time when we
first left the Channel—it would put a stopper on this fire.
Wouldn't it?' I remarked irrelevantly, 'Do you remember
the rats?'

"We fought the fire and sailed the ship too as carefully as
though nothing had been the matter. The steward cooked
and attended on us. Of the other twelve men, eight worked
while four rested. Everyone took his turn, captain included.
There was equality, and if not exactly fraternity, then a
deal of good feeling. Sometimes a man, as he dashed a
bucketful of water down the hatchway, would yell out, 'Hur-
rah for Bangkok!' and the rest laughed. But generally we
were taciturn and serious—and thirsty. Oh! how thirsty!
And we had to be careful with the water. Strict allowance.
The ship smoked, the sun blazed. . . . Pass the bottle.

"We tried everything. We even made an attempt to dig
down to the fire. No good, of course. No man could remain more than a minute below. Mahon, who went first,
fainted there, and the man who went to fetch him out did
likewise. We lugged them out on deck. Then I leaped
down to show how easily it could be done. They had learned
wisdom by that time, and contented themselves by fishing for
me with a chain-hook tied to a broom-handle, I believe. I
did not offer to go and fetch up my shovel, which was left
down below.

"Things began to look bad. We put the long-boat into
the water. The second boat was ready to swing out. We
had also another, a 14-foot thing, on davits aft, where it was
quite safe.

"Then, behold, the smoke suddenly decreased. We redoubled our efforts to flood the bottom of the ship.   In two days there was no smoke at all.   Everybody was on the broad grin.   This was on a Friday.   On Saturday no work, but sailing the ship of course, was done.   The men washed their clothes and their faces for the first time in a fortnight, and had a special dinner given them.   They spoke of spontaneous combustion with contempt, and implied *they* were the boys to put out combustions.   Somehow we all felt as though we each had inherited a large fortune.   But a beastly smell of burning hung about the ship.   Captain Beard had hollow eyes and sunken cheeks.   I had never noticed so much before how twisted and bowed he was.   He and Mahon prowled soberly about hatches and ventilators, sniffing.   It struck me suddenly poor Mahon was a very, very old chap.   As to me, I was as pleased and proud as though I had helped to win a great naval battle.   O youth!

"The night was fine.   In the morning a homeward-bound ship passed us hull down—the first we had seen for months; but we were nearing the land at last, Java Head being about 190 miles off, and nearly due north.

"Next day it was my watch on deck from eight to twelve. At breakfast the captain observed, 'It's wonderful how that smell hangs about the cabin.'   About ten, the mate being on the poop, I stepped down on the main-deck for a moment. The carpenter's bench stood abaft the mainmast: I leaned against it sucking at my pipe, and the carpenter, a young chap, came to talk to me.   He remarked, 'I think we have done very well, haven't we?' and then I perceived with annoyance the fool was trying to tilt the bench.   I said curtly, 'Don't, Chips,' and immediately became aware of a queer sensation, of an absurd delusion,—I seemed somehow to be in the air.   I heard all round me like a pent-up breath released —as if a thousand giants simultaneously had said 'Phoo!'—and felt a dull concussion which made my ribs ache suddenly. No doubt about it—I was in the air, and my body was

describing a short parabola.   But short as it was, I had the
time to think several thoughts in, as far as I can remember,
the following order: 'This can't be the carpenter—What is
it?—Some accident—Submarine volcano?—Coals, gas!—By
Jove! we are being blown up—Everybody's dead—I am
falling into the after-hatch—I see fire in it.'

"The coal-dust suspended in the air of the hold had glowed
dull-red at the moment of the explosion.   In the twinkling of
an eye, in an infinitesimal fraction of a second since the first
tilt of the bench, I was sprawling full length on the cargo.
I picked myself up and scrambled out.   It was quick like a
rebound.   The deck was a wilderness of smashed timber, lying
crosswise like trees in a wood after a hurricane; an immense
curtain of soiled rags waved gently before me—it was the
mainsail blown to strips.   I thought, The masts will be toppling over directly; and to get out of the way bolted on
all fours towards the poop ladder.   The first person I saw was
Mahon, with eyes like saucers, his mouth open, and the long
white hair standing straight on end round his head like a silver
halo.   He was just about to go down when the sight of the
main-deck stirring, heaving up, and changing into splinters
before his eyes, petrified him on the top step.   I stared at him
in unbelief, and he stared at me with a queer kind of shocked
curiosity.   I did not know that I had no hair, no eyebrows,
no eyelashes, that my young mustache was burnt off, that
my face was black, one cheek laid open, my nose cut, and
my chin bleeding.   I had lost my cap, one of my slippers, and
my shirt was torn to rags.   Of all this I was not aware.   I
was amazed to see the ship still afloat, the poop deck whole—
and, most of all, to see anybody alive.   Also the peace of the
sky and the serenity of the sea were distinctly surprising.   I
suppose I expected to see them convulsed with horror. . . .
Pass the bottle.

"There was a voice hailing the ship from somewhere—in
the air, in the sky—I couldn't tell.   Presently I saw the cap-

tain—and he was mad. He asked me eagerly, 'Where's the cabin table?' and to hear such a question was a frightful shock. I had just been blown up, you understand, and vibrated with that experience,—I wasn't quite sure whether I was alive. Mahon began to stamp with both feet and yelled at him, 'Good God! don't you see the deck's blown out of her?' I found my voice, and stammered out as if conscious of some gross neglect of duty, 'I don't know where the cabin table is.' It was like an absurd dream.

"Do you know what he wanted next? Well, he wanted to trim the yards. Very placidly, and as if lost in thought, he insisted on having the foreyard squared. 'I don't know if there's anybody alive,' said Mahon, almost tearfully. 'Surely,' he said, gently, 'there will be enough left to square the fore-yard.'

"The old chap, it seems, was in his own berth winding up the chronometers, when the shock sent him spinning. Immediately it occurred to him—as he said afterwards—that the ship had struck something, and he ran out into the cabin. There he saw the cabin table had vanished somewhere. The deck being blown up, it had fallen down into the lazarette, of course. Where we had our breakfast that morning he saw only a great hole in the floor. This appeared to him so awfully mysterious, and impressed him so immensely, that what he saw and heard after he got on deck were mere trifles in comparison. And, mark, he noticed directly the wheel deserted and his barque off her course—and his only thought was to get that miserable, stripped, undecked, smoldering shell of a ship back again with her head pointing at her port of destination. Bangkok! That's what he was after. I tell you this quiet, bowed, bandy-legged, almost deformed little man was immense in the singleness of his idea and in his placid ignorance of our agitation. He motioned us forward with a commanding gesture, and went to take the wheel himself.

"Yes; that was the first thing we did—trim the yards of

that wreck!　No one was killed, or even disabled, but everyone was more or less hurt.　You should have seen them!
Some were in rags, with black faces, like coal-heavers, like
sweeps, and had bullet heads that seemed closely cropped, but
were in fact singed to the skin.　Others, of the watch below,
awakened by being shot out from their collapsing bunks,
shivered incessantly, and kept on groaning even as we went
about our work.　But they all worked.　That crew of Liverpool hard cases had in them the right stuff.　It's my experience they always have.　It is the sea that gives it—the
vastness, the loneliness surrounding their dark stolid souls.
Ah well! we stumbled, we crept, we fell, we barked our shins
on the wreckage, we hauled.　The masts stood, but we did
not know how much they might be charred down below.　It
was nearly calm, but a long swell ran from the west and
made her roll.　They might go at any moment.　We looked
at them with apprehension.　One could not foresee which
way they would fall.

"Then we retreated aft and looked about us.　The deck
was a tangle of planks on edge, of planks on end, of splinters,
of ruined woodwork.　The masts rose from that chaos like
big trees above a matted undergrowth.　The interstices of that
mass of wreckage were full of something whitish, sluggish,
stirring—of something that was like a greasy fog.　The
smoke of the invisible fire was coming up again, was trailing,
like a poisonous thick mist in some valley choked with dead
wood.　Already lazy wisps were beginning to curl upwards
amongst the mass of splinters.　Here and there a piece of
timber, stuck upright, resembled a post.　Half of a fife rail
had been shot through the foresail, and the sky made a patch
of glorious blue in the ignobly soiled canvas.　A portion of
several boards holding together had fallen across the rail, and
one end protruded overboard, like a gangway leading upon
nothing, like a gangway leading over the deep sea, leading to

death—as if inviting us to walk the plank at once and be done with our ridiculous troubles. And still the air, the sky —a ghost, something invisible was hailing the ship.

"Someone had the sense to look over, and there was the helmsman, who had impulsively jumped overboard, anxious to come back. He yelled and swam lustily like a merman, keeping up with the ship. We threw him a rope, and presently he stood amongst us streaming with water and very crest-fallen. The captain had surrendered the wheel, and apart, elbow on rail and chin in hand, gazed at the sea wistfully. We asked ourselves, What next? I thought, Now, this is something like. This is great. I wonder what will happen. O youth!

"Suddenly Mahon sighted a steamer far astern. Captain Beard said, 'We may do something with her yet.' We hoisted two flags, which said in the international language of the sea, 'On fire. Want immediate assistance.' The steamer grew bigger rapidly, and by and by spoke with two flags on her foremast, 'I am coming to your assistance.'

"In half an hour she was abreast, to windward, within hail, and rolling slightly, with her engines stopped. We lost our composure, and yelled all together with excitement, 'We've been blown up.' A man in a white helmet, on the bridge, cried, 'Yes! All right! all right!' and he nodded his head, and smiled, and made soothing motions with his hand as though at a lot of frightened children. One of the boats dropped in the water, and walked towards us upon the sea with her long oars. Four Calashes pulled a swinging stroke. This was my first sight of Malay seamen. I've known them since, but what struck me then was their unconcern: they came alongside, and even the bowman standing up and holding to our main-chains with the boat and hook did not deign to lift his head for a glance. I thought people who had been blown up deserved more attention.

"A little man, dry like a chip and agile like a monkey,

clambered up.   It was the mate of the steamer.   He gave one look, and cried, 'O boys—you had better quit.'

"We were silent.   He talked apart with the captain for a time,—seemed to argue with him.   Then they went away together to the steamer.

"When our skipper came back we learned that the steamer was the *Somerville*, Captain Nash, from West Australia to Singapore *via* Batavia with mails, and that the agreement was she should tow us to Anjer or Batavia, if possible, where we could extinguish the fire by scuttling, and then proceed on our voyage—to Bangkok!   The old man seemed excited. 'We will do it yet,' he said to Mahon, fiercely.   He shook his fist at the sky.   Nobody else said a word.

"At noon the steamer began to tow.   She went ahead slim and high, and what was left of the *Judea* followed at the end of seventy fathom of towrope,—followed her swiftly like a cloud of smoke with mastheads protruding above.   We went aloft to furl the sails.   We coughed on the yards, and were careful about the bunts.   Do you see the lot of us there, putting a neat furl on the sails of that ship doomed to arrive nowhere?   There was not a man who didn't think that at any moment the masts would topple over.   From aloft we could not see the ship for smoke, and they worked carefully, passing the gaskets with even turns.   'Harbor furl—aloft there!' cried Mahon from below.

"You understand this?   I don't think one of those chaps expected to get down in the usual way.   When we did I heard them saying to each other, 'Well, I thought we would come down overboard, in a lump—sticks and all—blame me if I didn't.'   'That's what I was thinking to myself,' would answer wearily another battered and bandaged scarecrow. And, mind, these were men without the drilled-in habit of obedience.   To an onlooker they would be a lot of profane scallawags without a redeeming point.   What made them do it—what made them obey me when I, thinking consciously

how fine it was, made them drop the bunt of the foresail twice
to try and do it better? What? They had no professional
reputation—no examples, no praise. It wasn't a sense of
duty; they all knew well enough how to shirk, and laze,
and dodge—when they had a mind to it—and mostly they
had. Was it the two pounds ten a month that sent them
there? They didn't think their pay half good enough. No;
it was something in them, something inborn and subtle and
everlasting. I don't say positively that the crew of a French
or German merchantman wouldn't have done it, but I doubt
whether it would have been done in the same way. There
was a completeness in it, something solid like a principle, and
masterful like an instinct—a disclosure of something secret
—of that hidden something, that gift of good or evil that
makes racial difference, that shapes the fate of nations.

"It was that night at ten that, for the first time since we
had been fighting it, we saw the fire. The speed of the
towing had fanned the smoldering destruction. A blue
gleam appeared forward, shining below the wreck of the
deck. It wavered in patches, it seemed to stir and creep like
the light of a glowworm. I saw it first, and told Mahon.
'Then the game's up,' he said. 'We had better stop this
towing, or she will burst out suddenly fore and aft before
we can clear out.' We set up a yell; rang bells to attract
their attention; they towed on. At last Mahon and I had
to crawl forward and cut the rope with an axe. There was
no time to cast off the lashings. Red tongues could be seen
licking the wilderness of splinters under our feet as we made
our way back to the poop.

"Of course they very soon found out in the steamer that
the rope was gone. She gave a loud blast of her whistle, her
lights were seen sweeping in a wide circle, she came up ranging close along-side, and stopped. We were all in a tight
group on the poop looking at her. Every man had saved a
little bundle or a bag. Suddenly a conical flame with a

twisted top shot up forward and threw upon the black sea a circle of light, with the two vessels side by side and heaving gently in its center. Captain Beard had been sitting on the gratings still and mute for hours, but now he rose slowly and advanced in front of us, to the mizzen-shrouds. Captain Nash hailed: 'Come along! Look sharp. I have mail bags on board. I will take you and your boats to Singapore.'

" 'Thank you! No!' said our skipper. 'We must see the last of the ship.'

" 'I can't stand by any longer,' shouted the other. 'Mails —you know.'

" 'Ay! ay! We are all right.'

" 'Very well! I'll report you in Singapore. . . . Good-bye!'

"He waved his hand. Our men dropped their bundles quietly. The steamer moved ahead, and passing out of the circle of light, vanished at once from our sight, dazzled by the fire which burned fiercely. And then I knew that I would see the East first as commander of a small boat. I thought it fine; and the fidelity to the old ship was fine. We should see the last of her. Oh, the glamour of youth! Oh, the fire of it, more dazzling than the flames of the burning ship, throwing a magic light on the wide earth, leaping audaciously to the sky, presently to be quenched by time, more cruel, more pitiless, more bitter than the sea—and, like the flames of the burning ship, surrounded by an impenetrable night.

*   *   *

"The old man warned us in his gentle and inflexible way that it was part of our duty to save for the underwriters as much as we could of the ship's gear. Accordingly we went to work aft, while she blazed forward to give us plenty of light. We lugged out a lot of rubbish. What didn't we save? An old barometer fixed with an absurd quantity of

screws nearly cost me my life: a sudden rush of smoke came
upon me, and I just got away in time. There were various
stores, bolts of canvas, coils of rope; the poop looked like a
marine bazaar, and the boats were lumbered to the gunwales.
One would have thought the old man wanted to take as much
as he could of his first command with him. He was very,
very quiet, but off his balance evidently. Would you believe it? He wanted to take a length of old stream-cable
and a kedge-anchor with him in the long-boat. We said,
'Ay, ay, sir,' deferentially, and on the quiet let the things
slip overboard. The heavy medicine-chest went that way,
two bags of green coffee, tins of paint—fancy, paint!—a
whole lot of things. Then I was ordered with two hands
into the boats to make a stowage and get them ready against
the time it would be proper for us to leave the ship.

"We put everything straight, stepped the long-boat's mast
for our skipper, who was to take charge of her, and I was
not sorry to sit down for a moment. My face felt raw,
every limb ached as if broken, I was aware of all my ribs,
and would have sworn to a twist in the backbone. The
boats, fast astern, lay in a deep shadow, and all around I
could see the circle of the sea lighted by the fire. A gigantic
flame arose forward straight and clear. It flared fierce, with
noises like the whirr of wings, with rumbles as of thunder.
There were cracks, detonations, and from the cone of flame
the sparks flew upwards, as man is born to trouble, to leaky
ships, and to ships that burn.

"What bothered me was that the ship, lying broadside to
the swell and to such wind as there was—a mere breath—
the boats would not keep astern where they were safe, but
persisted, in a pig-headed way boats have, in getting under
the counter and then swinging alongside. They were knocking about dangerously and coming near the flame, while the
ship rolled on them, and, of course, there was always the
danger of the masts going over the side at any moment. I

and my two boat-keepers kept them off as best we could,
with oars and boat-hooks; but to be constantly at it became
exasperating, since there was no reason why we should not
leave at once.   We could not see those on board, nor could we
imagine what caused the delay.   The boat-keepers were
swearing feebly, and I had not only my share of the work
but also had to keep at it two men who showed a constant
inclination to lay themselves down and let things slide.

"At last I hailed, 'On deck there,' and someone looked
over.   'We're ready here,' I said.   The head disappeared,
and very soon popped up again.   'The captain says, All
right, sir, and to keep the boats well clear of the ship.'

"Half an hour passed.   Suddenly there was a frightful
racket, rattle, clanking of chain, hiss of water, and millions
of sparks flew up into the shivering column of smoke that
stood leaning slightly above the ship.   The catheads had
burned away, and the two red-hot anchors had gone to the
bottom, tearing out after them two hundred fathom of red-
hot chain.   The ship trembled, the mass of flame swayed
as if ready to collapse, and the fore topgallant mast fell.   It
darted down like an arrow of fire, shot under, and instantly
leaping up within an oar's length of the boats, floated quietly,
very black on the luminous sea.   I hailed the deck again.
After some time a man in an unexpectedly cheerful but also
muffled tone, as though he had been trying to speak with his
mouth shut, informed me, 'Coming directly, sir,' and vanished.   For a long time I heard nothing but the whirr and
roar of the fire.   There were also whistling sounds.   The
boats jumped, tugged at the painters, ran at each other playfully, knocked their sides together, or, do what we would,
swung in a bunch against the ship's side.   I couldn't stand
it any longer, and swarming up a rope, clambered aboard
over the stern.

"It was as bright as day.   Coming up like this, the sheet
of fire facing me was a terrifying sight, and the heat seemed

hardly bearable at first. On a settee cushion dragged out of the cabin Captain Beard, his legs drawn up and one arm under his head, slept with the light playing on him. Do you know what the rest were busy about? They were sitting on deck right aft, round an open case, eating bread and cheese and drinking bottled stout.

"On the background of flames twisting in fierce tongues above their heads they seemed at home like salamanders, and looked like a band of desperate pirates. The fire sparkled in the whites of their eyes, gleamed on patches of white skin seen through the torn shirts. Each had the marks as of a battle about him—bandaged heads, tied-up arms, a strip of dirty rag round a knee—and each man had a bottle between his legs and a chunk of cheese in his hand. Mahon got up. With his handsome and disreputable head, his hooked profile, his long white beard, and with an uncorked bottle in his hand, he resembled one of those reckless sea-robbers of old making merry amidst violence and disaster. 'The last meal on board,' he explained solemnly. 'We had nothing to eat all day, and it was no use leaving all this.' He flourished the bottle and indicated the sleeping skipper. 'He said he couldn't swallow anything, so I got him to lie down,' he went on; and as I stared, 'I don't know whether you are aware, young fellow, the man had no sleep to speak of for days—and there will be dam' little sleep in the boats.' 'There will be no boats by and by if you fool about much longer,' I said, indignantly. I walked up to the skipper and shook him by the shoulder. At last he opened his eyes, but did not move. 'Time to leave her, sir,' I said quietly.

"He got up painfully, looked at the flames, at the sea sparkling round the ship, and black, black as ink farther away; he looked at the stars shining dim through a thin veil of smoke in a sky black, black as Erebus.

" 'Youngest first,' he said.

"And the ordinary seaman, wiping his mouth with the

back of his hand, got up, clambered over the taffrail, and vanished. Others followed. One, on the point of going over, stopped short to drain his bottle, and with a great swing of his arm flung it at the fire. 'Take this!' he cried.

"The skipper lingered disconsolately, and we left him to commune alone for a while with his first command. Then I went up again and brought him away at last. It was time. The ironwork on the poop was hot to the touch.

"Then the painter of the longboat was cut, and the three boats, tied together, drifted clear of the ship. It was just sixteen hours after the explosion when we abandoned her. Mahon had charge of the second boat, and I had the smallest —the 14-foot thing. The longboat would have taken the lot of us; but the skipper said we must save as much property as we could—for the underwriters—and so I got my first command. I had two men with me, a bag of biscuits, a few tins of meat, and a breaker of water. I was ordered to keep close to the longboat, that in case of bad weather we might be taken into her.

"And do you know what I thought? I thought I would part company as soon as I could. I wanted to have my first command all to myself. I wasn't going to sail in a squadron if there were a chance for independent cruising. I would make land by myself. I would beat the other boats. Youth! All youth! The silly, charming, beautiful youth.

"But we did not make a start at once. We must see the last of the ship. And so the boats drifted about that night, heaving and setting on the swell. The men dozed, waked, sighed, groaned. I looked at the burning ship.

"Between the darkness of earth and heaven she was burning fiercely upon a disc of purple sea shot by the blood-red play of gleams; upon a disc of water glittering and sinister. A high, clear flame, an immense and lonely flame, ascended from the ocean, and from its summit the black smoke poured continuously at the sky. She burned furiously; mournful

and imposing like a funeral pile kindled in the night, surrounded by the sea, watched over by the stars.   A magnificent death had come like a grace, like a gift, like a reward to
that old ship at the end of her laborious days.   The surrender
of her weary ghost to the keeping of stars and sea was stirring
like the sight of a glorious triumph.   The masts fell just
before daybreak, and for a moment there was a burst and
turmoil of sparks that seemed to fill with flying fire the night
patient and watchful, the vast night lying silent upon the
sea.   At daylight she was only a charred shell, floating still
under a cloud of smoke and bearing a glowing mass of coal
within.

"Then the oars were got out, and the boats, forming in a
line, moved round her remains as if in procession—the long-
boat leading.   As we pulled across her stern a slim dart of
fire shot out viciously at us, and suddenly she went down,
head first, in a great hiss of steam.   The unconsumed stern
was the last to sink; but the paint had gone, had cracked,
had peeled off, and there were no letters, there was no word,
no stubborn device that was like her soul, to flash at the
rising sun her creed and her name.

"We made our way north.   A breeze sprang up, and about
noon all the boats came together for the last time.   I had no
mast or sail in mine, but I made a mast out of a spare oar
and hoisted a boat awning for a sail, with a boat hook for a
yard.   She was certainly overmasted, but I had the satisfaction of knowing that with the wind aft I could beat the
other two.   I had to wait for them.   Then we all had a look
at the captain's chart, and, after a sociable meal of hard bread
and water, got our last instructions.   These were simple:
steer north, and keep together as much as possible.   'Be careful with that jury rig, Marlow,' said the captain; and Mahon,
as I sailed proudly past his boat, wrinkled his curved nose
and hailed, 'You will sail that ship of yours under water, if
you don't look out, young fellow.'   He was a malicious old

man—and may the deep sea where he sleeps now rock him gently, rock him tenderly to the end of time!

"Before sunset a thick rain-squall passed over the two boats, which were far astern, and that was the last I saw of them for a time. Next day I sat steering my cockleshell —my first command—with nothing but water and sky around me. I did sight in the afternoon the upper sails of a ship far away, but said nothing, and my men did not notice her. You see, I was afraid she might be homeward bound, and I had no mind to turn back from the portals of the East. I was steering for Java—another blessed name—like Bangkok, you know. I steered many days.

"I need not tell you what it is to be knocking about in an open boat. I remember nights and days of calm, when we pulled, we pulled, and the boat seemed to stand still, as if bewitched within the circle of the sea horizon. I remember the heat, the deluge of rain-squalls that kept us bailing for dear life (but filled our water cask), and I remember sixteen hours on end with a mouth dry as a cinder and a steering-oar over the stern to keep my first command head on to a breaking sea. I did not know how good a man I was till then. I remember the drawn faces, the dejected figures of my two men, and I remember my youth and the feeling that will never come back any more—the feeling that I could last forever, outlast the sea, the earth, and all men; the deceitful feeling that lures us on to joys, to perils, to love, to vain effort—to death; the triumphant conviction of strength, the heat of life in the handful of dust, the glow in the heart that with every year grows dim, grows cold, grows small, and expires—and expires, too soon, too soon— before life itself.

"And this is how I see the East. I have seen its secret places and have looked into its very soul; but now I see it always from a small boat, a high outline of mountains, blue and afar in the morning; like faint mist at noon; a jagged wall of purple at sunset. I have the feel of the oar in my hand, the vision of a scorching blue sea in my eyes. And I see a bay, a wide bay, smooth as glass and polished like ice, shimmering in the dark. A red light burns far off upon the gloom of the land, and the night is soft and warm. We drag at the oars with aching arms, and suddenly a puff of wind, a puff faint and tepid and laden with strange odors of blossoms, of aromatic wood, comes out of the still night— the first sigh of the East on my face. That I can never forget. It was impalpable and enslaving, like a charm, like a whispered promise of mysterious delight.

"We had been pulling this finishing spell for eleven hours. Two pulled, and he whose turn it was to rest sat at the tiller. We had made out the red light in that bay and steered for it, guessing it must mark some small coasting port. We passed two vessels, outlandish and high-sterned, sleeping at anchor, and, approaching the light, now very dim, ran the boat's nose against the end of a jutting wharf. We were blind with fatigue. My men dropped the oars and fell off the thwarts as if dead. I made fast to a pile. A current rippled softly. The scented obscurity of the shore was grouped into vast masses, a density of colossal clumps of vegetation, probably—mute and fantastic shapes. And at their foot the semicircle of a beach gleamed faintly, like an illusion. There was not a light, not a stir, not a sound. The mysterious East faced me, perfumed like a flower, silent like death, dark like a grave.

"And I sat weary beyond expression, exulting like a conqueror, sleepless and entranced as if before a profound, a fateful enigma.

"A splashing of oars, a measured dip reverberating on the level of water, intensified by the silence of the shore into loud claps, made me jump up. A boat, a European boat, was coming in. I invoked the name of the dead; I hailed: *Judea* ahoy! A thin shout answered.

"It was the captain. I had beaten the flagship by three hours, and I was glad to hear the old man's voice again, tremulous and tired. 'Is it you, Marlow?' 'Mind the end of that jetty, sir,' I cried.

"He approached cautiously, and brought up with the deep-sea lead line which we had saved—for the underwriters. I eased my painter and fell alongside. He sat, a broken figure at the stern, wet with dew, his hands clasped in his lap. His men were asleep already. 'I had a terrible time of it,' he murmured. 'Mahon is behind—not very far.' We conversed in whispers, in low whispers, as if afraid to wake up the land. Guns, thunder, earthquakes would not have awakened the men just then.

"Looking round as we talked, I saw away at sea a bright light traveling in the night. 'There's a steamer passing the bay,' I said. She was not passing, she was entering, and she even came close and anchored. 'I wish,' said the old man, 'you would find out whether she is English. Perhaps they could give us a passage somewhere.' He seemed nervously anxious. So by dint of punching and kicking I started one of my men into a state of somnambulism, and giving him an oar, took another and pulled towards the lights of the steamer.

"There was a murmur of voices in her, metallic hollow clangs of the engine-room, footsteps on the deck. Her ports shone, round like dilated eyes. Shapes moved about, and there was a shadowy man high up on the bridge. He heard my oars.

"And then, before I could open my lips, the East spoke to me, but it was in a Western voice. A torrent of words was poured into the enigmatical, the fateful silence; outlandish, angry words, mixed with words and even whole sentences of good English, less strange but even more surprising. The voice swore and cursed violently; it riddled the solemn peace of the bay by a volley of abuse. It began by calling me Pig, and from that went crescendo into unmentionable adjectives—in English. The man up there raged aloud in two languages, and with a sincerity in his fury that almost convinced me I had, in some way, sinned against the harmony of the universe. I could hardly see him, but began to think he would work himself into a fit.

"Suddenly he ceased, and I could hear him snorting and blowing like a porpoise. I said—

" 'What steamer is this, pray?'

" 'Eh? What's this? And who are you?'

" 'Castaway crew of an English barque burnt at sea. We came here tonight. I am the second mate. The captain is in the longboat, and wishes to know if you would give us a passage somewhere.'

" 'Oh, my goodness! I say. . . . This is the *Celestial* from Singapore on her return trip. I'll arrange with your captain in the morning, . . . and, . . . I say, . . . did you hear me just now?'

" 'I should think the whole bay heard you.'

" 'I thought you were a shore boat. Now, look here— this infernal lazy scoundrel of a caretaker has gone to sleep again—curse him. The light is out, and I nearly ran foul of the end of this damned jetty. This is the third time he plays me this trick. Now, I ask you, can anybody stand this kind of thing? It's enough to drive a man out of his mind. I'll report him. . . . I'll get the Assistant Resident to give him the sack, by . . . ! See—there's no light. It's out, isn't it? I take you to witness the light's out. There should be a light, you know. A red light on the——'

" 'There was a light,' I said, mildly.

" 'But it's out, man! What's the use of talking like this? You can see for yourself it's out—don't you? If you had to take a valuable steamer along this God-forsaken coast you would want a light, too. I'll kick him from end to end of his miserable wharf. You'll see if I don't. I will——'

"'So I may tell my captain you'll take us?' I broke in.
"'Yes, I'll take you. Good-night,' he said, brusquely.

"I pulled back, made fast again to the jetty, and then
went to sleep at last. I had faced the silence of the East.
I had heard some of its language. But when I opened my
eyes again the silence was as complete as though it had never
been broken. I was lying in a flood of light, and the sky
had never looked so far, so high, before. I opened my eyes
and lay without moving.

"And then I saw the men of the East—they were looking
at me. The whole length of the jetty was full of people.
I saw brown, bronze, yellow faces, the black eyes, the glitter,
the color of an Eastern crowd. And all these beings stared
without a murmur, without a sigh, without a movement.
They stared down at the boats, at the sleeping men who at
night had come to them from the sea. Nothing moved.
The fronds of palms stood still against the sky. Not a
branch stirred along the shore, and the brown roofs of
hidden houses peeped through the green foliage, through the
big leaves that hung shining and still like leaves forged of
heavy metal. This was the East of the ancient navigators,
so old, so mysterious, resplendent and somber, living and un-
changed, full of danger and promise. And these were the
men. I sat up suddenly. A wave of movement passed
through the crowd from end to end, passed along the heads,
swayed the bodies, ran along the jetty like a ripple on the
water, like a breath of wind on a field—and all was still
again. I see it now—the wide sweep of the bay, the glittering sands, the wealth of green infinite and varied, the sea
blue like the sea of a dream, the crowd of attentive faces, the
blaze of vivid color—the water reflecting it all, the curve of
the shore, the jetty, the high-sterned outlandish craft floating still, and the three boats with the tired men from the
West sleeping, unconscious of the land and the people and
of the violence of sunshine. They slept thrown across the

thwarts, curled on bottom boards, in the careless attitudes
of death. The head of the old skipper, leaning back in the
stern of the longboat, had fallen on his breast, and he looked
as though he would never wake. Farther out old Mahon's
face was upturned to the sky, with the long white beard
spread out on his breast, as though he had been shot where
he sat at the tiller; and a man, all in a heap in the bows of the
boat, slept with both arms embracing the stem-head and
with his cheek laid on the gunwale. The East looked at them
without a sound.

"I have known its fascination since; I have seen the mysterious shores, the still water, the lands of brown nations,
where a stealthy Nemesis lies in wait, pursues, overtakes so
many of the conquering race, who are proud of their wisdom,
of their knowledge, of their strength. But for me all the
East is contained in that vision of my youth. It is all in
that moment when I opened my young eyes on it. I came
upon it from a tussle with the sea—and I was young—and I
saw it looking at me. And this is all that is left of it! Only
a moment; a moment of strength, of romance, of glamour
—of youth! . . . A flick of sunshine upon a strange shore,
the time to remember, the time for a sigh, and—good-bye!—
Night—Good-bye . . . !"

He drank.

"Ah! The good old time—the good old time. Youth
and the sea. Glamour and the sea! The good, strong sea,
the salt, bitter sea, that could whisper to you and roar at you
and knock your breath out of you."

He drank again.

"By all that's wonderful it is the sea, I believe, the sea
itself—or is it youth alone? Who can tell? But you here—
you all had something out of life: money, love—whatever
one gets on shore—and, tell me, wasn't that the best time,
that time when we were young at sea; young and had nothing, on the sea that gives nothing, except hard knocks—

and sometimes a chance to feel your strength—that only
—what you all regret?"

And we all nodded at him: the man of finance, the man
of accounts, the man of law, we all nodded at him over the
polished table that like a still sheet of brown water reflected
our faces, lined, wrinkled; our faces marked by toil, by de-
ceptions, by success, by love; our weary eyes looking still,
looking always, looking anxiously for something out of life,
that while it is expected is already gone—has passed unseen,
in a sigh, in a flash—together with the youth, with the
strength, with the romance of illusions.

THE ERA OF EXAMINATIONS

[In this section, Conrad has grouped the amusing ordeal of his
three examinations: for third mate in 1880; for mate, 1883; for
"the certificate of competency as master," 1886.]

I have a small handful of sea appreciations, signed by
various masters, yellowing slowly in my writing-table's left-
hand drawer, rustling under my reverent touch, like a handful of dry leaves plucked for a tender memento from the tree
of knowledge. Strange! It seems that it is for these few
bits of paper, headed by the names of a few ships and signed
by the names of a few Scottish and English shipmasters, that
I have faced the astonished indignations, the mockeries, and
the reproaches of a sort hard to bear for a boy of fifteen;
that I have been charged with the want of patriotism, the
want of sense, and the want of heart too; that I went through
agonies of self-conflict and shed secret tears not a few, and
had the beauties of the Furca Pass spoiled for me, and have
been called an "incorrigible Don Quixote," in allusion to the
book-born madness of the knight. For that spoil! They
rustle, those bits of paper—some dozen of them in all. In

that faint, ghostly sound there live the memories of twenty years, the voices of rough men now no more, the strong voice of the everlasting winds, and the whisper of a mysterious spell, the murmur of the great sea, which must have somehow reached my inland cradle and entered my unconscious ear, like that formula of Mohammedan faith the Mussulman father whispers into the ear of his new-born infant, making him one of the faithful almost with his first breath. I do not know whether I have been a good seaman, but I know I have been a very faithful one. And after all there is that handful of "characters" from various ships to prove that all these years have not been altogether a dream. There they are, brief, and monotonous in tone, but as suggestive bits of writing to me as any inspired page to be found in literature. But then, you see, I have been called romantic. Well, that can't be helped. But stay. I seem to remember that I have been called a realist also. And as that charge too can be made out, let us try to live up to it, at whatever cost, for a change. With this end in view, I will confide to you coyly, and only because there is no one about to see my blushes by the light of the midnight lamp, that these suggestive bits of quarter-deck appreciation one and all contain the words "strictly sober."

Did I overhear a civil murmur, "That's very gratifying, to be sure"? Well, yes, it is gratifying—thank you. It is at least as gratifying to be certified sober as to be certified romantic, though such certificates would not qualify one for the secretaryship of a temperance association or for the post of official troubadour to some lordly democratic institution such as the London County Council, for instance.

As to my sea-sobriety, that is quite properly certified under the sign-manual of several trustworthy shipmasters of some standing in their time. I seem to hear your polite murmur that "Surely this might have been taken for granted." Well, no. It might not have been. That august academical body

of the Marine Department of the Board of Trade takes nothing for granted in the granting of its learned degrees.   By
its regulations issued under the first Merchant Shipping Act,
the very word *sober* must be written, or a whole sackful, a
ton, a mountain of the most enthusiastic appreciation will
avail you nothing.   The door of the examination rooms
shall remain closed to your tears and entreaties.   The most
fanatical advocate of temperance could not be more pitilessly
fierce in his rectitude than the Marine Department of the
Board of Trade.   As I have been face to face at various times
with all the examiners of the Port of London, in my genera-
tion, there can be no doubt as to the force and the continuity
of my abstemiousness.   Three of them were examiners in
seamanship, and it was my fate to be delivered into the hands
of each of them at proper intervals of sea service.   The first
of all, tall, spare, with a perfectly white head and mustache,
a quiet, kindly manner, and an air of benign intelligence,
must, I am forced to conclude, have been unfavorably impressed by something in my appearance.   His old thin hands
loosely clasped resting on his crossed legs, he began by an
elementary question in a mild voice, and went on, went on
. . . It lasted for hours, for hours.   Had I been a strange
microbe with potentialities of deadly mischief to the Merchant Service I could not have been submitted to a more
microscopic examination.   Greatly reassured by his apparent
benevolence, I had been at first very alert in my answers.
But at length the feeling of my brain getting addled crept
upon me.   And still the passionless process went on, with a
sense of untold ages having been spent already on mere
preliminaries.   Then I got frightened.   I was not frightened of being plucked; that eventuality did not even present
itself to my mind.   It was something much more serious,
and weird.   "This ancient person," I said to myself, terrified, "is so near his grave that he must have lost all notion
of time.   He is considering this examination in terms of

eternity. It is all very well for him. His race is run. But I may find myself coming out of this room into the world of men, a stranger, friendless, forgotten by my very landlady, even were I able after this endless experience to remember the way to my hired home." This statement is not so much of a verbal exaggeration as may be supposed. Some very queer thoughts passed through my head while I was considering my answers; thoughts which had nothing to do with seamanship, nor yet with anything reasonable known to this earth. I verily believe that at times I was lightheaded in a sort of languid way. At last there fell a silence, and that, too, seemed to last for ages, while, bending over his desk, the examiner wrote out my pass slip slowly with a noiseless pen. He extended the scrap of paper to me without a word, inclined his white head gravely to my parting bow . . .

When I got out of the room I felt limply flat, like a squeezed lemon, and the doorkeeper in his glass cage, where I stopped to get my hat and tip him a shilling, said:

"Well! I thought you were never coming out."

"How long have I been in there?" I asked faintly.

He pulled out his watch.

"He kept you, sir, just under three hours. I don't think this ever happened with any of the gentlemen before."

It was only when I got out of the building that I began to walk on air. And the human animal being averse from change and timid before the unknown, I said to myself that I would not mind really being examined by the same man on a future occasion. But when the time of ordeal came round again the doorkeeper let me into another room, with the now familiar paraphernalia of models of ships and tackle, a board for signals on the wall, a big long table covered with official forms, and having an unrigged mast fixed to the edge. The solitary tenant was unknown to me by sight, though not by reputation, which was simply execrable. Short and sturdy as far as I could judge, clad in an old brown morning suit,

he sat leaning on his elbow, his hand shading his eyes, and
half averted from the chair I was to occupy on the other
side of the table. He was motionless, mysterious, remote,
enigmatical, with something mournful too in the pose, like
that statue of Giuliano (I think) de Medici shading his face
on the tomb by Michelangelo, though, of course, he was far,
far from being beautiful. He began by trying to make me
talk nonsense. But I had been warned of that fiendish trait,
and contradicted him with great assurance. After a while
he left off. So far, good. But his immobility, the thick
elbow on the table, the abrupt, unhappy voice, the shaded
and averted face grew more and more impressive. He kept
inscrutably silent for a moment, and then, placing me in a
ship of a certain size at sea, under certain conditions of
weather, season, locality, etc., etc.—all very clear and precise
—ordered me to execute a certain maneuver. Before I was
half through with it he did some material damage to the
ship. Directly I had grappled with the difficulty, he caused
another to present itself; and when that too was met he
stuck another ship before me, creating a very dangerous
situation. I felt slightly outraged by this ingenuity in piling
up trouble upon a man.

"I wouldn't have got into that mess," I suggested mildly.
"I could have seen that ship before."

He never stirred the least bit.

"No, you couldn't. The weather's thick."

"Oh! I didn't know," I apologized blankly. I suppose
that after all I managed to stave off the smash with sufficient
approach to verisimilitude, and the ghastly business went on.
You must understand that the scheme of the test he was
applying to me was, I gathered, a homeward passage—the
sort of passage I would not wish to my bitterest enemy.
That imaginary ship seemed to labor under a most compre-
hensive curse. It's no use enlarging on these never-ending
misfortunes; suffice it to say that long before the end I would

have welcomed with gratitude an opportunity to exchange into the *Flying Dutchman*. Finally he shoved me into the North Sea (I suppose) and provided me with a leeshore with outlying sandbanks—the Dutch coast presumably. Distance, eight miles. The evidence of such implacable animosity deprived me of speech for quite half a minute.

"Well," he said—for our pace had been very smart indeed till then.

"I will have to think a little, sir."

"Doesn't look as if there were much time to think," he muttered sardonically from under his hand.

"No, sir," I said with some warmth. "Not on board a ship I could see. But so many accidents have happened that I really can't remember what there's left for me to work with."

Still half averted, and with his eyes concealed, he made unexpectedly a grunting remark.

"You've done very well."

"Have I the two anchors at the bow, sir?" I asked.

"Yes."

I prepared myself then, as a last hope for the ship, to let them both go in the most effectual manner, when his infernal system of testing resourcefulness came into play again.

"But there's only one cable. You've lost the other."

It was exasperating.

"Then I would back them, if I could, and tail the heaviest hawser on board on the end of the chain before letting go, and if she parted from that, which is quite likely, I would just do nothing. She would have to go."

"Nothing more to do, eh?"

"No, sir. I could do no more."

He gave a bitter half-laugh.

"You could always say your prayers."

He got up, stretched himself, and yawned slightly. It was a sallow, strong, unamiable face. He put me in a surly,

bored fashion through the usual questions as to lights and
signals, and I escaped from the room thankfully—passed!
Forty minutes! And again I walked on air along Tower
Hill, where so many good men had lost their heads, because,
I suppose, they were not resourceful enough to save them.
And in my heart of hearts I had no objection to meeting
that examiner once more when the third and last ordeal
became due in another year or so. I even hoped I should.
I knew the worst of him now, and forty minutes is not
an unreasonable time. Yes, I distinctly hoped . . .

But not a bit of it. When I presented myself to be examined for Master, the examiner who received me was short,
plump, with a round, soft face in gray, fluffy whiskers, and
fresh loquacious lips.

He commenced operations with an easy-going "Let's see.
H'm. Suppose you tell me all you know of charter parties."
He kept it up in that style all through, wandering off in the
shape of comment into bits out of his own life, then pulling
himself up short and returning to the business in hand. It
was very interesting. "What's your idea of a jury rudder,
now?" he queried suddenly, at the end of an instructive
anecdote bearing upon a point of stowage.

I warned him that I had no experience of a lost rudder at
sea, and gave him two classical examples of makeshifts out of
a textbook. In exchange he described to me a jury rudder
he had invented himself years before, when in command of a
3000-ton steamer. It was, I declare, the cleverest contrivance
imaginable. "May be of use to you some day," he concluded. "You will go into steam presently. Everybody
goes into steam."

There he was wrong. I never went into steam—not really.
If I only live long enough I shall become a bizarre relic of a
dead barbarism, a sort of monstrous antiquity, the only seaman of the dark ages who had never gone into steam—not
really.

Before the examination was over he imparted to me a few interesting details of the transport service in the time of the Crimean War.

"The use of wire rigging became general about that time, too," he observed. "I was a very young master then. That was before you were born."

"Yes, sir. I am of the year 1857."

"The Mutiny year," he commented, as if to himself, adding in a louder tone that his ship happened then to be in the Gulf of Bengal, employed under a Government charter.

Clearly the transport service had been the making of this examiner, who so unexpectedly had given me an insight into his existence, awakening in me the sense of the continuity of that sea-life into which I had stepped from outside; giving a touch of human intimacy to the machinery of official relations. I felt adopted. His experience was for me, too, as though he had been an ancestor.

Writing my long name (it has twelve letters) with laborious care on the slip of blue paper, he remarked:

"You are of Polish extraction."

"Born there, sir."

He laid down the pen and leaned back to look at me as it were for the first time.

"Not many of your nationality in our service, I should think. I never remember meeting one either before or after I left the sea. Don't remember ever hearing of one. An inland people, aren't you?"

I said yes—very much so. We were remote from the sea not only by situation, but also from a complete absence of indirect association, not being a commercial nation at all, but purely agricultural. He made then the quaint reflection that it was "a long way for me to come out to begin a sea-life"; as if sea-life were not precisely a life in which one goes a long way from home.

I told him, smiling, that no doubt I could have found a

ship much nearer my native place, but I had thought to myself that if I was to be a seaman then I would be a British
seaman and no other.   It was a matter of deliberate choice.

He nodded slightly at that; and as he kept on looking at me
interrogatively, I enlarged a little, confessing that I had spent
a little time on the way in the Mediterranean and in the
West Indies.   I did not want to present myself to the British
Merchant Service in an altogether green state.   It was no
use telling him that my mysterious vocation was so strong
that my very wild oats had to be sown at sea.   It was the
exact truth, but he would not have understood the somewhat
exceptional psychology of my sea-going, I fear.

"I suppose you've never come across one of your country-
men at sea.   Have you, now?"

I admitted I never had.   The examiner had given himself
up to the spirit of gossiping idleness.   For myself, I was
in no haste to leave that room.   Not in the least.   The era
of examinations was over.   I would never again see that
friendly man who was a professional ancestor, a sort of
grandfather in the craft.   Moreover, I had to wait till he dismissed me, and of that there was no sign.   As he remained
silent, looking at me, I added:

"But I have heard of one, some years ago.   He seems to
have been a boy serving his time on board a Liverpool ship,
if I am not mistaken."

"What was his name?"

I told him.

"How did you say that?" he asked, puckering up his eyes
at the uncouth sound.

I repeated the name very distinctly.

"How do you spell it?"

I told him.   He moved his head at the impracticable nature
of that name, and observed:

"It's quite as long as your own—isn't it?"

There was no hurry.   I had passed for Master, and I had

all the rest of my life before me to make the best of it. That seemed a long time. I went leisurely through a small mental calculation, and said:

"Not quite. Shorter by two letters, sir."

"Is it?" The examiner pushed the signed blue slip across the table to me, and rose from his chair. Somehow this seemed a very abrupt ending of our relations, and I felt almost sorry to part from that excellent man, who was master of a ship before the whisper of the sea had reached my cradle. He offered me his hand and wished me well. He even made a few steps towards the door with me, and ended with good-natured advice.

"I don't know what may be your plans, but you ought to go into steam. When a man has got his master's certificate it's the proper time. If I were you I would go into steam."

I thanked him, and shut the door behind me definitely on the era of examinations. But that time I did not walk on air, as on the first two occasions. I walked across the Hill of many beheadings with measured steps. It was a fact, I said to myself, that I was now a British master mariner beyond a doubt. It was not that I had an exaggerated sense of that very modest achievement, with which, however, luck, opportunity, or any extraneous influence could have had nothing to do. That fact, satisfactory and obscure in itself, had for me a certain ideal significance.

FIRST COMMAND

(From *The Shadow Line*)

[The autobiographical material in this section is taken from *The Shadow Line,* which Conrad meant originally to bear the title *First Command.* Fortunately it was found possible to select the important, significant passages without interrupting the course of the narrative.

"That piece of work," says Conrad, "is not a story really but an

exact autobiography."—"The very speeches are (I won't say authentic, they are that absolutely) I believe verbally accurate. And
all this happened in March-April, 1887."—"A confession—for from
a certain point of view, it is that—and essentially as sincere as any
confession can be."

For identification of ships and places, see the Chronological Table
1887, 1888, 1889.]

The Green Sickness of Early Youth

ONLY the young have such moments. I don't mean the
very young. No. The very young have, properly speaking, no moments. It is the privilege of early youth to live
in advance of its days in all the beautiful continuity of hope
which knows no pauses and no introspection.

One closes behind one the little gate of mere boyishness—
and enters an enchanted garden. Its very shades glow with
promise. Every turn of the path has its seduction. And it
isn't because it is an undiscovered country. One knows well
enough that all mankind had streamed that way. It is the
charm of universal experience from which one expects an
uncommon or personal sensation—a bit of one's own.

One goes on recognizing the landmarks of the predecessors,
excited, amused, taking the hard luck and the good luck together—the kicks and the halfpence, as the saying is—the
picturesque common lot that holds so many possibilities for
the deserving, or perhaps for the lucky. Yes. One goes on.
And the time, too, goes on—till one perceives ahead a
shadow line warning one that the region of early youth, too,
must be left behind.

This is the period of life in which such moments of which
I have spoken are likely to come. What moments? Why,
the moments of boredom, of weariness, of dissatisfaction.
Rash moments. I mean moments when the still young are
inclined to commit rash actions, such as getting married suddenly or else throwing up a job for no reason.

This is not a marriage story. It wasn't so bad as that with me. My action, rash as it was, had more the character of divorce—almost of desertion. For no reason on which a sensible person could put a finger I threw up my job—chucked my berth—and left the ship, of which the worst that could be said was that she was a steamship and therefore, perhaps, not entitled to that blind loyalty which . . . . However, it's no use trying to put a gloss on what even at the time I myself half suspected to be a caprice.

It was in an Eastern port. She was an Eastern ship, inasmuch as then she belonged to that port. She traded among dark islands on a blue reef-scarred sea, with the Red Ensign over the taffrail and at her masthead a house-flag, also red, but with a green border and with a white crescent in it. For an Arab owned her, and a Syed at that. Hence the green border on the flag. He was the head of a great House of Straits Arabs, but as loyal a subject of the complex British Empire as you could find east of the Suez Canal. World politics did not trouble him at all, but he had a great occult power amongst his own people.

It was all one to us who owned the ship. He had to employ white men in the shipping part of his business, and many of those he so employed had never set eyes on him from the first to the last day. I myself saw him but once, quite accidentally on a wharf—an old, dark little man blind in one eye, in a snowy robe and yellow slippers. He was having his hand severely kissed by a crowd of Malay pilgrims to whom he had done some favor, in the way of food and money. His almsgiving, I have heard, was most extensive, covering almost the whole Archipelago. For isn't it said that "The charitable man is the friend of Allah"?

Excellent (and picturesque) Arab owner, about whom one needed not to trouble one's head, a most excellent Scottish ship—for she was that from the keel up—excellent sea-boat, easy to keep clean, most handy in every way, and, if it had not been for her internal propulsion, worthy of any man's love, I cherish to this day a profound respect for her memory. As to the kind of trade she was engaged in and the character of my shipmates, I could not have been happier if I had had the life and the men made to my order by a benevolent Enchanter.

And suddenly I left all this. I left it in that, to us, inconsequential manner in which a bird flies away from a comfortable branch. It was as though all unknowing I had heard a whisper or seen something. Well—perhaps! One day I was perfectly right, and the next everything was gone —glamour, flavor, interest, contentment—everything. It was one of those moments, you know. The green sickness of late youth descended on me and carried me off. Carried me off that ship, I mean.

We were only four white men on board, with a large crew of Calashes and two Malay petty officers. The Captain stared hard as if wondering what ailed me. But he was a sailor, and he, too, had been young at one time. Presently a smile came to lurk under his thick iron-gray mustache, and he observed that, of course, if I felt I must go he couldn't keep me by main force. And it was arranged that I should be paid off the next morning. As I was going out of the chart-room he added suddenly, in a peculiar, wistful tone, that he hoped I would find what I was so anxious to go and look for. A soft, cryptic utterance which seemed to reach deeper than any diamond-hard tool could have done. I do believe he understood my case.

The Right Man for the Job

Captain Giles . . . . began to haul at his gorgeous gold chain till at last the watch came up from the deep pocket like solid truth from a well. Solemnly he lowered it down again and only then said:

"Just three o'clock. You will be in time—if you don't lose any, that is."

"In time for what?" I asked.

"Good Lord! For the Harbor Office. . . ."

I muttered that I didn't think—it was nothing to me.

"Nothing!" repeated Captain Giles, giving some signs of quiet, deliberate indignation. "Kent warned me you were a peculiar young fellow. You will tell me next that a command is nothing to you—and after all the trouble I've taken, too."

"The trouble!" I murmured, uncomprehending. What trouble? All I could remember was being mystified and bored by his conversation for a solid hour after tiffin. And he called that taking a lot of trouble.

He was looking at me with a self-complacency which would have been odious in any other man. . . .

And still I did not move. Captain Giles lost his patience a little. With an angry puff at his pipe he turned his back on my hesitation.

But it was not hesitation on my part. I had been, if I may express myself so, put out of gear mentally. But as soon as I had convinced myself that this stale, unprofitable world of my discontent contained such a thing as a command to be seized, I recovered my powers of locomotion.

It's a good step from the Officers' Home to the Harbor Office; but with the magic word "Command" in my head I found myself suddenly on the quay as if transported there in the twinkling of an eye, before a portal of dressed white stone above a flight of shallow white steps.

All this seemed to glide towards me swiftly. The whole great roadstead to the right was just a mere flicker of blue, and the dim cool hall swallowed me up out of the heat and glare of which I had not been aware till the very moment I passed in from it.

The broad inner staircase insinuated itself under my feet somehow.   Command is a strong magic. . . .

The next thing I saw was the top-knot of silver hair surmounting Captain Ellis' smooth red face, which would have been apoplectic if it hadn't had such a fresh appearance.

Our deputy-Neptune had no beard on his chin, and there was no trident to be seen standing in a corner anywhere, like an umbrella.   But his hand was holding a pen—the official pen, far mightier than the sword in making or marring the fortune of simple toiling men.   He was looking over his shoulder at my advance. . . .

I said . . . . that I had heard there was a master needed for some vessel, and being a sailing-ship man I thought I would apply. . . .

He interrupted me.   "Why! Hang it! *You* are the right man for that job—if there had been twenty others after it.   But no fear of that.   They are all afraid to catch hold. . . . ."

He was very irritated.   I said innocently: "Are they, sir? I wonder why?"

"Why!" he fumed.   "Afraid of the sails.   Afraid of a white crew.   Too much trouble.   Too much work.   Too long out here.   Easy life and deck chairs more their mark. . . . ."

I only smiled kindly down on him, and he seemed to recollect himself, and asked me to take a seat.   He explained that the master of a British ship having died in Bangkok the Consul-General had cabled to him a request for a competent man to be sent out to take command.

Apparently, in his mind, I was the man from the first. . . . . An agreement had already been prepared.   He gave it to me to read, and when I handed it back to him with the remark that I accepted its terms, the deputy-Neptune signed it, stamped it with his own exalted hand, folded it in **four** (it was a sheet of blue foolscap), and presented it to me—a gift of extraordinary potency, for, as I put it in my pocket, my head swam a little.

"This is your appointment to the command," he said with a certain gravity. "An official appointment binding the owners to conditions which you have accepted. Now—when will you be ready to go?"

I said I would be ready that very day if necessary. He caught me at my word with great readiness. The steamer *Melita* was leaving for Bangkok that evening about seven. He would request her captain officially to give me a passage and wait for me till ten o'clock.

Then he rose from his office chair, and I got up too. My head swam, there was no doubt about it, and I felt a heaviness of limbs as if they had grown bigger since I had sat down on that chair. I made my bow.

A subtle change in Captain Ellis' manner became perceptible as though he had laid aside the trident of deputy-Neptune. In reality, it was only his official pen that he had dropped on getting up.

He shook hands with me: "Well, there you are, on your own, appointed officially under my responsibility."

He was actually walking with me to the door. What a distance off it seemed! I moved like a man in bonds. But we reached it at last. I opened it with the sensation of dealing with mere dream-stuff, and then at the last moment the fellowship of seamen asserted itself, stronger than the difference of age and station. It asserted itself in Captain Ellis' voice.

"Good-bye—and good luck to you," he said so heartily that I could only give him a grateful glance.

The next ten minutes might have been ten seconds or ten centuries for all my consciousness had to do with it. People might have been falling dead around me, houses crumbling, guns firing. I wouldn't have known. I was thinking: "By Jove! I have got it." *It* being the command. . . .

I perceived that my imagination had been running in conventional channels and that my hopes had always been drab stuff. I had envisaged a command as a result of a slow course of promotion in the employ of some highly respectable firm. The reward of faithful service. Well, faithful service was all right. One would naturally give that for one's own sake, for the sake of the ship, for the love of the life of one's choice; not for the sake of the reward.

There is something distasteful in the notion of a reward.

And now here I had my command, absolutely in my pocket, in a way undeniable indeed, but most unexpected; beyond my imaginings, outside all reasonable expectations . . .

A strange sense of exultation began to creep into me. If I had worked for that command ten years or more there would have been nothing of the kind. I was a little frightened.

"Let us be calm," I said to myself.

What I really needed was to be alone for a bit . . . . My bedroom was a quiet refuge. . . . Having absolutely nothing to do (for I had not unpacked my things), I sat down on the bed and abandoned myself to the influences of the hour. To the unexpected influences. . . .

And first I wondered at my state of mind. Why was I not more surprised? Why? Here I was, invested with a command in the twinkling of an eye, not in the common course of human affairs, but more as if by enchantment. I ought to have been lost in astonishment. But I wasn't. I was very much like people in fairy tales. Nothing ever astonishes them. When a fully appointed gala coach is produced out of a pumpkin to take her to a ball, Cinderella does not exclaim. She gets in quietly and drives away to her high fortune.

Captain Ellis (a fierce sort of fairy) had produced a command out of a drawer almost as unexpectedly as in a fairy tale. But a command is an abstract idea, and it seemed a sort of "lesser marvel" till it flashed upon me that it involved the concrete existence of a ship.

A ship! My ship! She was mine, more absolutely mine for possession and care than anything in the world; an object of responsibility and devotion. She was there waiting for me, spellbound, unable to move, to live, to get out into the world (till I came), like an enchanted princess. Her call had come to me as if from the clouds. I had never suspected her existence. I didn't know how she looked, I had barely heard her name, and yet we were indissolubly united for a certain portion of our future, to sink or swim together!

A sudden passion of anxious impatience rushed through my veins and gave me such a sense of the intensity of existence as I have never felt before or since. I discovered how much of a seaman I was, in heart, in mind, and, as it were, physically—a man exclusively of sea and ships; the sea the only world that counted, and the ships the test of manliness, of temperament, of courage and fidelity—and of love.

I had an exquisite moment. It was unique also. Jumping up from my seat, I paced up and down my room for a long time. But when I came into the dining-room I behaved with sufficient composure. Only I couldn't eat anything at dinner.

"That's Your Ship, Captain"

Having declared my intention not to drive but to walk down to the quay, I must render the wretched Steward justice that he bestirred himself to find me some coolies for the luggage. They departed, carrying all my worldly possessions (except a little money I had in my pocket) slung from a long pole. Captain Giles volunteered to walk down with me.

We followed the somber, shaded alley across the Esplanade. It was moderately cool there under the trees.

. . . I prepared to take my leave of Captain Giles, who stood there with an air as though his mission were drawing to a close. It could not be denied that he had done it all. And while I hesitated about an appropriate sentence, he made himself heard:

"I expect you'll have your hands pretty full of tangled-up business."

I asked him what made him think so; and he answered that it was his general experience of the world. Ship a long time away from her port, owners inaccessible by cable, and the only man who could explain matters dead and buried.

"And you yourself new to the business in a way," he concluded in a sort of unanswerable tone.

"Don't insist," I said. "I know it only too well. I only wish you could impart to me some small portion of your experience before I go. As it can't be done in ten minutes I had better not begin to ask you. There's that harbor-launch waiting for me too. But I won't feel really at peace till I have that ship of mine out in the Indian Ocean."

He remarked casually that from Bangkok to the Indian Ocean was a pretty long step. And this murmur, like a dim flash from a dark lantern, showed me for a moment the broad belt of islands and reefs between that unknown ship, which was mine, and the freedom of the great waters of the globe.

But I felt no apprehension. I was familiar enough with the Archipelago by that time. Extreme patience and extreme care would see me through the region of broken land, of faint airs, and of dead water to where I would feel at last my command swing on the great swell and list over to the great breath of regular winds, that would give her the feeling of a

large, more intense life.   The road would be long.   All roads
are long that lead towards one's heart's desire.   But this road
my mind's eye could see on a chart, professionally, with all
its complications and difficulties, yet simple enough in a way.
One is a seaman or one is not.   And I had no doubt of being
one.

The only part I was a stranger to was the Gulf of Siam.
And I mentioned this to Captain Giles.   Not that I was
concerned very much.   It belonged to the same region the
nature of which I knew, into whose very soul I seemed to
have looked during the last months of that existence with
which I had broken now, suddenly, as one parts with some
enchanting company.

"The Gulf . . . Ay!   A funny piece of water—that,"
said Captain Giles.

Funny, in this connection, was a vague word.   The whole
thing sounded like an opinion uttered by a cautious person
mindful of actions for slander.

I didn't inquire as to the nature of that funniness.   There
was really no time.   But at the very last he volunteered a
warning.

"Whatever you do, keep to the east side of it.   The west
side is dangerous at this time of the year.   Don't let anything tempt you over.   You'll find nothing but trouble
there."

Though I could hardly imagine what could tempt me to
involve my ship amongst the currents and reefs of the Malay
shore, I thanked him for the advice.

He gripped my extended arm warmly, and the end of our
acquaintance came suddenly in the words: "Good-night."

That was all he said: "Good-night."   Nothing more.   I
don't know what I intended to say, but surprise made me
swallow it, whatever it was.   I choked slightly, and then
exclaimed with a sort of nervous haste: "Oh!   Good-night,
Captain Giles, good-night."

His movements were always deliberate, but his back had receded some distance along the deserted quay before I collected myself enough to follow his example and made a half turn in the direction of the jetty.

Only my movements were not deliberate. I hurried down to the steps and leaped into the launch. Before I had fairly landed in her stern sheets the slim little craft darted away from the jetty with a sudden swirl of her propeller and the hard, rapid puffing of the exhaust in her vaguely gleaming brass funnel amidships.

The misty churning at her stern was the only sound in the world. The shore lay plunged in the silence of the deepest slumber. I watched the town recede still and soundless in the hot night, till the abrupt hail "Steam-launch, ahoy!" made me spin round face forwards. We were close to a white, ghostly steamer. Lights shone on her decks, in her port holes. And the same voice shouted from her: "Is that our passenger?"

"It is," I yelled.

Her crew had been obviously on the jump. I could hear them running about. The modern spirit of haste was loudly vocal in the orders to "Heave away on the cable"—to "Lower the side-ladder," and in urgent requests to me to "Come along, sir! We have been delayed three hours for you. . . . Our time is seven o'clock, you know!"

I stepped on the deck. I said, "No! I don't know." The spirit of modern hurry was embodied in a thin, long-armed, long-legged man, with a closely clipped gray beard. His meager hand was hot and dry. He declared feverishly:

"I am hanged if I would have waited another five minutes —harbor-master or no harbor-master."

"That's your own business," I said. "I didn't ask you to wait for me."

"I hope you don't expect any supper," he burst out. "This isn't a boarding-house afloat. You are the first passenger I ever had in my life and I hope to goodness you will be the last."

I made no answer to this hospitable communication; and, indeed, he didn't wait for any, bolting away on to his bridge to get his ship under way.

For the four days he had me on board he did not depart from that half-hostile attitude. His ship having been delayed three hours on my account, he couldn't forgive me for not being a more distinguished person. He was not exactly outspoken about it, but that feeling of annoyed wonder was peeping out perpetually in his talk.

He was absurd.

He was also a man of much experience, which he liked to trot out; but no greater contrast with Captain Giles could have been imagined. He would have amused me if I had wanted to be amused. But I did not want to be amused. I was like a lover looking forward to a meeting. Human hostility was nothing to me. I thought of my unknown ship. It was amusement enough, torment enough, occupation enough.

He perceived my state, for his wits were sufficiently sharp for that, and he poked sly fun at my preoccupation in the manner some nasty, cynical old men assume towards the dreams and illusions of youth. I, on my side, refrained from questioning him as to the appearance of my ship, though I knew that being in Bangkok every month or so he must have known her by sight. I was not going to expose the ship, my ship! to some slighting reference.

He was the first really unsympathetic man I had ever come in contact with. My education was far from being finished, though I didn't know it. No! I didn't know it.

All I knew was that he disliked me and had some contempt for my person. Why? Apparently because his ship had been delayed three hours on my account. Who was I to have such a thing done for me? Such a thing had never been done for him. It was a sort of jealous indignation.

My expectation, mingled with fear, was wrought to its highest pitch. How slow had been the days of the passage, and how soon they were over! One morning, early, we crossed the bar, and while the sun was rising splendidly over the flat spaces of the land we steamed up the innumerable bends, passed under the shadow of the great gilt pagoda, and reached the outskirts of the town.

There it was, spread largely on both banks, the Oriental capital which had as yet suffered no white conqueror; an expanse of brown houses of bamboo, of mats, of leaves, of a vegetable-matter style of architecture, sprung out of the brown soil on the banks of the muddy river. It was amazing to think that in those miles of human habitation there was not, probably, half a dozen pounds of nails. Some of those houses of sticks and grass, like the nests of an aquatic race, clung to the low shores. Others seemed to grow out of the water; others again floated in long anchored rows in the very middle of the stream. Here and there in the distance, above the crowded mob of low, brown roof ridges, towered great piles of masonry, King's Palace, temples, gorgeous and dilapidated, crumbling under the vertical sunlight, tremendous, overpowering, almost palpable, which seemed to enter one's breast with the breath of one's nostrils and soak into one's limbs through every pore of one's skin.

The ridiculous victim of jealousy had, for some reason or other, to stop his engines just then. The steamer drifted slowly up with the tide. Oblivious of my new surroundings I walked the deck, in anxious, deadened abstraction, a commingling of romantic reverie with a very practical survey of my qualifications. For the time was approaching for me to behold my command and to prove my worth in the ultimate test of my profession.

Suddenly I heard myself called by that imbecile. He was beckoning me to come up on his bridge.

I didn't care very much for that, but as it seemed that he had something particular to say I went up the ladder.

He laid his hand on my shoulder and gave me a slight turn, pointing with his other arm at the same time.

"There! That's your ship, Captain," he said. I felt a thump in my breast—only one, as if my heart had then ceased to beat. There were ten or more ships moored along the bank, and the one he meant was partly hidden from my sight by her next astern. He said: "We'll drift abreast her in a moment."

What was his tone? Mocking? Threatening? Or only indifferent? I could not tell. I suspected some malice in this unexpected manifestation of interest.

He left me, and I leaned over the rail of the bridge looking over the side. I dared not raise my eyes. Yet it had to be done—and, indeed, I could not have helped myself. I believe I trembled.

But directly my eyes had rested on my ship all my fear vanished. It went off swiftly, like a bad dream. Only that a dream leaves no shame behind it, and that I felt a momentary shame at my unworthy suspicions.

Yes, there she was. Her hull, her rigging filled my eye with a great content. That feeling of life-emptiness which had made me so restless for the last few months lost its bitter plausibility, its evil influence, dissolved in a flow of joyous emotion.

At the first glance I saw that she was a high-class vessel, a harmonious creature in the lines of her fine body, in the proportioned tallness of her spars. Whatever her age and her history, she had preserved the stamp of her origin. She was one of those craft that in virtue of their design and complete finish will never look old. Amongst her companions moored to the bank, and all bigger than herself, she looked like a creature of high breed—an Arab steed in a string of cart-horses.

A voice behind me said in a nasty equivocal tone: "I hope you are satisfied with her, Captain." I did not even turn my head. It was the master of the steamer, and whatever he meant, whatever he thought of her, I knew that, like some rare women, she was one of those creatures whose mere existence is enough to awaken an unselfish delight. One feels that it is good to be in the world in which she has her being.

That illusion of life and character which charms one in men's finest handiwork radiated from her. An enormous baulk of teak-wood timber swung over her hatchway; lifeless matter, looking heavier and bigger than anything aboard of her. When they started lowering it, the surge of the tackle sent a quiver through her from water-line to the trucks up the fine nerves of her rigging, as though she had shuddered at the weight. It seemed cruel to load her so. . . .

Half an hour later, putting my foot on her deck for the first time, I received the feeling of deep physical satisfaction. Nothing could equal the fullness of that moment, the ideal completeness of that emotional experience which had come to me without the preliminary toil and disenchantment of an obscure career.

My rapid glance ran over her, enveloped, appropriated the form concreting the abstract sentiment of my command. A lot of details perceptible to a seaman struck my eye vividly in that instant. For the rest, I saw her disengaged from the material conditions of her being. The shore to which she was moored was as if it did not exist. What were to me all the countries of the globe? In all the parts of the world washed by navigable waters our relation to each other would be the same—and more intimate than there are words to express in the language. Apart from that, every scene and episode would be a mere passing show. The very gang of yellow coolies busy about the main hatch was less substantial than the stuff dreams are made of. For who on earth would dream of Chinamen? . . .

I went aft, ascended the poop, where, under the awning, gleamed the brasses of the yacht-like fittings, the polished surfaces of the rails, the glass of the skylights. Right aft two seamen, busy cleaning the steering gear, with the reflected ripples of light running playfully up their bent backs, went on with their work, unaware of me and of the almost affectionate glance I threw at them in passing towards the companion-way of the cabin.

The doors stood wide open, the slide was pushed right back. The half-turn of the staircase cut off the view of the lobby. A low humming ascended from below, but it stopped abruptly at the sound of my descending footsteps.

The Captains' Succession

The first thing I saw down there was the upper part of a man's body projecting backwards, as it were, from one of the doors at the foot of the stairs. His eyes looked at me very wide and still. In one hand he held a dinner plate, in the other a cloth.

"I am your new captain," I said quietly.

In a moment, in the twinkling of an eye, he had got rid of the plate and the cloth and jumped to open the cabin door. As soon as I passed into the saloon he vanished, but only to reappear instantly, buttoning up a jacket he had put on with the swiftness of a "quick-change" artist.

"Where's the chief mate?" I asked.

"In the hold, I think, sir. I saw him go down the after-hatch ten minutes ago."

"Tell him I am on board."

The mahogany table under the skylight shone in the twilight like a dark pool of water. The sideboard, surmounted by a wide looking-glass in an ormolu frame, had a marble top. It bore a pair of silver-plated lamps and some other pieces—obviously a harbor display. The saloon itself was paneled in two kinds of wood in the excellent, simple taste prevailing when the ship was built.

I sat down in the arm-chair at the head of the table—the captain's chair, with a small telltale compass swung above it—a mute reminder of unremitting vigilance.

A succession of men had sat in that chair. I became aware of that thought suddenly, vividly, as though each had left a little of himself between the four walls of these ornate bulkheads; as if a sort of composite soul, the soul of command, had whispered suddenly to mine of long days at sea and of anxious moments.

"You, too!" it seemed to say, "you, too, shall taste of that peace and that unrest in a searching intimacy with your own self—obscure as we were and as supreme in the face of all the winds and all the seas, in an immensity that receives no impress, preserves no memories, and keeps no reckoning of lives."

Deep within the tarnished ormolu frame, in the hot half-light sifted through the awning, I saw my own face propped between my hands. And I stared back at myself with the perfect detachment of distance, rather with curiosity than with any other feeling, except of some sympathy for this latest representative of what for all intents and purposes was a dynasty; continuous not in blood, indeed, but in its experience, in its training, in its conception of duty, and in the blessed simplicity of its traditional point of view on life.

It struck me that this quietly staring man whom I was watching, both as if he were myself and somebody else, was not exactly a lonely figure. He had his place in a line of men whom he did not know, of whom he had never heard; but who were fashioned by the same influences, whose souls in relation to their humble life's work had no secrets for him.

Suddenly I perceived that there was another man in the saloon, standing a little on one side and looking intently at me. The chief mate. His long, red mustache determined

the character of his physiognomy, which struck me as pug-
nacious in (strange to say) a ghastly sort of way.

How long had he been there looking at me, appraising me
in my unguarded day-dreaming state? I would have been
more disconcerted if, having the clock set in the top of the
mirror frame right in front of me, I had not noticed that its
long hand had hardly moved at all.

I could not have been in that cabin more than two minutes
altogether. Say three. . . . . So he could not have been
watching me more than a mere fraction of a minute, luckily.
Still, I regretted the occurrence.

But I showed nothing of it as I rose leisurely (it had to be
leisurely) and greeted him with perfect friendliness.

There was something reluctant and at the same time attentive in his bearing. His name was Burns. We left the cabin
and went round the ship together. His face in the full light
of day appeared very worn, meager, even haggard. Somehow I had a delicacy as to looking too often at him; his eyes,
on the contrary, remained fairly glued on my face. They
were greenish and had an expectant expression.

He answered all my questions readily enough, but my ear
seemed to catch a tone of unwillingness. The second officer,
with three or four hands, was busy forward. The mate mentioned his name, and I nodded to him in passing. He was
very young. He struck me as rather a cub.

When we returned below I sat down on one end of a deep,
semi-circular, or, rather, semi-oval settee, upholstered in red
plush. It extended right across the whole after-end of the
cabin. Mr. Burns, motioned to sit down, dropped into one
of the swivel chairs round the table, and kept his eyes on me
as persistently as ever, and with that strange air as if all this
were make-believe and he expected me to get up, burst into a
laugh, slap him on the back, and vanish from the cabin.

There was an odd stress in the situation which began to

make me uncomfortable. I tried to react against this vague feeling.

"It's only my inexperience," I thought.

In the face of that man, several years, I judged, older than myself, I became aware of what I had left already behind me —my youth. And that was indeed poor comfort. Youth is a fine thing, a mighty power—as long as one does not think of it. I felt I was becoming self-conscious. Almost against my will I assumed a moody gravity. I said: "I see you have kept her in very good order, Mr. Burns."

Directly I had uttered these words I asked myself angrily why the deuce did I want to say that? Mr. Burns in answer had only blinked at me. What on earth did he mean?

I fell back on a question which had been in my thoughts for a long time—the most natural question on the lips of any seaman whatever joining a ship. I voiced it (confound this self-consciousness) in a *dégagé* cheerful tone: "I suppose she can travel—what?"

Now a question like this might have been answered normally, either in accents of apologetic sorrow or with a visibly suppressed pride, in a "I don't want to boast, but you shall see" sort of tone. There are sailors, too, who would have been roughly outspoken: "Lazy brute," or openly delighted: "She's a flyer." Two ways, if four manners.

But Mr. Burns found another way, a way of his own, which had, at all events, the merit of saving his breath, if no other.

Again he did not say anything. He only frowned. And it was an angry frown. I waited. Nothing more came.

"What's the matter? . . . . Can't you tell after being nearly two years in the ship?" I addressed him sharply.

He looked as startled for a moment as though he had discovered my presence only that very moment. But this passed off almost at once. He put on an air of indifference. But I suppose he thought it better to say something. He said that a ship needed, just like a man, the chance to show the best she could do, and that this ship had never had a chance since he had been on board of her. Not that he could remember. The last captain . . . He paused.

"Has he been so very unlucky?" I asked with frank incredulity. Mr. Burns turned his eyes away from me. No, the late captain was not an unlucky man. One couldn't say that. But he had not seemed to want to make use of his luck.

Mr. Burns—man of enigmatic moods—made this statement with an inanimate face and staring wilfully at the rudder-casing. The statement itself was obscurely suggestive. I asked quietly:

"Where did he die?"

"In this saloon. Just where you are sitting now," answered Mr. Burns.

I repressed a silly impulse to jump up; but upon the whole I was relieved to hear that he had not died in the bed which was now to be mine. I pointed out to the chief mate that what I really wanted to know was where he had buried his late captain.

Mr. Burns said that it was at the entrance to the Gulf. A roomy grave; a sufficient answer. But the mate, overcoming visibly something within him—something like a curious reluctance to believe in my advent (as an irrevocable fact, at any rate), did not stop at that—though, indeed, he may have wished to do so.

As a compromise with his feelings, I believe, he addressed himself persistently to the rudder-casing, so that to me he had the appearance of a man talking in solitude, a little unconsciously, however.

His tale was that at seven bells in the forenoon watch he had all hands mustered on the quarter-deck and told them that they had better go down to say good-bye to the captain.

Those words, as if grudged to an intruding personage,

were enough for me to evoke vividly that strange ceremony:
The bare-footed, bare-headed seamen crowding shyly into that
cabin, a small mob pressed against that sideboard, uncomfortable rather than moved, shirts open on sunburnt chests,
weather-beaten faces, and all staring at the dying man with
the same grave and expectant expression.

"Was he conscious?" I asked.

"He didn't speak, but he moved his eyes to look at them,"
said the mate.

After waiting a moment, Mr. Burns motioned the crew to
leave the cabin, but he detained the two eldest men to stay
with the captain while he went on deck with his sextant to
"take the sun." It was getting towards noon and he was
anxious to obtain a good observation for latitude. When he
returned below to put his sextant away he found that the
two men had retreated out into the lobby. Through the
open door he had a view of the captain lying easy against the
pillows. He had "passed away" while Mr. Burns was taking
his observation. As near noon as possible. He had hardly
changed his position.

Mr. Burns sighed, glanced at me inquisitively, as much as
to say, "Aren't you going yet?" and then turned his thoughts
from his new captain back to the old, who, being dead, had
no authority, was not in anybody's way, and was much easier
to deal with.

I might have smiled if I had not been busy with my own
sensations, which were not those of Mr. Burns. I was already
the man in command. My sensations could not be like those
of any other man on board. In that community I stood, like
a king in his country, in a class all by myself. I mean an
hereditary king, not a mere elected head of a state. I was
brought there to rule by an agency as remote from the
people, and as inscrutable almost to them, as the Grace of
God.

Delay

. . . . The future brought in a lot of trouble. There
were days when I used to remember Captain Giles with nothing short of abhorrence. His confounded acuteness had let
me in for this job; while his prophecy that I "would have my
hands full" coming true, made it appear as if done on purpose to play an evil joke on my young innocence.

Yes. I had my hands full of complications which were
most valuable as "experience." People have a great opinion
of the advantages of experience. But in that connection
experience means always something disagreeable as opposed to
the charm and innocence of illusions.

I must say I was losing mine rapidly. But on these instructive complications I must not enlarge more than to say that
they could all be resumed in the one word: Delay.

A mankind which has invented the proverb, "Time is
money," will understand my vexation. The word "Delay"
entered the secret chamber of my brain, resounded there like
a tolling bell which maddens the ear, affected all my senses,
took on a black coloring, a bitter taste, a deadly meaning.

"I am really sorry to see you worried like this. Indeed, I
am . . ."

It was the only humane speech I used to hear at that time.
And it came from a doctor, appropriately enough.

A doctor is humane by definition. But that man was so
in reality. His speech was not professional. I was not ill.
But other people were, and that was the reason of his visiting
the ship.

He was the doctor of our Legation, and, of course, of the
Consulate too. He looked after the ship's health, which generally was poor, and trembling, as it were, on the verge of
a break-up. Yes. The men ailed. And thus time was not
only money, but life as well.

I had never seen such a steady ship's company. As the

doctor remarked to me: "You seem to have a most respectable lot of seamen." Not only were they consistently sober, but they did not even want to go ashore. Care was taken to expose them as little as possible to the sun. They were employed on light work under the awnings. And the humane doctor commended me.

"Your arrangements appear to me to be very judicious, my dear Captain."

It is difficult to express how much that pronouncement comforted me. The doctor's round full face framed in a light-colored whisker was the perfection of a dignified amenity. He was the only human being in the world who seemed to take the slightest interest in me. He would generally sit in the cabin for half an hour or so at every visit.

I said to him one day:

"I suppose the only thing now is to take care of them as you are doing, till I can get the ship to sea?"

He inclined his head, shutting his eyes under the large spectacles, and murmured:

"The sea . . . undoubtedly."

The first member of the crew fairly knocked over was the steward—the first man to whom I had spoken on board. He was taken ashore (with choleraic symptoms) and died there at the end of a week. Then, while I was still under the startling impression of this first home-thrust of the climate, Mr. Burns gave up and went to bed in a raging fever without saying a word to anybody.

I believe he had partly fretted himself into that illness; the climate did the rest with the swiftness of an invisible monster ambushed in the air, in the water, in the mud of the river bank. Mr. Burns was a predestined victim.

I discovered him lying on his back, glaring sullenly and radiating heat on one like a small furnace. He would hardly answer my questions, and only grumbled: Couldn't a man take an afternoon off duty with a bad headache—for once?

That evening, as I sat in the saloon after dinner, I could hear him muttering continuously in his room. Ransome, who was clearing the table, said to me:

"I am afraid, sir, I won't be able to give the mate all the attention he's likely to need. I will have to be forward in the galley a great part of my time."

Ransome was the cook. The mate had pointed him out to me the first day, standing on the deck, his arms crossed on his broad chest, gazing on the river.

Even at a distance his well-proportioned figure, something thoroughly sailor-like in his poise, made him noticeable. On nearer view the intelligent, quiet eyes, a well-bred face, the disciplined independence of his manner made up an attractive personality. When, in addition, Mr. Burns told me he was the best seaman in the ship, I expressed my surprise that in his earliest prime and of such appearance he should sign on as cook on board a ship.

"It's his heart," Mr. Burns had said. "There's something wrong with it. He mustn't exert himself too much or he may drop dead suddenly."

And he was the only one the climate had not touched— perhaps because, carrying a deadly enemy in his breast, he had schooled himself into a systematic control of feelings and movements. When one was in the secret this was apparent in his manner. After the poor steward died, and as he could not be replaced by a white man in this Oriental port, Ransome had volunteered to do the double work.

"I can do it all right, sir, as long as I go about it quietly," he had assured me.

But obviously he couldn't be expected to take up sick-nursing in addition. Moreover, the doctor peremptorily ordered Mr. Burns ashore.

With a seaman on each side holding him up under the arms, the mate went over the gangway more sullen than ever. We built him up with pillows in the gharry, and he made an effort to say brokenly:

"Now—you've got—what you wanted—got me out of—the ship."

"You were never more mistaken in your life, Mr. Burns," I said quietly, duly smiling at him; and the trap drove off to a sort of sanatorium, a pavilion of bricks which the doctor had in the grounds of his residence.

Then, one day, suddenly, a burst of downright panic burst through all this craziness.

If I left him [Burns] behind in this deadly place, he would die. He felt it, he was certain of it. But I wouldn't have the heart to leave him ashore. He had a wife and child in Sydney.

He produced his wasted fore-arms from under the sheet which covered him and clasped his fleshless claws. He would die! He would die here. . . .

He absolutely managed to sit up, but only for a moment, and when he fell back I really thought that he would die there and then. I called to the Bengali dispenser, and hastened away from the room.

Next day he upset me thoroughly by renewing his entreaties. I returned an evasive answer, and left him the picture of ghastly despair. The day after I went in with reluctance, and he attacked me at once in a much stronger voice and with an abundance of argument which was quite startling. He presented his case with a sort of crazy vigor, and asked me finally how would I like to have a man's death on my conscience? He wanted me to promise that I would not sail without him.

I said that I really must consult the doctor first. He cried out at that. The doctor! Never! That would be a death sentence.

The effort had exhausted him. He closed his eyes, but

went on rambling in a low voice.   I had hated him from the
start.   The late captain had hated him, too.   Had wished
him dead.   Had wished all hands dead. . . .

"What do you want to stand in with that wicked corpse
for, sir?   He'll have you too," he ended, blinking his glazed
eyes vacantly.

"Mr. Burns," I cried, very much discomposed, "what on
earth are you talking about?"

He seemed to come to himself, though he was too weak
to start.

"I don't know," he said languidly.   "But don't ask that
doctor, sir.   You and I are sailors.   Don't ask him, sir.
Some day perhaps you will have a wife and child yourself."

And again he pleaded for the promise that I would not
leave him behind.   I had the firmness of mind not to give it
to him.   Afterwards this sternness seemed criminal; for my
mind was made up.   That prostrated man, with hardly
strength enough to breathe and ravaged by a passion of fear,
was irresistible.   And, besides, he had happened to hit on
the right words.   He and I were sailors.   That was a claim,
for I had no other family.   As to the wife-and-child (some
day) argument, it had no force.   It sounded merely bizarre.

I could imagine no claim that would be stronger and more
absorbing than the claim of that ship, of these men snared
in the river by silly commercial complications, as if in some
poisonous trap.

However, I had nearly fought my way out.   Out to sea.
The sea—which was pure, safe, and friendly.   Three days
more.

Under Way

When Mr. Burns appeared at the gangway carried on a
stretcher, the doctor himself walked by its side.   The program had been altered in so far that this transportation had

been left to the last moment, on the very morning of our departure.

It was barely an hour after sunrise. The doctor waved his big arm to me from the shore and walked back at once to his trap, which had followed him empty to the riverside. Mr. Burns, carried across the quarter-deck, had the appearance of being absolutely lifeless. Ransome went down to settle him in his cabin. I had to remain on deck to look after the ship, for the tug had got hold of our towrope already.

The splash of our shore-fasts falling in the water produced a complete change of feeling in me. It was like the imperfect relief of awakening from a nightmare. But when the ship's head swung down the river away from that town, Oriental and squalid, I missed the expected elation of that striven-for moment. What there was, undoubtedly, was a relaxation of tension which translated itself into a sense of weariness after an inglorious fight.

About midday we anchored a mile outside the bar. The afternoon was busy for all hands. Watching the work from the poop, where I remained all the time, I detected in it some of the languor of the six weeks spent in the steaming heat of the river. The first breeze would blow that away. Now the calm was complete. I judged that the second officer—a callow youth with an unpromising face—was not, to put it mildly, of that invaluable stuff from which a commander's right hand is made. But I was glad to catch along the main deck a few smiles on those seamen's faces at which I had hardly had time to have a good look as yet. Having thrown off the mortal coil of shore affairs, I felt myself familiar with them and yet a little strange, like a long-lost wanderer among his kin.

Ransome flitted continually to and fro between the galley and the cabin. It was a pleasure to look at him. The man

positively had grace.   He alone of all the crew had not had
a day's illness in port.   But with the knowledge of that
uneasy heart within his breast I could detect the restraint he
put on the natural sailor-like agility of his movements.   It
was as though he had something very fragile or very explosive
to carry about his person and was all the time aware of it.

I had occasion to address him once or twice.   He answered
me in his pleasant quiet voice and with a faint, slightly wistful smile.   Mr. Burns appeared to be resting.   He seemed
fairly comfortable.

After sunset I came out on deck again to meet only a still
void.   The thin, featureless crust of the coast could not be
distinguished.   The darkness had risen around the ship like a
mysterious emanation from the dumb and lonely waters.   I
leaned on the rail and turned my ear to the shadows of the
night.   Not a sound.   My command might have been a
planet flying vertiginously on its appointed path in a space
of infinite silence.   I clung to the rail as if my sense of balance were leaving me for good.   How absurd!   I hailed
nervously.

"On deck there!"

The immediate answer, "Yes, sir," broke the spell.   The
anchor-watch man ran up the poop ladder smartly.   I told
him to report at once the slightest sign of a breeze coming.

Going below I looked in on Mr. Burns.   In fact, I could
not avoid seeing him, for his door stood open.   The man
was so wasted that, in that white cabin, under a white sheet,
and with his diminished head sunk in the white pillow, his
red mustaches captured one's eyes exclusively, like something
artificial—a pair of mustaches from a shop exhibited there in
the harsh light of the bulkhead-lamp without a shade.

While I stared with a sort of wonder he asserted himself
by opening his eyes and even moving them in my direction.
A minute stir.

"Dead calm, Mr. Burns," I said resignedly.

In an unexpectedly distinct voice Mr. Burns began a rambling speech. Its tone was very strange, not as if affected by his illness, but as if of a different nature. It sounded unearthly. As to the matter, I seemed to make out that it was the fault of the "old man"—the late captain—ambushed down there under the sea with some evil intention. It was a weird story.

I listened to the end; then stepping into the cabin I laid my hand on the mate's forehead. It was cool. He was lightheaded only from extreme weakness. Suddenly he seemed to become aware of me, and in his own voice—of course, very feeble—he asked regretfully:

"Is there no chance at all to get under way, sir?"

"What's the good of letting go our hold of the ground only to drift, Mr. Burns?" I answered.

He sighed, and I left him to his immobility. His hold on life was as slender as his hold on sanity. I was oppressed by my lonely responsibilities. I went into my cabin to seek relief in a few hours' sleep, but almost before I closed my eyes the man on deck came down reporting a light breeze. Enough to get under way with, he said.

And it was no more than just enough. I ordered the windlass manned, the sails loosed, and the topsails set. But by the time I had cast the ship I could hardly feel any breath of wind. Nevertheless, I trimmed the yards and put everything on her. I was not going to give up the attempt.

A Double Fight

Slight puffs came and went, and whenever they were strong enough to wake up the black water the murmur alongside ran through my very heart in a delicate crescendo of delight and died away swiftly. I was bitterly tired. The very stars seemed weary of waiting for daybreak. It came at last with a mother-of-pearl sheen at the zenith, such as I had never seen before in the tropics, unglowing, almost grey, with a strange reminder of high latitudes.

The voice of the lookout man hailed from forward:

"Land on the port bow, sir."

"All right."

Leaning on the rail I never raised my eyes. The motion of the ship was imperceptible. Presently Ransome brought me the cup of morning coffee. After I had drunk it I looked ahead, and in the still streak of very bright pale orange light I saw the land profiled flatly as if cut out of black paper and seeming to float on the water as light as cork. But the rising sun turned it into mere dark vapor, a doubtful, massive shadow trembling in the hot glare.

The watch finished washing decks. I went below and stopped at Mr. Burns' door (he could not bear to have it shut), but hesitated to speak to him till he moved his eyes. I gave him the news.

"Sighted Cape Liant at daylight. About fifteen miles."

He moved his lips then, but I heard no sound till I put my ear down, and caught the peevish comment:

"This is crawling. . . . No luck."

"Better luck than standing still, anyhow," I pointed out resignedly, and left him to whatever thoughts or fancies haunted his hopeless prostration.

Later that morning, when relieved by my second officer, I threw myself on my couch, and for some three hours or so I really found oblivion. It was so perfect that on waking up I wondered where I was. Then came the immense relief of the thought: on board my ship! At sea! At sea!

Through the port-holes I beheld an unruffled, sun-smitten horizon. The horizon of a windless day. But its spaciousness alone was enough to give me a sense of a fortunate escape, a momentary exultation of freedom.

I stepped out into the saloon with my heart lighter than

it had been for days.   Ransome was at the sideboard preparing to lay the table for the first sea dinner of the passage.   He
turned his head, and something in his eyes checked my modest
elation.

Instinctively I asked: "What is it now?" not expecting in
the least the answer I got.   It was given with that sort of
contained serenity which was characteristic of the man.

"I am afraid we haven't left all sickness behind us, sir."

"We haven't!   What's the matter?"

He told me then that two of our men had been taken bad
with fever in the night.   One of them was burning and the
other was shivering, but he thought that it was pretty much
the same thing.   I thought so too.   I felt shocked by the
news.   "One burning, the other shivering, you say?   No.
We haven't left the sickness behind.   Do they look very ill?"

"Middling bad, sir."   Ransome's eyes gazed steadily into
mine.   We exchanged smiles.   Ransome's a little wistful, as
usual, mine no doubt grim enough, to correspond with my
secret exasperation.

I asked:

"Was there any wind at all this morning?"

"Can hardly say that, sir.   We've moved all the time
though.   The land ahead seems a little nearer."

That was it.   A little nearer.   Whereas if we had only
had a little more wind, only a very little more, we might, we
should, have been abreast of Liant by this time and increasing our distance from that contaminated shore.   And it was
not only the distance.   It seemed to me that a stronger breeze
would have blown away the infection which clung to the
ship.   It obviously did cling to the ship.   Two men.   One
burning, one shivering.   I felt a distinct reluctance to go
and look at them.   What was the good?   Poison is poison.
Tropical fever is tropical fever.   But that it should have
stretched its claw after us over the sea seemed to me an
extraordinary and unfair license.   I could hardly believe that

it could be anything worse than the last desperate pluck of the evil from which we were escaping into the clean breath of the sea. If only that breath had been a little stronger! However, there was the quinine against the fever. I went into the spare cabin where the medicine chest was kept to prepare two doses. I opened it full of faith as a man opens a miraculous shrine. The upper part was inhabited by a collection of bottles, all square-shouldered and as like each other as peas. Under that orderly array there were two drawers, stuffed as full of things as one could imagine—paper packages, bandages, cardboard boxes officially labeled. The lower of the two, in one of its compartments, contained our provision of quinine.

There were five bottles, all round and all of a size. One was about a third full. The other four remained still wrapped up in paper and sealed. But I did not expect to see an envelope lying on top of them. A square envelope, belonging, in fact, to the ship's stationery.

It lay so that I could see it was not closed down, and on picking it up and turning it over I perceived that it was addressed to myself. It contained a half-sheet of notepaper, which I unfolded with a queer sense of dealing with the uncanny, but without any excitement, as people meet and do extraordinary things in a dream.

"My dear Captain," it began, but I ran to the signature. The writer was the doctor. The date was that of the day on which, returning from my visit to Mr. Burns in the hospital, I had found the excellent doctor waiting for me in the cabin; and when he told me that he had been putting in time inspecting the medicine chest for me. How bizarre! While expecting me to come in at any moment he had been amusing himself by writing me a letter, and then as I came in had hastened to stuff it into the medicine chest drawer. A rather incredible proceeding. I turned to the text in wonder.

In a large, hurried, but legible hand the good, sympathetic man, for some reason, either of kindness or more likely impelled by the irresistible desire to express his opinion, with which he didn't want to damp my hopes before, was warning me not to put my trust in the beneficial effects of a change from land to sea. "I didn't want to add to your worries by discouraging your hopes," he wrote. "I am afraid that, medically speaking, the end of your troubles is not yet." In short, he expected me to have to fight a probable return of tropical illness. Fortunately I had a good provision of quinine. I should put my trust in that, and administer it steadily, when the ship's health would certainly improve.

I crumpled up the letter and rammed it into my pocket. Ransome carried off two big doses to the men forward. As to myself, I did not go on deck as yet. I went instead to the door of Mr. Burns' room, and gave him that news too.

It is impossible to say the effect it had on him. At first I thought that he was speechless. His head lay sunk in the pillow. He moved his lips enough, however, to assure me that he was getting much stronger; a statement shockingly untrue on the face of it.

That afternoon I took my watch as a matter of course. A great over-heated stillness enveloped the ship and seemed to hold her motionless in a flaming ambience composed in two shades of blue. Faint, hot puffs eddied nervelessly from her sails. And yet she moved. She must have. For, as the sun was setting, we had drawn abreast of Cape Liant and dropped it behind us; an ominous retreating shadow in the last gleams of twilight.

In the evening, under the crude glare of his lamp, Mr. Burns seemed to have come more to the surface of his bedding. It was as if a depressing hand had been lifted off him. He answered my few words by a comparatively long, connected speech. He asserted himself strongly. If he escaped being smothered by this stagnant heat, he said, he was confident that in a very few days he would be able to come up on deck and help me.

While he was speaking I trembled lest this effort of energy should leave him lifeless before my eyes. But I cannot deny that there was something comforting in his willingness. I made a suitable reply, but pointed out to him that the only thing that could really help us was wind—a fair wind.

He rolled his head impatiently on the pillow. And it was not comforting in the least to hear him begin to mutter crazily about the late captain, that old man buried in latitude 8° 20′, right in our way—ambushed at the entrance of the Gulf.

"Are you still thinking of your late captain, Mr. Burns?" I said. "I imagine the dead feel no animosity against the living. They care nothing for them."

"You don't know that one," he breathed out feebly.

"No. I didn't know him, and he didn't know me. And so he can't have any grievance against me, anyway."

"Yes. But there's all the rest of us on board," he insisted.

I felt the inexpugnable strength of common sense being insidiously menaced by this gruesome, by this insane delusion. And I said:

"You mustn't talk so much. You will tire yourself."

"And there is the ship herself," he persisted in a whisper.

"Now, not a word more," I said, stepping in and laying my hand on his cool forehead. It proved to me that this atrocious absurdity was rooted in the man himself and not in the disease, which, apparently, had emptied him of every power, mental and physical, except that one fixed idea.

I avoided giving Mr. Burns any opening for conversation for the next few days. I merely used to throw him a hasty, cheery word when passing his door. I believe that if he had had the strength he would have called out after me more than once. But he hadn't the strength. Ransome, however, observed to me one afternoon that the mate "seemed to be picking up wonderfully."

"Did he talk any nonsense to you of late?" I asked casually.

"No, sir." Ransome was startled by the direct question: but after a pause, he added equably: "He told me this morning, sir, that he was sorry he had to bury our late captain right in the ship's way, as one may say, out of the Gulf."

"Isn't this nonsense enough for you?" I asked, looking confidently at the intelligent, quiet face on which the secret uneasiness in the man's breast had thrown a transparent veil of care.

Ransome didn't know. He had not given a thought to the matter. And with a faint smile he flitted away from me on his never-ending duties, with his usual guarded activity.

Two more days passed. We had advanced a little way— a very little way—into the larger space of the Gulf of Siam. Seizing eagerly upon the elation of the first command thrown into my lap, by the agency of Captain Giles, I had yet an uneasy feeling that such luck as this has got perhaps to be paid for in some way. I had held, professionally, a review of my chances. I was competent enough for that. At least, I thought so. I had a general sense of my preparedness which only a man pursuing a calling he loves can know. That feeling seemed to me the most natural thing in the world. As natural as breathing. I imagined I could not have lived without it.

I don't know what I expected. Perhaps nothing else than that special intensity of existence which is the quintessence of youthful aspirations. Whatever I expected, I did not expect to be beset by hurricanes. I knew better than that. In the Gulf of Siam there are no hurricanes. But neither did I expect to find myself bound hand and foot to the hopeless extent which was revealed to me as the days went on.

Not that the evil spell held us always motionless. Mysterious currents drifted us here and there, with a stealthy power made manifest by the changing vistas of the islands fringing the east shore of the Gulf. And there were winds too, fitful and deceitful. They raised hopes only to dash them into the bitterest disappointment, promises of advance ending in lost ground, expiring in sighs, dying into dumb stillness in which the currents had it all their own way—their own inimical way.

The Island of Koh-ring, a great, black, upheaved ridge amongst a lot of tiny islets, lying upon the glassy water like a triton amongst minnows, seemed to be the center of the fatal circle. It seemed impossible to get away from it. Day after day it remained in sight. More than once, in a favorable breeze, I would take its bearing in the fast ebbing twilight, thinking that it was for the last time. Vain hope. A night of fitful airs would undo the gains of temporary favor, and the rising sun would throw out the black relief of Koh-ring, looking more barren, inhospitable, and grim than ever.

"It's like being bewitched, upon my word," I said once to Mr. Burns, from my usual position in the doorway.

He was sitting up in his bed-place. He was progressing towards the world of living men, if he could hardly have been said to have rejoined it yet. He nodded to me his frail and bony head in a wisely mysterious assent.

"Oh, yes, I know what you mean," I said, "but you cannot expect me to believe that a dead man has the power to put out of joint the meteorology of this part of the world. Though indeed it seems to have gone utterly wrong. The land and sea breezes have got broken up into small pieces. We cannot depend upon them for five minutes together."

"It won't be very long now before I can come up on deck," muttered Mr. Burns, "and then we shall see."

Whether he meant this for a promise to grapple with super-

natural evil I couldn't tell.   At any rate, it wasn't the kind
of assistance I needed.   On the other hand, I had been living
on deck practically night and day so as to take advantage
of every chance to get my ship a little more to the southward.
The mate, I could see, was extremely weak yet, and not quite
rid of his delusion, which to me appeared but a symptom of
his disease.   At all events, the hopefulness of an invalid was
not to be discouraged.   I said:

"You will be most welcome there, I am sure, Mr. Burns.
If you go on improving at this rate you'll be presently one of
the healthiest men in the ship."

This pleased him, but his extreme emaciation converted his
self-satisfied smile into a ghastly exhibition of long teeth
under the red mustache.

"Aren't the fellows improving, sir?" he asked soberly,
with an extremely sensible expression of anxiety on his face.

I answered him only with a vague gesture and went away
from the door.   The fact was that disease played with us
capriciously very much as the winds did.   It would go from
one man to another with a lighter or heavier touch, which
always left its mark behind, staggering some, knocking others
over for a time, leaving this one, returning to another, so
that all of them had now an invalidish aspect and a hunted,
apprehensive look in their eyes; while Ransome and I, the
only two completely untouched, went amongst them assidu-
ously distributing quinine.   It was a double fight.   The
adverse weather held us in front and the disease pressed on
our rear. . . .

A Dirty Trick

Down below, in his cabin, Mr. Burns had advanced so
far as not only to be able to sit up, but even to draw up his
legs.   Clasping them with bony arms, like an animated skeleton, he emitted deep, impatient sighs.

"The great thing to do, sir," he would tell me on every

occasion, when I gave him the chance, "the great thing is to get the ship past 8° 20′ of latitude. Once she's past that we're all right."

At first I used only to smile at him, though, God knows, I had not much heart left for smiles. But at last I lost my patience.

"Oh, yes. The latitude 8° 20′. That's where you buried your late captain, isn't it?" Then with severity: "Don't you think, Mr. Burns, it's about time you dropped all that nonsense?"

He rolled at me his deep-sunken eyes in a glance of invincible obstinacy. But for the rest, he only muttered, just loud enough for me to hear, something about "Not surprised . . . find . . . play us some beastly trick yet . . ."

Such passages as this were not exactly wholesome for my resolution. The stress of adversity was beginning to tell on me. At the same time I felt a contempt for that obscure weakness of my soul. I said to myself disdainfully that it should take much more than that to affect in the smallest degree my fortitude.

I didn't know then how soon and from what unexpected direction it would be attacked.

It was the very next day. The sun had risen clear of the southern shoulder of Koh-ring, which still hung, like an evil attendant, on our port quarter. It was intensely hateful to my sight. During the night we had been heading all round the compass, trimming the yards again and again, to what I fear must have been for the most part imaginary puffs of air. Then just about sunrise we got for an hour an inexplicable, steady breeze, right in our teeth. There was no sense in it. It fitted neither with the season of the year, nor with the secular experience of seamen as recorded in books, nor with the aspect of the sky. Only purposeful malevolence could account for it. It sent us traveling at a great pace away from our proper course; and if we had been out on pleasure sailing bent it would have been a delightful breeze, with the awakened sparkle of the sea, with the sense of motion and a feeling of unwonted freshness.   Then all at once, as if disdaining to carry farther the sorry jest, it dropped and died out completely in less than five minutes. The ship's head swung where it listed; the stilled sea took on the polish of a steel plate in the calm.

I went below, not because I meant to take some rest, but simply because I couldn't bear to look at it just then.   The indefatigable Ransome was busy in the saloon.   It had become a regular practice with him to give me an informal health report in the morning.   He turned away from the sideboard with his usual pleasant, quiet gaze.   No shadow rested on his intelligent forehead.

"There are a good many of them middling bad this morning, sir," he said in a calm tone.

"What?   All knocked out?"

"Only two actually in their bunks, sir, but . . ."

"It's the last night that has done for them.   We have had to pull and haul all the blessed time."

"I heard, sir.   I had a mind to come out and help, only, you know . . ."

"Certainly not.   You mustn't. . . .   The fellows lie at night about the decks, too.   It isn't good for them."

Ransome assented.   But men couldn't be looked after like children.   Moreover, one could hardly blame them for trying for such coolness and such air as there were to be found on deck.   He himself, of course, knew better.

He was, indeed, a reasonable man.   Yet it would have been hard to say that the others were not.   The last few days had been for us like the ordeal of the fiery furnace.   One really couldn't quarrel with their common, imprudent humanity making the best of the moments of relief, when the night brought in the illusion of coolness and the starlight twinkled through the heavy, dew-laden air.   Moreover, most of them were so weakened that hardly anything could be done without everybody that could totter mustering on the braces. No, it was no use remonstrating with them. But I fully believed that quinine was of very great use indeed.

I believed in it. I pinned my faith to it. It would save the men, the ship, break the spell by its medicinal virtue, make time of no account, the weather but a passing worry, and, like a magic powder working against mysterious malefices, secure the first passage of my first command against the evil powers of calms and pestilence. I looked upon it as more precious than gold, and unlike gold, of which there ever hardly seems to be enough anywhere, the ship had a sufficient store of it. I went in to get it with the purpose of weighing out doses. I stretched my hand with the feeling of a man reaching for an unfailing panacea, took up a fresh bottle and unrolled the wrapper, noticing as I did so that the ends, both top and bottom, had come unsealed. . . .

But why record all the swift steps of the appalling discovery? You have guessed the truth already. There was the wrapper, the bottle, and the white powder inside, some sort of powder! But it wasn't quinine. One look at it was quite enough. I remember that at the very moment of picking up the bottle, before I even dealt with the wrapper, the weight of the object I had in my hand gave me an instant of premonition. Quinine is as light as feathers; and my nerves must have been exasperated into an extraordinary sensibility. I let the bottle smash itself on the floor. The stuff, whatever it was, felt gritty under the sole of my shoe. I snatched up the next bottle and then the next. The weight alone told the tale. One after another they fell, breaking at my feet, not because I threw them down in my dismay, but slipping through my fingers as if this disclosure were too much for my strength.

It is a fact that the very greatness of a mental shock helps one to bear up against it, by producing a sort of temporary insensibility. I came out of the stateroom stunned, as if something heavy had dropped on my head. From the other side of the saloon, across the table, Ransome, with a duster in his hand, stared open-mouthed. I don't think that I looked wild. It is quite possible that I appeared to be in a hurry because I was instinctively hastening up on deck. An example of this training become instinct. The difficulties, the dangers, the problems of a ship at sea must be met on deck.

To this fact, as it were of nature, I responded instinctively; which may be taken as a proof that for a moment I must have been robbed of my reason.

I was certainly off my balance, a prey to impulse, for at the bottom of the stairs I turned and flung myself at the doorway of Mr. Burns' cabin. The wildness of his aspect checked my mental disorder. He was sitting up in his bunk, his body looking immensely long, his head drooping a little sideways, with affected complacency. He flourished, in his trembling hand, on the end of a forearm no thicker than a stout walking-stick, a shining pair of scissors which he tried before my very eyes to jab at his throat.

I was to a certain extent horrified; but it was rather a secondary sort of effect, not really strong enough to make me yell at him in some such manner as: "Stop!" . . . "Heavens!" . . . "What are you doing?"

In reality he was simply overtaxing his returning strength in a shaky attempt to clip off the thick growth of his red beard. A large towel was spread over his lap, and a shower of stiff hairs, like bits of copper wire, was descending on it at every snip of the scissors.

He turned to me his face grotesque beyond the fantasies of mad dreams, one cheek all bushy as if with a swollen flame, the other denuded and sunken, with the untouched long mustache on that side asserting itself, lonely and fierce. And while he stared thunderstruck, with the gaping scissors on his fingers, I shouted my discovery at him fiendishly, in six

words, without comment.   Mr. Burns glared spectrally, but
otherwise wonderfully composed.

"I always thought he would play us some deadly trick,"
he said, with a peculiar emphasis on the *he*.

It gave me a mental shock, but I had neither the mind
nor the heart nor the spirit to argue with him.   My form of
sickness was indifference.   The creeping paralysis of a hopeless outlook.   So I only gazed at him.   Mr. Burns broke
into further speech.

"Eh?   What?   No!   You won't believe it?   Well, how
do you account for this?   How do you think it could have
happened?"

"Happened?"   I repeated dully.   "Why, yes, how in the
name of the infernal powers did this thing happen?"

Indeed, on thinking it out, it seemed incomprehensible that
it should just be like this: the bottles emptied, refilled, re-
wrapped, and replaced.   A sort of plot, a sinister attempt to
deceive, a thing resembling sly vengeance—but for what?—
or else a fiendish joke.   But Mr. Burns was in possession of
a theory.   It was simple, and he uttered it solemnly in a
hollow voice.

"I suppose they have given him about fifteen pounds in
Haiphong for that little lot."

"Mr. Burns!"   I cried.

He nodded grotesquely over his raised legs, like two broom-
sticks in the pyjamas, with enormous bare feet at the end.

"Why not?   The stuff is pretty expensive in this part of
the world, and they were very short of it in Tonkin.   And
what did he care?   You have not known him.   I have, and I
have defied him.   He feared neither God, nor devil, nor
man, nor wind, nor sea, nor his own conscience.   And I
believe he hated everybody and everything.   But I think he
was afraid to die.   I believe I am the only man who ever
stood up to him.   I faced him in that cabin where you live
now, when he was sick, and I cowed him then.   He thought

I was going to twist his neck for him. If he had had his way we would have been beating up against the northeast monsoon, as long as he lived and afterwards too, for ages and ages. Acting the Flying Dutchman in the China Sea! Ha! Ha!"

"But why should he replace the bottles like this?" I began.

"Why shouldn't he? Why should he want to throw the bottles away? They fit the drawer. They belong to the medicine chest."

"And they were wrapped up," I cried.

"Well, the wrappers were there. Did it from habit, I suppose, and as to refilling, there is always a lot of stuff they send in paper parcels that burst after a time. And then, who can tell? I suppose you didn't taste it, sir? But, of course, you are sure . . ."

"No," I said. "I didn't taste it. It is all overboard now."

Behind me, a soft cultivated voice said: "I have tasted it. It seemed a mixture of all sorts, sweetish, saltish, very horrible."

Ransome, stepping out of the pantry, had been listening for some time, as it was very excusable in him to do.

"A dirty trick," said Mr. Burns. "I always said he would."

The magnitude of my indignation was unbounded. And the kind, sympathetic doctor too. The only sympathetic man I ever knew . . . instead of writing that warning letter, the very refinement of sympathy, why didn't the man make a proper inspection? But, as a matter of fact, it was hardly fair to blame the doctor. The fittings were in order and the medicine chest is an officially arranged affair. There was nothing really to arouse the slightest suspicion. The person I could never forgive was myself. Nothing should ever be taken for granted. The seed of everlasting remorse was sown in my breast.

"I feel it's all my fault," I exclaimed, "mine, and nobody else's. That's how I feel. I shall never forgive myself."

"That's very foolish, sir," said Mr. Burns fiercely.

And after this effort he fell back exhausted on his bed. He closed his eyes, he panted; this affair, this abominable surprise had shaken him up, too. As I turned away I perceived Ransome looking at me blankly. He appreciated what it meant, but he managed to produce his pleasant, wistful smile. Then he stepped back into his pantry, and I rushed up on deck again to see whether there was any wind, any breath under the sky, any stir of the air, any sign of hope. The deadly stillness met me again.

Worthy of My Undying Regard

The only spot of light in the ship at night was that of the compass-lamps, lighting up the faces of the succeeding helmsmen; for the rest we were lost in the darkness, I walking the poop and the men lying about the decks. They were all so reduced by sickness that no watches could be kept. Those who were able to walk remained all the time on duty, lying about in the shadows of the main deck, till my voice raised for an order would bring them to their enfeebled feet, a tottering little group, moving patiently about the ship, with hardly a murmur, a whisper amongst them all. And every time I had to raise my voice it was with a pang of remorse and pity.

Then about four o'clock in the morning a light would gleam forward in the galley. The unfailing Ransome with the uneasy heart, immune, serene, and active, was getting ready the early coffee for the men. Presently he would bring me a cup up on the poop, and it was then that I allowed myself to drop into my deck chair for a couple of hours of real sleep. No doubt I must have been snatching short dozes when leaning against the rail for a moment in sheer exhaustion; but, honestly, I was not aware of them, except in the painful form of convulsive starts that seemed to come on me even while I walked. From about five, however, until after seven I would sleep openly under the fading stars.

I would say to the helmsman: "Call me at need," and drop into that chair and close my eyes, feeling that there was no more sleep for me on earth. And then I would know nothing till, some time between seven and eight, I would feel a touch on my shoulder and look up at Ransome's face, with its faint, wistful smile and friendly, gray eyes, as though he were tenderly amused at my slumbers. Occasionally the second mate would come up and relieve me at early coffee time. But it didn't really matter. Generally it was a dead calm, or else faint airs so changing and fugitive that it really wasn't worth while to touch a brace for them. If the air steadied at all the seaman at the helm could be trusted for a warning shout: "Ship's all aback, sir!" which like a trumpet-call would make me spring a foot above the deck. Those were the words which, it seemed to me, would have made me spring up from eternal sleep. But this was not often. I have never met since such breathless sunrises. And if the second mate happened to be there (he had generally one day in three free of fever) I would find him sitting on the sky-light half-senseless, as it were, and with an idiotic gaze fastened on some object near by—a rope, a cleat, a belaying pin, a ringbolt.

That young man was rather troublesome. He remained cubbish in his sufferings. He seemed to have become completely imbecile; and when the return of fever drove him to his cabin below, the next thing would be that we would miss him from there. The first time it happened Ransome and I were very much alarmed. We started a quiet search, and ultimately Ransome discovered him curled up in the sail-locker, which opened into the lobby by a sliding door. When remonstrated with, he muttered sulkily, "It's cool in there." That wasn't true. It was only dark there.

The fundamental defects of his face were not improved

by its uniform livid hue. It was not so with many of the men. The wastage of ill-health seemed to idealize the general character of the features, bringing out the unsuspected nobility of some, the strength of others, and in one case revealing an essentially comic aspect. He was a short, gingery, active man with a nose and chin of the Punch type, whom his shipmates called "Frenchy." I don't know why. He may have been a Frenchman, but I have never heard him utter a single word in French.

To see him coming aft to the wheel comforted one. The blue dungaree trousers turned up the calf, one leg a little higher than the other, the clean check shirt, the white canvas cap, evidently made by himself, made up a whole of peculiar smartness, and the persistent jauntiness of his gait, even, poor fellow, when he couldn't help tottering, told of his invincible spirit. There was also a man called Gambril. He was the only grizzled person in the ship. His face was of an austere type. But if I remember all their faces, wasting tragically before my eyes, most of their names have vanished from my memory.

The words that passed between us were few and puerile in regard of the situation. I had to force myself to look them in the face. I expected to meet reproachful glances. There were none. The expression of suffering in their eyes was indeed hard enough to bear. But that they couldn't help. For the rest, I ask myself whether it was the temper of their souls or the sympathy of their imagination that made them so wonderful, so worthy of my undying regard.

For myself, neither my soul was highly tempered, nor my imagination properly under control. There were moments when I felt, not only that I would go mad, but that I had gone mad already; so that I dared not open my lips for fear of betraying myself by some insane shriek. Luckily I had only orders to give, and an order has a steadying influence upon him who has to give it. Moreover, the seaman, the officer of the watch, in me was sufficiently sane. I was like a mad carpenter making a box. Were he ever so convinced that he was King of Jerusalem, the box he would make would be a sane box. What I feared was a shrill note escaping me involuntarily and upsetting my balance. Luckily, again, there was no necessity to raise one's voice. The brooding stillness of the world seemed sensitive to the slightest sound like a whispering gallery. The conversational tone would almost carry a word from one end of the ship to the other. The terrible thing was that the only voice that I ever heard was my own. At night especially it reverberated very lonely amongst the planes of the unstirring sails.

"You'll Do"

The barrier of awful stillness which had encompassed us for so many days as though we had been accursed was broken. I felt that. I let myself fall on to the skylight seat. A faint white ridge of foam, thin, very thin, broke alongside. The first for ages—for ages. I could have cheered, if it hadn't been for the sense of guilt which clung to all my thoughts secretly. Ransome stood before me.

And I steered, too tired for anxiety, too tired for connected thought. I had moments of grim exultation and then my heart would sink awfully at the thought of that forecastle at the other end of the dark deck, full of fever-stricken men—some of them dying. By my fault. But never mind. Remorse must wait. I had to steer.

In the small hours the breeze weakened, then failed altogether. About five it returned, gentle enough, enabling us to head for the roadstead.

As we had a signal for medical assistance flying on the mizzen it is a fact that before the ship was fairly at rest three steam-launches from various men-of-war arrived alongside; and at least five naval surgeons clambered on board. They stood in a knot gazing up and down the empty main deck, then looked aloft—where not a man could be seen either.

I went towards them—a solitary figure in a blue and gray striped sleeping suit and a pipe-clayed cork helmet on its head. Their disgust was extreme. They had expected surgical cases. Each one had brought his carving tools with him. But they soon got over their little disappointment. In less than five minutes one of the steam-launches was rushing shorewards to order a big boat and some hospital people for the removal of the crew. The big steam-pinnace went off to her ship to bring over a few bluejackets to furl my sails for me.

One of the surgeons had remained on board. He came out of the forecastle looking impenetrable, and noticed my inquiring gaze.

"There's nobody dead in there, if that's what you want to know," he said deliberately. Then added in a tone of wonder: "The whole crew!"

"And very bad?"

"And very bad," he repeated.

When I returned on deck everything was ready for the removal of the men. It was the last ordeal of that episode which had been maturing and tempering my character—though I did not know it.

It was awful. They passed under my eyes one after another—each of them an embodied reproach of the bitterest kind, till I felt a sort of revolt wake up in me. . . . .

It is strange how on coming ashore I was struck by the springy step, the lively eyes, the strong vitality of everyone I met. It impressed me enormously. And amongst those I met there was Captain Giles, of course. It would have been very extraordinary if I had not met him. A prolonged stroll in the business part of the town was the regular employment of all his mornings when he was ashore.

I caught the glitter of the gold watch-chain across his chest ever so far away. He radiated benevolence.

"What is it I hear?" he queried with a "kind uncle" smile, after shaking hands. "Twenty-one days from Bangkok?"

"Is this all you've heard?" I asked. "You must come to tiffin with me. I want you to know exactly what you have let me in for."

He hesitated for almost a minute.

"Well—I will," he decided condescendingly at last.

We turned into the hotel. I found to my surprise that I could eat quite a lot. Then over the cleared table-cloth I unfolded to Captain Giles all the story since I took command in all its professional and emotional aspects, while he smoked patiently the big cigar I had given him.

Then he observed sagely:

"You must feel jolly well tired by this time."

"No," I said. "Not tired. But I'll tell you, Captain Giles, how I feel. I feel old. And I must be. All of you on shore look to me just a lot of skittish youngsters that have never known a care in the world."

He didn't smile. He looked insufferably exemplary. He declared:

"That will pass. But you do look older—it's a fact."

"Aha!" I said.

"No! No! The truth is that one must not make too much of anything in life, good or bad."

"Live at half-speed," I murmured perversely. "Not everybody can do that."

"You'll be glad enough presently if you can keep going even at that rate," he retorted with his air of conscious virtue. "And there's another thing: a man should stand up to his bad luck, to his mistakes, to his conscience, and all

that sort of thing. Why—what else would you have to
fight against?"

I kept silent. I don't know what he saw in my face,
but he asked abruptly:

"Why—you aren't faint-hearted?"

"God only knows, Captain Giles," was my sincere answer.

"That's all right," he said calmly. "You will learn soon
how not to be faint-hearted. A man has got to learn everything—and that's what so many of those youngsters don't
understand."

"Well, I am no longer a youngster."

"No," he conceded. "Are you leaving soon?"

"I am going on board directly," I said. "I shall pick up
one of my anchors and heave it to half-cable on the other
as soon as my new crew comes on board, and I shall be off
at daylight tomorrow."

"You will?" grunted Captain Giles approvingly. "That's
the way. You'll do."

TORRES STRAIT

[After the many disappointments on the *Otago,* related in the
preceding section, Conrad finally began to realize the satisfactions
of command. His most exciting experience on the Bangkok-
Sydney-Mauritius route he relates in the following passage. The
owners of the ship, apparently sharing Captain Giles's verdict,
"You'll do," allowed Conrad, on something like a whim, to sail for
Mauritius by way of the dangerous Torres Strait.]

It was in 1888, when in command of a ship loading in
Sydney a mixed cargo for Mauritius, that, one day, all of a
sudden, all the deep-lying historic sense of the exploring adventures in the Pacific surged up to the surface of my being.
Almost without reflection I sat down and wrote a letter to
my owners suggesting that, instead of the usual southern

route, I should take the ship to Mauritius by way of Torres
Strait.   I ought to have received a severe rap on the knuckles,
if only for wasting their time in submitting an unheard-of
proposition.

I must say I awaited the reply with some trepidation.   It
came in due course, but instead of beginning with the
chiding words, "We fail to understand," etc., etc., it simply
called my attention in the first paragraph to the fact that
"there would be an additional insurance premium to pay
for that route," and so on, and so on.   And it ended like
this: "Upon the whole, however, we have no objection to
your taking the ship through Torres Strait if you are certain
that the season is not too far advanced to endanger the
success of your passage by the calms which, as you know,
prevail at times in the Arafura Sea."

I read, and in my heart I felt compunctions.   The season
was somewhat advanced.   I had not been scrupulously
honest in my argumentation.   Perhaps it was because I never
expected it to be effective.   And here it was all left to my
responsibility.   My letter must have struck a lucky day in
Messrs. H. Simpson & Sons' offices—a romantic day.   I
won't pretend that I regret my lapse from strict honesty,
for what would the memory of my sea life have been for me
if it had not included a passage through Torres Strait, in its
fullest extent, from the mouth of the great Fly River right
on along the track of the early navigators?

The season being advanced, I insisted on leaving Sydney
during a heavy southeast gale.   Both the pilot and the tug-
master were scandalized by my obstinacy, and they hastened
to leave me to my own devices while still inside Sydney
Heads.   The fierce southeaster caught me up on its wings,
and no later than the ninth day I was outside the entrance of
Torres Strait, named after the undaunted and reticent
Spaniard who, in the seventeenth century, first sailed that
way without knowing where he was, without suspecting he

had New Guinea on one side of him and the whole solid Australian continent on the other—he thought he was passing through an archipelago—the strait whose existence for a century and a half had been doubted, argued about, squabbled over by geographers, and even denied by the disreputable but skilful navigator, Abel Tasman, who thought it was a large bay, and whose true contours were first laid down on the map by James Cook, the navigator without fear and without reproach, the greatest in achievement and character of the later seamen fathers of militant geography. If the dead haunt the scenes of their earthly exploits, then I must have been attended benevolently by those three shades —the inflexible Spaniard of such lofty spirit that in his report he disdains to say a single word about the appalling hardships and dangers of his passage; the pig-headed Hollander who, having made up his mind that there was no passage there, missed the truth by only fifty miles or so; and the great Englishman, a son of the soil, a great commander and a great professional seaman, who solved that question among many others and left no unsolved problems of the Pacific behind him. Great shades! All friends of my youth!

It was not without a certain emotion that, commanding very likely the first, and certainly the last, merchant ship that carried a cargo that way—from Sydney to Mauritius— I put her head at daybreak for Bligh's Entrance, and packed on her every bit of canvas she could carry. Windswept, sunlit empty waters were all around me, half-veiled by a brilliant haze. The first thing that caught my eye upon the play of green white-capped waves was a black speck marking conveniently the end of a low sandbank. It looked like the wreck of some small vessel.

I altered the course slightly in order to pass close, with the hope of being able to read the letters on her stern. They were already faded. Her name was *Honolulu*. The name of the port I could not make out. The story of her life is known by now to God alone, and the winds must have drifted long ago around her remains a quiet grave of the very sand on which she had died. Thirty-six hours afterwards, of which about nine were spent at anchor, approaching the other end of the Strait, I sighted a gaunt, gray wreck of a big American ship lying high and dry on the southernmost of the Warrior Reefs. She had been there for years. I had heard of her. She was legendary. She loomed up, a sinister and enormous *memento mori* raised by the refraction of this serene afternoon above the far-away line of the horizon drawn under the sinking sun.

And thus I passed out of Torres Strait before the dusk settled on its waters. Just as a clear sun sank ahead of my ship I took a bearing of a little island for a fresh departure, an insignificant crumb of dark earth, lonely, like an advanced sentinel of that mass of broken land and water, to watch the approaches from the side of the Arafura Sea. But to me it was a hallowed spot, for I knew that the *Endeavour* had been hove to off it in the year 1762 for her captain, whose name was James Cook, to go ashore for half an hour. What he could possibly want to do I cannot imagine. Perhaps only to be alone with his thoughts for a moment. The dangers and the triumphs of exploration and discovery were over for that voyage. All that remained to do was to go home, and perhaps his great and equable soul, tempered in the incessant perils of a long exploration, wanted to commune with itself at the end of its task. It may be that on this dry crumb of the earth's crust which I was setting by compass he had tasted for a moment of perfect peace. I could depict to myself the famous seaman navigator, a lonely figure in a three-cornered hat and square-skirted laced coat, pacing to and fro slowly on the rocky shore, while in the ship's boat, lying off on her oars, the coxswain kept his eyes open for the slightest sign of the captain's hand.

Thus the sea has been for me a hallowed ground, thanks to those books of travel and discovery which have peopled it with unforgettable shades of the masters in the calling which, in a humble way, was to be mine, too; men great in their endeavor and in hard-won successes of militant geography; men who went forth each according to his lights and with varied motives, laudable or sinful, but each bearing in his breast a spark of the sacred fire.

THE CONGO
(From *Heart of Darkness*)

[Uneasiness about his uncle's health caused Conrad to resign from the *Otago* and return to Europe. A long period of enforced leisure followed. He was well fitted to take a command, but no command was to be found. Although still only thirty-three, he began to dream dreams of his past. Evoking from his memory the people and scenes of Borneo, and following again what he was accustomed to call an "inexplicable impulse," he wrote the opening chapters of his first novel, *Almayer's Folly*. Yet he meant to live rather than dream his life. Suddenly given an opportunity, which allowed him to fulfill a boyhood boast, he accepted the command of a river boat on the Congo. The experience in the African jungle proved epochal, for the lingering Congo fever, which he brought back to Europe, forced him finally to give up the active life of the sea and to follow completely that "inexplicable impulse" that had led him to begin *Almayer's Folly*.

The following selections from *Heart of Darkness* show not only his experiences in the Congo but his growing interest in the nature of man and in the response that man makes to his environment.

For the sake of clearness it should be said that "the pilgrims" mentioned in the following narrative were the various traders who accompanied Conrad from Kinchassa to Stanley Falls. The term Conrad uses, of course, ironically, for all of them were a part of this "vilest scramble for loot."]

GOING up that river was like traveling back to the earliest beginnings of the world, when vegetation rioted on the earth and the big trees were kings. An empty stream, a great silence, an impenetrable forest. The air was warm, thick, heavy, sluggish. There was no joy in the brilliance of sunshine. The long stretches of the waterway ran on, deserted, into the gloom of overshadowed distances. On silvery sandbanks hippos and alligators sunned themselves side by side. The broadening waters flowed through a mob of wooded islands; you lost your way on that river as you would in a desert, and butted all day long against shoals, trying to find the channel, till you thought yourself bewitched and cut off forever from everything you had known once— somewhere—far away—in another existence, perhaps. There were moments when one's past came back to one, as it will sometimes when you have not a moment to spare to yourself; but it came in the shape of an unrestful and noisy dream, remembered with wonder amongst the overwhelming realities of this strange world of plants, and water, and silence. And this stillness of life did not in the least resemble a peace. It was the stillness of an implacable force brooding over an inscrutable intention. It looked at you with a vengeful aspect. I got used to it afterwards; I did not see it any more; I had no time. I had to keep guessing at the channel; I had to discern, mostly by inspiration, the signs of hidden banks; I watched for sunken stones; I was learning to clap my teeth smartly before my heart flew out, when I shaved by a fluke some infernal sly old snag that would have ripped the life out of the tin-pot steamboat and drowned all the pilgrims; I had to keep a lookout for the signs of dead wood we could cut up in the night for next day's steaming. When you have to attend to things of that sort, to the mere incidents of the surface, the reality—the reality, I tell you—fades. The inner truth is hidden— luckily, luckily But I felt it all the same; I felt often its mysterious stillness watching me at my monkey tricks, just as it watches you fellows performing on your respective tight-ropes for—what is it? Half-a-crown a tumble——

We penetrated deeper and deeper into the heart of darkness. It was very quiet there. At night sometimes the roll of drums behind the curtain of trees would run up the river and remain sustained faintly, as if hovering in the air high over our heads, till the first break of day. Whether it meant war, peace, or prayer we could not tell. The dawns were heralded by the descent of a chill stillness; the wood-cutters slept, their fires burned low; the snapping of a twig would make you start. We were wanderers on a prehistoric earth, on an earth that wore the aspect of an unknown planet. We could have fancied ourselves the first of men taking possession of an accursed inheritance, to be subdued at the cost of profound anguish and of excessive toil. But suddenly, as we struggled round a bend, there would be a glimpse of rush walls, of peaked grass-roofs, a burst of yells, a whirl of black limbs, a mass of hands clapping, of feet stamping, of bodies swaying, of eyes rolling, under the droop of heavy and motionless foliage. The steamer toiled along slowly on the edge of a black and incomprehensible frenzy. The pre-historic man was cursing us, praying to us, welcoming us—who could tell? We were cut off from the comprehension of our surroundings; we glided past like phantoms, wonder-ing and secretly appalled, as sane men would be before an enthusiastic outbreak in a madhouse. We could not under-stand because we were too far and could not remember, because we were traveling in the night of first ages, of those ages that are gone, leaving hardly a sign—and no memories.

The earth seemed unearthly. We are accustomed to look upon the shackled form of a conquered monster, but there—there you could look at a thing monstrous and free. It was unearthly, and the men were—— No, they were not in-human. Well, you know, that was the worst of it—this suspicion of their not being inhuman. It would come slowly

to one.   They howled and leaped, and spun and made horrid
faces; but what thrilled you was just the thought of their
humanity—like yours—the thought of your remote kinship
with this wild and passionate uproar.   Ugly.   Yes, it was
ugly enough; but if you were man enough you would admit
to yourself that there was in you just the faintest trace of a
response to the terrible frankness of that noise, a dim suspicion
of there being a meaning in it which you—you so remote
from the night of first ages—could comprehend.   And why
not?   The mind of man is capable of anything—because
everything is in it, all the past as well as all the future.   What
was there, after all?   Joy, fear, sorrow, devotion, valor,
rage—who can tell?—but truth—truth stripped of its cloak
of time.   Let the fool gape and shudder—the man knows,
and can look on without a wink.   But he must at least be as
much of a man as these on the shore.   He must meet that
truth with his own true stuff—with his own inborn strength.
Principles won't do.   Acquisitions, clothes, pretty rags—
rags that would fly off at the first good shake.   No; you
want a deliberate belief.   An appeal to me in this fiendish
row—is there?   Very well; I hear; I admit, but I have a
voice, too, and for good or evil mine is the speech that cannot
be silenced.   Of course, a fool, what with sheer fright and
fine sentiments, is always safe.   Who's that grunting?   You
wonder I didn't go ashore for a howl and a dance?   Well,
no—I didn't.   Fine sentiments, you say?   Fine sentiments,
be hanged!   I had no time.   I had to mess about with white-
lead and strips of woolen blanket helping to put bandages
on those leaky steampipes—I tell you.   I had to watch the
steering, and circumvent those snags, and get the tin-pot
along by hook or by crook.   There was surface-truth enough
in these things to save a wiser man.   And between whiles I
had to look after the savage who was fireman.   He was an
improved specimen; he could fire up a vertical boiler.   He
was there below me, and, upon my word, to look at him was

as edifying as seeing a dog in a parody of breeches and a feather hat, walking on his hind legs. A few months of training had done for that really fine chap. He squinted at the steam-gauge and at the water-gauge with an evident effort of intrepidity—and he had filed teeth, too, the poor devil, and the wool of his pate shaved into queer patterns, and three ornamental scars on each of his cheeks. He ought to have been clapping his hands and stamping his feet on the bank, instead of which he was hard at work, a thrall to strange witchcraft, full of improving knowledge. He was useful because he had been instructed; and what he knew was this—that should the water in that transparent thing disappear, the evil spirit inside the boiler would get angry through the greatness of his thirst, and take a terrible vengeance. So he sweated and fired up and watched the glass fearfully (with an impromptu charm, made of rags, tied to his arm, and a piece of polished bone, as big as a watch, stuck flatways through his lower lip), while the wooded banks slipped past us slowly, the short noise was left behind, the interminable miles of silence. . . . .

When the sun rose there was a white fog, very warm and clammy, and more blinding than the night. It did not shift or drive; it was just there, standing all round you like something solid. At eight or nine, perhaps, it lifted as a shutter lifts. We had a glimpse of the towering multitude of trees, of the immense matted jungle, with the blazing little ball of the sun hanging over it—all perfectly still— and then the white shutter came down again, smoothly, as if sliding in greased grooves. I ordered the chain, which we had begun to heave in, to be paid out again. Before it stopped running with a muffled rattle, a cry, a very loud cry, as of infinite desolation, soared slowly in the opaque air. It ceased. A complaining clamor, modulated in savage dis- cords, filled our ears. The sheer unexpectedness of it made my hair stir under my cap. I don't know how it struck the others; to me it seemed as though the mist itself had screamed, so suddenly, and apparently from all sides at once, did this tumultuous and mournful uproar arise. It culminated in a hurried outbreak of almost intolerably excessive shrieking, which stopped short, leaving us stiffened in a variety of silly attitudes, and obstinately listening to the nearly as appalling and excessive silence. "Good God! What is the mean-ing——" stammered at my elbow one of the pilgrims—a little fat man, with sandy hair and red whiskers, who wore side-spring boots, and pink pyjamas tucked into his socks. Two others remained open-mouthed a whole minute, then dashed into the little cabin, to rush out incontinently and stand darting scared glances, with Winchesters at "Ready!" in their hands. What we could see was just the steamer we were on, her outlines blurred as though she had been on the point of dissolving, and a misty strip of water, perhaps two feet broad, around her—and that was all. The rest of the world was nowhere, as far as our eyes and ears were con-cerned. Just nowhere. Gone, disappeared; swept off with-out leaving a whisper or a shadow behind.

I went forward, and ordered the chain to be hauled in short, so as to be ready to trip the anchor and move the steamboat at once if necessary. "Will they attack?" whis-pered an awed voice. "We will be all butchered in this fog," murmured another. The faces twitched with the strain, the hands trembled slightly, the eyes forgot to wink. It was very curious to see the contrast of expressions of the white men and of the black fellows of our crew, who were as much strangers to that part of the river as we, though their homes were only eight hundred miles away. The whites, of course greatly discomposed, had besides a curious look of being painfully shocked by such an out-rageous row. The others had an alert, naturally interested expression; but their faces were essentially quiet, even those of the one or two who grinned as they hauled at the chain.

Several exchanged short, grunting phrases, which seemed to settle the matter to their satisfaction. Their headman, a young, broad-chested black, severely draped in dark-blue fringed cloths, with fierce nostrils and his hair all done up artfully in oily ringlets, stood near me. "Aha!" I said, just for good fellowship's sake. "Catch 'im," he snapped, with a bloodshot widening of his eyes and a flash of sharp teeth— "catch 'im. Give 'im to us." "To you, eh?" I asked; "what would you do with them?" "Eat 'im!" he said, curtly, and, leaning his elbow on the rail, looked out into the fog in a dignified and profoundly pensive attitude. I would no doubt have been properly horrified, had it not occurred to me that he and his chaps must be very hungry; that they must have been growing increasingly hungry for at least this month past. They had been engaged for six months (I don't think a single one of them had any clear idea of time, as we at the end of countless ages have. They still belonged to the beginnings of time—had no inherited experience to teach them, as it were), and of course, as long as there was a piece of paper written over in accordance with some farcical law or other made down the river, it didn't enter anybody's head to trouble how they would live. Certainly they had brought with them some rotten hippo-meat, which couldn't have lasted very long, anyway, even if the pilgrims hadn't, in the midst of a shocking hullabaloo, thrown a considerable quantity of it overboard. It looked like a high-handed proceeding; but it was really a case of legitimate self-defense. You can't breathe dead hippo waking, sleeping, and eating, and at the same time keep your precarious grip on existence. Besides that, they had given them every week three pieces of brass wire, each about nine inches long; and the theory was they were to buy their provisions with that currency in riverside villages. You can see how *that* worked. There were either no villages, or the people were hostile, or the director—who, like the rest of us, fed out of tins, with an occasional old he-goat thrown in—didn't want to stop the steamer for some more or less recondite reason. So, unless they swallowed the wire itself, or made loops of it to snare the fishes with, I don't see what good their extravagant salary could be to them. I must say it was paid with a regularity worthy of a large and honorable trading company. For the rest, the only thing to eat—though it didn't look eatable in the least—I saw in their possession was a few lumps of some stuff like half-cooked dough, of a dirty lavender color, they kept wrapped in leaves, and now and then swallowed a piece of, but so small that it seemed done more for the looks of the thing than for any serious purpose of sustenance. Why in the name of all the gnawing devils of hunger they didn't go for us—they were thirty to five— and have a good tuck-in for once, amazes me now when I think of it. They were big powerful men, with not much capacity to weigh the consequences, with courage, with strength, even yet, though their skins were no longer glossy and their muscles no longer hard. And I saw that some-thing restraining, one of those human secrets that baffle probability, had come into play there. I looked at them with a swift quickening of interest—not because it occurred to me I might be eaten by them before very long, though I own to you that just then I perceived—in a new light, as it were —how unwholesome the pilgrims looked, and I hoped, yes, I positively hoped, that my aspect was not so—what shall I say?—so—unappetizing: a touch of fantastic vanity which fitted well with the dream-sensation that pervaded all my days at that time. Perhaps I had a little fever, too. One can't live with one's finger everlastingly on one's pulse. I had often "a little fever," or a little touch of other things— the playful paw-strokes of the wilderness, the preliminary trifling before the more serious onslaught which came in due course. Yes; I looked on them as you would on any human being, with a curiosity of their impulses, motives, capacities, weaknesses, when brought to the test of an inexorable physical necessity. Restraint! What possible restraint? Was it superstition, disgust, patience, fear—or some kind of primitive humor? No fear can stand up to hunger, no patience can wear it out, disgust simply does not exist where hunger is; and as to superstition, beliefs, and what you may call principles, they are less than chaff in the breeze. Don't you know the devilry of lingering starvation, its exasperating torment, its black thoughts, its somber and brooding ferocity? Well, I do. It takes a man all his inborn strength to fight hunger properly. It's really easier to face bereavement, dishonor, and the perdition of one's soul—than this kind of prolonged hunger. Sad, but true. And these chaps, too, had no earthly reason for any kind of scruple. Restraint! I would just as soon have expected restraint from a hyena prowling amongst the corpses of a battlefield. But there was the fact facing me—the fact dazzling, to be seen, like the foam on the depths of the sea, like a ripple on an unfathomable enigma, a mystery greater—when I thought of it—than the curious, inexplicable note of desperate grief in this savage clamor that had swept by us on the river bank, behind the blind whiteness of the fog.

Well, you may guess I watched the fog for the signs of lifting as a cat watches a mouse; but for anything else our eyes were of no more use to us than if we had been buried miles deep in a heap of cotton-wool. It felt like it, too—choking, warm, stifling. Besides, all I said, though it sounded extravagant, was absolutely true to fact. What we afterwards alluded to as an attack was really an attempt at repulse. The action was very far from being aggressive—it was not even defensive, in the usual sense: it was undertaken under the stress of desperation, and in its essence was purely protective.

It developed itself, I should say, two hours after the fog lifted. . . .

One of my hungry and forbearing friends was sounding in the bows just below me. This steamboat was exactly like a decked scow. On the deck, there were two little teak-wood houses, with doors and windows. The boiler was in the fore-end, and the machinery right astern. Over the whole there was a light roof, supported on stanchions. The funnel projected through that roof, and in front of the funnel a small cabin built of light planks served for a pilot-house. It contained a couch, two camp-stools, a loaded Martini-Henry leaning in one corner, a tiny table, and the steering wheel. It had a wide door in front and a broad shutter at each side. All these were always thrown open, of course. . . .

An athletic black belonging to some coast tribe, and educated by my poor predecessor, was the helmsman. He sported a pair of brass earrings, wore a blue cloth wrapper from the waist to the ankles, and thought all the world of himself. He was the most unstable kind of fool I had ever seen. He steered with no end of a swagger while you were by; but if he lost sight of you, he became instantly the prey of an abject funk, and would let that cripple of a steamboat get the upper hand of him in a minute.

I was looking down at the sounding-pole, and feeling much annoyed to see at each try a little more of it stick out of that river, when I saw my poleman give up the business suddenly, and stretch himself flat on the deck, without even taking the trouble to haul his pole in. He kept hold on it though, and it trailed in the water. At the same time the fireman, whom I could also see below me, sat down abruptly before his furnace and ducked his head. I was amazed. Then I had to look at the river mighty quick, because there was a snag in the fairway. Sticks, little sticks, were flying about—thick: they were whizzing before my nose, dropping below me, striking behind me against my pilot-house. All this time the river, the shore, the woods, were very quiet—perfectly quiet. I could only hear the heavy splashing thump of the stern-wheel and the patter of these things. We cleared the snag clumsily. Arrows, by Jove! We were being shot at! I stepped in quickly to close the shutter on the land-side. That fool-helmsman, his hands on the spokes, was lifting his knees high, stamping his feet, champing his mouth, like a reined-in horse. Confound him! And we were staggering within ten feet of the bank. I had to lean right out to swing the heavy shutter, and I saw a face amongst the leaves on the level with my own, looking at me very fierce and steady; and then suddenly, as though a veil had been removed from my eyes, I made out, deep in the tangled gloom, naked breasts, arms, legs, glaring eyes,—the bush was swarming with human limbs in movement, glistening, of bronze color. The twigs shook, swayed, and rustled, the arrows flew out of them, and then the shutter came to. "Steer her straight," I said to the helmsman. He held his head rigid, face forward; but his eyes rolled, he kept on lifting and setting down his feet gently, his mouth foamed a little. "Keep quiet!" I said in a fury. I might just as well have ordered a tree not to sway in the wind. I darted out. Below me there was a great scuffle of feet on the iron deck; confused exclamations; a voice screamed, "Can you turn back?" I caught sight of a V-shaped ripple on the water ahead. What? Another snag! A fusillade burst out under my feet. The pilgrims had opened with their Winchesters, and were simply squirting lead into that bush. A deuce of a lot of smoke came up and drove slowly forward. I swore at it. Now I couldn't see the ripple, or the snag either. I stood in the doorway, peering, and the arrows came in swarms. They might have been poisoned, but they looked as though they wouldn't kill a cat. The bush began to howl. Our wood-cutters raised a warlike whoop; the report of a rifle just at my back deafened me. I glanced over my shoulder, and the pilot-house was yet full of noise and smoke when I made a

dash at the wheel.   The fool nigger had dropped everything,
to throw the shutter open and let off that Martini-Henry.
He stood before the wide opening, glaring, and I yelled at him
to come back, while I straightened the sudden twist out of
that steamboat.   There was no room to turn even if I had
wanted to, the snag was somewhere very near ahead in that
confounded smoke, there was no time to lose, so I just
crowded her into the bank—right into the bank, where I
knew the water was deep.

We tore slowly along the overhanging bushes in a whirl
of broken twigs and flying leaves.   The fusillade below
stopped short, as I had foreseen it would when the squirts got
empty.   I threw my head back to a glinting whizz that
traversed the pilot-house, in at one shutter-hole and out at
the other.   Looking past that mad helmsman, who was shaking the empty rifle and yelling at the shore, I saw vague
forms of men running bent double, leaping, gliding, distinct,
incomplete, evanescent.   Something big appeared in the air
before the shutter, the rifle went overboard, and the man
stepped back swiftly, looked at me over his shoulder in an
extraordinary, profound, familiar manner, and fell upon my
feet.   The side of his head hit the wheel twice, and the
end of what appeared a long cane clattered round and
knocked over a little camp-stool.   It looked as though after
wrenching that thing from somebody ashore he had lost his
balance in the effort.   The thin smoke had blown away, we
were clear of the snag, and looking ahead I could see that in
another hundred yards or so I would be free to sheer off,
away from the bank; but my feet felt so very warm and wet
that I had to look down.   The man had rolled on his back
and stared straight up at me; both his hands clutched that
cane.   It was the shaft of a spear that, either thrown or
lunged through the opening, had caught him in the side just
below the ribs; the blade had gone in out of sight, after mak-

ing a frightful gash; my shoes were full; a pool of blood lay very still, gleaming dark-red under the wheel; his eyes shone with an amazing luster. The fusillade burst out again. He looked at me anxiously, gripping the spear like something precious, with an air of being afraid I would try to take it away from him. I had to make an effort to free my eyes from his gaze and attend to the steering. With one hand I felt above my head for the line of the steam whistle, and jerked out screech after screech hurriedly. The tumult of angry and warlike yells was checked instantly, and then from the depths of the woods went out such a tremulous and prolonged wail of mournful fear and utter despair as may be imagined to follow the flight of the last hope from the earth. There was a great commotion in the bush; the shower of arrows stopped, a few dropping shots rang out sharply—then silence, in which the languid beat of the stern-wheel came plainly to my ears. I put the helm hard a-starboard at the moment when the pilgrim in pink pyjamas, very hot and agitated, appeared in the doorway. "The manager sends me——," he began in an official tone, and stopped short. "Good God!" he said, glaring at the wounded man.

We two whites stood over him, and his lustrous and inquiring glance enveloped us both. I declare it looked as though he would presently put to us some question in an understandable language; but he died without uttering a sound, without moving a limb, without twitching a muscle. Only in the very last moment, as though in response to some sign we could not see, to some whisper we could not hear, he frowned heavily, and that frown gave to his black death-mask an inconceivably somber, brooding, and menacing expression.

I missed my late helmsman awfully,—I missed him even while his body was still lying in the pilot-house. Perhaps

you will think it passing strange, this regret for a savage who
was no more account than a grain of sand in a black Sahara.
Well, don't you see, he had done something, he had steered;
for months I had him at my back—a help—an instrument.
It was a kind of partnership.   He steered for me—I had to
look after him, I worried about his deficiencies, and thus a
subtle bond had been created, of which I only became aware
when it was suddenly broken.   And the intimate profundity
of that look he gave me when he received his hurt remains
to this day in my memory—like a claim of distant kinship
affirmed in a supreme moment.

Poor fool!   If he had only left the shutter alone.   He had
no restraint, no restraint . . . . a tree swayed by the wind.
As soon as I had put on a dry pair of slippers, I dragged him
out, after first jerking the spear out of his side, which operation I confess I performed with my eyes shut tight.   His
heels leaped together over the little door-step; his shoulders
were pressed to my breast; I hugged him from behind desperately.   Oh! he was heavy, heavy; heavier than any man
on earth, I should imagine.   Then without more ado I tipped
him overboard.   The current snatched him as though he had
been a wisp of grass, and I saw the body roll over twice before
I lost sight of it forever.   All the pilgrims and the manager
were then congregated on the awning-deck about the pilot-
house, chattering at each other like a flock of excited mag-
pies, and there was a scandalized murmur at my heartless
promptitude.   What they wanted to keep that body hanging about for I can't guess.   Embalm it, maybe.   But I had
also heard another, and a very ominous, murmur on the deck
below.   My friends the wood-cutters were likewise scandalized, and with a better show of reason—though I admit
that the reason itself was quite inadmissible.   Oh, quite!   I
had made up my mind that if my late helmsman was to be
eaten, the fishes alone should have him.   He had been a very
second-rate helmsman while alive, but now he was dead

he might have become a first-class temptation, and possibly cause some startling trouble. . . . .

When next day we left at noon, the crowd, of whose presence behind the curtain of trees I had been acutely conscious all the time, flowed out of the woods again, filled the clearing, covered the slope with a mass of naked, breathing, quivering, bronze bodies. I steamed up a bit, then swung downstream, and two thousand eyes followed the evolutions of the splashing, thumping, fierce river-demon beating the water with its terrible tail and breathing black smoke into the air. In front of the first rank, along the river, three men, plastered with bright red earth from head to foot, strutted to and fro restlessly. When we came abreast again, they faced the river, stamped their feet, nodded their horned heads, swayed their scarlet bodies; they shook towards the fierce river-demon a bunch of black feathers, a mangy skin with a pendent tail—something that looked like a dried gourd; they shouted periodically together strings of amazing words that resembled no sounds of human language; and the deep murmurs of the crowd, interrupted suddenly, were like the responses of some satanic litany.

THE "TORRENS": EXPERIENCES WITH PASSENGERS

[In January, 1891, Conrad returned to Europe from Africa, but illness necessitated some months of compulsory leisure. By November, 1891, he felt sufficiently strong to accept the second command of the famous clipper *Torrens* (Plymouth-Adelaide-Cape Town). When on the fifteenth of October, 1893, he parted from her in London Dock, he stepped, as he said, out of his sea life altogether.]

My two years in the *Torrens* is my only professional experience of passengers; and though we—officers brought up in strenuous Indiamen and famous wool clippers—did not think much of passengers, regarding them as derogatory nuisances with delicate feelings which prevented one driving one's ship till all was blue, I will confess that this experience was most fortunate from every point of view, marking the end of my sea life with pleasant memories, new impressions, and precious friendships. The pleasant memories include the excellent ship's companies it was my luck to work with on each of my two voyages. But the *Torrens* had a fame which attracted the right kind of sailor, and when engaging her crew her chief officer had always a large and promising crowd to pick and choose from. There was in it always a certain proportion of men who had served in her before and were anxious to join again; for apart from her more brilliant qualities, such as her speed and her celebrated good looks (which by themselves go a long way with a sailor), she was regarded as a "comfortable ship" in a strictly professional sense, which means that she was known to handle easily and to be a good sea boat in heavy weather. I cannot say that during my time in her we ever experienced really heavy weather; but we had the usual assortment of winds, up to "very strong gales" (log-book style), from various directions; and I can testify that, on every point of sailing, the way that ship had of letting big seas slip under her did one's heart good to watch. It resembled so much an exhibition of intelligent grace and unerring skill that it could fascinate even the least seamanlike of our passengers. A passage under sail brings out in the course of days whatever there may be of sea love and sea sense in any individual whose soul is not indissolubly wedded to the pedestrian shore.

There are, of course, degrees of landsmanism—even to the incurable. A gentleman whom we had on board on my first voyage presented an extreme instance of it. It, however, trenched upon the morbid in its excessive sea fright, which had its pathetic as well as comic moments. We had not been more than ten days out from Plymouth when he took it into his head that his shattered constitution could not stand the voyage. Note that he had not had as much as an hour of seasickness. He maintained, however, that a few more days at sea would certainly kill him. He was absolutely certain of it, and he pleaded day after day with a persistent agonized earnestness to be put ashore on the first convenient bit of land, which in this case would have been Teneriffe. But it is not so easy for a sailing ship to make an unexpected call without losing much time. Any deviation from a direct course of the voyage (unless in case of actual distress) would have invalidated the ship's insurance. It was not to be thought of, especially as the man looked fit enough, and the doctor had reported that he could not find the slightest evidence of organic disease of any sort. I was sorry for my captain. He could not refuse to listen to the man. Neither could he accede to his request. It was absurd. And yet! . . . who could tell? It became worse when he began to offer progressive bribes up to £300 or more. I don't know why I was called to one of those awful conferences. The even, low flow of argument from those trembling lips impressed me. He exhibited to us his bank passbook to prove that he had the means to buy his life from us. Our doctor stood by in grim silence. The captain looked dead tired, but kept his temper wonderfully under the implication of callous heartlessness. It was I who could not stand the inclusive anguish of the situation. It was not so long since I had been neurasthenic myself. At the very next pause I remarked in a loud and cheery tone, "I suppose I had better get the anchors ready first thing tomorrow." The captain glared at me speechlessly, as well he might. But the effect of the hopeful word "anchors" had an instantaneous soothing effect on our passenger. As if satisfied that there was at last somebody on his side he was willing to leave it at that. He went out.

I need not say that next day the anchors were not touched.

But we sighted Teneriffe at thirty miles off, to windward—a towering and majestic shadow against the sky. Our passenger spent the day leaning over the rail, watching it till it melted away in the dusk. It was the confirmation of a death sentence for him, I suppose. He took it very well.

He gave me the opportunity to admire for many days an exhibition of consistent stoicism. He never repined. He withdrew within himself. Though civil enough when addressed directly, he had very few words to give to anybody—as though his fund of speech had been expended while pleading in vain for his life. But his heart was burning with indignant anger. He went ashore unreadable but unforgiving, without taking notice of any one in the ship. I was the only exception. Poor futile creature as I was, he remembered that I at least had seemed to be "on his side." If I may take an Irishman's privilege, I will say that if he had really died he could not have abhorred the ship and everyone in her more. To have been exposed to live for seventy days under a sentence of death was a soul-searing outrage, and he very properly resented it to the last.

I must say that, in general, our passengers would begin very soon to look thoroughly at home in the ship. Its life was homely enough and far removed from the ideals of the Ritz Hotel. The monotony of the sea is easier to bear than the boredom of the shore, if only because there is no visible remedy and no contrasts at hand to keep discontent alive. The world contains, or contained then, some people who could put up with a sense of peace for three months. The feeling of close confinement in a sailing ship, with her propelling power working in the open air, and with her daily life going on in public sight, and presenting the varied interests of human character and individual exertion, is always less oppressive than in a steamer even many times her size. Besides, in a sailing ship there are neither vibration nor mechanical noises to grow actively wearisome. Another advantage was that the sailing passenger ships of that epoch were never crowded. The cabins of the *Torrens* had two berths only, but they were roomy and not overfurnished with all sorts of inadequate contrivances for comfort, so called. I have seen the cabins of a modern passenger steamship with three or four berths (their very couches being numbered) which were not half as big as ours. Not half as big—in fact, some of our passengers who seized the opportunity of learning to dance the hornpipe from our boatswain (an agile professor), could pursue their studies in their own rooms. And that art requires for its practice more space than the proverbial swinging of a cat, I can assure you. Much more.

The *Torrens* was launched in 1875, only a few months after I had managed, after lots of trouble, to launch myself on the waters of the Mediterranean. Thus we began our careers about the same time. . . . I joined her . . . . on the 2nd of November, 1891, in London, and I ceased to "belong to her," as the saying is (it was a wrench), on the 15th of October, 1893, when, in London Dock, I took a long look from the quay at that last of ships I ever had under my care, and, stepping round the corner of a tall warehouse, parted from her forever, and at the same time stepped (in merciful ignorance) out of my sea life altogether.

In the end her body of iron and wood, so fair to look upon, had to be broken up—I hope with fitting reverence; and as I sit here, thirty years, almost to a day, since I last set eyes on her, I love to think that her perfect form found a merciful end on the shores of the sunlit sea of my boyhood's dreams, and that her fine spirit has returned to dwell in the regions of the great winds, the inspirers and the companions of her swift, renowned, sea-tossed life, which I, too, have been permitted to share for a little while.

THE WRITER

[Conrad, it might be said, first lived a life; then after he had something to say, he wrote. As previous introductory notes have shown, his life as a seaman and his career as a writer overlapped. While still a seaman in 1889, he began writing his first novel; but the transition, which he accomplished "insensibly," he did not consider complete until 1897.

Notwithstanding a resulting discrepancy in chronological order, it has been thought best to group together all autobiographical passages that have to do with his career as a writer. The first group of passages concerns English, the language of his adoption. It should be understood that Conrad knew—thoroughly knew—three languages: Polish, his mother-tongue, in which he never wrote for print, but which he used whenever necessity arose; French, almost a second mother-tongue, which he continued to read, speak, and write as long as he lived; and English, which he began to learn at the age of twenty. How thoroughly he mastered the written language his books best show. But in his conversation when he was thirty-five, John Galsworthy noted a "strong foreign accent"; and two or more years after that, when reading aloud some newly written manuscript to Edward Garnett, "he mispronounced so many words," Garnett said, "that I followed him with difficulty. I found that he had never once heard these English words spoken but had learned them all from books."

As to what books they were, there is much evidence. In *Youth* he speaks of rejoining his ship with "a complete set of Byron's works." At sea he "read and reread" Shakespeare. He considered Dickens "a great man." Keats was his favorite poet. "The manliness, the clearness of Dr. Johnson's *The Lives of the Poets*" commanded his admiration. Jeremy Taylor he read "not for what he says, but for the language, the exquisite music." He "never regretted his surrender" to Marryat and Cooper: "the youthful glamour, the headlong vitality" of the one; "the profound sympathy, the artistic insight" of the other. Henry James's books stood on his shelves "in a place whose accessibility" proclaimed "the habit of frequent communion." Books, to use his own phrase, were an integral part of his life.]

"ENGLISH—THE SPEECH OF MY SECRET CHOICE"

THERE are ships I have met more than once and known well by sight whose names I have forgotten; but the name of that ship seen once so many years ago in the clear flush of a cold pale sunrise I have not forgotten. How could I—the first English ship on whose side I ever laid my hand! The name —I read it letter by letter on the bow—was *James Westoll*. Not very romantic, you will say. The name of a very considerable, well-known, and universally respected North-country shipowner, I believe. James Westoll! What better name could an honorable hard-working ship have? To me the very grouping of the letters is alive with the romantic feeling of her reality as I saw her floating motionless, and borrowing an ideal grace from the austere purity of the light.

We were then very near her, and, on a sudden impulse, I volunteered to pull bow in the dinghy which shoved off at once to put the pilot on board, while our boat, fanned by the faint air which had attended us all through the night, went on gliding gently past the black glistening length of the ship. A few strokes brought us alongside, and it was then [in 1874 or 1875, while associating with the pilots of Marseilles] that, for the very first time in my life, I heard myself addressed in English—the speech of my secret choice, of my future, of long friendships, of the deepest affections, of hours of toil and hours of ease, and of solitary hours too, of books read, of thoughts pursued, of remembered emotions—of my very dreams! And if (after being thus fashioned by it in that part of me which cannot decay) I dare not claim it aloud as my own, then, at any rate, the speech of my children. Thus

small events grow memorable by the passage of time.   As to
the quality of the address itself, I cannot say it was very
striking.   Too short for eloquence and devoid of all charm
of tone, it consisted precisely of the three words "Look out
there," growled out huskily above my head.

The North Sea had been for some time the schoolroom of
my trade.   On it, I may safely say, I had learned, too, my
first words of English.   A wild and stormy abode, sometimes,
was that confined, shallow-water academy of seamanship
from which I launched myself on the wide oceans.   My
teachers had been the sailors of the Norfolk shore; coast men,
with steady eyes, mighty limbs, and gentle voice; men of
very few words, which at least were never bare of meaning.
Honest, strong, steady men, sobered by domestic ties, one and
all, as far as I can remember.

After hearing it spoken and when I could talk enough, I
read.   I have still a thick, green-covered volume of Shakespeare I bought with my first earnings.   It had beastly print,
but it had everything in it, including the sonnets.   I had
read the whole of Shakespeare by 1880 and I reread him in
the following years.   While I was at sea there was another
book I used to read a lot, and it pulled my English together.
That was Mill's *Political Economy*.   It was most interesting,
but also it was an excellent soporific—Mill charms your mind
into sleep.

But perhaps I could say I learned English by reading the
newspapers.   I learned a great deal from the old *Standard*
when it was under Mudford.   He was a remarkable journalist, a cultured man; and in those days they paid great
attention to style.   "Telegraphese" and "punch" were unknown to English journalism. . . .

Now look at that word "punch"—all the meanings it has.
It is a technical noun and it is several other common things.

Also there is the "punch" immortalized by Dickens in *Pickwick*. Can you wonder that I experienced enormous difficulty in learning the English language? Look at the words pronounced alike and meaning different things—words ending in "ough" for instance. The phonetics of English is indeed a dismal thing for foreigners.

St. Anne's [in Cracow, Poland] where I was a scholar . . . . was on the classical side, you know, along old-fashioned lines. . . . I was good at mathematics, fairly good at history, and my composition could always pull me up in the class. But I was no good at grammar. Oh, what a grind I had when (later) I tried to get hold of English grammar! As I had always been a reading boy I remained a reader after going to sea, and reading is the best way to pick up any language. But I still absolutely refused to learn grammar . . . . After all, grammar is so arbitrary; why bother about it?

The fact of my not writing in my native language has been, of course, commented upon frequently in reviews and notices of my various works and in the more extended critical articles. I suppose that was unavoidable; and indeed these comments were of the most flattering kind to one's vanity. But in that matter I have no vanity that could be flattered. I could not have it. The first object of this note is to disclaim any merit there might have been in an act of deliberate volition.

The impression of my having exercised a choice between the two languages, French and English, both foreign to me, has got abroad somehow. That impression is erroneous. . . .

The truth of the matter is that my faculty to write in English is as natural as any other aptitude with which I might have been born. I have a strange and overpowering feeling that it had always been an inherent part of myself. English was for me neither a matter of choice nor adoption. The merest idea of choice had never entered my head. And as to adoption—well, yes, there was adoption; but it was I who was adopted by the genius of the language, which, directly I came out of the stammering stage, made me its own so completely that its very idioms, I truly believe, had a direct action on my temperament and fashioned my still plastic character.

When I wrote the first words of *Almayer's Folly*, I had been already for years and years *thinking* in English. I began to think in English long before I mastered, I won't say the style (I haven't done that yet), but the mere uttered speech. Is it thinkable that anybody possessed of some effective inspiration should contemplate for a moment such a frantic thing as translating it into another tongue? And there are also other considerations: such as the sheer appeal of the language, my quickly awakened love for its prose cadences, a subtle and unforeseen accord of my emotional nature with its genius . . . You may take it from me that if I had not known English I wouldn't have written a line for print, in my life.

THE FIRST BOOK
(*Almayer's Folly*)

[The materials for *Almayer's Folly* Conrad gathered on board the *Vidar* in 1887–8 on the wild coast and up the rivers of Borneo, Celebes, and Sumatra. He began the book itself in London in 1889. The next year the unfinished manuscript, like himself, narrowly survived the Congo expedition. Its very first reader was the "reserved" *Torrens* passenger of 1892–3. He did not complete the manuscript until 1894, five years after writing those first chapters in London. "Line by line, rather than page by page," he said, "was the growth of *Almayer's Folly*."]

THE MAN ALMAYER

What I am certain of is that I was very far from thinking of writing a story, though it is possible and even likely that I was thinking of the man Almayer.

I had seen him for the first time some four years before from the bridge of a steamer moored to a rickety little wharf forty miles up, more or less, a Bornean river. . . . The forests above and below and on the opposite bank looked black and dank; wet dripped from the rigging upon the tightly stretched deck awnings, and it was in the middle of a shuddering yawn that I caught sight of Almayer. He was moving across a patch of burnt grass, a blurred, shadowy shape with the blurred bulk of a house behind him, a low house of mats, bamboos, and palm-leaves, with a high-pitched roof of grass.

He stepped upon the jetty. He was clad simply in flapping pyjamas of cretonne pattern (enormous flowers with yellow petals on a disagreeable blue ground) and a thin cotton singlet with short sleeves. His arms, bare to the elbow, were crossed on his chest. His black hair looked as if it had not been cut for a very long time, and a curly wisp of it strayed across his forehead. I had heard of him at Singapore; I had heard of him on board; I had heard of him early in the morning and late at night; I had heard of him at tiffin and at dinner; I had heard of him in a place called Pulo Laut from a half-caste gentleman there, who described himself as the manager of a coal mine; which sounded civilized and progressive till you heard that the mine could not be worked at present because it was haunted by some particularly atrocious ghosts. I had heard of him in a place called Dongola, in the Island of Celebes, when the Rajah of that little-known seaport (you can get no anchorage there in less than fifteen fathom, which is extremely inconvenient) came on board in a friendly way with only two attendants, and drank bottle after bottle of

soda water on the after-skylight with my good friend and
commander Captain C——.   At least I heard his name distinctly pronounced several times in a lot of talk in Malay
language.   Oh, yes, I heard it quite distinctly—Almayer, Almayer—and saw Captain C—— smile while the fat, dingy
Rajah laughed audibly.   To hear a Malay Rajah laugh out-
right is a rare experience, I can assure you.   And I overheard
more of Almayer's name amongst our deck passengers (mostly
wandering traders of good repute) as they sat all over the
ship—each man fenced round with bundles and boxes—on
mats, on pillows, on quilts, on billets of wood, conversing of
Island affairs.   Upon my word, I heard the mutter of Almayer's name faintly at midnight, while making my way aft
from the bridge to look at the patent taffrail-log tinkling its
quarter-miles in the great silence of the sea.   I don't mean to
say that our passengers dreamed aloud of Almayer, but it is
indubitable that two of them at least, who could not sleep
apparently and were trying to charm away the trouble of
insomnia by a little whispered talk at that ghostly hour, were
referring in some way or other to Almayer.   It was really
impossible on board that ship to get away definitely from
Almayer; and a very small pony tied up forward and whisk-
ing its tail inside the galley, to the great embarrassment of our
Chinaman cook, was destined for Almayer.   What he wanted
with a pony goodness only knows, since I am perfectly certain he could not ride it; but here you have the man, am-
bitious, aiming at the grandiose, importing a pony, whereas
in the whole settlement at which he used to shake daily his
impotent fist, there was only one path that was practicable
for a pony: a quarter of a mile at most, hedged in by hundreds of square leagues of virgin forest.   But who knows?
The importation of that Bali pony might have been part of
some deep scheme, of some diplomatic plan, of some hopeful
intrigue.   With Almayer one could never tell.   He gov-
erned his conduct by considerations removed from the obvi-

ous, by incredible assumptions, which rendered his logic impenetrable to any reasonable person. I learned all this later. That morning, seeing the figure in pyjamas moving in the mist, I said to myself: "That's the man."

He came quite close to the ship's side and raised a harassed countenance, round and flat, with that curl of black hair over the forehead and a heavy, pained glance.

"Good morning."

"Good morning."

He looked hard at me: I was a new face, having just replaced the chief mate he was accustomed to see; and I think that this novelty inspired him, as things generally did, with deep-seated mistrust. . . .

"Have you been long out from Europe?" he asked me.

"Not very. Not quite eight months," I told him. "I left a ship in Samarang with a hurt back and have been in the hospital in Singapore some weeks."

He sighed.

"Trade is very bad here."

"Indeed!"

"Hopeless! . . . See these geese?"

With the hand holding the letters he pointed out to me what resembled a patch of snow creeping and swaying across the distant part of his compound. It disappeared behind some bushes.

"The only geese on the East Coast," Almayer informed me in a perfunctory mutter without a spark of faith, hope, or pride. Thereupon, with the same absence of any sort of sustaining spirit, he declared his intention to select a fat bird and send him on board for us not later than next day.

I had heard of these largesses before. He conferred a goose as if it were a sort of Court decoration given only to the tried friends of the house. I had expected more pomp in the ceremony. The gift had surely its special quality, multiple and rare. From the only flock on the East Coast! He did not make half enough of it. That man did not understand his opportunities. However, I thanked him at some length.

"You see," he interrupted abruptly in a very peculiar tone, "the worst of this country is that one is not able to realize . . . it's impossible to realize . . ." His voice sank into a languid mutter. "And when one has very large interests . . . very important interests . . ." he finished faintly . . . "up the river."

We looked at each other. He astonished me by giving a start and making a very queer grimace.

"Well, I must be off," he burst out hurriedly. "So long!"

At the moment of stepping over the gangway he checked himself, though, to give me a mumbled invitation to dine at his house that evening with my captain, an invitation which I accepted. I don't think it could have been possible for me to refuse. . . . A refusal would have appeared perverse and insane. Nobody unless a surly lunatic would have refused. But if I had not got to know Almayer pretty well it is almost certain there would never have been a line of mine in print.

I accepted then—and I am paying yet the price of my sanity. The possessor of the only flock of geese on the East Coast is responsible for the existence of some fourteen volumes, so far. The number of geese he had called into being under adverse climatic conditions was considerably more than fourteen. The tale of volumes will never overtake the counting of heads, I am safe to say; but my ambitions point not exactly that way, and whatever the pangs the toil of writing has cost me, I have always thought kindly of Almayer.

I wonder, had he known anything of it, what his attitude would have been? This is something not to be discovered in this world. But if we ever meet in the Elysian Fields—where I cannot depict him to myself otherwise than attended in the distance by his flock of geese (birds sacred to Jupiter) and he addresses me in the stillness of that passionless region, neither light nor darkness, neither sound nor silence, and heaving endlessly with billowy mists from the impalpable multitudes of the swarming dead, I think I know what answer to make.

I would say, after listening courteously to the unvibrating tone of his measured remonstrances, which should not disturb, of course, the solemn eternity of stillness in the least—I would say something like this:

"It is true, Almayer, that in the world below I have converted your name to my own uses. But that is a very small larceny. What's in a name, O Shade? If so much of your old mortal weakness clings to you yet as to make you feel aggrieved (it was the note of your earthly voice, Almayer), then, I entreat you, seek speech without delay with our sublime fellow-Shade—with him who, in his transient existence as a poet, commented upon the smell of the rose. He will comfort you. You came to me stripped of all prestige by men's queer smiles and the disrespectful chatter of every vagrant trader in the Islands. Your name was the common property of the winds: it, as it were, floated naked over the waters about the Equator. I wrapped round its unhonored form the royal mantle of the tropics and have essayed to put into the hollow sound the very anguish of paternity—feats which you did not demand from me—but remember that all the toil and all the pain were mine. In your earthly life you haunted me, Almayer. Consider that this was taking a great liberty. Since you were always complaining of being lost to the world, you should remember that if I had not believed enough in your existence to let you haunt my rooms in Bessborough Gardens you would have been much more lost. You affirm that, had I been capable of looking at you with a more perfect detachment and a greater simplicity, I might have perceived better the inward marvelousness which, you insist, attended your career upon that tiny pin point of light, hardly visible, far, far below us, where both our graves lie. No doubt! But reflect, O complaining Shade, that this was not so much my fault as your crowning misfortune. I believed

in you in the only way it was possible for me to believe.   It
was not worthy of your merits? So be it. But you were
always an unlucky man, Almayer.   Nothing was ever quite
worthy of you. What made you so real to me was that you
held this lofty theory with some force of conviction and with
an admirable consistency."

It is with some such words translated into the proper
shadowy expressions that I am prepared to placate Almayer
in the Elysian Abode of Shades, since it has come to pass that,
having parted many years ago, we are never to meet again in
this world.

Almayer's Folly was never dismissed from my mind, even
when the hope of ever finishing it was very faint. Many
things came in its way: daily duties, new impressions, old
memories. It was not the outcome of a need—the
famous need of self-expression which artists find in their
search for motives. The necessity which impelled me was a
hidden, obscure necessity, a completely masked and unac-
countable phenomenon. Or perhaps some idle and frivolous
magician (there must be magicians in London) had cast a
spell over me through his parlor window as I explored the
maze of streets east and west in solitary leisurely walks without chart and compass. Till I began to write that novel I
had written nothing but letters, and not very many of these.
I never made a note of a fact, of an impression, or of an anecdote in my life. The conception of a planned book was
entirely outside my mental range when I sat down to write;
the ambition of being an author had never turned up amongst
these gracious imaginary existences one creates fondly for
oneself at times in the stillness and immobility of a day-
dream: yet it stands clear as the sun at noonday that from
the moment I had done blackening over the first manuscript
page of *Almayer's Folly* (it contained about two hundred
words, and this proportion of words to a page has remained

with me through the fifteen years of my writing life), from the moment I had, in the simplicity of my heart and the amazing ignorance of my mind, written that page, the die was cast.   Never had Rubicon been more blindly forded, without invocation to the gods, without fear of men.

THE FIRST READER OF "ALMAYER'S FOLLY"

It would be on my part the greatest ingratitude ever to forget the sallow, sunken face and the deep-set, dark eyes of the young Cambridge man (he was a "passenger for his health" on board the good ship *Torrens* outward bound to Australia) who was the first reader of *Almayer's Folly*—the very first reader I ever had.   "Would it bore you very much reading a manuscript in a handwriting like mine?"   I asked him one evening on a sudden impulse at the end of a longish conversation whose subject was Gibbon's History.   Jacques (that was his name) was sitting in my cabin one stormy dog-watch below, after bringing me a book to read from his own traveling store.

"Not at all," he answered with his courteous intonation and a faint smile.   As I pulled a drawer open his suddenly aroused curiosity gave him a watchful expression.   I wonder what he expected to see.   A poem, maybe.   All that's beyond guessing now.   He was not a cold, but a calm man, still more subdued by disease—a man of few words and of an unassuming modesty in general intercourse, but with something uncommon in the whole of his person which set him apart from the undistinguished lot of our sixty passengers.   His eyes had a thoughtful, introspective look.   In his attractive, reserved manner, and in a veiled, sympathetic voice, he asked:

"What is this?"   "It is a sort of tale," I answered with an effort.   "It is not even finished yet.   Nevertheless, I would like to know what you think of it."   He put the manuscript in the breast pocket of his jacket; I remember perfectly his thin brown fingers folding it lengthwise. "I will read it to-morrow," he remarked, seizing the door handle, and then watching the roll of the ship for a propitious moment, he opened the door and was gone. In the moment of his exit I heard the sustained booming of the wind, the swish of the water on the decks of the *Torrens,* and the subdued, as if distant, roar of the rising sea. I noted the growing disquiet in the great restlessness of the ocean, and responded professionally to it with the thought that at eight o'clock, in another half-hour or so at the furthest, the topgallant sails would have to come off the ship.

Next day, but this time in the first dogwatch, Jacques entered my cabin. He had a thick, woolen muffler round his throat, and the manuscript was in his hand. He tendered it to me with a steady look but without a word. I took it in silence. He sat down on the couch and still said nothing. I opened and shut a drawer under my desk, on which a filled-up log slate lay wide open in its wooden frame waiting to be copied neatly into the sort of book I was accustomed to write with care, the ship's log book. I turned my back squarely on the desk. And even then Jacques never offered a word. "Well, what do you say?" I asked at last. "Is it worth finishing?" This question expressed exactly the whole of my thoughts.

"Distinctly," he answered in his sedate veiled voice, and then coughed a little.

"Were you interested?" I inquired further, almost in a whisper.

"Very much!"

In a pause I went on meeting instinctively the heavy rolling of the ship, and Jacques put his feet upon the couch. The curtain of my bedplace swung to and fro as it were a punkah, the bulkhead lamp circled in its gimbals, and now and then the cabin door rattled slightly in the gusts of wind. It

was in latitude 40° south, and nearly in the longitude of
Greenwich, as far as I can remember, that these quiet rites
of Almayer's and Nina's resurrection were taking place. In
the prolonged silence it occurred to me that there was a good
deal of retrospective writing in the story as far as it went.
Was it intelligible in its action, I asked myself, as if already
the story teller were being born into the body of a seaman.
But I heard on deck the whistle of the officer of the watch
and remained on the alert to catch the order that was to follow this call to attention. It reached me as a faint, fierce
shout to "Square the yards." "Aha!" I thought to myself,
"a westerly blow coming on." Then I turned to my very
first reader, who, alas! was not to live long enough to know
the end of the tale.

"Now let me ask you one more thing: Is the story quite
clear to you as it stands?"

He raised his dark, gentle eyes to my face and seemed surprised.

"Yes!   Perfectly."

This was all I was to hear from his lips concerning the
merits of *Almayer's Folly*. We never spoke together of the
book again. A long period of bad weather set in and I had
no thoughts left but for my duties, whilst poor Jacques
caught a fatal cold and had to keep close in his cabin. When
we arrived at Adelaide the first reader of my prose went at
once up-country, and died rather suddenly in the end, either
in Australia or, it may be, on the passage while going home
through the Suez Canal. I am not sure which it was now,
and I do not think I ever heard precisely; though I made inquiries about him from some of our return passengers who,
wandering about to "see the country" during the ship's stay
in port, had come upon him here and there. At last we
sailed, homeward bound, and still not one line was added to
the careless scrawl of the many pages which poor Jacques had
had the patience to read with the very shadows of Eternity

gathering already in the hollows of his kind, steadfast eyes.

The purpose instilled into me by his simple and final "Distinctly" remained dormant, yet alive to await its opportunity. I dare say I am compelled, unconsciously compelled, now to write volume after volume, as in past years I was compelled to go to sea, voyage after voyage. Leaves must follow upon each other as leagues used to follow in the days gone by, on and on to the appointed end, which, being Truth itself, is One—one for all men and for all occupations.

I do not know which of the two impulses has appeared more mysterious and more wonderful to me. Still, in writing, as in going to sea, I had to wait my opportunity. Let me confess here that I was never one of those wonderful fellows that would go afloat in a washtub for the sake of the fun, and if I may pride myself upon my consistency it was ever just the same with my writing. Some men, I have heard, write in railway carriages and could do it, perhaps, sitting cross-legged on a clothesline; but I must confess that my sybaritic disposition will not consent to write without something at least resembling a chair. Line by line, rather than page by page, was the growth of *Almayer's Folly*.

"WHY NOT WRITE ANOTHER?"

An Outcast of the Islands is my second novel in the absolute sense of the word; second in conception, second in execution, second as it were in its essence. There was no hesitation, half-formed plan, vague idea, or the vaguest reverie of anything else between it and *Almayer's Folly*. The only doubt I suffered from, after the publication of *Almayer's Folly*, was whether I should write another line for print. Those days, now grown so dim, had their poignant moments. Neither in my mind nor in my heart had I then given up the sea. In truth I was clinging to it desperately, all the more desperately because, against my will, I could not help feeling that there was something changed in my relation to it. *Almayer's Folly* had been finished and done with. The mood itself was gone. But it had left the memory of an experience that, both in thought and emotion, was unconnected with the sea, and I suppose that part of my moral being which is rooted in consistency was badly shaken. I was a victim of contrary stresses which produced a state of immobility. I gave myself up to indolence. Since it was impossible for me to face both ways I had elected to face nothing. The discovery of new values in life is a very chaotic experience; there is a tremendous amount of jostling and confusion and a momentary feeling of darkness. I let my spirit float supine over that chaos.

A phrase of Edward Garnett's is, as a matter of fact, responsible for this book. The first of the friends I made for myself by my pen, it was but natural that he should be the recipient, at that time, of my confidences. One evening when we had dined together and he had listened to the account of my perplexities (I fear he must have been growing a little tired of them) he pointed out that there was no need to determine my future absolutely. Then he added: "You have the style, you have the temperament; why not write another?" I believe that as far as one man may wish to influence another man's life Edward Garnett had a great desire that I should go on writing. At that time, and, I may say, ever afterwards, he was always very patient and gentle with me. What strikes me most, however, in the phrase quoted above, which was offered to me in a tone of detachment, is not its gentleness but its effective wisdom. Had he said, "Why not go on writing?" it is very probable he would have scared me away from pen and ink forever; but there was nothing either to frighten one or arouse one's antagonism in the mere suggestion to "write another." And thus a dead point in the revolution of my affairs was insidiously got over. The word "another" did it. At about eleven o'clock of a nice London night, Edward and I walked along interminable streets talking of many things, and I remember that on getting home I sat down and wrote about half a page of *An Outcast of the Islands* before I slept.   This was committing myself definitely. I won't say to another life, but to another book.   There is apparently something in my character which will not allow me to abandon for good any piece of work I have begun.   I have laid aside many beginnings.   I have laid them aside with sorrow, with disgust, with rage, with melancholy, and even with self-contempt; but even at the worst I had an uneasy consciousness that I would have to go back to them.

HENCEFORTH—TO BE A WRITER

From that evening when James Wait joined the ship—late for the muster of the crew—to the moment when he left us in the open sea, shrouded in sailcloth, through the open port, I had much to do with him.   He was in my watch.   A negro in a British forecastle is a lonely being.   He has no chums.   Yet James Wait, afraid of death and making her his accomplice, was an impostor of some character—mastering our compassion, scornful of our sentimentalism, triumphing over our suspicions.

But in the book he is nothing; he is merely the center of the ship's collective psychology and the pivot of the action. Yet he, who in the family circle and amongst my friends is familiarly referred to as "The Nigger," remains very precious to me.   For the book written round him is not the sort of thing that can be attempted more than once in a lifetime. . . .

After writing the last words of that book, in the revulsion of feeling before the accomplished task, I understood that I had done with the sea, and that henceforth I had to be a writer.   And almost without laying down the pen I wrote a preface, trying to express the spirit in which I was entering on the task of my new life.

THE ARTIST'S CREED
(Being the Preface to *The Nigger of the "Narcissus"*)

A work that aspires, however humbly, to the condition of art should carry its justification in every line.   And art itself may be defined as a single-minded attempt to render the highest kind of justice to the visible universe, by bringing to light the truth, manifold and one, underlying its every aspect.   It is an attempt to find in its forms, in its colors, in its light, in its shadows, in the aspects of matter and in the facts of life, what of each is fundamental, what is enduring and essential —their one illuminating and convincing quality—the very truth of their existence.   The artist, then, like the thinker or the scientist, seeks the truth and makes his appeal.   Impressed by the aspect of the world the thinker plunges into ideas, the scientist into facts—whence, presently, emerging they make their appeal to those qualities of our being that fit us best for the hazardous enterprise of living.   They speak authoritatively to our common sense, to our intelligence, to our desire of peace or to our desire of unrest; not seldom to our prejudices, sometimes to our fears, often to our egoism— but always to our credulity.   And their words are heard with reverence, for their concern is with weighty matters: with the cultivation of our minds and the proper care of our bodies, with the attainment of our ambitions, with the perfection of the means and the glorification of our precious aims.

It is otherwise with the artist.

Confronted by the same enigmatical spectacle the artist descends within himself, and in that lonely region of stress and strife, if he be deserving and fortunate, he finds the terms of his appeal.   His appeal is made to our less obvious capacities: to that part of our nature which, because of the warlike conditions of existence, is necessarily kept out of sight within the more resisting and hard qualities—like the vulnerable

body within a steel armor.   His appeal is less loud, more profound, less distinct, more stirring—and sooner forgotten.
Yet its effect endures forever.   The changing wisdom of
successive generations discards ideas, questions facts, demol-
ishes theories.   But the artist appeals to that part of our
being which is not dependent on wisdom: to that in us which
is a gift and not an acquisition—and, therefore, more perma-
nently enduring.   He speaks to our capacity for delight and
wonder, to the sense of mystery surrounding our lives; to our
sense of pity, and beauty, and pain; to the latent feeling of
fellowship with all creation—and to the subtle but invincible conviction of solidarity that knits together the loneliness
of innumerable hearts, to the solidarity in dreams, in joy, in
sorrow, in aspirations, in illusions, in hope, in fear, which
binds men to each other, which binds together all humanity
—the dead to the living and the living to the unborn.

It is only some such train of thought, or rather of feeling,
that can in a measure explain the aim of the attempt, made
in the tale which follows, to present an unrestful episode in
the obscure lives of a few individuals out of all the disregarded multitude of the bewildered, the simple, and the voice-
less.   For, if any part of truth dwells in the belief confessed
above, it becomes evident that there is not a place of splendor or a dark corner of the earth that does not deserve if
only a passing glance of wonder and pity.   The motive, then,
may be held to justify the matter of the work; but this preface, which is simply an avowal of endeavor, cannot end here
—for the avowal is not yet complete.

Fiction—if it at all aspires to be art—appeals to temperament.   And in truth it must be, like painting, like music,
like all art, the appeal of one temperament to all the other
innumerable temperaments whose subtle and resistless power
endows passing events with their true meaning, and creates
the moral, the emotional atmosphere of the place and time.
Such an appeal, to be effective, must be an impression con-

veyed through the senses; and, in fact, it cannot be made in any other way, because temperament, whether individual or collective, is not amenable to persuasion. All art, therefore, appeals primarily to the senses, and the artistic aim when expressing itself in written words must also make its appeal through the senses, if its high desire is to reach the secret spring of responsive emotions. It must strenuously aspire to the plasticity of sculpture, to the color of painting, and to the magic suggestiveness of music—which is the art of arts. And it is only through complete, unswerving devotion to the perfect blending of form and substance; it is only through an unremitting, never-discouraged care for the shape and ring of sentences that an approach can be made to plasticity, to color, and that the light of magic suggestiveness may be brought to play for an evanescent instant over the common- place surface of words: of the old, old words, worn thin, de- faced by ages of careless usage.

The sincere endeavor to accomplish that creative task, to go as far on that road as his strength will carry him, to go undeterred by faltering, weariness, or reproach, is the only valid justification for the worker in prose. And if his con- science is clear, his answer to those who in the fullness of a wisdom which looks for immediate profit, demand specifi- cally to be edified, consoled, amused; who demand to be promptly improved, or encouraged, or frightened, or shocked, or charmed, must run thus:—My task which I am trying to achieve is, by the power of the written word, to make you hear, to make you feel—it is, before all, to make you *see*. That—and no more, and it is everything. If I succeed, you shall find there, according to your deserts, encouragement, consolation, fear, charm—all you demand—and, perhaps, also that glimpse of truth for which you have forgotten to ask.

To snatch, in a moment of courage, from the remorseless rush of time a passing phase of life, is only the beginning of the task. The task approached in tenderness and faith is to hold up unquestioningly, without choice and without fear, the rescued fragment before all eyes in the light of a sincere mood.   It is to show its vibration, its color, its form; and through its movement, its form, and its color, reveal the substance of its truth—disclose its inspiring secret: the stress and passion within the core of each convincing moment.   In a single-minded attempt of that kind, if one be deserving and fortunate, one may perchance attain to such clearness of sincerity that at last the presented vision of regret or pity, of terror or mirth, shall awaken in the hearts of the beholders that feeling of unavoidable solidarity; of the solidarity in mysterious origin, in toil, in joy, in hope, in uncertain fate, which binds men to each other and all mankind to the visible world.

It is evident that he who, rightly or wrongly, holds by the convictions expressed above cannot be faithful to any one of the temporary formulas of his craft.   The enduring part of them—the truth which each only imperfectly veils—should abide with him as the most precious of his possessions, but they all—Realism, Romanticism, Naturalism, even the unofficial Sentimentalism (which, like the poor, is exceedingly difficult to get rid of,)—all these gods must, after a short period of fellowship, abandon him—even on the very threshold of the temple—to the stammerings of his conscience and to the outspoken consciousness of the difficulties of his work.   In that uneasy solitude the supreme cry of Art for Art itself loses the exciting ring of its apparent immorality. It sounds far off.   It has ceased to be a cry and is heard only as a whisper, often incomprehensible, but at times and faintly encouraging.

Sometimes, stretched at ease in the shade of a roadside tree, we watch the motions of a laborer in a distant field, and after a time, begin to wonder languidly as to what the fellow may be at.   We watch the movements of his body, the waving of his arms; we see him bend down, stand up, hesitate, begin again. It may add to the charm of an idle hour to be told the purpose of his exertions. If we know he is trying to lift a stone, to dig a ditch, to uproot a stump, we look with a more real interest at his efforts; we are disposed to condone the jar of his agitation upon the restfulness of the landscape; and even, if in a brotherly frame of mind, we may bring ourselves to forgive his failure. We understood his object, and, after all, the fellow has tried, and perhaps he had not the strength—and perhaps he had not the knowledge. We forgive, go on our way—and forget.

And so it is with the workman of art. Art is long and life is short, and success is very far off. And thus, doubtful of strength to travel so far, we talk a little about the aim—the aim of art, which, like life itself, is inspiring, difficult—obscured by mists. It is not in the clear logic of a triumphant conclusion; it is not in the unveiling of one of those heartless secrets which are called the Laws of Nature. It is not less great, but only more difficult.

To arrest, for the space of a breath, the hands busy about the work of the earth, and compel men entranced by the sight of distant goals to glance for a moment at the surrounding vision of form and color, of sunshine and shadows; to make them pause for a look, for a sigh, for a smile—such is the aim, difficult and evanescent, and reserved only for a very few to achieve. But sometimes, by the deserving and the fortunate, even that task is accomplished. And when it is accomplished—behold!—all the truth of life is there: a moment of vision, a sigh, a smile—and the return to an eternal rest.

THE WRITER AT WORK

[In 1897, at the age of forty, Conrad wrote, in an introductory note to The Nigger of the "Narcissus," "I understood that I had done with the sea and that henceforth I had to be a writer." Until his death in 1924, he continued to write; and an account of his life during this period would be principally an account of the composition of his works. "There was no time in these years," he said, "to turn my head away from the table. There were whole days when I did not know whether the sun shone or not."

In prefaces written in 1917–1920 for a new edition of his books, as well as in letters and autobiographical works, he grants the reader, as he says, "the right to come and look over my shoulder." There follow some glimpses of Conrad in his workshop.]

Give me the right word and the right accent and I will move the world . . . Let me only find the right word! Surely it must be lying somewhere among the wreckage of all the plaints and all the exultations poured out aloud since the first day when hope, the undying, came down on earth. It may be there, close by, disregarded, invisible, quite at hand. But it's no good. I believe there are men who can lay hold of a needle in a pottle of hay at the first try. For myself, I have never had such luck.

And then there is that accent. Another difficulty. For who is going to tell whether the accent is right or wrong till the word is shouted, and fails to be heard, perhaps, and goes down-wind, leaving the world unmoved?

I am always worrying about the right phrase and saying "This will never do!" of something I have written. A man might be disdainfully careless, or angrily careless, but as a matter of course a man must surely write the best he can. It is inconceivable that a man should compose less well than he is able to compose. It is like a man walking lame when he is perfectly well.

My Jim [Lord Jim] is not a type of wide commonness. But I can safely assure my readers that he is not the product of coldly perverted thinking. He's not a figure of Northern Mists either. One sunny morning in the commonplace surroundings of an Eastern roadstead, I saw his form pass by—

appealing—significant—under a cloud—perfectly silent. Which is as it should be.   It was for me, with all the sympathy of which I was capable, to seek fit words for his meaning.   He was "one of us."

The end of L[ord] J[im] has been pulled off with a steady drag of 21 hours.   I sent wife and child out of the house (to London) and sat down at 9 A. M. with a desperate resolve to be done with it.   Now and then I took a walk round the house, out at one door in at the other.   Ten-minute meals. A great hush.   Cigarette ends growing into a mound similar to a cairn over a dead hero.   Moon rose over the barn, looked in at the window, and climbed out of sight.   Dawn broke, brightened.   I put the lamp out and went on, with the morning breeze blowing the sheets of MS. all over the room.   Sun rose.   I wrote the last word and went into the dining-room. . . . Felt very well, only sleepy; had a bath at seven and at 1:30 was on my way to London.

In 1875 or '6, when very young, in the West Indies—or rather in the Gulf of Mexico . . . I heard the story of some man who was supposed to have stolen single-handed a whole lighter-full of silver, somewhere on the Tierra Firme seaboard during the troubles of a revolution.

On the face of it, this was something of a feat.   But I heard no details, and having no particular interest in crime *qua* crime I was not likely to keep that one in my mind. And I forgot it till twenty-six or seven years afterwards I came upon the very thing in a shabby volume picked up outside a second-hand bookshop. . . . Yet I did not see anything at first in the mere story.   A rascal steals a large parcel of a valuable commodity—so people say.   It's either true or untrue; and in any case it has no value in itself.   To invent a circumstantial account of the robbery did not appeal to me, because my talents not running that way I did not think that the game was worth the candle.   It was only when it dawned upon me that the purloiner of the treasure need not necessarily be a confirmed rogue, that he could be even a man of character, an actor, and possibly a victim in the changing scenes of a revolution, it was only then that I had the first vision of a twilight country which was to become the province of Sulaco, with its high shadowy Sierra and its misty Campo for mute witnesses of events flowing from the passions of men shortsighted in good and evil.

Such are in very truth the obscure origins of *Nostromo*— the book.   From that moment, I suppose, it had to be.   Yet even then I hesitated, as if warned by the instinct of self-preservation from venturing on a distant and toilsome journey into a land full of intrigues and revolutions.   But it had to be done.

It took the best part of the years 1903–1904 to do; with many intervals of renewed hesitation, lest I should lose myself in the ever-enlarging vistas opening before me as I progressed deeper in my knowledge of the country.   Often, also, when I had thought myself to a standstill over the tangled-up affairs of the Republic, I would, figuratively speaking, pack my bag, rush away from Sulaco for a change of air and write a few pages of *The Mirror of the Sea*.   But generally, as I've said before, my sojourn on the Continent of Latin America, famed for its hospitality, lasted for about two years.   On my return I found (speaking somewhat in the style of Captain Gulliver) my family all well, my wife heartily glad to learn that the fuss was all over, and our small boy considerably grown during my absence.

THE WRITER CAUGHT IN THE EXERCISE OF HIS CRAFT

"Life," in the words of an immortal thinker of, I should say, bucolic origin, but whose perishable name is lost to the worship of posterity—"life is not all beer and skittles."

Neither is the writing of novels. It isn't really. *Je vous donne ma parole d'honneur* that it—is—not. Not all. I am thus emphatic because some years ago, I remember, the daughter of a general. . . .

Sudden revelations of the profane world must have come now and then to hermits in their cells, to the cloistered monks of Middle Ages, to lonely sages, men of science, reformers; the revelations of the world's superficial judgment, shocking to the souls concentrated upon their own bitter labor in the cause of sanctity, or of knowledge, or of temperance, let us say, or of art, if only the art of cracking jokes or playing the flute. And thus this general's daughter came to me—or I should say one of the general's daughters did. There were three of these bachelor ladies, of nicely graduated ages, who held a neighboring farmhouse in a united and more or less military occupation. The eldest warred against the decay of manners in the village children, and executed frontal attacks upon the village mothers for the conquest of curtseys. It sounds futile, but it was really a war for an idea. The second skirmished and scouted all over the country; and it was that one who pushed a reconnaissance right to my very table—I mean the one who wore stand-up collars. She was really calling upon my wife in the soft spirit of afternoon friendliness, but with her usual martial determination. She marched into my room swinging her stick . . . but no—I mustn't exaggerate. It is not my specialty. I am not a humoristic writer. In all soberness, then, all I am certain of is that she had a stick to swing.

No ditch or wall encompassed my abode. The window was open; the door, too, stood open to that best friend of my work, the warm, still sunshine of the wide fields. They lay around me infinitely helpful, but truth to say I had not known for weeks whether the sun shone upon the earth and whether the stars above still moved on their appointed courses. I was just then giving up some days of my allotted span to the last chapters of the novel *Nostromo,* a tale of an imaginary (but true) seaboard, which is still mentioned now and again, and indeed kindly, sometimes in connection with the word *failure* and sometimes in conjunction with the word *astonishing.* I have no opinion on this discrepancy. It's the sort of difference that can never be settled. All I know is that, for twenty months, neglecting the common joys of life that fall to the lot of the humblest on this earth, I had, like the prophet of old, "wrestled with the Lord" for my creation, for the headlands of the coast, for the darkness of the Placid Gulf, the light on the snows, the clouds on the sky, and for the breath of life that had to be blown into the shapes of men and women, of Latin and Saxon, of Jew and Gentile. These are, perhaps, strong words, but it is difficult to characterize otherwise the intimacy and the strain of a creative effort in which mind and will and conscience are engaged to the full, hour after hour, day after day, away from the world, and to the exclusion of all that makes life really lovable and gentle—something for which a material parallel can only be found in the everlasting somber stress of the westward winter passage round Cape Horn. For that, too, is the wrestling of men with the might of their Creator, in a great isolation from the world, without the amenities and consolations of life, a lonely struggle under a sense of over-matched littleness, for no reward that could be adequate, but for the mere winning of a longitude. Yet a certain longitude, once won, cannot be disputed. The sun and the stars and the shape of your earth are the witnesses of your gain; whereas a handful of pages, no matter how much you have made them your own, are, at best, but an obscure and questionable spoil. Here they are. "Failure"—"Astonishing": take your choice; or perhaps both, or neither—a mere rustle and flutter of pieces of paper settling down in the night, and undistinguishable, like the snowflakes of a great drift destined to melt away in sunshine.

"How do you do?"

It was the greeting of the general's daughter. I had heard nothing—no rustle, no footsteps. I had felt only a moment before a sort of premonition of evil; I had the sense of an inauspicious presence—just that much warning and no more; and then came the sound of the voice and the jar as of a terrible fall from a great height—a fall, let us say, from the highest of the clouds floating in gentle procession over the fields in the faint westerly air of that July afternoon. I picked myself up quickly, of course; in other words, I jumped up from my chair stunned and dazed, every nerve quivering with the pain of being uprooted out of one world and flung down into another—perfectly civil.

"Oh! How do you do? Won't you sit down?"

That's what I said. This horrible but, I assure you, perfectly true reminiscence tells you more than a whole volume of confessions *à la* Jean Jacques Rousseau would do. Observe! I didn't howl at her, or start upsetting furniture, or throw myself on the floor and kick, or allow myself to hint in any other way at the appalling magnitude of the disaster. The whole world of Costaguana (the country, you may remember, of my seaboard tale), men, women, headlands, houses, mountains, town, *campo* (there was not a single brick, stone, or grain of sand of its soil I had not placed in position with my hands); all the history, geography, politics, finance; the wealth of Charles Gould's silver-mine, and the splendor of the magnificent Capataz de Cargadores, whose name, cried out in the night (Dr. Monygham heard it pass over his head —in Linda Viola's voice), dominated even after death the dark gulf containing his conquests of treasure and love—all that had come down crashing about my ears. I felt I could never pick up the pieces—and in that very minute I was saying, "Won't you sit down?"

The sea is strong medicine. Behold what the quarter-deck training even in a merchant ship will do! This episode

should give you a new view of the English and Scottish seamen (a much-caricatured folk) who had the last say in the
formation of my character. One is nothing if not modest,
but in this disaster I think I have done some honor to their
simple teaching. "Won't you sit down?" Very fair; very
fair indeed. She sat down. Her amused glance strayed all
over the room. There were pages of manuscript on the table
and under the table, a batch of typed copy on a chair, single
leaves had fluttered away into distant corners; there were
there living pages, pages scored and wounded, dead pages
that would be burnt at the end of the day—the litter of a
cruel battlefield, of a long, long and desperate fray. Long!
I suppose I went to bed sometimes, and got up the same number of times. Yes, I suppose I slept, and ate the food put
before me, and talked connectedly to my household on suitable occasions. But I had never been aware of the even flow
of daily life, made easy and noiseless for me by a silent,
watchful, tireless affection. Indeed, it seemed to me that I
had been sitting at that table surrounded by the litter of a
desperate fray for days and nights on end. It seemed so,
because of the intense weariness of which that interruption
had made me aware—the awful disenchantment of a mind
realizing suddenly the futility of an enormous task, joined to
a bodily fatigue such as no ordinary amount of fairly heavy
physical labor could ever account for. I have carried bags
of wheat on my back, bent almost double under a ship's
deck-beams, from six in the morning till six in the evening
(with an hour and a half off for meals), so I ought to know.

   And I love letters. I am jealous of their honor and concerned for the dignity and comeliness of their service. I
was, most likely, the only writer that neat lady had ever
caught in the exercise of his craft, and it distressed me not
to be able to remember when it was that I dressed myself
last, and how. No doubt that would be all right in essen-
tials. The fortune of the house included a pair of gray-blue

watchful eyes that would see to that. But I felt somehow as grimy as a Costaguana *lepero* after a day's fighting in the streets, rumpled all over and disheveled down to my very heels. And I am afraid I blinked stupidly. All this was bad for the honor of letters and the dignity of their service. Seen indistinctly through the dust of my collapsed universe, the good lady glanced about the room with a slightly amused serenity. And she was smiling. What on earth was she smiling at? She remarked casually:

"I am afraid I interrupted you."

"Not at all."

She accepted the denial in perfect good faith. And it was strictly true. Interrupted—indeed! She had robbed me of at least twenty lives, each infinitely more poignant and real than her own, because informed with passion, possessed of convictions, involved in great affairs created out of my own substance for an anxiously meditated end.

She remained silent for a while, then said with a last glance all round at the litter of the fray:

"And you sit like this here writing your—your . . ."

"I—what? Oh, yes! I sit here all day."

"It must be perfectly delightful."

I suppose that, being no longer very young, I might have been on the verge of having a stroke; but she had left her dog in the porch, and my boy's dog, patrolling the field in front, had espied him from afar. He came on straight and swift like a cannon ball, and the noise of the fight, which burst suddenly upon our ears, was more than enough to scare away a fit of apoplexy. We went out hastily and separated the gallant animals. Afterwards I told the lady where she would find my wife—just round the corner, under the trees. She nodded and went off with her dog, leaving me appalled before the death and devastation she had lightly made—and with the awfully instructive sound of the word "delightful" lingering in my ears.

THE ORIGIN OF A HEROINE

Since this Note is mostly concerned with personal contacts
and the origins of the persons in the tale, I am bound also to
speak of Lena, because if I were to leave her out it would
look like a slight; and nothing would be further from my
thoughts than putting a slight on Lena. If of all the personages involved in the "mystery of Samburan" I have lived
longest with Heyst (or with him I call Heyst), it was at her,
whom I call Lena, that I have looked the longest and with a
most sustained attention. This attention originated in idleness for which I have a natural talent. One evening I wandered into a café, in a town not of the tropics but of the
South of France. It was filled with tobacco smoke, the hum
of voices, the rattling of dominoes, and the sounds of strident
music. The orchestra was rather smaller than the one that
performed at Schomberg's hotel, had the air more of a family
party than of an enlisted band, and I must confess, seemed
rather more respectable than the Zangiacomo musical enterprise. It was less pretentious also, more homely and familiar,
so to speak, insomuch that in the intervals when all the performers left the platform one of them went amongst the
marble tables collecting offerings of sous and francs in a battered tin receptacle recalling the shape of a sauceboat. It
was a girl. Her detachment from her task seems to me now
to have equaled or even surpassed Heyst's aloofness from all
the mental degradations to which a man's intelligence is exposed in its way through life. Silent and wide-eyed she went
from table to table with the air of a sleep-walker, and with
no other sound but the slight rattle of the coins to attract
attention. It was long after the sea chapter of my life had
been closed, but it is difficult to discard completely the characteristics of half a lifetime, and it was in something of the
jack-ashore spirit that I dropped a five-franc piece into the
sauceboat; whereupon the sleepwalker turned her head to

gaze at me and said *"Merci, Monsieur,"* in a tone in which there was no gratitude, but only surprise. I must have been idle indeed to take the trouble to remark on such slight evidence that the voice was very charming, and when the performers resumed their seats I shifted my position slightly in order not to have that particular performer hidden from me by the little man with the beard who conducted and who might for all I know have been her father, but whose real mission in life was to be a model for the Zangiacomo of *Victory*. Having got a clear line of sight I naturally (being idle) continued to look at the girl through all the second part of the program. The shape of her dark head inclined over the violin was fascinating, and, while resting between the pieces of that interminable program, she was, in her white dress and with her brown hands reposing in her lap, the very image of dreamy innocence. The mature, bad-tempered woman at the piano might have been her mother, though there was not the slightest resemblance between them. All I am certain of in their personal relation to each other is that cruel pinch on the upper part of the arm. That I am sure I have seen! There could be no mistake. I was in a too idle mood to imagine such a gratuitous barbarity. It may have been playfulness, yet the girl jumped up as if she had been stung by a wasp. It may have been playfulness. Yet I saw plainly poor "dreamy innocence" rub gently the affected place as she filed off with the other performers down the middle aisle between the marble tables in the uproar of voices, the rattling of dominoes, through a blue atmosphere of tobacco smoke. I believe that those people left the town next day.

Or perhaps they had only migrated to the other big café, on the other side of the Place de la Comédie. It is very possible. I did not go across to find out. It was my perfect idleness that had invested the girl with a peculiar charm, and I did not want to destroy it by any superfluous exertion.

The receptivity of my indolence made the impression so
permanent that when the moment came for her meeting with
Heyst I felt that she would be heroically equal to every demand of the risky and uncertain future. I was so convinced
of it that I let her go with Heyst, I won't say without a pang,
but certainly without misgivings. And in view of her triumphant end, what more could I have done for her rehabili-
tation and her happiness?

[A Note on *Victory,* by Mrs. Conrad: I remember the day so
well this novel was finished. He had been having many troubled
days fighting his way to the end of it. He had been very erratic,
and had taken his meals mostly alone for two or three weeks. . . .
I was feeling the strain little less than he, and the day on which the
last words were added, I had gone into the garden, finding it impossible to rest in the house. I stood talking to the old gardener in
low tones, when the window above me was thrown violently open,
and Conrad thrust his head out. His voice was hoarse, and his appearance disheveled; the gardener lifted a scared face. "She's dead,
Jess!" "Who?" I asked, suddenly feeling sick. "Why, Lena, of
course, and I have got the title; it is *Victory.*" He flung the
cigarette out of the window and muttered the injunction, "Don't
come near me. I am going to lie down."]

VERDICTS AND REBUTTALS

[Although Conrad continued his creative writing until his death
in 1924, he had begun some years before that to take stock, as it
were,—to evaluate his works, and to generalize on the literary
principles which they embodied. This closing section brings together some passages that reveal his high seriousness both as an artist
and as a man. Having early proclaimed the creed of the artist in
the famous preface to *The Nigger of the "Narcissus,"* he now sub-
jected his whole work to a more experienced judgment. Having
grown prone by the writing of novels to examine human motives
and human values, he naturally and inevitably returned from time
to time to self-portrayal and self-examination.]

I proceed to admit that, upon the whole, my previous state of existence was not a good equipment for a literary life. Perhaps I should not have used the word *literary*. That word presupposes an intimacy of acquaintance with letters, a turn of mind and a manner of feeling to which I dare lay no claim. I only love letters; but the love of letters does not make a literary man, any more than the love of the sea makes a seaman. And it is very possible, too, that I love the letters in the same way a literary man may love the sea he looks at from the shore—a scene of great endeavor and of great achievements changing the face of the world, the great open way to all sorts of undiscovered countries. No, perhaps I had better say that the life at sea—and I don't mean a mere taste of it, but a good broad span of years, something that really counts as real service—is not, upon the whole, a good equipment for a writing life. God forbid, though, that I should be thought of as denying my masters of the quarter-deck. I am not capable of that sort of apostasy. I have confessed my attitude of piety towards their shades in three or four tales, and if any man on earth more than another needs to be true to himself as he hopes to be saved, it is certainly the writer of fiction.

What I meant to say, simply, is that the quarter-deck training does not prepare one sufficiently for the reception of literary criticism. Only that, and no more. But this defect is not without gravity. If it be permissible to twist, invert, adapt, (and spoil) M. Anatole France's definition of a good critic, then let us say that the good author is he who contemplates without marked joy or excessive sorrow the adventures of his soul amongst criticisms. Far be from me the intention to mislead an attentive public into the belief that there is no criticism at sea. That would be dishonest, and even impolite. Everything can be found at sea, according to the spirit of your quest—strife, peace, romance, naturalism of the most pronounced kind, ideals, boredom.

disgust, inspiration, and every conceivable opportunity, including the opportunity to make a fool of yourself—exactly as in the pursuit of literature. But the quarter-deck criticism is somewhat different from literary criticism. This much they have in common, that before the one and the other the answering back, as a general rule, does not pay.

Perhaps you won't find it presumption if after twenty-two years of work, I may say that I have not been very well understood. I have been called a writer of the sea, of the tropics, a descriptive writer, a romantic writer, and also a realist. But as a matter of fact all my concern has been with the *ideal* value of things, events, and people. That and nothing else. The humorous, the pathetic, the passionate, the sentimental aspects came in of themselves—*mais en vérité c'est valeurs idéales des faits et gestes humains qui se sont imposés à mon activité artistique.*

Whatever dramatic and narrative gifts I may have are always, instinctively, used with that object—to get at, to bring forth *les valeurs idéales.*

THE ROMANTIC FEELING OF REALITY

A reviewer observed that I liked to write of men who go to sea or live on lonely islands untrammeled by the pressure of worldly circumstances because such characters allowed freer play to my imagination, which in their case was only bounded by natural laws and the universal human conventions. There is a certain truth in this remark, no doubt. It is only the suggestion of deliberate choice that misses its mark. I have not sought for special imaginative freedom or a larger play of fancy in my choice of characters and subjects. The nature of the knowledge, suggestions, or hints used in my imaginative work has depended directly on the conditions of my active life. It depended more on contacts,

and very slight contacts at that, than on actual experience;
because my life as a matter of fact is far from being adventurous in itself. Even now when I look back on it with
a certain regret (who would not regret his youth?) and
positive affection, its coloring wears the sober hue of hard
work and exacting calls of duty; things which in themselves
are not much charged with a feeling of romance. If these
things appeal strongly to me even in retrospect, it is, I suppose, because the romantic feeling of reality was in me an
inborn faculty. This in itself may be a curse, but, when disciplined by a sense of personal responsibility and a recognition of the hard facts of existence shared with the rest of
mankind, becomes but a point of view from which the very
shadows of life appear endowed with an internal glow. And
such romanticism is not a sin. It is none the worse for the
knowledge of truth. It only tries to make the best of it,
hard as it may be; and in this hardness discovers a certain
aspect of beauty.

I am speaking here of romanticism in relation to life, not
of romanticism in relation to imaginative literature, which,
in its early days, was associated simply with mediæval subjects, or, at any rate, with subjects sought for in a remote
past. My subjects are not mediæval, and I have a natural
right to them because my past is very much my own. If
their course lie out of the beaten path of organized social
life, it is, perhaps, because I myself did in a sort break away
from it early in obedience to an impulse which must have
been very genuine since it has sustained me through all the
dangers of disillusion. But that origin of my literary work
was very far from giving a larger scope to my imagination.
On the contrary, the mere fact of dealing with matters outside the general run of everyday experience laid me under
the obligation of a more scrupulous fidelity to the truth of
my own sensations. The problem was to make unfamiliar
things credible. To do that I had to create for them, to

reproduce for them, to envelop them in their proper atmosphere of actuality. This was the hardest task of all and the most important, in view of that conscientious rendering of truth in thought and fact which has been always my aim.

SEA STUFF

You know yourself very well that in the body of my work barely one-tenth is what may be called sea stuff, and even of that, the bulk, that is *Nigger* and *Mirror*, has a very special purpose . . . . Of course, there are seamen in a good many of my books. That doesn't make them sea stories any more than the existence of de Barral in *Chance* (and he occupies there as much space as Captain Anthony) makes that novel a story about the financial world . . .

Youth has been called a fine sea-story. Is it? Well, I won't bore you with a discussion of fundamentals. But surely those stories of mine where the sea enters can be looked at from another angle. In the *Nigger* I give the psychology of a group of men and render certain aspects of nature. But the problem that faces them is not a problem of the sea, it is merely a problem that has arisen on board a ship where the conditions of complete isolation from all land entanglements make it stand out with a particular force and coloring. In other of my tales the principal point is the study of a particular man, or a particular event. My only sea book, and the only tribute to a life which I have lived in my own particular way, is *The Mirror of the Sea.*

As a matter of fact I have written of the sea very little if the pages were counted. It has been the scene, but very seldom the aim, of my endeavor. It is too late after all those years to try to keep back the truth; so I will confess here that when I launched my first paper boats in the days of my literary childhood, I aimed at an element as restless, as dangerous, as changeable as the sea, and even more vast;—the unappeasable ocean of human life.

THE ARTIST AND MANKIND

As for the writing of novels . . . . I have always approached my task in the spirit of love for mankind.

I would not like to be left standing as a mere spectator on the bank of the great stream carrying onward so many lives. I would fain claim for myself the faculty of so much insight as can be expressed in a voice of sympathy and compassion.

I am content to sympathize with common mortals, no matter where they live; in houses or in tents, in the streets under a fog, or in the forests behind the dark line of dismal mangroves that fringe the vast solitude of the sea. For, their land—like ours—lies under the inscrutable eyes of the Most High. Their hearts—like ours—must endure the load of the gifts from Heaven: the curse of facts and the blessing of illusions, the bitterness of our wisdom and the deceptive consolation of our folly.

There are those who say that a native will not speak to a white man. Error. No man will speak to his master; but to a wanderer and a friend, to him who does not come to teach or to rule, to him who asks for nothing and accepts all things, words are spoken by the camp fires, in the shared solitude of the sea, in riverside villages, in resting places surrounded by forests—words are spoken that take no account of race or color. One heart speaks—another one listens; and the earth, the sea, the sky, the passing wind and the stirring leaf, hear also the futile burden of life.

I think that all ambitions are lawful except those which climb upward on the miseries or credulities of mankind. All intellectual and artistic ambitions are permissible, up to and even beyond the limit of prudent sanity. They can hurt no one. If they are mad, then so much the worse for the artist. Indeed, as virtue is said to be, such ambitions are their own reward.

As in political, so in literary action, a man wins friends for himself mostly by the passion of his prejudices and by the consistent narrowness of his outlook. But I have never been able to love what was not lovable or hate what was not hateful out of deference for some general principle. Whether there be any courage in making this admission, I know not. After the middle turn of life's way we consider dangers and joys with a tranquil mind. So I proceed in peace to declare that I have always suspected, in the effort to bring into play the extremities of emotions, the debasing touch of insincerity. In order to move others deeply we must deliberately allow ourselves to be carried away beyond the bounds of our normal sensibility—innocently enough, perhaps, and of necessity, like an actor who raises his voice on the stage above the pitch of natural conversation—but still we have to do that. And surely this is no great sin. But the danger lies in the writer becoming the victim of his own exaggeration, losing the exact notion of sincerity, and in the end coming to despise truth itself as something too cold, too blunt for his purpose—as, in fact, not good enough for his insistent emotion. From laughter and tears the descent is easy to snivelling and giggles.

I do not mean to hint that anybody had ever done me the injury (I don't mean insult, I mean injury) of charging a single one of my pages with didactic purpose. But every subject in the region of intellect and emotion must have a morality of its own if it is treated at all sincerely; and even the most artful of writers will give himself (and his morality) away in about every third sentence. The varied shades of moral significance which have been discovered in my writings are very numerous. None of them, however, has provoked a hostile manifestation. It may have happened to me to sin against taste now and then, but apparently I have never sinned against the basic feelings and elementary convictions which make life possible to the mass of mankind, and, by establishing a standard of judgment, set their idealism free to look for plainer ways, for higher feelings, for deeper purposes.

The ethical view of the universe involves us at last in so many cruel and absurd contradictions, where the last vestiges of faith, hope, charity, and even of reason itself, seem ready to perish, that I have come to suspect that the aim of creation cannot be ethical at all. I would fondly believe that its object is purely spectacular; a spectacle for awe, love, adoration, or hate, if you like, but in this view—and in this view alone—never for despair! Those visions, delicious or poignant, are a moral end in themselves. The rest is our affair—the laughter, the tears, the tenderness, the indignation, the high tranquillity of a steeled heart, the detached curiosity of a subtle mind—that's our affair! And the unwearied self-forgetful attention to every phase of the living universe reflected in our consciousness may be our appointed task on this earth—a task in which fate has perhaps engaged nothing of us except our conscience, gifted with a voice in order to bear true testimony to the visible wonder, the haunting terror, the infinite passion, and the illimitable serenity; to the supreme law and the abiding mystery of the sublime spectacle.

Of him from whose armory of phrases one in a hundred thousand may perhaps hit the far-distant and elusive mark of art I would ask that in his dealings with mankind he

should be capable of giving a tender recognition to their
obscure virtues. I would not have him impatient with their
small failings and scornful of their errors. I would not have
him expect too much gratitude from that humanity whose
fate, as illustrated in individuals, it is open to him to depict
as ridiculous or terrible. I would wish him to look with a
large forgiveness at men's ideas and prejudices, which are by
no means the outcome of malevolence, but depend on their
education, their social status, even their professions. The
good artist should expect no recognition of his toil and no
admiration of his genius, because his toil can with difficulty
be appraised and his genius cannot possibly mean anything
to the illiterate who, even from the dreadful wisdom of their
evoked dead, have, so far, culled nothing but inanities and
platitudes. I would wish him to enlarge his sympathies by
patient and loving observation while he grows in mental
power. It is in the impartial practice of life, if anywhere,
that the promise of perfection for his art can be found,
rather than in the absurd formulas trying to prescribe this
or that particular method of technique or conception. Let
him mature the strength of his imagination amongst the
things of this earth, which it is his business to cherish and
know, and refrain from calling down his inspiration ready-
made from some heaven of perfection of which he knows
nothing. And I would not grudge him the proud illusion
that will come sometimes to a writer: the illusion that his
achievement has almost equalled the greatness of his dream.

PART TWO

CONRAD'S FICTION

A book is a deed, . . . the writing of it is an enterprise as much as the conquest of a colony.

INTRODUCTION TO CONRAD'S FICTION

The fiction of Conrad is essentially the re-presentation of the life he had lived. Many of his stories grew entirely out of his own experience, and even those that had their basis either in his imagination or in some once-current tale he had heard and stored away in memory are colored by his experience and are given direction by his philosophy of life. Marlow in *Youth* is Conrad himself; the newly appointed captain in *The Secret Sharer,* faced with the problems of a strange ship and a strange crew, also sprang full-sized from Conrad's own life; likewise, the captain in *The Shadow Line* (See "First Command,") fighting the discouraging battle against an epidemic of tropical fever, is Conrad. The story found in *Typhoon* is largely an imaginative one, although Conrad had been told the story of a steamship full of coolies returning from Singapore to some port in northern China. But the remarkable description of the typhoon he did create out of his intimate knowledge of the gales that menace ships in Eastern waters. Moreover, of the captain of the *Nan-Shan* Conrad says: "MacWhirr is not the acquaintance of a few hours, or a few weeks, or a few months. He is the product of twenty years of life. My own life."

Conrad lived his life and then wrote, and since so much of his life was lived on the sea, much of the writing of Conrad is "sea stuff." Again and again the sea recurs as setting, and in some of the novels it seems to dominate. In *The Nigger of the "Narcissus"* it is practically a *dramatis persona*; in *Typhoon* it seems, like Egdon Heath in *The Return*

of the Native, or better, like the great whale in *Moby Dick,*
to symbolize Fate.   Nor could the actual descriptions of
the sea be easily surpassed—the unforgettable dramatic
storms of *Typhoon* and *The Nigger of the "Narcissus";* the
foaming shallow sea of *The Rescue;* its mystery and wonder
in *The Secret Sharer.* Superficially, then Conrad appears to
belong to the long list of writers of the sea—a list including
Marryat, Stevenson, and Sabatini. Actually he does not belong there. From the uproarious entertainment of *Mr. Mid-
shipman Easy,* the pure adventure of *Treasure Island,* or the
romance of *Captain Blood,* it is a far cry to the subtle char-
acterization of the captain in *The Secret Sharer* and the
penetrating study of cowardice and courage in *Lord Jim.*

For after all, Conrad is concerned primarily with men and
women, whom he offers in the fullness of their being.   And
as his handling of character is fundamentally psychological,
the action in his novels proceeds from, and in accordance
with, character.   Thus it is no surprise that Arsat makes his
final heroic resolution, or that MacWhirr is staunch in the
face of a typhoon.   Conrad never tells a story for the sake
of the story alone.   The element of suspense potential in
every page and culminating in a great moment of dramatic
intensity is there artistically, not merely for narrative but
for character.   It is not that Peyrol and Jim die, but *why*
they die.   The completion of a *Rover* or *Typhoon* is not the
end of a tale, but the full and sympathetic comprehension of
a human soul.

Even the sea, then, a word used almost synonymously with
Conrad's name, is incidental.   He has no intention of merely
depicting ships and the exciting incidents of life at sea.
The ambition of Conrad is made of sterner stuff; he is sailing not only the ocean known to sailors, but the more
profound "ocean of human thought." The sea happens to
be his raw material, just as Dorset was for Hardy, and New
England for Hawthorne.   With deliberate intention he em-

ploys the tools and medium most available to his genius to create his interpretation of life.

Conrad's treatment of material is often called romantic realism. The realism derives from knowledge, the romanticism from feeling. In realistic description Conrad is a consummate artist. He conjures up before us with precise details the smoky, huddled forecastle of the *Narcissus*, the terrible rage of a typhoon, the brilliant fertility of tropical Sambir. This Conrad does with sure craft, for he knows of what he speaks. He sailed in the *Narcissus;* he endured storms in the China Sea; he saw Almayer in his island home. But more than mere memory of things seen was requisite; Conrad had also the imagination and the conscientiousness of the artist. His diction tends toward both preciseness and imagery. He searches for the right word: "Give me the right word . . . . and I will move the world." He strives to find the phrase that will express just the *nuance* that will harmonize with the rhythm of the whole. In *The Secret Sharer* the beauty and suggestiveness of the opening description anticipate the sense of calm and mystery inherent in the entire story. Even when Conrad employs abstract terms, as he often does, they are not perfunctory; they gleam with sincerity and have a significance profound and exciting: "O youth! The strength of it, the faith of it, the imagination of it!" So, too, his technical knowledge of sea, ships, and seamanship has the ring of truth. This technical knowledge, after all, is the foundation upon which are reared such structures as *Typhoon* and *The Secret Sharer;* yet never is the realism obtrusive—the idiom so glitters with life and imaginative appeal.

But real as the *Nan-Shan* and the China Sea may be, Conrad's approach is essentially romantic. This does not mean that he is concerned merely with themes of love and adventure; *Victory* and *Youth* are certainly far removed from *Ivanhoe* and *Quentin Durward*. Conrad interprets life in terms of idealism. His characters are real yet ideal. We visualize white-headed, bronze-faced Singleton with his spectacles and *Pelham;* Heyst with his bald head, yellow mustache, and blue eyes; Arlette dark of hair and red of mouth. We visualize his characters, but we scarcely expect to encounter them. They are derived from actuality: the progenitor of Lingard and Peyrol is a *padrone* of the early Mediterranean days; of the Nigger, a black named Wait; of the narrator of *Youth,* Joseph Conrad himself. But over them has played the romantic imagination of a creator, and the result is a galaxy of men and women of unusual personality and heroic proportion.

The technique of Conrad offers a twofold obstacle to the unwary. In the first place, he makes use of the so-called retrogressive method, a method, of course, not unusual. In *Silas Marner* George Eliot goes back fifteen years to the life of Marner in Lantern Yard. Wren's *Beau Geste* opens with the strange events at Zinderneuf, reverts some ten or fifteen years to the childhood of the Gestes, and advances once more to Zinderneuf. But Conrad uses a retrogressive method more frequently and more subtly. At the end of the first chapter of *Typhoon* Captain MacWhirr stands in the chartroom confronted by the fall of the barometer. Time stops. At the beginning of the fourth chapter Captain MacWhirr is still standing in the chartroom observing the steady fall of the barometer. Time begins. The reader, having meanwhile learned an amazing amount concerning the *Nan-Shan,* the mate, the engineer, and the captain—not to forget his wife and his umbrella—is ready to observe and comprehend the acts of the characters on their approaching remarkable voyage. Again and again, through the mind of a character, we retreat to years and incidents and even thoughts in the past. Almayer, gazing at sundown over the gold-flowing river of Pantai, dreamily thinks of Lingard and Nina, of Hudig and Macassar. In such a method there is nothing haphazard or unnatural. A word, an inflection will free a stream of thoughts in the human consciousness. Nor is Conrad irrelevant. These apparent mental digressions fill gaps of the past and assist in comprehension of character. In short, Conrad is apt to disregard the purely chronological sequence of events and to proceed rather by the wholly natural sequence of suggestion and idea.

In the second place, many of the stories are told by a narrator, or even, as in *Lord Jim,* by several narrators. This is not a unique method. In McFee's *The Harbourmaster,* Mr. Spenlove, sitting on the passenger deck of the *Camotan* anchored off Puerto Balboa, spins his tale of Captain Fraley and his wife. *Beau Geste* is told in both the third and first persons. The danger in such a method is the possibility of a disjointed, artificial result. The purpose, in Conrad's stories at least, is to gain credibility, objectivity, and suspense; in the author's words, it is in part to make unfamiliar things seem credible. So we, hearing a tale from the lips of Marlow, hearing him talk in a matter-of-fact digressive way, are lulled into acceptance; the effect is like that of a play within a play. Again, since his characters tell the story, Conrad the author seems detached. In *Lord Jim,* where the purpose clearly is objectivity, the story is told in different lights through different mediums. It is for the reader to harmonize the parts and to weigh judgment.

The Lagoon, The Secret Sharer, and *Typhoon* in this volume are fairly representative of Conrad. They have the glamour of ships, the mystery of the sea, and the resplendence of the East. Here the nobility of men's souls is tested by the conflict of love, friendship, and honor. Here is the suffering of the world, and the beauty and wonder of life. Here, too, Conrad's technique is apparent: a great deal of *The Lagoon* is told in the first person; in *Typhoon* objectivity is achieved by an analysis of the feelings of various individuals in the same situation; in *The Secret Sharer* there is suspense, both physical and spiritual. In all, the diction combines precision with picturesqueness.

Truly the new reader of the stories of Joseph Conrad faces an exciting experience. A new world is here, a world of unusual and heroic figures set against a vivid exotic background, engaged in adventures strange and dramatic. From the time the first page is turned, the characters and scenes become a part of the reader's very life: Tuan Jim, the heroic coward; Peyrol, the magnanimous rover; Wait, the towering, superb negro; and all the seething Malay Archipelago— Lingard's secret river, Java, Sumatra, and Mindanao.

Admiration for the work means respect for the man. An author, says Conrad, reveals himself in every third sentence. Conrad would bear an examination creditably. There is essential truth in McFee's dictum that "the cunning, the avaricious, and the ignoble are not admirers of Conrad." Dignity and sincerity shine through his thought and his expression. He could, as he says, no more think of writing ill when he could write well than of walking lame when he could walk perfectly. Honor, fidelity, and idealism characterize that long gallery from Captain Lingard to Jean Peyrol. Perhaps even steady, sober MacWhirr would admit that he earned his pay. The baser, too, like Almayer, and Willems of *The Outcast of the Islands*, have a depth and universality that arouse pity. But Conrad, interpreting life, presents the weak as well as the strong. Like his Nigger, he has from a pinnacle surveyed the virtues and foibles of the world; but unlike the Nigger, he has looked with tolerance. His irony contains no bitterness, only quiet humor and sympathy for those bewildered by fate or circumstance. With true nobility and infinite compassion Joseph Conrad accepts all mankind: "He was one of us."

THE LAGOON

THE white man, leaning with both arms over the roof of the little house in the stern of the boat, said to the steersman—

"We will pass the night in Arsat's clearing. It is late."

The Malay only grunted, and went on looking fixedly at the river. The white man rested his chin on his crossed arms and gazed at the wake of the boat. At the end of the straight avenue of forests cut by the intense glitter of the river, the sun appeared unclouded and dazzling, poised low over the water that shone smoothly like a band of metal. The forests, somber and dull, stood motionless and silent on each side of the broad stream. At the foot of big, towering trees, trunkless nipa palms rose from the mud of the bank, in bunches of leaves enormous and heavy, that hung unstirring over the brown swirl of eddies. In the stillness of the air every tree, every leaf, every bough, every tendril of creeper and every petal of minute blossoms seemed to have been bewitched into an immobility perfect and final. Nothing moved on the river but the eight paddles that rose flashing regularly, dipped together with a single splash; while the steersman swept right and left with a periodic and sudden flourish of his blade describing a glinting semicircle above his head. The churned-up water frothed alongside with a confused murmur. And the white man's canoe, advancing upstream in the short-lived disturbance of its own making, seemed to enter the portals of a land from which the very memory of motion had forever departed.

The white man, turning his back upon the setting sun,

looked along the empty and broad expanse of the sea-reach. For the last three miles of its course the wandering, hesitating river, as if enticed irresistibly by the freedom of an open horizon, flows straight into the sea, flows straight to the east —to the east that harbors both light and darkness. Astern of the boat the repeated call of some bird, a cry discordant and feeble, skipped along over the smooth water and lost itself, before it could reach the other shore, in the breathless silence of the world.

The steersman dug his paddle into the stream, and held hard with stiffened arms, his body thrown forward. The water gurgled aloud; and suddenly the long straight reach seemed to pivot on its center, the forests swung in a semicircle, and the slanting beams of sunset touched the broadside of the canoe with a fiery glow, throwing the slender and distorted shadows of its crew upon the streaked glitter of the river. The white man turned to look ahead. The course of the boat had been altered at right-angles to the stream, and the carved dragon-head of its prow was pointing now at a gap in the fringing bushes of the bank. It glided through, brushing the overhanging twigs, and disappeared from the river like some slim and amphibious creature leaving the water for its lair in the forests.

The narrow creek was like a ditch: tortuous, fabulously deep; filled with gloom under the thin strip of pure and shining blue of the heaven. Immense trees soared up, invisible behind the festooned draperies of creepers. Here and there, near the glistening blackness of the water, a twisted root of some tall tree showed amongst the tracery of small ferns, black and dull, writhing and motionless, like an arrested snake. The short words of the paddlers reverberated loudly between the thick and somber walls of vegetation. Darkness oozed out from between the trees, through the tangled maze of the creepers, from behind the great fantastic and unstirring leaves; the darkness, mysterious and invincible; the darkness scented and poisonous of impenetrable forests.

The men poled in the shoaling water. The creek broadened, opening out into a wide sweep of a stagnant lagoon. The forests receded from the marshy bank, leaving a level strip of bright green, reedy grass to frame the reflected blueness of the sky. A fleecy pink cloud drifted high above, trailing the delicate coloring of its image under the floating leaves and the silvery blossoms of the lotus. A little house, perched on high piles, appeared black in the distance. Near it, two tall nibong palms, that seemed to have come out of the forests in the background, leaned slightly over the ragged roof, with a suggestion of sad tenderness and care in the droop of their leafy and soaring heads.

The steersman, pointing with his paddle, said, "Arsat is there. I see his canoe fast between the piles."

The polers ran along the sides of the boat glancing over their shoulders at the end of the day's journey. They would have preferred to spend the night somewhere else than on this lagoon of weird aspect and ghostly reputation. Moreover, they disliked Arsat, first as a stranger, and also because he who repairs a ruined house, and dwells in it, proclaims that he is not afraid to live amongst the spirits that haunt the places abandoned by mankind. Such a man can disturb the course of fate by glances or words; while his familiar ghosts are not easy to propitiate by casual wayfarers upon whom they long to wreak the malice of their human master. White men care not for such things, being unbelievers and in league with the Father of Evil, who leads them unharmed through the invisible dangers of this world. To the warnings of the righteous they oppose an offensive pretence of disbelief. What is there to be done?

So they thought, throwing their weight on the end of their long poles. The big canoe glided on swiftly, noiselessly, and smoothly, towards Arsat's clearing, till, in a great rattling of poles thrown down, and the loud murmurs of "Allah be praised!" it came with a gentle knock against the crooked piles below the house.

The boatmen with uplifted faces shouted discordantly, "Arsat! O Arsat!" Nobody came. The white man began to climb the rude ladder giving access to the bamboo platform before the house. The juragan of the boat said sulkily, "We will cook in the sampan, and sleep on the water."

"Pass my blankets and the basket," said the white man, curtly.

He knelt on the edge of the platform to receive the bundle. Then the boat shoved off, and the white man, standing up, confronted Arsat, who had come out through the low door of his hut. He was a man young, powerful, with broad chest and muscular arms. He had nothing on but his sarong. His head was bare. His big, soft eyes stared eagerly at the white man, but his voice and demeanor were composed as he asked, without any words of greeting—

"Have you medicine, Tuan?"

"No," said the visitor in a startled tone. "No. Why? Is there sickness in the house?"

"Enter and see," replied Arsat, in the same calm manner, and turning short round, passed again through the small doorway. The white man, dropping his bundles, followed.

In the dim light of the dwelling he made out on a couch of bamboos a woman stretched on her back under a broad sheet of red cotton cloth. She lay still, as if dead; but her big eyes, wide open, glittered in the gloom, staring upwards at the slender rafters, motionless and unseeing. She was in a high fever, and evidently unconscious. Her cheeks were sunk slightly, her lips were partly open, and on the young face there was the ominous and fixed expression—the absorbed, contemplating expression of the unconscious who are going to die. The two men stood looking down at her in silence.

"Has she been long ill?" asked the traveler.

"I have not slept for five nights," answered the Malay,

in a deliberate tone. "At first she heard voices calling her from the water and struggled against me who held her. But since the sun of today rose she hears nothing—she hears not me. She sees nothing. She sees not me—me!"

He remained silent for a minute, then asked softly—

"Tuan, will she die?"

"I fear so," said the white man, sorrowfully. He had known Arsat years ago, in a far country in times of trouble and danger, when no friendship is to be despised. And since his Malay friend had come unexpectedly to dwell in the hut on the lagoon with a strange woman, he had slept many times there, in his journeys up and down the river. He liked the man who knew how to keep faith in council and how to fight without fear by the side of his white friend. He liked him—not so much perhaps as a man likes his favorite dog—but still he liked him well enough to help and ask no questions, to think sometimes vaguely and hazily in the midst of his own pursuits, about the lonely man and the long-haired woman with audacious face and triumphant eyes, who lived together hidden by the forests—alone and feared.

The white man came out of the hut in time to see the enormous conflagration of sunset put out by the swift and stealthy shadows that, rising like a black and impalpable vapor above the tree-tops, spread over the heaven, extinguishing the crimson glow of floating clouds and the red brilliance of departing daylight. In a few moments all the stars came out above the intense blackness of the earth and the great lagoon, gleaming suddenly with reflected lights, resembled an oval patch of night sky flung down into the hopeless and abysmal night of the wilderness. The white man had some supper out of the basket, then collecting a few sticks that lay about the platform, made up a small fire, not for warmth, but for the sake of the smoke, which would keep off the mosquitoes. He wrapped himself in the blankets and sat with his back against the reed wall of the house, smoking thoughtfully.

Arsat came through the doorway with noiseless steps and squatted down by the fire. The white man moved his outstretched legs a little.

"She breathes," said Arsat in a low voice, anticipating the expected question. "She breathes and burns as if with a great fire. She speaks not; she hears not—and burns!"

He paused for a moment, then asked in a quiet, incurious tone—

"Tuan . . . will she die?"

The white man moved his shoulders uneasily and muttered in a hesitating manner—

"If such is her fate."

"No, Tuan," said Arsat, calmly. "If such is my fate. I hear, I see, I wait. I remember . . . Tuan, do you remember the old days? Do you remember my brother?"

"Yes," said the white man. The Malay rose suddenly and went in. The other, sitting still outside, could hear the voice in the hut. Arsat said: "Hear me! Speak!" His words were succeeded by a complete silence. "O Diamelen!" he cried, suddenly. After that cry there was a deep sigh. Arsat came out and sank down again in his old place.

They sat in silence before the fire. There was no sound within the house, there was no sound near them; but far away on the lagoon they could hear the voices of the boatmen ringing fitful and distinct on the calm water. The fire in the bows of the sampan shone faintly in the distance with a hazy red glow. Then it died out. The voices ceased. The land and the water slept invisible, unstirring, and mute. It was as though there had been nothing left in the world but the glitter of stars streaming, ceaseless and vain, through the black stillness of the night.

The white man gazed straight before him into the darkness with wide-open eyes. The fear and fascination, the inspiration and the wonder of death—of death near, unavoidable, and unseen—soothed the unrest of his race and stirred the most indistinct, the most intimate of his thoughts. The ever-ready suspicion of evil, the gnawing suspicion that lurks in our hearts, flowed out into the stillness round him— into the stillness profound and dumb—and made it appear untrustworthy and infamous, like the placid and impenetrable mask of an unjustifiable violence. In that fleeting and powerful disturbance of his being the earth enfolded in the starlight peace became a shadowy country of inhuman strife, a battle-field of phantoms terrible and charming, august or ignoble, struggling ardently for the possession of our helpless hearts. An unquiet and mysterious country of inextinguishable desires and fears.

A plaintive murmur rose in the night; a murmur saddening and startling, as if the great solitudes of surrounding woods had tried to whisper into his ear the wisdom of their immense and lofty indifference. Sounds hesitating and vague floated in the air round him, shaped themselves slowly into words; and at last flowed on gently in a murmuring stream of soft and monotonous sentences. He stirred like a man waking up and changed his position slightly. Arsat, motionless and shadowy, sitting with bowed head under the stars, was speaking in a low and dreamy tone—

". . . for where can we lay down the heaviness of our trouble but in a friend's heart? A man must speak of war and of love. You, Tuan, know what war is, and you have seen me in time of danger seek death as other men seek life! A writing may be lost; a lie may be written; but what the eye has seen is truth and remains in the mind!"

"I remember," said the white man, quietly. Arsat went on with mournful composure—

"Therefore I shall speak to you of love. Speak in the night. Speak before both night and love are gone—and the eye of day looks upon my sorrow and my shame; upon my blackened face; upon my burnt-up heart."

A sigh, short and faint, marked an almost imperceptible pause, and then his words flowed on, without a stir, without a gesture.

"After the time of trouble and war was over and you went away from my country in the pursuit of your desires, which we, men of the islands, cannot understand, I and my brother became again, as we had been before, the sword-bearers of the Ruler. You know we were men of family, belonging to a ruling race, and more fit than any to carry on our right shoulder the emblem of power. And in the time of prosperity Si Dendring showed us favor, as we, in time of sorrow, had showed to him the faithfulness of our courage. It was a time of peace. A time of deer-hunts and cock-fights; of idle talks and foolish squabbles between men whose bellies are full and weapons are rusty. But the sower watched the young rice-shoots grow up without fear, and the traders came and went, departed lean and returned fat into the river of peace. They brought news, too. Brought lies and truth mixed together, so that no man knew when to rejoice and when to be sorry. We heard from them about you also. They had seen you here and had seen you there. And I was glad to hear, for I remembered the stirring times, and I always remembered you, Tuan, till the time came when my eyes could see nothing in the past, because they had looked upon the one who is dying there—in the house."

He stopped to exclaim in an intense whisper, "O Mara bahia! O Calamity!" then went on speaking a little louder:

"There's no worse enemy and no better friend than a brother, Tuan, for one brother knows another, and in perfect knowledge is strength for good or evil. I loved my brother. I went to him and told him that I could see nothing but one face, hear nothing but one voice. He told me: 'Open your heart so that she can see what is in it—and wait. Patience is wisdom. Inchi Midah may die or our Ruler may throw off his fear of a woman! . . . I waited! . . . You remember the lady with the veiled face, Tuan, and the fear of our Ruler before her cunning and temper. And if she wanted her servant, what could I do? But I fed the hunger of my heart on short glances and stealthy words. I loitered on the path to the bathhouses in the daytime, and when the sun had fallen behind the forest I crept along the jasmine hedges of the women's courtyard. Unseeing, we spoke to one another through the scent of flowers, through the veil of leaves, through the blades of long grass that stood still before our lips; so great was our prudence, so faint was the murmur of our great longing. The time passed swiftly . . . and there were whispers amongst women—and our enemies watched—my brother was gloomy, and I began to think of killing and of a fierce death. . . . We are of a people who take what they want—like you whites. There is a time when a man should forget loyalty and respect. Might and authority are given to rulers, but to all men is given love and strength and courage. My brother said, 'You shall take her from their midst. We are two who are like one.' And I answered, 'Let it be soon, for I find no warmth in sunlight that does not shine upon her.' Our time came when the Ruler and all the great people went to the mouth of the river to fish by torchlight. There were hundreds of boats, and on the white sand, between the water and the forests, dwellings of leaves were built for the households of the Rajahs. The smoke of cooking-fires was like a blue mist of the evening, and many voices rang in it joyfully. While they were making the boats ready to beat up the fish, my brother came to me and said, 'Tonight!' I looked to my weapons, and when the time came our canoe took its place in the circle of boats carrying the torches. The lights blazed on the water, but behind the boats there was darkness. When the shouting began and the excitement made them like mad we dropped out. The water swallowed our fire, and we floated back to the shore that was dark with only here and there the glimmer of embers. We could hear the talk of slave-girls amongst the sheds. Then we found a place deserted and silent. We waited there. She came. She came running along the shore, rapid and leaving no trace, like a leaf driven by the wind into the sea. My brother said gloomily, 'Go and take her; carry her into our boat.' I lifted her in my arms. She panted. Her heart was beating against my breast. I said, 'I take you from those people. You came to the cry of my heart, but my arms take you into my boat against the will of the great!' 'It is right,' said my brother. 'We are men who take what we want and can hold it against many. We should have taken her in daylight.' I said, 'Let us be off'; for since she was in my boat I began to think of our Ruler's many men. 'Yes. Let us be off,' said my brother. 'We are cast out and this boat is our country now—and the sea is our refuge.' He lingered with his foot on the shore, and I entreated him to hasten, for I remembered the strokes of her heart against my breast and thought that two men cannot withstand a hundred. We left, paddling down-stream close to the bank; and as we passed by the creek where they were fishing, the great shouting had ceased, but the murmur of voices was loud like the humming of insects flying at noonday. The boats floated, clustered together, in the red light of torches, under a black roof of smoke; and men talked of their sport. Men that boasted, and praised, and jeered—men that would have been our friends in the morning, but on that night were already our enemies. We paddled swiftly past. We had no more friends in the country of our birth. She sat in the middle of the canoe with covered face; silent as she is now; unseeing as she is now—and I had no regret at what I was leaving because I could hear her breathing close to me—as I can hear her now."

He paused, listened with his ear turned to the doorway, then shook his head and went on:

"My brother wanted to shout the cry of challenge—one cry only—to let the people know we were freeborn robbers who trusted our arms and the great sea. And again I begged him in the name of our love to be silent. Could I not hear her breathing close to me? I knew the pursuit would come quick enough. My brother loved me. He dipped his paddle without a splash. He only said, 'There is half a man in you now—the other half is in that woman. I can wait. When you are a whole man again, you will come back with me here to shout defiance. We are sons of the same mother.' I made no answer. All my strength and all my spirit were in my hands that held the paddle—for I longed to be with her in a safe place beyond the reach of men's anger and of women's spite. My love was so great, that I thought it could guide me to a country where death was unknown, if I could only escape from Inchi Midah's fury and from our Ruler's sword. We paddled with haste, breathing through our teeth. The blades bit deep into the smooth water. We passed out of the river; we flew in clear channels amongst the shallows. We skirted the black coast; we skirted the sand beaches where the sea speaks in whispers to the land; and the gleam of white sand flashed back past our boat, so swiftly she ran upon the water. We spoke not. Only once I said, 'Sleep, Diamelen, for soon you may want all your strength.' I heard the sweetness of her voice, but I never turned my head. The sun rose and still we went on. Water fell from my face like rain from a cloud. We flew in the light and heat. I never looked back, but I knew that my brother's eyes, behind me, were looking steadily ahead, for the boat went as straight as a bushman's dart, when it leaves the end of the sumpitan. There was no better paddler, no better steersman than my brother. Many times, together, we had won races in that canoe. But we never had

put out our strength as we did then—then, when for the
last time we paddled together! There was no braver or
stronger man in our country than my brother. I could not
spare the strength to turn my head and look at him, but
every moment I heard the hiss of his breath getting louder
behind me. Still he did not speak. The sun was high.
The heat clung to my back like a flame of fire. My ribs
were ready to burst, but I could no longer get enough air
into my chest. And then I felt I must cry out with my
last breath, 'Let us rest!' . . . 'Good!' he answered; and his
voice was firm. He was strong. He was brave. He knew
not fear and no fatigue . . . My brother!"

A murmur powerful and gentle, a murmur vast and faint;
the murmur of trembling leaves, of stirring boughs, ran
through the tangled depths of the forests, ran over the starry
smoothness of the lagoon, and the water between the piles
lapped the slimy timber once with a sudden splash. A
breath of warm air touched the two men's faces and passed
on with a mournful sound—a breath loud and short like an
uneasy sigh of the dreaming earth.

Arsat went on in an even, low voice.

"We ran our canoe on the white beach of a little bay close
to a long tongue of land that seemed to bar our road; a long
wooded cape going far into the sea. My brother knew that
place. Beyond the cape a river has its entrance, and
through the jungle of that land there is a narrow path. We
made a fire and cooked rice. Then we lay down to sleep on
the soft sand in the shade of our canoe, while she watched.
No sooner had I closed my eyes than I heard her cry of
alarm. We leaped up. The sun was halfway down the sky
already, and coming in sight in the opening of the bay we
saw a prau manned by many paddlers. We knew it at once;
it was one of our Rajah's praus. They were watching the
shore, and saw us. They beat the gong, and turned the head
of the prau into the bay. I felt my heart become weak

within my breast. Diamelen sat on the sand and covered
her face. There was no escape by sea. My brother laughed.
He had the gun you had given him, Tuan, before you went
away, but there was only a handful of powder. He spoke
to me quickly: 'Run with her along the path. I shall keep
them back, for they have no firearms, and landing in the
face of a man with a gun is certain death for some. Run
with her. On the other side of that wood there is a fisher-
man's house—and a canoe. When I have fired all the shots
I will follow. I am a great runner, and before they can
come up we shall be gone. I will hold out as long as I can,
for she is but a woman—that can neither run nor fight, but
she has your heart in her weak hands.' He dropped behind
the canoe. The prau was coming. She and I ran, and as
we rushed along the path I heard shots. My brother fired—
once—twice—and the booming of the gong ceased. There
was silence behind us. That neck of land is narrow. Before
I heard my brother fire the third shot I saw the shelving
shore, and I saw the water again; the mouth of a broad river.
We crossed a grassy glade. We ran down to the water. I
saw a low hut above the black mud, and a small canoe hauled
up. I heard another shot behind me. I thought, 'That is
his last charge.' We rushed down to the canoe; a man came
running from the hut, but I leaped on him, and we rolled
together in the mud. Then I got up, and he lay still at my
feet. I don't know whether I had killed him or not. I and
Diamelen pushed the canoe afloat. I heard yells behind me,
and I saw my brother run across the glade. Many men were
bounding after him. I took her in my arms and threw her
into the boat, then leaped in myself. When I looked back
I saw that my brother had fallen. He fell and was up again,
but the men were closing round him. He shouted, 'I am
coming!' The men were close to him. I looked. Many
men. Then I looked at her. Tuan, I pushed the canoe! I
pushed it into deep water. She was kneeling forward look-

ing at me, and I said, 'Take your paddle.' while I struck the water with mine. Tuan, I heard him cry. I heard him cry my name twice; and I heard voices shouting, 'Kill! Strike!' I never turned back. I heard him calling my name again with a great shriek, as when life is going out together with the voice—and I never turned my head. My own name! . . . My brother! Three times he called—but I was not afraid of life. Was she not there in that canoe? And could I not with her find a country where death is forgotten—where death is unknown!"

The white man sat up. Arsat rose and stood, an indistinct and silent figure above the dying embers of the fire. Over the lagoon a mist drifting and low had crept, erasing slowly the glittering images of the stars. And now a great expanse of white vapor covered the land: it flowed cold and gray in the darkness, eddied in noiseless whirls round the tree-trunks and about the platform of the house, which seemed to float upon a restless and impalpable illusion of a sea. Only far away the tops of the trees stood outlined on the twinkle of heaven, like a somber and forbidding shore—a coast deceptive, pitiless, and black.

Arsat's voice vibrated loudly in the profound peace.

"I had her there! I had her! To get her I would have faced all mankind. But I had her—and——"

His words went out ringing into the empty distances. He paused, and seemed to listen to them dying away very far—beyond help and beyond recall. Then he said quietly—

"Tuan, I loved my brother."

A breath of wind made him shiver. High above his head, high above the silent sea of mist, the drooping leaves of the palms rattled together with a mournful and expiring sound. The white man stretched his legs. His chin rested on his chest, and he murmured sadly without lifting his head—

"We all love our brothers."

Arsat burst out with an intense whispering violence—

"What did I care who died? I wanted peace in my own heart."

He seemed to hear a stir in the house—listened—then stepped noiselessly. The white man stood up. A breeze was coming in fitful puffs. The stars shone paler as if they had retreated into the frozen depths of immense space. After a chill gust of wind there were a few seconds of perfect calm and absolute silence. Then from behind the black and wavy line of the forests a column of golden light shot up into the heavens and spread over the semicircle of the eastern horizon. The sun had risen. The mist lifted, broke into drifting patches, vanished into thin flying wreaths; and the unveiled lagoon lay, polished and black, in the heavy shadows at the foot of the wall of trees. A white eagle rose over it with a slanting and ponderous flight, reached the clear sunshine and appeared dazzlingly brilliant for a moment, then soaring higher, became a dark and motionless speck before it vanished into the blue as if it had left the earth forever. The white man, standing gazing upwards before the doorway, heard in the hut a confused and broken murmur of distracted words ending with a loud groan. Suddenly Arsat stumbled out with outstretched hands, shivered, and stood still for some time with fixed eyes. Then he said—

"She burns no more."

Before his face the sun showed its edge above the tree tops, rising steadily. The breeze freshened; a great brilliance burst upon the lagoon, sparkled on the rippling water. The forests came out of the clear shadows of the morning, became distinct, as if they had rushed nearer—to stop short in a great stir of leaves, of nodding boughs, of swaying branches. In the merciless sunshine the whisper of unconscious life grew louder, speaking in an incomprehensible voice round the dumb darkness of that human sorrow. Arsat's eyes wandered slowly, then stared at the rising sun.

"I can see nothing," he said half aloud to himself.

"There is nothing," said the white man, moving to the edge of the platform and waving his hand to his boat. A shout came faintly over the lagoon and the sampan began to glide towards the abode of the friend of ghosts.

"If you want to come with me, I will wait all the morning," said the white man, looking away upon the water.

"No, Tuan," said Arsat, softly. "I shall not eat or sleep in this house, but I must first see my road. Now I can see nothing—see nothing! There is no light and no peace in the world; but there is death—death for many. We are sons of the same mother—and I left him in the midst of enemies; but I am going back now."

He drew a long breath and went on in a dreamy tone:

"In a little while I shall see clear enough to strike—to strike. But she has died, and . . . now . . . darkness."

He flung his arms wide open, let them fall along his body, then stood still with unmoved face and stony eyes, staring at the sun. The white man got down into his canoe. The polers ran smartly along the sides of the boat, looking over their shoulders at the beginning of a weary journey. High in the stern, his head muffled up in white rags, the juragan sat moody, letting his paddle trail in the water. The white man, leaning with both arms over the grass roof of the little cabin, looked back at the shining ripple of the boat's wake. Before the sampan passed out of the lagoon into the creek he lifted his eyes. Arsat had not moved. He stood lonely in the searching sunshine; and he looked beyond the great light of a cloudless day into the darkness of a world of illusions.

THE SECRET SHARER[1]

ON MY right hand there were lines of fishing-stakes resembling a mysterious system of half-submerged bamboo fences, incomprehensible in its division of the domain of tropical fishes, and crazy of aspect as if abandoned forever by some nomad tribe of fishermen now gone to the other end of the ocean; for there was no sign of human habitation as far as the eye could reach. To the left a group of barren islets, suggesting ruins of stone walls, towers, and block-houses, had its foundations set in a blue sea that itself looked solid, so still and stable did it lie below my feet; even the track of light from the westering sun shone smoothly, without that animated glitter which tells of an imperceptible ripple. And when I turned my head to take a parting glance at the tug which had just left us anchored outside the bar, I saw the straight line of the flat shore joined to the stable sea, edge to edge, with a perfect and unmarked closeness, in one leveled floor half brown, half blue under the enormous dome of the sky. Corresponding in their insignificance to the islets of the sea, two small clumps of trees, one on each side of the only fault in the impeccable joint, marked the mouth of the river Meinam we had just left on the first pre-

[1]The story on which *The Secret Sharer* is based was, says Conrad, "the common possession of the whole fleet of merchant ships trading to Australia, India, and China." The actual facts were these: In 1880, the mate of the English clipper *Cutty Sark*, Penarth to Anjer, murdered a negro of the crew, who was "particularly incapable and clumsy." The mate, by reputation a tough customer, was later smuggled to an American ship, the *Colorado,* whose captain was in need of a man-handler. The crew of the *Cutty Sark,* learning of the escape, almost mutinied, and the captain, fearing an investigation, stepped overboard when four days out of Anjer. The murderer eventually got seven years in England and lost his papers. After release from prison, he rose again to command—*From* The Log of the *Cutty Sark,* Lubbock.

paratory stage of our homeward journey; and, far back on
the inland level, a larger and loftier mass, the grove surrounding the great Paknam pagoda, was the only thing on
which the eye could rest from the vain task of exploring the
monotonous sweep of the horizon.   Here and there gleams
as of a few scattered pieces of silver marked the windings
of the great river; and on the nearest of them, just within
the bar, the tug steaming right into the land became lost
to my sight, hull and funnel and masts, as though the impassive earth had swallowed her up without an effort, without a tremor   My eye followed the light cloud of her
smoke, now here, now there, above the plain, according to
the devious curves of the stream, but always fainter and
farther away, till I lost it at last behind the miter-shaped hill
of the great pagoda.   And then I was left alone with my
ship, anchored at the head of the Gulf of Siam.

She floated at the starting-point of a long journey, very
still in an immense stillness, the shadows of her spars flung
far to the eastward by the setting sun.   At that moment I
was alone on her decks.   There was not a sound in her—and
around us nothing moved, nothing lived, not a canoe on the
water, not a bird in the air, not a cloud in the sky.   In this
breathless pause at the threshold of a long passage we seemed
to be measuring our fitness for a long and arduous enterprise,
the appointed task of both our existences to be carried out,
far from all human eyes, with only sky and sea for specta-
tors and judges.

There must have been some glare in the air to interfere
with one's sight, because it was only just before the sun left
us that my roaming eyes made out beyond the highest ridge
of the principal islet of the group something which did away
with the solemnity of perfect solitude.   The tide of darkness flowed swiftly; and with tropical suddenness a swarm of
stars came out above the shadowy earth, while I lingered

yet, my hand resting lightly on my ship's rail as if on the
shoulder of a trusted friend. But, with all that multitude
of celestial bodies staring down at one, the comfort of quiet
communion with her was gone for good. And there were
also disturbing sounds by this time—voices, footsteps forward; the steward flitted along the main-deck, a busily min-
istering spirit; a hand-bell tinkled urgently under the poop-
deck. . . .

I found my two officers waiting for me near the supper
table in the lighted cuddy. We sat down at once, and as I
helped the chief mate, I said:

"Are you aware that there is a ship anchored inside the
islands? I saw her mastheads above the ridge as the sun
went down."

He raised sharply his simple face, overcharged by a terrible growth of whisker, and emitted his usual ejaculation:
"Bless my soul, sir! You don't say so!"

My second mate was a round-cheeked, silent young man,
grave beyond his years, I thought; but as our eyes happened
to meet I detected a slight quiver on his lips. I looked down
at once. It was not my part to encourage sneering on board
my ship. It must be said too that I knew very little of my
officers. In consequence of certain events of no particular
significance, except to myself, I had been appointed to the
command only a fortnight before. Neither did I know
much of the hands forward. All these people had been
together for eighteen months or so, and my position was that
of the only stranger on board. I mention this because it has
some bearing on what is to follow. But what I felt most
was my being a stranger to the ship; and if all the truth must
be told, I was somewhat of a stranger to myself. The
youngest man on board (barring the second mate), and un-
tried as yet by a position of the fullest responsibility, I was
willing to take the adequacy of the others for granted. They

had simply to be equal to their tasks; but I wondered how far I should turn out faithful to that ideal conception of one's own personality every man sets up for himself secretly.

Meanwhile the chief mate, with an almost visible effect of collaboration on the part of his round eyes and frightful whiskers, was trying to evolve a theory of the anchored ship. His dominant trait was to take all things into earnest consideration. He was of a painstaking turn of mind. As he used to say, he "liked to account to himself" for practically everything that came his way, down to a miserable scorpion he had found in his cabin the week before. The why and wherefore of that scorpion—how it got on board and came to select his room rather than the pantry (which was a dark place and more what a scorpion would be partial to), and how on earth it managed to drown itself in the inkwell of his writing desk—had exercised him infinitely. The ship within the islands was much more easily accounted for; and just as we were about to rise from table, he made his pronouncement. She was, he doubted not, a ship from home lately arrived. Probably she drew too much water to cross the bar except at the top of spring tides. Therefore she went into that natural harbor to wait for a few days in preference to remaining in an open roadstead.

"That's so," confirmed the second mate, suddenly, in his slightly hoarse voice. "She draws over twenty feet. She's the Liverpool ship *Sephora* with a cargo of coal. Hundred and twenty-three days from Cardiff."

We looked at him in surprise.

"The tugboat skipper told me when he came on board for your letters, sir," explained the young man. "He expects to take her up the river the day after tomorrow."

After thus overwhelming us with the extent of his information, he slipped out of the cabin. The mate observed regretfully that he "could not account for that young fellow's whims." What prevented him telling us all about it at once, he wanted to know.

I detained him as he was making a move. For the last two days the crew had had plenty of hard work, and the night before they had very little sleep. I felt painfully that I—a stranger—was doing something unusual when I directed him to let all hands turn in without setting an anchor-watch. I proposed to keep on deck till one o'clock or thereabouts. I would get the second mate to relieve me at that hour.

"He will turn out the cook and the steward at four," I concluded, "and then give you a call. Of course at the slightest sign of any sort of wind we'll have the hands up and make a start at once."

He concealed his astonishment. "Very well, sir." Outside the cuddy he put his head in the second mate's door to inform him of my unheard-of caprice to take a five hours' anchor-watch on myself. I heard the other raise his voice incredulously— "What? The captain himself?" Then a few more murmurs, a door closed, then another. A few moments later I went on deck.

My strangeness, which had made me sleepless, had prompted that unconventional arrangement, as if I had expected in those solitary hours of the night to get on terms with the ship of which I knew nothing, manned by men of whom I knew very little more. Fast alongside a wharf, littered like any ship in port with a tangle of unrelated things, invaded by unrelated shore people, I had hardly seen her yet properly. Now, as she lay cleared for sea, the stretch of her main-deck seemed to me very fine under the stars. Very fine, very roomy for her size, and very inviting. I descended the poop and paced the waist, my mind picturing to myself the coming passage through the Malay Archipelago, down the Indian Ocean, and up the Atlantic. All its phases were familiar enough to me, every characteristic, all the alternatives which were likely to face me on the

high seas—everything! . . . Except the novel responsibility
of command. But I took heart from the reasonable thought
that the ship was like other ships, the men like other men,
and that the sea was not likely to keep any special surprises
expressly for my discomfiture.

Arrived at that comforting conclusion, I bethought myself of a cigar and went below to get it. All was still down
there. Everybody at the after end of the ship was sleeping
profoundly. I came out again on the quarter-deck, agree-
ably at ease in my sleeping-suit on that warm breathless
night, barefooted, a glowing cigar in my teeth, and, going
forward, I was met by the profound silence of the fore end
of the ship. Only as I passed the door of the forecastle I
heard a deep, quiet, trustful sigh of some sleeper inside. And
suddenly I rejoiced in the great security of the sea as compared with the unrest of the land, in my choice of that un-
tempted life presenting no disquieting problems, invested
with an elementary moral beauty by the absolute straight-
forwardness of its appeal and by the singleness of its purpose.

The riding-light in the fore-rigging burned with a clear,
untroubled, as if symbolic, flame, confident and bright in the
mysterious shades of the night. Passing on my way aft
along the other side of the ship, I observed that the rope
side-ladder, put over, no doubt, for the master of the tug
when he came to fetch away our letters, had not been hauled
in as it should have been. I became annoyed at this, for
exactitude in small matters is the very soul of discipline.
Then I reflected that I had myself peremptorily dismissed
my officers from duty, and by my own act had prevented
the anchor-watch from being formally set and things properly attended to. I asked myself whether it was wise ever
to interfere with the established routine of duties even from
the kindest of motives. My action might have made me
appear eccentric. Goodness only knew how that absurdly
whiskered mate would "account" for my conduct, and what

the whole ship thought of the informality of their new captain. I was vexed with myself.

Not from compunction certainly, but, as it were mechanically, I proceeded to get the ladder in myself. Now a side-ladder of that sort is a light affair and comes in easily, yet my vigorous tug, which should have brought it flying aboard, merely recoiled upon my own body in a totally unexpected jerk. What the devil! . . . I was so astounded by the immovableness of that ladder that I remained stock-still, trying to account for it to myself like that imbecile mate of mine. In the end, of course, I put my head over the rail.

The side of the ship made an opaque belt of shadow on the darkling glassy shimmer of the sea. But I saw at once something elongated and pale floating very close to the ladder. Before I could form a guess a faint flash of phosphorescent light, which seemed to issue suddenly from the naked body of a man, flickered in the sleeping water with the elusive, silent play of summer lightning in a night sky. With a gasp I saw revealed to my stare a pair of feet, the long legs, a broad livid back immersed right up to the neck in a greenish cadaverous glow. One hand, awash, clutched the bottom rung of the ladder. He was complete but for the head. A headless corpse! The cigar dropped out of my gaping mouth with a tiny plop and a short hiss quite audible in the absolute stillness of all things under heaven. At that I suppose he raised up his face, a dimly pale oval in the shadow of the ship's side. But even then I could only barely make out down there the shape of his black-haired head. However, it was enough for the horrid frost-bound sensation which had gripped me about the chest to pass off. The moment of vain exclamations was past, too. I only climbed on the spare spar and leaned over the rail as far as I could, to bring my eyes nearer to that mystery floating alongside.

As he hung by the ladder, like a resting swimmer, the sea-lightning played about his limbs at every stir; and he appeared in it ghastly, silvery, fish-like. He remained as mute as a fish, too. He made no motion to get out of the water, either. It was inconceivable that he should not attempt to come on board, and strangely troubling to suspect that perhaps he did not want to. And my first words were prompted by just that troubled incertitude.

"What's the matter?" I asked in my ordinary voice, speaking down to the face upturned exactly under mine.

"Cramp," it answered, no louder. Then slightly anxious, "I say, no need to call anyone."

"I was not going to," I said.

"Are you alone on deck?"

"Yes."

I had somehow the impression that he was on the point of letting go the ladder to swim away beyond my ken—mysterious as he came. But, for the moment, this being appearing as if he had risen from the bottom of the sea (it was certainly the nearest land to the ship), wanted only to know the time. I told him. And he, down there, tentatively:

"I suppose your captain's turned in?"

"I am sure he isn't," I said.

He seemed to struggle with himself, for I heard something like the low, bitter murmur of doubt. "What's the good?" His next words came out with a hesitating effort.

"Look here, my man. Could you call him out quietly?"

I thought the time had come to declare myself.

"I am the captain."

I heard a "By Jove!" whispered at the level of the water. The phosphorescence flashed in the swirl of the water all about his limbs, his other hand seized the ladder.

"My name's Leggatt."

The voice was calm and resolute. A good voice. The self-possession of that man had somehow induced a corresponding state in myself. It was very quietly that I remarked:

"You must be a good swimmer."

"Yes. I've been in the water practically since nine o'clock. The question for me is whether I am to let go this ladder and go on swimming till I sink from exhaustion, or— to come on board here."

I felt this was no mere formula of desperate speech, but a real alternative in the view of a strong soul. I should have gathered from this that he was young; indeed, it is only the young who are ever confronted by such clear issues. But at the time it was pure intuition on my part. A mysterious communication was already established between us two— in the face of that silent, darkened, tropical sea. I was young, too; young enough to make no comment. The man in the water began suddenly to climb up the ladder, and I hastened away from the rail to fetch some clothes.

Before entering the cabin I stood still, listening in the lobby at the foot of the stairs. A faint snore came through the closed door of the chief mate's room. The second mate's door was on the hook, but the darkness in there was absolutely soundless. He, too, was young and could sleep like a stone. Remained the steward, but he was not likely to wake up before he was called. I got a sleeping-suit out of my room and, coming back on deck, saw the naked man from the sea sitting on the main hatch, glimmering white in the darkness, his elbows on his knees and his head in his hands. In a moment he had concealed his damp body in a sleeping-suit of the same gray-stripe pattern as the one I was wearing and followed me like my double on the poop. Together we moved right aft, barefooted, silent.

"What is it?" I asked in a deadened voice, taking the lighted lamp out of the binnacle, and raising it to his face.

"An ugly business."

He had rather regular features; a good mouth; light eyes under somewhat heavy, dark eyebrows; a smooth, square forehead; no growth on his cheeks; a small, brown mustache, and a well-shaped, round chin. His expression was concentrated, meditative, under the inspecting light of the lamp I held up to his face—such as a man thinking hard in solitude might wear. My sleeping-suit was just right for his size. A well-knit young fellow of twenty-five at most. He caught his lower lip with the edge of white, even teeth.

"Yes," I said, replacing the lamp in the binnacle. The warm, heavy tropical night closed upon his head again.

"There's a ship over there," he murmured.

"Yes, I know. The *Sephora*. Did you know of us?"

"Hadn't the slightest idea. I am the mate of her——" He paused and corrected himself.—"I should say I was."

"Aha! Something wrong?"

"Yes. Very wrong indeed. I've killed a man."

"What do you mean? Just now?"

"No, on the passage. Weeks ago. Thirty-nine south. When I say a man——"

"Fit of temper," I suggested confidently.

The shadowy, dark head, like mine, seemed to nod imperceptibly above the ghostly gray of my sleeping-suit. It was, in the night, as though I had been faced by my own reflection in the depths of a somber and immense mirror.

"A pretty thing to have to own up to for a *Conway* boy," murmured my double distinctly.

"You're a *Conway* boy?"

"I am," he said, as if startled. Then, slowly . . . "Perhaps you too——"

It was so; but being a couple of years older I had left before he joined. After a quick interchange of dates a silence fell; and I thought suddenly of my absurd mate with his terrific whiskers and the "Bless my soul—you don't say so" type of intellect. My double gave me an inkling of his thoughts by saying:

"My father's a parson in Norfolk. Do you see me before a judge and jury on that charge? For myself I can't see the

necessity. There are fellows that an angel from heaven——
And I am not that. He was one of those creatures that are
just simmering all the time with a silly sort of wickedness.
Miserable devils that have no business to live at all. He
wouldn't do his duty and wouldn't let anybody else do theirs.
But what's the good of talking! You know well enough the
sort of ill-conditioned snarling cur——"

He appealed to me as if our experiences had been as identical as our clothes. And I knew well enough the pestiferous
danger of such a character where there are no means of legal
repression. And I knew well enough also that my double
there was no homicidal ruffian. I did not think of asking
him for details, and he told me the story roughly in brusque,
disconnected sentences. I needed no more. I saw it all
going on as though I were myself inside that other sleeping-
suit.

"It happened while we were setting a reefed foresail at
dusk. Reefed foresail! You understand the sort of
weather. The only sail we had left to keep the ship running; so you may guess what it had been like for days.
Anxious sort of job, that. He gave me some of his cursed
insolence at the sheet. I tell you I was overdone with this
terrific weather that seemed to have no end to it. Terrific,
I tell you—and a deep ship. I believe the fellow himself
was half crazed with funk. It was no time for gentlemanly reproof, so I turned around and felled him like an
ox. He up and at me. We closed just as an awful sea made
for the ship. All hands saw it coming and took to the rigging, but I had him by the throat and went on shaking him
like a rat, the men above us yelling, 'Look out! Look out!'
Then a crash as if the sky had fallen on my head. They
say that for over ten minutes hardly anything was to be
seen of the ship—just the three masts and a bit of the forecastle head and of the poop all awash driving along in a
smother of foam. It was a miracle that they found us,

jammed together behind the fore-bits. It's clear that I meant business, because I was holding him by the throat still when they picked us up. He was black in the face. It was too much for them. It seems they rushed us aft together, gripped as we were, screaming 'Murder!' like a lot of lunatics, and broke into the cuddy. And the ship running for her life, touch and go, all the time, in a sea fit to turn your hair gray only a-looking at it. I understand that the skipper, too, started raving like the rest of them. The man had been deprived of sleep for more than a week, and to have this sprung on him at the height of a furious gale nearly drove him out of his mind. I wonder they didn't fling me overboard after getting the carcass of their precious shipmate out of my fingers. They had rather a job to separate us, I've been told. A sufficiently fierce story to make an old judge and a respectable jury sit up a bit. The first thing I heard when I came to myself was the maddening howling of that endless gale, and on that the voice of the old man. He was hanging on to my bunk, staring into my face out of his sou'wester.

" 'Mr. Leggatt, you have killed a man. You can no longer act as mate of this ship.' "

His care to subdue his voice made it sound monotonous. He rested a hand on the end of the skylight to steady himself with, and all that time did not stir a limb, so far as I could see. "Nice little tale for a quiet tea-party," he concluded in the same tone.

One of my hands, too, rested on the end of the skylight; neither did I stir a limb, so far as I knew. We stood less than a foot from each other. It occurred to me that if old "Bless my soul—you don't say so" were to put his head up the companion and catch sight of us, he would think he was seeing double, or imagine himself come upon a scene of weird witchcraft; the strange captain having a quiet confabulation by the wheel with his own gray ghost. I became very much concerned to prevent anything of the sort. I heard the other's soothing undertone.

"My father's a parson in Norfolk," it said. Evidently he had forgotten he had told me this important fact before. Truly a nice little tale.

"You had better slip down into my stateroom now," I said, moving off stealthily. My double followed my movements; our bare feet made no sound; I let him in, closed the door with care, and, after giving a call to the second mate, returned on deck for my relief.

"Not much sign of any wind yet," I remarked when he approached. "No, sir. Not much," he assented, sleepily, in his hoarse voice, with just enough deference, no more, and barely suppressing a yawn.

"Well, that's all you have to look out for. You have got your orders."

"Yes, sir."

I paced a turn or two on the poop and saw him take up his position face forward with his elbow in the ratlines of the mizzen-rigging before I went below. The mate's faint snoring was still going on peacefully. The cuddy lamp was burning over the table on which stood a vase with flowers, a polite attention from the ship's provision merchant—the last flowers we should see for the next three months at the very least. Two bunches of bananas hung from the beam symmetrically, one on each side of the rudder-casing. Everything was as before in the ship—except that two of her captain's sleeping-suits were simultaneously in use, one motionless in the cuddy, the other keeping very still in the captain's stateroom.

It must be explained here that my cabin had the form of a capital letter L, the door being within the angle and opening into the short part of the letter. A couch was to the left, the bed-place to the right; my writing-desk and the chronometer's table faced the door; but anyone opening it, unless he stepped right inside, had no view of what I call the long (or vertical) part of the letter. It contained some lockers surmounted by a bookcase; and a few clothes, a thick jacket or two, caps, oilskin coat, and such like, hung on hooks. There was at the bottom of that part a door opening into my bathroom, which could be entered also directly from the saloon. But that way was never used.

The mysterious arrival had discovered the advantage of this particular shape. Entering my room, lighted strongly by a big bulkhead lamp swung on gimbals above my writing-desk, I did not see him anywhere till he stepped out quietly from behind the coats hung in the recessed part.

"I heard somebody moving about, and went in there at once," he whispered.

I, too, spoke under my breath.

"Nobody is likely to come in here without knocking and getting permission."

He nodded. His face was thin and the sunburn faded, as though he had been ill. And no wonder. He had been, I heard presently, kept under arrest in his cabin for nearly seven weeks. But there was nothing sickly in his eyes or in his expression. He was not a bit like me, really; yet, as we stood leaning over my bed-place, whispering side by side, with our dark heads together and our backs to the door, anybody bold enough to open it stealthily would have been treated to the uncanny sight of a double captain busy talking in whispers with his other self.

"But all this doesn't tell me how you came to hang on to our side-ladder," I inquired, in the hardly audible murmurs we used, after he had told me something more of the proceedings on board the *Sephora* once the bad weather was over.

"When we sighted Java Head I had had time to think all those matters out several times over. I had six weeks of doing nothing else, and with only an hour or so every eve-ning for a tramp on the quarter-deck."

He whispered, his arms folded on the side of my bed-place, staring through the open port. And I could imagine perfectly the manner of this thinking out—a stubborn, if not a steadfast, operation; something of which I should have been perfectly incapable.

"I reckoned it would be dark before we closed with the land," he continued, so low that I had to strain my hearing, near as we were to each other, shoulder touching shoulder almost. "So I asked to speak to the old man. He always seemed very sick when he came to see me—as if he could not look me in the face. You know, that foresail saved the ship. She was too deep to have run long under bare poles. And it was I that managed to set it for him. Anyway, he came. When I had him in my cabin—he stood by the door looking at me as if I had the halter around my neck already—I asked him right away to leave my cabin door unlocked at night while the ship was going through Sunda Straits. There would be the Java coast within two or three miles, off Angier Point. I wanted nothing more. I've had a prize for swimming my second year in the Con-way."

"I can believe it," I breathed out.

"God only knows why they locked me in every night. To see some of their faces you'd have thought they were afraid I'd go about at night strangling people. Am I a murdering brute? Do I look it? By Jove! if I had been he wouldn't have trusted himself like that inside my room. You'll say I might have chucked him aside and bolted out, there and then—it was dark already. Well, no. And for the same reason I wouldn't think of trying to smash the door. There would have been a rush to stop me at the noise, and I did not mean to get into a confounded scrim-mage. Somebody else might have got killed—for I would

not have broken out only to get chucked back in—and I
did not want any more of that work. He refused, looking
more sick than ever. He was afraid of the men, and also of
that old second mate of his who had been sailing with him
for years—a gray-headed old humbug; and his steward, too,
had been with him devil knows how long—seventeen years
or more—a dogmatic sort of loafer who hated me like poison,
just because I was chief mate. No chief mate ever made
more than one voyage in the *Sephora,* you know. Those two
old chaps ran the ship. Devil only knows what the skipper
wasn't afraid of (all his nerve went to pieces altogether in
that hellish spell of bad weather we had)—of what the law
would do to him—of his wife, perhaps. Oh, yes! she's on
board. Though I don't think she would have meddled. She
would have been only too glad to have me out of the ship
in any way. The 'brand of Cain' business, don't you see. I
was ready enough to go off wandering on the face of the
earth—and that was price enough to pay for an Abel of that
sort. Anyhow, he wouldn't listen to me. 'This thing must
take its course. I represent the law here.' He was shaking
like a leaf. 'So you won't?' 'No!' 'Then I hope you will
be able to sleep on that,' I said, and turned my back on him.
'I wonder that *you* can,' cries he, and locks the door.

"Well, after that, I couldn't. Not very well. That was
three weeks ago. We have had a slow passage through the
Java Sea; drifted about Carimata for ten days. When we
anchored here they thought, I suppose, that it was all right.
The nearest land (and that's five miles) is the ship's destination; the consul would soon set about catching me; and there
would have been no object in bolting to these islets here. I
don't suppose there's a drop of water on them. I don't know
how it was, but tonight that steward, after bringing me my
supper, went out to let me eat it, and left the door unlocked.
And I ate it—all there was, too. After I had finished I
strolled out on the quarter-deck. I don't know that I meant

to do anything.   A breath of fresh air was all I wanted, I believe.   Then a sudden temptation came over me.   I kicked off my slippers and was in the water before I had made up my mind fairly.   Somebody heard the splash and they raised an awful hullabaloo.   'He's gone!   Lower the boats!   He's committed suicide.   No, he's swimming.'   Certainly I was swimming.   It's not so easy for a swimmer like me to commit suicide by drowning.   I landed on the nearest islet before the boat left the ship's side.   I heard them pulling about in the dark, hailing, and so on, but after a bit they gave it up.   Everything quieted down, and the anchorage became as still as death.   I sat down on a stone and began to think. I felt certain they would start searching for me at daylight. There was no place to hide on those stony things—and if there had been, what would have been the good?   But now I was clear of that ship, I was not going back.   So after a while I took off all my clothes, tied them in a bundle with a stone inside, and dropped them in the deep water on the outer side of that islet.   That was suicide enough for me. Let them think what they liked, but I didn't mean to drown myself.   I meant to swim till I sank—but that's not the same thing.   I struck out for another of these little islets, and it was from that one that I first saw your riding-light.   Something to swim for.   I went on easily, and on the way I came upon a flat rock a foot or two above the water.   In the daytime, I dare say, you might make it out with a glass from your poop.   I scrambled up on it and rested myself for a bit. Then I made another start.   That last spell must have been over a mile."

His whisper was getting fainter and fainter, and all the time he stared straight out through the porthole, in which there was not even a star to be seen.   I had not interrupted him.   There was something that made comment impossible in his narrative; or perhaps in himself; a sort of feeling, a quality, which I can't find a name for.   And when he ceased,

all I found was a futile whisper: "So you swam for our
light?"

"Yes—straight for it. It was something to swim for.
I couldn't see any stars low down because the coast was in
the way, and I couldn't see the land, either. The water was
like glass. One might have been swimming in a confounded
thousand-feet deep cistern with no place for scrambling out
anywhere; but what I didn't like was the prospect of swimming round and round like a crazed bullock before I gave
out; and as I didn't mean to go back . . . No. Do you
see me being hauled back, stark naked, off one of these little
islands by the scruff of the neck and fighting like a wild
beast? Somebody would have got killed for certain, and I
did not want any of that. So I went on. Then your ladder——"

"Why didn't you hail the ship?" I asked, a little louder.

He touched my shoulder lightly. Lazy footsteps came
right over our heads and stopped. The second mate had
crossed from the other side of the poop and might have been
hanging over the rail, for all we knew.

"He couldn't hear us talking—could he?" my double
breathed into my ear, anxiously.

His anxiety was an answer, a sufficient answer, to the
question I had put to him. An answer containing all the
difficulty of the situation. I closed the porthole quietly,
to make sure. A louder word might have been overheard.

"Who's that?" he whispered then.

"My second mate. But I don't know much more about
the fellow than you do."

And I told him a little about myself. I had been appointed to take charge while I least expected anything of
the sort, not quite a fortnight ago. I didn't know either
the ship or the people. Hadn't had time in port to look
about me or size anybody up. And as to the crew, all they
knew was that I was appointed to take the ship home. For

the rest, I was almost as much of a stranger on board as himself, I said. And at the moment I felt it most acutely. I felt that it would take very little to make me a suspect person in the eyes of the ship's company.

He had turned about meanwhile; and we, the two strangers in the ship, faced each other in identical attitudes.

"Your ladder——" he murmured, after a silence. "Who'd have thought of finding a ladder hanging over at night in a ship anchored out here! I felt just then a very unpleasant faintness. After the life I've been leading for nine weeks, anybody would have got out of condition. I wasn't capable of swimming around as far as your rudder-chains. And lo and behold! there was a ladder to get hold of. After I gripped it I said to myself, 'What's the good?' When I saw a man's head looking over I thought I would swim away presently and leave him shouting—in whatever language it was. I didn't mind being looked at. I—I liked it. And then you speaking to me so quietly—as if you had expected me—made me hold on a little longer. It had been a confoundedly lonely time—I don't mean while swimming. I was glad to talk a little to somebody that didn't belong to the *Sephora*. As to asking for the captain, that was a mere impulse. It could have been no use, with all the ship knowing about me and the other people pretty certain to be around here in the morning. I don't know—I wanted to be seen, to talk to somebody, before I went on. I don't know what I would have said. . . . 'Fine night, isn't it?' or something of the sort."

"Do you think they will be around here presently?" I asked with some incredulity.

"Quite likely," he said, faintly.

He looked extremely haggard all of a sudden. His head rolled on his shoulders.

"H'm. We shall see then. Meanwhile get into that bed," I whispered. "Want help? There."

It was a rather high bed-place with a set of drawers underneath. This amazing swimmer really needed the lift I gave him by seizing his leg. He tumbled in, rolled over on his back, and flung one arm across his eyes. And then, with his face nearly hidden, he must have looked exactly as I used to look in that bed. I gazed upon my other self for a while before drawing across carefully the two green serge curtains which ran on a brass rod. I thought for a moment of pinning them together for greater safety, but I sat down on the couch, and once there I felt unwilling to rise and hunt for a pin. I was extremely tired, in a peculiarly intimate way, by the strain of stealthiness, by the effort of whispering and the general secrecy of this excitement. It was three o'clock now and I had been on my feet since nine, but I was not sleepy; I could not have gone to sleep. I sat there, fagged out, looking at the curtains, trying to clear my mind of the confused sensation of being in two places at once, and greatly bothered by an exasperating knocking in my head. It was a relief to discover suddenly that it was not in my head at all, but on the outside of the door. Before I could collect myself the words "Come in" were out of my mouth, and the steward entered with a tray, bringing in my morning coffee. I had slept, after all, and I was so frightened that I shouted, "This way! I am here, steward," as though he had been miles away. He put down the tray on the table next the couch and only then said, very quietly, "I can see you are here, sir." I felt him give me a keen look, but I dared not meet his eyes just then. He must have wondered why I had drawn the curtains of my bed before going to sleep on the couch. He went out, hooking the doors open as usual.

I heard the crew washing the decks above me. I knew I would have been told at once if there had been any wind. Calm, I thought, and I was doubly vexed. Indeed, I felt more dual than ever. The steward reappeared suddenly in the doorway. I jumped up from the couch so quickly that he gave a start.

"What do you want here?"

"Close your port, sir—they are washing decks."

"It is closed," I said, reddening.

"Very well, sir." But he did not move from the doorway and returned my stare in an extraordinary, equivocal manner for a time. Then his eyes wavered, all his expression changed, and in a voice unusually gentle, almost coaxingly:

"May I come in to take the empty cup away, sir?"

"Of course!" I turned my back on him while he popped in and out. Then I unhooked and closed the door and even pushed the bolt. This sort of thing could not go on very long. The cabin was as hot as an oven, too. I took a peep at my double, and discovered that he had not moved, his arm was still over his eyes; but his chest heaved; his hair was wet; his chin glistened with perspiration. I reached over him and opened the port.

"I must show myself on deck," I reflected.

Of course, theoretically, I could do what I liked, with no one to say me nay within the whole circle of the horizon; but to lock my cabin door and take the key away I did not dare. Directly I put my head out of the companion I saw the group of my two officers, the second mate barefooted, the chief mate in long india-rubber boots, near the break of the poop, and the steward halfway down the poop-ladder talking to them eagerly. He happened to catch sight of me and dived, the second ran down on the main-deck shouting some order or other, and the chief mate came to meet me, touching his cap.

There was a sort of curiosity in his eye that I did not like. I don't know whether the steward had told them that I was "queer" only, or downright drunk, but I know the man meant to have a good look at me. I watched him coming with a smile which, as he got into point-blank range, took effect and froze his very whiskers. I did not give him time to open his lips.

"Square the yards by lifts and braces before the hands go to breakfast."

It was the first particular order I had given on board that ship; and I stayed on deck to see it executed, too. I had felt the need of asserting myself without loss of time. That sneering young cub got taken down a peg or two on that occasion, and I also seized the opportunity of having a good look at the face of every foremast man as they filed past me to go to the after braces. At breakfast time, eating nothing myself, I presided with such frigid dignity that the two mates were only too glad to escape from the cabin as soon as decency permitted; and all the time the dual working of my mind distracted me almost to the point of insanity. I was constantly watching myself, my secret self, as dependent on my actions as my own personality, sleeping in that bed, behind that door which faced me as I sat at the head of the table. It was very much like being mad, only it was worse because one was aware of it.

I had to shake him for a solid minute, but when at last he opened his eyes it was in the full possession of his senses, with an inquiring look.

"All's well so far," I whispered. "Now you must vanish into the bathroom."

He did so, as noiseless as a ghost, and I then rang for the steward, and facing him boldly, directed him to tidy up my stateroom while I was having my bath— "and be quick about it." As my tone admitted of no excuses, he said, "Yes, sir," and ran off to fetch his dust-pan and brushes. I took a bath and did most of my dressing, splashing and whistling softly for the steward's edification, while the secret sharer of my life stood drawn up bolt upright in that little space, his face looking very sunken in daylight, his eyelids lowered under the stern, dark line of his eyebrows drawn together by a slight frown.

When I left him there to go back to my room, the steward was finishing the dusting. I sent for the mate and engaged him in some insignificant conversation. It was, as it were, trifling with the terrific character of his whiskers; but my object was to give him an opportunity for a good look at my cabin. And then I could at last shut, with a clear conscience, the door of my stateroom and get my double back into the recessed part. There was nothing else for it. He had to sit still on a small folding stool, half smothered by heavy coats hanging there. We listened to the steward going into the bathroom out of the saloon, filling the water-bottles there, scrubbing down the bath, setting things to rights, whisk, bang, clatter—out again into the saloon—turn the key —click. Such was my scheme for keeping my second self invisible. Nothing better could be contrived under the circumstances. And there we sat; I at my writing-desk, ready to appear busy with some papers, he behind me, out of sight of the door. It would not have been prudent to talk in daytime; and I could not have stood the excitement of that queer sense of whispering to myself. Now and then, glancing back over my shoulder, I saw him far back there, sitting rigidly on the low stool, his bare feet close together, his arms folded, his head hanging on his breast—and perfectly still. Anybody would have taken him for me.

I was fascinated by it myself. Every moment I had to glance over my shoulder. I was looking at him when a voice outside the door said:

"Beg pardon, sir."

"Well!" . . . I kept my eyes on him, and so, when the voice outside the door announced, "There's a ship's boat coming our way, sir," I saw him give a start—the first movement he had made for hours. But he did not raise his bowed head.

"All right.   Get the ladder over."

I hesitated.   Should I whisper something to him?   But what?   His immobility seemed to have been never disturbed. What could I tell him he did not know already? . . . Finally I went on deck.

II

The skipper of the *Sephora* had a thin red whisker all round his face, and the sort of complexion that goes with hair of that color; also the particular, rather smeary shade of blue in the eyes.   He was not exactly a showy figure; his shoulders were high, his stature but middling—one leg slightly more bandy than the other.   He shook hands, looking vaguely around.   A spiritless tenacity was his main characteristic, I judged.   I behaved with a politeness which seemed to disconcert him.   Perhaps he was shy.   He mumbled to me as if he were ashamed of what he was saying; gave his name (it was something like Archbold—but at this distance of years I am hardly sure), his ship's name, and a few other particulars of that sort, in the manner of a criminal making a reluctant and doleful confession.   He had had terrible weather on the passage out—terrible—terrible—wife aboard, too.

By this time we were seated in the cabin and the steward brought in a tray with a bottle and glasses.   "Thanks! No!"   Never took liquor.   Would have some water, though. He drank two tumblerfuls.   Terrible thirsty work.   Ever since daylight had been exploring the islands round his ship.

"What was that for—fun?" I asked, with an appearance of polite interest.

"No!"   He sighed.   "Painful duty."

As he persisted in his mumbling and I wanted my double to hear every word, I hit upon the notion of informing him that I regretted to say I was hard of hearing.

"Such a young man, too!" he nodded, keeping his smeary blue, unintelligent eyes fastened upon me. What was the cause of it—some disease? he inquired, without the least sympathy and as if he thought that, if so, I'd got no more than I deserved.

"Yes; disease," I admitted in a cheerful tone which seemed to shock him. But my point was gained, because he had to raise his voice to give me his tale. It is not worth while to record that version. It was just over two months since all this had happened, and he had thought so much about it that he seemed completely muddled as to its bearings, but still immensely impressed.

"What would you think of such a thing happening on board your own ship? I've had the *Sephora* for these fifteen years. I am a well-known shipmaster."

He was densely distressed—and perhaps I should have sympathized with him if I had been able to detach my mental vision from the unsuspected sharer of my cabin as though he were my second self. There he was on the other side of the bulkhead, four or five feet from us, no more, as we sat in the saloon. I looked politely at Captain Archbold (if that was his name), but it was the other I saw, in a gray sleeping-suit, seated on a low stool, his bare feet close together, his arms folded, and every word said between us falling into the ears of his dark head bowed on his chest.

"I have been at sea now, man and boy, for seven-and-thirty years, and I've never heard of such a thing happening in an English ship. And that it should be my ship. Wife on board, too."

I was hardly listening to him.

"Don't you think," I said, "that the heavy sea which, you told me, came aboard just then might have killed the man? I have seen the sheer weight of a sea kill a man very neatly, by simply breaking his neck."

"Good God!" he uttered impressively, fixing his smeary

blue eyes on me. "The sea! No man killed by the sea ever looked like that." He seemed positively scandalized by my suggestion. And as I gazed at him, certainly not prepared for anything original on his part, he advanced his head close to mine and thrust his tongue out at me so suddenly that I couldn't help starting back.

After scoring over my calmness in this graphic way, he nodded wisely. If I had seen the sight, he assured me, I would never forget it as long as I lived. The weather was too bad to give the corpse a proper sea burial. So next day at dawn they took it up on the poop, covering its face with a bit of bunting; he read a short prayer, and then, just as it was, in its oilskins and long boots, they launched it amongst those mountainous seas that seemed ready every moment to swallow up the ship herself and the terrified lives on board of her.

"That reefed foresail saved you," I threw in.

"Under God—it did," he exclaimed fervently. "It was by a special mercy, I firmly believe, that it stood some of those hurricane squalls."

"It was the setting of that sail which——" I began.

"God's own hand in it," he interrupted me. "Nothing less could have done it. I don't mind telling you that I hardly dared give the order. It seemed impossible that we could touch anything without losing it, and then our last hope would have been gone."

The terror of that gale was on him yet. I let him go on for a bit, then said, casually—as if returning to a minor subject:

"You were very anxious to give up your mate to the shore people, I believe?"

He was. To the law. His obscure tenacity on that point had in it something incomprehensible and a little awful; something, as it were, mystical, quite apart from his anxiety that he should not be suspected of "countenancing any doings

of that sort." Seven-and-thirty virtuous years at sea, of
which over twenty of immaculate command, and the last fifteen in the *Sephora,* seemed to have laid him under some pitiless obligation.

"And you know," he went on, groping shamefacedly
among his feelings, "I did not engage that young fellow.
His people had some interest with my owners. I was in a
way forced to take him on. He looked very smart, very
gentlemanly, and all that. But do you know—I never liked
him, somehow. I am a plain man. You see, he wasn't exactly the sort for the chief mate of a ship like the *Sephora.*"

I had become so connected in thoughts and impressions
with the secret sharer of my cabin that I felt as if I, person-
ally, were being given to understand that I, too, was not the
sort that would have done for chief mate of a ship like the
Sephora. I had no doubt of it in my mind.

"Not at all the style of man. You understand," he insisted, superfluously, looking hard at me.

I smiled urbanely. He seemed at a loss for a while.

"I suppose I must report a suicide."

"Beg pardon?"

"Sui-cide! That's what I'll have to write to my owners
directly I get in."

"Unless you manage to recover him before tomorrow,"
I assented, dispassionately. . . . "I mean, alive."

My lack of excitement, of curiosity, of surprise, of any
sort of pronounced interest, began to arouse his distrust. But
except for the felicitous pretense of deafness I had not tried
to pretend anything. I had felt utterly incapable of playing the part of ignorance properly, and therefore was afraid
to try. It is also certain that he had brought some ready-
made suspicions with him, and that he viewed my politeness
as a strange and unnatural phenomenon. And yet how else
could I have received him? Not heartily! That was impossible for psychological reasons, which I need not state

here. My only object was to keep off his inquiries. Surlily?
Yes, but surliness might have provoked a point-blank question. From its novelty to him and from its nature, punctili-
ous courtesy was the manner best calculated to restrain the
man. But there was danger of his breaking through my
defense bluntly. I could not, I think, have met him by a
direct lie, also for psychological (not moral) reasons. If he
had only known how afraid I was of his putting my feeling
of identity with the other to the test! But, strangely enough
(I thought of it only afterwards), I believe that he was not
a little disconcerted by the reverse side of that weird situation, by something in me that reminded him of the man he
was seeking—suggested a mysterious similitude to the young
fellow he had disturbed and disliked from the first.

However that might have been, the silence was not very
prolonged. He took another oblique step.

"I reckon I had no more than a two-mile pull to your
ship. Not a bit more."

"And quite enough, too, in this awful heat," I said.

Another pause full of mistrust followed. Necessity, they
say, is mother of invention, but fear, too, is not barren of
ingenious suggestions. And I was afraid he would ask me
point-blank for news of my other self.

"Nice little saloon, isn't it?" I remarked, as if noticing
for the first time the way his eyes roamed from one closed
door to the other. "And very well fitted out, too. Here,
for instance," I continued, reaching over the back of my
seat negligently and flinging the door open, "is my bathroom."

He made an eager movement, but hardly gave it a glance.
I got up, shut the door of the bathroom, and invited him to
have a look around, as if I were very proud of my accommo-
dation. He had to rise and be shown round, but he went
through the business without any raptures whatever.

"And now we'll have a look at my stateroom," I declared,

in a voice as loud as I dared make it, crossing the cabin to the
starboard side with purposely heavy steps.

He followed me in and gazed around. My intelligent
double had vanished. I played my part.

"Very convenient—isn't it?"

"Very nice. Very comf . . ." He didn't finish, and
went out brusquely as if to escape from some unrighteous
wiles of mine. But it was not to be. I had been too frightened not to feel vengeful; I felt I had him on the run, and
I meant to keep him on the run. My polite insistence must
have had something menacing in it, because he gave in suddenly. And I did not let him off a single item; mate's room,
pantry, storerooms, the very sail-locker which was also under
the poop—he had to look in all of them. When at last I
showed him out on the quarter-deck he drew a long, spiritless sigh, and mumbled dismally that he must really be going
back to his ship now. I desired my mate, who had joined
us, to see to the captain's boat.

The man of whiskers gave a blast on the whistle which he
used to wear hanging round his neck, and yelled, "*Sephora's*
away!" My double down there in my cabin must have
heard, and certainly could not feel more relieved than I.
Four fellows came running out from somewhere forward and
went over the side, while my own men, appearing on deck
too, lined the rail. I escorted my visitor to the gangway
ceremoniously, and nearly overdid it. He was a tenacious
beast. On the very ladder he lingered, and in that unique,
guiltily conscientious manner of sticking to the point:

"I say . . . you . . . you don't think that——"

I covered his voice loudly.

"Certainly not . . . I am delighted. Good-bye."

I had an idea of what he meant to say, and just saved
myself by the privilege of defective hearing. He was too
shaken generally to insist, but my mate, close witness of that
parting, looked mystified and his face took on a thoughtful

cast.　As I did not want to appear as if I wished to avoid all communication with my affairs, he had the opportunity to address me.

"Seems a very nice man.　His boat's crew told our chaps a very extraordinary story, if what I am told by the steward is true.　I suppose you had it from the captain, sir?"

"Yes.　I had a story from the captain."

"A very horrible affair—isn't it, sir?"

"It is."

"Beats all these tales we hear about murders in Yankee ships."

"I don't think it beats them.　I don't think it resembles them in the least."

"Bless my soul—you don't say so!　But of course I've no acquaintance whatever with American ships, not I, so I couldn't go against your knowledge.　It's horrible enough for me. . . . But the queerest part is that those fellows seemed to have some idea the man was hidden aboard here. They had really.　Did you ever hear of such a thing?"

"Preposterous—isn't it?"

We were walking to and fro athwart the quarter-deck. No one of the crew forward could be seen (the day was Sunday), and the mate pursued:

"There was some little dispute about it.　Our chaps took offense.　'As if we would harbor a thing like that,' they said. 'Wouldn't you like to look for him in our coal-hole?'　Quite a tiff.　But they made it up in the end.　I suppose he did drown himself.　Don't you, sir?"

"I don't suppose anything."

"You have no doubt in the matter, sir?"

"None whatever."

I left him suddenly.　I felt I was producing a bad impression, but with my double down there it was most trying to be on deck.　And it was almost as trying to be below. Altogether a nerve-trying situation.　But on the whole I felt less torn in two when I was with him. There was no one in the whole ship whom I dared to take into my confidence. Since the hands had got to know his story, it would have been impossible to pass him off for any one else, and an accidental discovery was to be dreaded now more than ever . . .

The steward being engaged in laying the table for dinner, we could talk only with our eyes when I first went down. Later in the afternoon we had a cautious try at whispering. The Sunday stillness of the ship was against us; the stillness of air and water around her was against us; the elements, the men were against us—everything was against us in our secret partnership; time itself—for this could not go on forever. The very trust in Providence was, I suppose, denied to his guilt. Shall I confess that this thought cast me down very much? And as to the chapter of accidents which counts for so much in the book of success, I could only hope that it was closed. For what favorable accident could be expected?

"Did you hear everything?" were my first words as soon as we took up our position side by side, leaning over my bed-place.

He had. And the proof of it was his earnest whisper, "The man told you he hardly dared give the order."

I understood the reference to be to that saving foresail.

"Yes. He was afraid of it being lost in the setting."

"I assure you he never gave the order. He may think he did, but he never gave it. He stood there with me on the break of the poop after the maintopsail blew away, and whimpered about our last hope—positively whimpered about it and nothing else—and the night coming on! To hear one's skipper go on like that in such weather was enough to drive any fellow out of his mind. It worked me up into a sort of desperation. I just took it into my own hands and went away from him, boiling, and—— But what's the use telling you? *You* know! . . . Do you think that if I had not been pretty fierce with them I should have got the men to do anything? Not it! The bos'n perhaps? Perhaps! It wasn't a heavy sea—it was a sea gone mad! I suppose the end of the world will be something like that; and a man may have the heart to see it coming once and be done with it— but to have to face it day after day—I don't blame anybody. I was precious little better than the rest. Only—I was an officer of that old coal-wagon, anyhow——"

"I quite understand," I conveyed that sincere assurance into his ear. He was out of breath with whispering; I could hear him pant slightly. It was all very simple. The same strung-up force which had given twenty-four men a chance, at least, for their lives, had, in a sort of recoil, crushed an unworthy mutinous existence.

But I had no leisure to weigh the merits of the matter—— Footsteps in the saloon, a heavy knock. "There's enough wind to get under way with, sir." Here was the call of a new claim upon my thoughts and even upon my feelings.

"Turn the hands up," I cried through the door. "I'll be on deck directly."

I was going out to make the acquaintance of my ship. Before I left the cabin our eyes met—the eyes of the only two strangers on board. I pointed to the recessed part where the little camp-stool awaited him and laid my finger on my lips. He made a gesture—somewhat vague—a little mysterious, accompanied by a faint smile, as if of regret.

This is not the place to enlarge upon the sensations of a man who feels for the first time a ship move under his feet to his own independent word. In my case they were not unalloyed. I was not wholly alone with my command; for there was that stranger in my cabin. Or, rather, I was not completely and wholly with her. Part of me was absent. That mental feeling of being in two places at once affected me physically as if the mood of secrecy had penetrated my very soul. Before an hour had elapsed since the ship had begun to move, having occasion to ask the mate (he stood by my side) to take a compass bearing of the Pagoda, I caught myself reaching up to his ear in whispers. I say I caught myself, but enough had escaped to startle the man. I can't describe it otherwise than by saying he shied. A grave, pre-occupied manner, as though he were in possession of some perplexing intelligence, did not leave him henceforth. A little later I moved away from the rail to look at the compass with such a stealthy gait that the helmsman noticed it —and I could not help noticing the unusual roundness of his eyes. These are trifling instances, though it's to no commander's advantage to be suspected of ludicrous eccentricities. But I was also more seriously affected. There are to a seaman certain words, gestures, that should in given conditions come as naturally, as instinctively as the winking of a menaced eye. A certain order should spring on to his lips without thinking; a certain sign should get itself made, so to speak, without reflection. But all unconscious alertness had abandoned me. I had to make an effort of will to recall myself back (from the cabin) to the conditions of the moment. I felt that I was appearing an irresolute commander to those people who were watching me more or less critically.

And, besides, there were the scares. On the second day out, for instance, coming off the deck in the afternoon (I had straw slippers on my bare feet) I stopped at the open pantry door and spoke to the steward. He was doing something there with his back to me. At the sound of my voice he nearly jumped out of his skin, as the saying is, and incidentally broke a cup.

"What on earth's the matter with you?" I asked, astonished.

He was extremely confused. "Beg your pardon, sir. I made sure you were in your cabin."

"You see I wasn't."

"No, sir. I could have sworn I had heard you moving in

there not a moment ago. It's most extraordinary . . . very sorry, sir."

I passed on with an inward shudder. I was so identified with my secret double that I did not even mention the fact in those scanty, fearful whispers we exchanged. I suppose he had made some slight noise of some kind or other. It would have been miraculous if he hadn't at one time or another. And yet, haggard as he appeared, he looked always perfectly self-controlled, more than calm—almost invulnerable. On my suggestion he remained almost entirely in the bathroom, which, upon the whole, was the safest place. There could be really no shadow of an excuse for any one ever wanting to go in there, once the steward had done with it. It was a very tiny place. Sometimes he reclined on the floor, his legs bent, his head sustained on one elbow. At others I would find him on the camp-stool, sitting in his gray sleeping-suit and with his cropped dark hair like a patient, unmoved convict. At night I would smuggle him into my bed-place and we would whisper together, with the regular footfalls of the officer of the watch passing and repassing over our heads. It was an infinitely miserable time. It was lucky that some tins of fine preserves were stowed in a locker in my stateroom: hard bread I could always get hold of; and so he lived on stewed chicken, pâté de foie gras, asparagus, cooked oysters, sardines—on all sorts of abominable sham delicacies out of tins. My early morning coffee he always drank; and it was all I dared do for him in that respect.

Every day there was the horrible maneuvering to go through with so that my room and then the bathroom should be done in the usual way. I came to hate the sight of the steward, to abhor the voice of that harmless man. I felt that it was he who would bring on the disaster of discovery. It hung like a sword over our heads.

The fourth day out, I think (we were then working down the east side of the Gulf of Siam)—the fourth day, I say, of this miserable juggling with the unavoidable, as we sat at our evening meal, that man, whose slightest movement I dreaded, after putting down the dishes, ran up on deck busily. This could not be dangerous. Presently he came down again; and then it appeared that he had remembered a coat of mine which I had thrown over a rail to dry after having been wetted in a shower which had passed over the ship in the afternoon. Sitting stolidly at the head of the table I became terrified at the sight of the garment on his arm. Of course he made for my door. There was no time to lose.

"Steward," I thundered. My nerves were so shaken that I could not govern my voice and conceal my agitation. This was the sort of thing that made my terrifically whiskered mate tap his forehead with his forefinger. I had detected him using that gesture while talking on deck with a confidential air to the carpenter. It was too far to hear a word, but I had no doubt that this pantomime could only refer to the strange new captain.

"Yes, sir," the pale-faced steward turned resignedly to me. It was this maddening course of being shouted at, checked without rhyme or reason, arbitrarily chased out of my cabin, suddenly called into it, sent flying out of his pantry on incomprehensible errands, that accounted for the growing wretchedness of his expression.

"Where are you going with that coat?"

"To your room, sir."

"Is there another shower coming?"

"I'm sure I don't know, sir. Shall I go up again and see, sir?"

"No! Never mind."

My object was attained, as of course my other self in there would have heard everything that passed. During this interlude my two officers never raised their eyes off their respective plates; but the lip of that confounded cub, the second mate, quivered visibly.

I expected the steward to hook my coat on and come out at once. He was very slow about it; but I dominated my nervousness sufficiently not to shout after him. Suddenly I became aware (it could be heard plainly enough) that the fellow for some reason or other was opening the door of the bathroom. It was the end. The place was literally not big enough to swing a cat in. My voice died in my throat and I went stony all over. I expected to hear a yell of surprise and terror, and made a movement, but had not the strength to get to my legs. Everything remained still. Had my second self taken the poor wretch by the throat? I don't know what I would have done next moment if I had not seen the steward come out of my room, close the door, and then stand quietly by the sideboard.

"Saved," I thought. "But, no! Lost! Gone! He was gone!"

I laid my knife and fork down and leaned back in my chair. My head swam. After a while, when sufficiently recovered to speak in a steady voice, I instructed my mate to put the ship round at eight o'clock himself.

"I won't come on deck," I went on. "I think I'll turn in, and unless the wind shifts I don't want to be disturbed before midnight. I feel a bit seedy."

"You did look middling bad a little while ago," the chief mate remarked without showing any great concern.

They both went out, and I stared at the steward clearing the table. There was nothing to be read on that wretched man's face. But why did he avoid my eyes, I asked myself. Then I thought I should like to hear the sound of his voice.

"Steward!"

"Sir!" Startled as usual.

"Where did you hang up that coat?"

"In the bathroom, sir." The usual anxious tone. "It's not quite dry yet, sir."

For some time longer I sat in the cuddy. Had my double

vanished as he had come? But of his coming there was an explanation, whereas his disappearance would be inexplicable. . . . I went slowly into my dark room, shut the door, lighted the lamp, and for a time dared not turn round. When at last I did, I saw him standing bolt upright in the narrow recessed part. It would not be true to say I had a shock, but an irresistible doubt of his bodily existence flitted through my mind. Can it be, I asked myself, that he is not visible to other eyes than mine? It was like being haunted. Motionless, with a grave face, he raised his hands slightly at me in a gesture which meant clearly, "Heavens! what a narrow escape!" Narrow indeed. I think I had come creeping quietly as near insanity as any man who has not actually gone over the border. That gesture restrained me, so to speak.

The mate with the terrific whiskers was now putting the ship on the other tack. In the moment of profound silence which follows upon the hands going to their stations I heard on the poop his raised voice: "Hard alee!" and the distant shout of the order repeated on the main-deck. The sails, in that light breeze, made but a faint fluttering noise. It ceased. The ship was coming round slowly; I held my breath in the renewed stillness of expectation; one wouldn't have thought that there was a single living soul on her decks. A sudden brisk shout, "Mainsail haul!" broke the spell, and in the noisy cries and rush overhead of the men running away with the main brace we two, down in my cabin, came together in our usual position by the bed-place.

He did not wait for my question. "I heard him fumbling here and just managed to squat myself down in the bath," he whispered to me. "The fellow only opened the door and put his arm in to hang the coat up. All the same——"

"I never thought of that," I whispered back, even more appalled than before at the closeness of the shave, and marveling at that something unyielding in his character which was carrying him through so finely. There was no agitation in his whisper. Whoever was being driven distracted, it was not he. He was sane. And the proof of his sanity was continued when he took up the whispering again.

"It would never do for me to come to life again."

It was something that a ghost might have said. But what he was alluding to was his old captain's reluctant admission of the theory of suicide. It would obviously serve his turn —if I understood at all the view which seemed to govern the unalterable purpose of his action.

"You must maroon me as soon as ever you can get amongst these islands off the Cambodje shore," he went on.

"Maroon you! We are not living in a boy's adventure tale," I protested. His scornful whispering took me up.

"We aren't indeed! There's nothing of a boy's tale in this. But there's nothing else for it. I want no more. You don't suppose I am afraid of what can be done to me? Prison or gallows or whatever they may please. But you don't see me coming back to explain such things to an old fellow in a wig and twelve respectable tradesmen, do you? What can they know whether I'm guilty or not—or of *what* I'm guilty, either? That's my affair. What does the Bible say? 'Driven off the face of the earth.' Very well. I am off the face of the earth now. As I came at night, so I shall go."

"Impossible!" I murmured. "You can't."

"Can't? . . . Not naked like a soul on the Day of Judgment. I shall freeze on to this sleeping-suit. The Last Day is not yet—and . . . you have understood thoroughly. Didn't you?"

I felt suddenly ashamed of myself. I may say truly that I understood—and my hesitation in letting that man swim away from my ship's side had been a mere sham sentiment, a sort of cowardice.

"It can't be done now till next night," I breathed out. "The ship is on the off-shore tack and the wind may fail us."

"As long as I know that you understand," he whispered. "But of course you do. It's a great satisfaction to have got somebody to understand. You seem to have been there on purpose." And in the same whisper, as if we two, whenever we talked, had to say things which were not fit for the world to hear, he added, "It's very wonderful."

We remained side by side talking in our secret way—but sometimes silent or just exchanging a whispered word or two at long intervals. And as usual he stared through the port. A breath of wind came now and again into our faces. The ship might have been moored in dock, so gently and on an even keel she slipped through the water, that did not murmur even at our passage, shadowy and silent like a phantom sea.

At midnight I went on deck, and to my mate's great surprise put the ship round on the other tack. His terrible whiskers flitted round me in silent criticism. I certainly should not have done it if it had been only a question of getting out of that sleepy gulf as quickly as possible. I believe he told the second mate, who relieved him, that it was a great want of judgment. The other only yawned. That intolerable cub shuffled about so sleepily and lolled against the rails in such a slack, improper fashion that I came down on him sharply.

"Aren't you properly awake yet?"

"Yes, sir! I am awake."

"Well, then, be good enough to hold yourself as if you were. And keep a lookout. If there's any current we'll be closing with some islands before daylight."

The east side of the gulf is fringed with islands, some solitary, others in groups. On the blue background of the high coast they seem to float on silvery patches of calm water, arid and gray, or dark green and rounded like clumps of evergreen bushes, with the larger ones, a mile or two long, showing the outlines of ridges, ribs of gray rock under the dark mantle of matted leafage. Unknown to trade, to

travel, almost to geography, the manner of life they harbor
is an unsolved secret.   There must be villages—settlements
of fishermen at least—on the largest of them, and some communication with the world is probably kept up by native
craft.   But all that forenoon, as we headed for them, fanned
along by the faintest of breezes, I saw no sign of man or
canoe in the field of the telescope I kept pointed on the scattered group.

At noon I gave no orders for a change of course, and the
mate's whiskers became much concerned and seemed to be
offering themselves unduly to my notice.   At last I said:

"I am going to stand right in.   Quite in—as far as I can
take her."

The stare of extreme surprise imparted an air of ferocity
also to his eyes, and he looked truly terrific for a moment.

"We're not doing well in the middle of the gulf," I continued casually.   "I am going to look for the land breezes
tonight."

"Bless my soul!   Do you mean, sir, in the dark amongst
the lot of them islands and reefs and shoals?"

"Well—if there are any regular land breezes at all on this
coast one must get close inshore to find them, mustn't one?"

"Bless my soul!" he exclaimed again under his breath.   All
that afternoon he wore a dreamy, contemplative appearance
which in him was a mark of perplexity.   After dinner I
went into my stateroom as if I meant to take some rest.
There we two bent our dark heads over a half-unrolled chart
lying on my bed.

"There," I said.   "It's got to be Koh-ring.   I've been
looking at it since sunrise.   It has got two hills and a low
point.   It must be inhabited.   And on the coast opposite
there is what looks like the mouth of a biggish river—with
some town, no doubt, not far up.   It's the best chance for
you that I can see."

"Anything.   Koh-ring let it be."

He looked thoughtfully at the chart as if surveying
chances and distances from a lofty height—and following
with his eyes his own figure wandering on the blank land
of Cochin-China, and then passing off that piece of paper
clean out of sight into uncharted regions.   And it was as
if the ship had two captains to plan her course for her.   I
had been so worried and restless running up and down that
I had not had the patience to dress that day.   I had remained
in my sleeping-suit, with straw slippers and a soft floppy hat.
The closeness of the heat in the gulf had been most oppressive, and the crew were used to seeing me wandering in that
airy attire.

"She will clear the south point as she heads now," I whispered into his ear.   "Goodness only knows when, but certainly after dark.   I'll edge her in to half a mile, as far as I
may be able to judge in the dark——"

"Be careful," he murmured, warningly—and I realized
suddenly that all my future, the only future for which I was
fit, would perhaps go irretrievably to pieces in any mishap to
my first command.

I could not stop a moment longer in the room.   I motioned him to get out of sight and made my way on the
poop.   That unplayful cub had the watch.   I walked up
and down for a while thinking things out, then beckoned
him over.

"Send a couple of hands to open the two quarter-deck
ports," I said mildly.

He actually had the impudence, or else so forgot himself
in his wonder at such an incomprehensible order, as to re-
peat:

"Open the quarter-deck ports!   What for, sir?"

"The only reason you need concern yourself about is because I tell you to do so.   Have them opened wide and
fastened properly."

He reddened and went off, but I believe made some jeer-

ing remark to the carpenter as to the sensible practice of
ventilating a ship's quarter-deck. I know he popped into
the mate's cabin to impart the fact to him because the whiskers came on deck, as it were by chance, and stole glances at
me from below—for signs of lunacy or drunkenness, I suppose.

A little before supper, feeling more restless than ever, I
rejoined, for a moment, my second self. And to find him
sitting so quietly was surprising, like something against
nature, inhuman.

I developed my plan in a hurried whisper.

"I shall stand in as close as I dare and then put her round.
I shall presently find means to smuggle you out of here into
the sail-locker, which communicates with the lobby. But
there is an opening, a sort of square for hauling the sails out,
which gives straight on the quarter-deck and which is never
closed in fine weather, so as to give air to the sails. When
the ship's way is deadened in stays and all hands are aft at
the main braces you shall have a clear road to slip out and
get overboard through the open quarter-deck port. I've had
them both fastened up. Use a rope's end to lower yourself
into the water so as to avoid a splash—you know. It could
be heard and cause some beastly complication."

He kept silent for a while, then whispered, "I understand."

"I won't be there to see you go," I began with an effort.

"The rest . . . I only hope I have understood, too."

"You have. From first to last"—and for the first time
there seemed to be a faltering, something strained in his whisper. He caught hold of my arm, but the ringing of the
supper bell made me start. He didn't, though; he only released his grip.

After supper I didn't come below again till well past eight
o'clock. The faint, steady breeze was loaded with dew; and
the wet, darkened sails held all there was of propelling power
in it. The night, clear and starry, sparkled darkly, and the

opaque, lightless patches shifting slowly against the low stars were the drifting islets. On the port bow there was a big one more distant and shadowily imposing by the great space of sky it eclipsed.

On opening the door I had a back view of my very own self looking at a chart. He had come out of the recess and was standing near the table.

"Quite dark enough," I whispered.

He stepped back and leaned against my bed with a level, quiet glance. I sat on the couch. We had nothing to say to each other. Over our heads the officer of the watch moved here and there. Then I heard him move quickly. I knew what that meant. He was making for the companion; and presently his voice was outside my door.

"We are drawing in pretty fast, sir. Land looks rather close."

"Very well," I answered. "I am coming on deck directly."

I waited till he was gone out of the cuddy, then rose. My double moved too. The time had come to exchange our last whispers, for neither of us was ever to hear the other's natural voice.

"Look here!" I opened a drawer and took out three sovereigns. "Take this, anyhow. I've got six and I'd give you the lot, only I must keep a little money to buy some fruit and vegetables for the crew from native boats as we go through the Sunda Straits."

He shook his head.

"Take it," I urged him, whispering desperately. "No one can tell what——"

He smiled and slapped meaningly the only pocket of the sleeping-jacket. It was not safe, certainly. But I produced a large old silk handkerchief of mine, and tying the three pieces of gold in a corner, pressed it on him. He was touched, I suppose, because he took it at last and tied it quickly round his waist under the jacket, on his bare skin.

Our eyes met; several seconds elapsed, till, our glances still mingled, I extended my hand and turned the lamp out. Then I passed through the cuddy, leaving the door of my room wide open. . . . "Steward!"

He was still lingering in the pantry in the greatness of his zeal, giving a rub-up to a plated cruet stand the last thing before going to bed. Being careful not to wake up the mate, whose room was opposite, I spoke in an undertone.

He looked around anxiously. "Sir!"

"Can you get me a little hot water from the galley?"

"I am afraid, sir, the galley fire's been out for some time now."

"Go and see."

He fled up the stairs.

"Now," I whispered loudly, into the saloon—too loudly, perhaps, but I was afraid I couldn't make a sound. He was by my side in an instant—the double captain slipped past the stairs—through the tiny dark passage . . . a sliding door. We were in the sail-locker, scrambling on our knees over the sails. A sudden thought struck me. I saw myself wandering barefooted, bareheaded, the sun beating on my dark poll. I snatched off my floppy hat and tried hurriedly in the dark to ram it on my other self. He dodged and fended off silently. I wonder what he thought had come over me before he understood and suddenly desisted. Our hands met gropingly, lingered united in a steady, motionless clasp for a second. . . . No word was breathed by either of us when they separated.

I was standing quietly by the pantry door when the steward returned.

"Sorry, sir. Kettle barely warm. Shall I light the spirit-lamp?"

"Never mind."

I came out on deck slowly. It was now a matter of conscience to shave the land as close as possible—for now he

must go overboard whenever the ship was put in stays. Must!
There could be no going back for him. After a moment I
walked over to leeward and my heart flew into my mouth at
the nearness of the land on the bow. Under any other circumstances I would not have held on a minute longer. The
second mate had followed me anxiously.

I looked on till I felt I could command my voice.

"She will weather," I said then in a quiet tone.

"Are you going to try that, sir?" he stammered out incredulously.

I took no notice of him and raised my tone just enough to
be heard by the helmsman.

"Keep her good full."

"Good full, sir."

The wind fanned my cheek, the sails slept, the world was
silent. The strain of watching the dark loom of the land
grow bigger and denser was too much for me. I had shut
my eyes—because the ship must go closer. She must! The
stillness was intolerable. Were we standing still?

When I opened my eyes the second view started my heart
with a thump. The black southern hill of Koh-ring seemed
to hang right over the ship like a towering fragment of the
everlasting night. On that enormous mass of blackness there
was not a gleam to be seen, not a sound to be heard. It was
gliding irresistibly toward us and yet seemed already within
reach of the hand. I saw the vague figures of the watch
grouped in the waist, gazing in awed silence.

"Are you going on, sir?" inquired an unsteady voice at my
elbow.

I ignored it. I had to go on.

"Keep her full. Don't check her way. That won't do
now," I said warningly.

"I can't see the sails very well," the helmsman answered
me, in strange, quavering tones.

Was she close enough? Already she was, I won't say in

the shadow of the land, but in the very blackness of it, already swallowed up as it were, gone too close to be recalled, gone from me altogether.

"Give the mate a call," I said to the young man who stood at my elbow as still as death. "And turn all hands up."

My tone had a borrowed loudness reverberated from the height of the land. Several voices cried out together: "We are all on deck, sir."

Then stillness again, with the great shadow gliding closer, towering higher, without a light, without a sound. Such a hush had fallen on the ship that she might have been a bark of the dead floating slowly under the very gate of Erebus.

"My God! Where are we?"

It was the mate moaning at my elbow. He was thunderstruck, and as it were deprived of the moral support of his whiskers. He clapped his hands and absolutely cried out, "Lost!"

"Be quiet," I said sternly.

He lowered his tone, but I saw the shadowy gesture of his despair. "What are we doing here?"

"Looking for the land wind."

He made as if to tear his hair and addressed me recklessly. "She will never get out of it. You have done it, sir. I knew it'd end in something like this. She will never weather, and you are too close now to stay. She'll drift ashore before she's round. O, my God!"

I caught his arm as he was raising it to batter his poor devoted head, and shook it vehemently.

"She's ashore already," he wailed, trying to tear himself away.

"Is she? . . . Keep good full there!"

"Good full, sir," cried the helmsman in a frightened, thin, childlike voice.

I hadn't let go the mate's arm and went on shaking it. "Ready about, do you hear? You go forward"—shake—

"and stop there"—shake—"and hold your noise"—shake—
"and see these head-sheets properly overhauled"—shake,
shake—shake.

And all the time I dared not look toward the land lest my
heart should fail me. I released my grip at last and he ran
forward as if fleeing for dear life.

I wondered what my double there in the sail-locker
thought of this commotion. He was able to hear everything—and perhaps he was able to understand why, on my
conscience, it had to be thus close—no less. My first order
"Hard alee!" reëchoed ominously under the towering shadow
of Koh-ring as if I had shouted in a mountain gorge. And
then I watched the land intently. In that smooth water
and light wind it was impossible to feel the ship coming to.
No! I could not feel her. And my second self was making
now ready to slip out and lower himself overboard. Perhaps he was gone already . . . ?

The great black mass brooding over our very mast-heads
began to pivot away from the ship's side silently. And now
I forgot the secret stranger ready to depart, and remembered only that I was a total stranger to the ship. Would
she do it? How was she to be handled?

I swung the mainyard and waited helplessly. She was
perhaps stopped, and her very fate hung in the balance, with
the black mass of Koh-ring like the gate of the everlasting
night towering over her taffrail. What would she do now?
Had she way on her yet? I stepped to the side swiftly, and
on the shadowy water I could see nothing except a faint
phosphorescent flash revealing the glassy smoothness of the
sleeping surface. It was impossible to tell—and I had not
learned yet the feel of my ship. Was she moving? What
I needed was something easily seen, a piece of paper, which I
could throw overboard and watch. I had nothing on me.
To run down for it I didn't dare. There was no time. All
at once my strained, yearning stare distinguished a white

object floating within a yard of the ship's side. White on
the black water. A phosphorescent flash passed under it.
What was that thing? . . . I recognized my own floppy hat.
It must have fallen off his head . . . and he didn't bother.
Now I had what I wanted—the saving mark for my eyes.
But I hardly thought of my other self, now gone from the
ship, to be hidden forever from all friendly faces, to be a
fugitive and a vagabond on the earth, with no brand of the
curse on his sane forehead to stay a slaying hand . . . too
proud to explain.

And I watched the hat—the expression of my sudden pity
for his mere flesh. It had been meant to save his homeless
head from the dangers of the sun. And now—behold—it
was saving the ship, by serving me for a mark to help out
the ignorance of my strangeness. Ha! It was drifting forward, warning me just in time that the ship had gathered
sternway.

"Shift the helm," I said in a low voice to the seaman standing like a statue.

The man's eyes glistened wildly in the binnacle light as he
jumped around to the other side and spun round the wheel.

I walked to the break of the poop. On the overshadowed
deck all hands stood by the forebraces waiting for my order.
The stars ahead seemed to be gliding from right to left. And
all was so still in the world that I heard the quiet remark
"She's round," passed in a tone of intense relief between two
seamen.

"Let go and haul."

The foreyards ran round with a great noise, amidst cheery
cries. And now the frightful whiskers made themselves
heard giving various orders. Already the ship was drawing
ahead. And I was alone with her. Nothing! no one in the
world should stand now between us, throwing a shadow on
the way of silent knowledge and mute affection, the perfect
communion of a seaman with his first command.

Walking to the taffrail, I was in time to make out on the very edge of a darkness thrown by a towering black mass like the very gateway of Erebus—yes, I was in time to catch an evanescent glimpse of my white hat left behind to mark the spot where the secret sharer of my cabin and my thoughts, as though he were my second self, had lowered himself into the water to take his punishment: a free man, a proud swimmer striking out for a new destiny.

TYPHOON

CAPTAIN MACWHIRR, of the steamer *Nan-Shan,* had a physiognomy that, in the order of material appearances, was the exact counterpart of his mind: it presented no marked characteristics of firmness or stupidity; it had no pronounced characteristics whatever; it was simply ordinary, irresponsive, and unruffled.

The only thing his aspect might have been said to suggest, at times, was bashfulness; because he would sit, in business offices ashore, sunburnt and smiling faintly, with downcast eyes. When he raised them, they were perceived to be direct in their glance and of blue color. His hair was fair and extremely fine, clasping from temple to temple the bald dome of his skull in a clamp as of fluffy silk. The hair of his face, on the contrary, carroty and flaming, resembled a growth of copper wire clipped short to the line of the lip; while, no matter how close he shaved, fiery metallic gleams passed, when he moved his head, over the surface of his cheeks. He was rather below the medium height, a bit round-shouldered, and so sturdy of limb that his clothes always looked a shade too tight for his arms and legs. As if unable to grasp what is due to the difference of latitudes, he wore a brown bowler hat, a complete suit of a brownish hue, and clumsy black boots. These harbor togs gave to his thick figure an air of stiff and uncouth smartness. A thin silver watch-chain looped his waistcoat, and he never left his ship for the shore without clutching in his powerful, hairy fist an elegant umbrella of the very best quality, but generally unrolled. Young Jukes, the chief mate, attending his commander to the gangway, would sometimes venture to say, with the greatest gentleness, "Allow me, sir"—and possessing himself of the umbrella deferentially, would elevate the ferule, shake the folds, twirl a neat furl in a jiffy, and hand it back; going through the performance with a face of such portentous gravity, that Mr. Solomon Rout, the chief engineer, smoking his morning cigar over the skylight, would turn away his head in order to hide a smile. "Oh! aye! The blessed gamp. . . . Thank 'ee, Jukes, thank 'ee," would mutter Captain MacWhirr, heartily, without looking up.

Having just enough imagination to carry him through each successive day, and no more, he was tranquilly sure of himself; and from the very same cause he was not in the least conceited. It is your imaginative superior who is touchy, overbearing, and difficult to please; but every ship Captain MacWhirr commanded was the floating abode of harmony and peace. It was, in truth, as impossible for him to take a flight of fancy as it would be for a watchmaker to put together a chronometer with nothing except a two-pound hammer and a whip-saw in the way of tools. Yet the uninteresting lives of men so entirely given to the actuality of the bare existence have their mysterious side. It was impossible in Captain MacWhirr's case, for instance, to understand what under heaven could have induced that perfectly satisfactory son of a petty grocer in Belfast to run away to sea. And yet he had done that very thing at the age of fifteen. It was enough, when you thought it over, to give you the idea of an immense, potent, and invisible hand thrust into the ant-heap of the earth, laying hold of shoulders, knocking heads together, and setting the unconscious faces of the multitude towards inconceivable goals and in undreamt-of directions.

His father never really forgave him for this undutiful stupidity. "We could have got on without him," he used to say later on, "but there's the business. And he an only

son, too!" His mother wept very much after his disappearance. As it had never occurred to him to leave word
behind, he was mourned over for dead till, after eight
months, his first letter arrived from Talcahuano. It was
short, and contained the statement: "We had very fine
weather on our passage out." But evidently, in the writer's
mind, the only important intelligence was to the effect that
his captain had, on the very day of writing, entered him
regularly on the ship's articles as Ordinary Seaman. "Because I can do the work," he explained. The mother again
wept copiously, while the remark, "Tom's an ass," expressed
the emotions of the father. He was a corpulent man, with
a gift for sly chaffing, which to the end of his life he exercised in his intercourse with his son, a little pityingly, as if
upon a half-witted person.

MacWhirr's visits to his home were necessarily rare, and
in the course of years he despatched other letters to his parents, informing them of his successive promotions and of his
movements upon the vast earth. In these missives could be
found sentences like this: "The heat here is very great." Or:
"On Christmas day at 4 p. m. we fell in with some icebergs."
The old people ultimately became acquainted with a good
many names of ships, and with the names of the skippers
who commanded them—with the names of Scots and English shipowners—with the names of seas, oceans, straits,
promontories—with outlandish names of lumber-ports, of
rice-ports, of cotton-ports—with the names of islands—with
the name of their son's young woman. She was called Lucy.
It did not suggest itself to him to mention whether he
thought the name pretty. And then they died.

The great day of MacWhirr's marriage came in due
course, following shortly upon the great day when he got
his first command.

All these events had taken place many years before the
morning when, in the chart-room of the steamer *Nan-Shan*,

he stood confronted by the fall of a barometer he had no reason to distrust. The fall—taking into account the excellence of the instrument, the time of the year, and the ship's position on the terrestrial globe—was of a nature ominously prophetic; but the red face of the man betrayed no sort of inward disturbance. Omens were as nothing to him, and he was unable to discover the message of a prophecy till the fulfilment had brought it home to his very door. "That's a fall, and no mistake," he thought. "There must be some uncommonly dirty weather knocking about."

The *Nan-Shan* was on her way from the southward to the treaty port of Fu-chau, with some cargo in her lower holds, and two hundred Chinese coolies returning to their village homes in the province of Fo-kien, after a few years of work in various tropical colonies. The morning was fine, the oily sea heaved without a sparkle, and there was a queer white misty patch in the sky like a halo of the sun. The foredeck, packed with Chinamen, was full of somber clothing, yellow faces, and pigtails, sprinkled over with a good many naked shoulders, for there was no wind, and the heat was close. The coolies lounged, talked, smoked, or stared over the rail; some, drawing water over the side, sluiced each other; a few slept on hatches, while several small parties of six sat on their heels surrounding iron trays with plates of rice and tiny teacups; and every single Celestial of them was carrying with him all he had in the world—a wooden chest with a ringing lock and brass on the corners, containing the savings of his labors: some clothes of ceremony, sticks of incense, a little opium maybe, bits of nameless rubbish of conventional value, and a small hoard of silver dollars; toiled for in coal lighters, won in gambling-houses or in petty trading, grubbed out of earth, sweated out in mines, on railway lines, in deadly jungle, under heavy burdens—amassed patiently, guarded with care, cherished fiercely.

A cross swell had set in from the direction of Formosa

Channel about ten o'clock, without disturbing these passengers much, because the *Nan-Shan*, with her flat bottom,
rolling chocks on bilges, and great breadth of beam, had the
reputation of an exceptionally steady ship in a sea-way.   Mr.
Jukes, in moments of expansion on shore, would proclaim
loudly that the "old girl was as good as she was pretty."   It
would never have occurred to Captain MacWhirr to express
his favorable opinion so loud or in terms so fanciful.

She was a good ship, undoubtedly, and not old either.
She had been built in Dumbarton less than three years before, to the order of a firm of merchants in Siam—Messrs.
Sigg and Son.   When she lay afloat, finished in every detail
and ready to take up the work of her life, the builders contemplated her with pride.

"Sigg has asked us for a reliable skipper to take her out,"
remarked one of the partners; and the other, after reflecting
for a while, said: "I think MacWhirr is ashore just at present."   "Is he?   Then wire him at once.   He's the very
man," declared the senior, without a moment's hesitation.

Next morning MacWhirr stood before them unperturbed,
having traveled from London by the midnight express after
a sudden but undemonstrative parting with his wife.   She
was the daughter of a superior couple who had seen better
days.

"We had better be going together over the ship, Captain," said the senior partner; and the three men started to
view the perfections of the *Nan-Shan* from stem to stern,
and from her keelson to the trucks of her two stumpy pole-
masts.

Captain MacWhirr had begun by taking off his coat,
which he hung on the end of a steam windlass embodying
all the latest improvements.

"My uncle wrote of you favorably by yesterday's mail to
our good friends—Messrs. Sigg, you know—and doubtless

they'll continue you out there in command," said the junior
partner. "You'll be able to boast of being in charge of the
handiest boat of her size on the coast of China, Captain," he
added.

"Have you? Thank 'ee," mumbled vaguely MacWhirr,
to whom the view of a distant eventuality could appeal no
more than the beauty of a wide landscape to a purblind
tourist; and his eyes happening at the moment to be at rest
upon the lock of the cabin door, he walked up to it, full of
purpose, and began to rattle the handle vigorously, while he
observed, in his low, earnest voice, "You can't trust the
workmen nowdays. A brand-new lock, and it won't act at
all. Stuck fast. See? See?"

As soon as they found themselves alone in their office
across the yard: "You praised that fellow up to Sigg. What
is it you see in him?" asked the nephew, with faint contempt.

"I admit he has nothing of your fancy skipper about him,
if that's what you mean," said the elder man, curtly. "Is
the foreman of the joiners on the *Nan-Shan* outside? . . .
Come in, Bates. How is it that you let Tait's people put
us off with a defective lock on the cabin door? The Captain could see directly he set eye on it. Have it replaced
at once. The little straws, Bates . . . the little straws. . . ."

The lock was replaced accordingly, and a few days afterwards the *Nan-Shan* steamed out to the East, without Mac-
Whirr having offered any further remark as to her fittings,
or having been heard to utter a single word hinting at pride
in his ship, gratitude for his appointment, or satisfaction at
his prospects.

With a temperament neither loquacious nor taciturn, he
found very little occasion to talk. There were matters of
duty, of course—directions, orders, and so on; but the past
being to his mind done with, and the future not there yet,

the more general actualities of the day required no comment—because facts can speak for themselves with overwhelming precision.

Old Mr. Sigg liked a man of few words, and one that "you could be sure would not try to improve upon his instructions." MacWhirr, satisfying these requirements, was continued in command of the *Nan-Shan,* and applied himself to the careful navigation of his ship in the China seas. She had come out on a British register, but after some time Messrs. Sigg judged it expedient to transfer her to the Siamese flag.

At the news of the contemplated transfer Jukes grew restless, as if under a sense of personal affront. He went about grumbling to himself, and uttering short, scornful laughs. "Fancy having a ridiculous Noah's Ark elephant in the ensign of one's ship," he said once at the engine-room door. "Dash me if I can stand it: I'll throw up the billet. Don't it make *you* sick, Mr. Rout?" The chief engineer only cleared his throat with the air of a man who knows the value of a good billet.

The first morning the new flag floated over the stern of the *Nan-Shan* Jukes stood looking at it bitterly from the bridge. He struggled with his feelings for a while, and then remarked, "Queer flag for a man to sail under, sir."

"What's the matter with the flag?" inquired Captain MacWhirr. "Seems all right to me." And he walked across to the end of the bridge to have a good look.

"Well, it looks queer to me," burst out Jukes, greatly exasperated, and flung off the bridge.

Captain MacWhirr was amazed at these manners. After a while he stepped quietly into the chart-room, and opened his International Signal Code-book at the plate where the flags of all the nations are correctly figured in gaudy rows. He ran his finger over them, and when he came to Siam he contemplated with great attention the red field and the white

elephant. Nothing could be more simple; but to make sure
he brought the book out on the bridge for the purpose of
comparing the colored drawing with the real thing at the
flag-staff astern. When next Jukes, who was carrying on
the duty that day with a sort of suppressed fierceness, happened on the bridge, his commander observed:

"There's nothing amiss with that flag."

"Isn't there?" mumbled Jukes, falling on his knees before
a deck-locker and jerking therefrom viciously a spare lead-
line.

"No. I looked up the book. Length twice the breadth
and the elephant exactly in the middle. I thought the people ashore would know how to make the local flag. Stands
to reason. You were wrong, Jukes. . . ."

"Well, sir," began Jukes, getting up excitedly, "all I can
say——" He fumbled for the end of the coil of line with
trembling hands.

"That's all right." Captain MacWhirr soothed him, sitting heavily on a little canvas folding-stool he greatly
affected. "All you have to do is to take care they don't hoist
the elephant upside-down before they get quite used to it."

Jukes flung the new lead-line over on the fore-deck with
a loud "Here you are, bos'n——don't forget to wet it thoroughly," and turned with immense resolution towards his
commander; but Captain MacWhirr spread his elbows on
the bridge-rail comfortably.

"Because it would be, I suppose, understood as a signal
of distress," he went on. "What do you think? That elephant there, I take it, stands for something in the nature of
the Union Jack in the flag. . . ."

"Does it!" yelled Jukes, so that every head on the Nan-
Shan's decks looked towards the bridge. Then he sighed,
and with sudden resignation: "It would certainly be a dam'
distressful sight," he said, meekly.

Later in the day he accosted the chief engineer with a

confidential, "Here, let me tell you the old man's latest."

Mr. Solomon Rout (frequently alluded to as Long Sol, Old Sol, or Father Rout), from finding himself almost invariably the tallest man on board every ship he joined, had acquired the habit of a stooping, leisurely condescension. His hair was scant and sandy, his flat cheeks were pale, his bony wrists and long scholarly hands were pale, too, as though he had lived all his life in the shade.

He smiled from on high at Jukes, and went on smoking and glancing about quietly, in the manner of a kind uncle lending an ear to the tale of an excited schoolboy. Then, greatly amused but impassive, he asked:

"And did you throw up the billet?"

"No," cried Jukes, raising a weary, discouraged voice above the harsh buzz of the *Nan-Shan's* friction winches. All of them were hard at work, snatching slings of cargo, high up, to the end of long derricks, only, as it seemed, to let them rip down recklessly by the run. The cargo chains groaned in the gins, clinked on coamings, rattled over the side; and the whole ship quivered, with her long gray flanks smoking in wreaths of steam. "No," cried Jukes, "I didn't. What's the good? I might just as well fling my resignation at this bulkhead. I don't believe you can make a man like that understand anything. He simply knocks me over."

At that moment Captain MacWhirr, back from the shore, crossed the deck, umbrella in hand, escorted by a mournful, self-possessed Chinaman, walking behind in paper-soled silk shoes, and who also carried an umbrella.

The master of the *Nan-Shan*, speaking just audibly and gazing at his boots as his manner was, remarked that it would be necessary to call at Fu-chau this trip, and desired Mr. Rout to have steam up tomorrow afternoon at one o'clock sharp. He pushed back his hat to wipe his forehead, observing at the same time that he hated going ashore anyhow; while overtopping him Mr. Rout, without deigning a

word, smoked austerely, nursing his right elbow in the palm
of his left hand. Then Jukes was directed in the same subdued voice to keep the forward 'tween-deck clear of cargo.
Two hundred coolies were going to be put down there. The
Bun Hin Company were sending that lot home. Twenty-
five bags of rice would be coming off in a sampan directly,
for stores. All seven-years' men they were, said Captain
MacWhirr, with a camphor-wood chest to every man. The
carpenter should be set to work nailing three-inch battens
along the deck below, fore and aft, to keep these boxes from
shifting in a sea-way. Jukes had better look to it at once.
"D'ye hear, Jukes?" This Chinaman here was coming with
the ship as far as Fu-chau—a sort of interpreter he would
be. Bun Hin's clerk he was, and wanted to have a look at
the space. Jukes had better take him forward. "D'ye hear,
Jukes?"

Jukes took care to punctuate these instructions in proper
places with the obligatory "Yes, sir," ejaculated without
enthusiasm. His brusque "Come along, John; make look
see" set the Chinaman in motion at his heels.

"Wanchee look see, all same look see can do," said Jukes,
who, having no talent for foreign languages, mangled the
very pidgin-English cruelly. He pointed at the open hatch.
"Catchee number one piecie place to sleep in. Eh?"

He was gruff, as became his racial superiority, but not unfriendly. The Chinaman, gazing sad and speechless into the
darkness of the hatchway, seemed to stand at the head of a
yawning grave.

"No catchee rain down there—savee?" pointed out Jukes.
"Suppose all'ee same fine weather, one piecie coolie-man
come topside," he pursued, warming up imaginatively.
"Make so—Phooooo!" He expanded his chest and blew out
his cheeks. "Savee, John? Breathe—fresh air. Good.
Eh? Washee him piecie pants, chow-chow topside—see,
John?"

With his mouth and hands he made exuberant motions of eating rice and washing clothes; and the Chinaman, who concealed his distrust of this pantomime under a collected demeanor tinged by a gentle and refined melancholy, glanced out of his almond eyes from Jukes to the hatch and back again. "Velly good," he murmured, in a disconsolate undertone, and hastened smoothly along the decks, dodging obstacles in his course. He disappeared, ducking low under a sling of ten dirty gunny-bags full of some costly merchandise and exhaling a repulsive smell.

Captain MacWhirr meantime had gone on the bridge, and into the chart-room, where a letter, commenced two days before, awaited termination. These long letters began with the words, "My darling wife," and the steward, between the scrubbing of the floors and the dusting of chronometer-boxes, snatched at every opportunity to read them. They interested him much more than they possibly could the woman for whose eye they were intended; and this for the reason that they related in minute detail each successive trip of the *Nan-Shan*.

Her master, faithful to facts, which alone his consciousness reflected, would set them down with painstaking care upon many pages. The house in a northern suburb to which these pages were addressed had a bit of garden before the bow-windows, a deep porch of good appearance, colored glass with imitation lead frame in the front door. He paid five-and-forty pounds a year for it, and did not think the rent too high, because Mrs. MacWhirr (a pretentious person with a scraggy neck and a disdainful manner) was admittedly ladylike, and in the neighborhood considered as "quite superior." The only secret of her life was her abject terror of the time when her husband would come home to stay for good. Under the same roof there dwelt also a daughter called Lydia and a son, Tom. These two were but slightly acquainted with their father. Mainly, they knew him as a rare but privileged visitor, who of an evening smoked his pipe in the dining-room and slept in the house. The lanky girl, upon the whole, was rather ashamed of him; the boy was frankly and utterly indifferent in a straight-forward, delightful, unaffected way manly boys have.

And Captain MacWhirr wrote home from the coast of China twelve times every year, desiring quaintly to be "re-membered to the children," and subscribing himself "your loving husband," as calmly as if the words so long used by so many men were, apart from their shape, worn-out things, and of a faded meaning.

The China seas north and south are narrow seas. They are seas full of every-day, eloquent facts, such as islands sand-banks, reefs, swift and changeable currents—tangled facts that nevertheless speak to a seaman in clear and defi-nite language. Their speech appealed to Captain Mac-Whirr's sense of realities so forcibly that he had given up his stateroom below and practically lived all his days on the bridge of his ship, often having his meals sent up, and sleep-ing at night in the chart-room. And he indited there his home letters. Each of them, without exception, contained the phrase, "The weather has been very fine this trip," or some other form of a statement to that effect. And this statement, too, in its wonderful persistence, was of the same perfect accuracy as all the others they contained.

Mr. Rout likewise wrote letters; only no one on board knew how chatty he could be pen in hand, because the chief engineer had enough imagination to keep his desk locked. His wife relished his style greatly. They were a childless couple, and Mrs. Rout, a big, high-bosomed, jolly woman of forty, shared with Mr. Rout's toothless and venerable mother a little cottage near Teddington. She would run over her correspondence, at breakfast, with lively eyes, and scream out interesting passages in a joyous voice at the deaf old lady, prefacing each extract by the warning shout.

"Solomon says!" She had the trick of firing off Solomon's utterances also upon strangers, astonishing them easily by the unfamiliar text and the unexpectedly jocular vein of these quotations. On the day the new curate called for the first time at the cottage, she found occasion to remark, "As Solomon says, 'The engineers that go down to the sea in ships behold the wonders of sailor nature' "—when a change in the visitor's countenance made her stop and stare.

"Solomon. . . . Oh! . . . . Mrs. Rout," stuttered the young man, very red in the face, "I must say . . . I don't. . . ."

"He's my husband," she announced in a great shout, throwing herself back in the chair. Perceiving the joke, she laughed immoderately with a handkerchief to her eyes, while he sat wearing a forced smile, and, from his inexperience of jolly women, fully persuaded that she must be deplorably insane. They were excellent friends afterwards; for, absolving her from irreverent intention, he came to think she was a very worthy person indeed; and he learned in time to receive without flinching other scraps of Solomon's wisdom.

"For my part," Solomon was reported by his wife to have said once, "give me the dullest ass for a skipper before a rogue. There is a way to take a fool; but a rogue is smart and slippery." This was an airy generalization drawn from the particular case of Captain MacWhirr's honesty, which, in itself, had the heavy obviousness of a lump of clay. On the other hand, Mr. Jukes, unable to generalize, unmarried, and unengaged, was in the habit of opening his heart after another fashion to an old chum and former shipmate, actually serving as second officer on board an Atlantic liner.

First of all he would insist upon the advantages of the Eastern trade, hinting at its superiority to the Western ocean service. He extolled the sky, the seas, the ships, and the easy life of the Far East. The *Nan-Shan*, he affirmed, was second to none as a sea-boat.

"We have no brass-bound uniforms, but then we are like brothers here," he wrote. "We all mess together and live like fighting-cocks. . . . All the chaps of the black-squad are as decent as they make that kind, and old Sol, the Chief, is a dry stick. We are good friends. As to our old man, you could not find a quieter skipper. Sometimes you would think he hadn't sense enough to see anything wrong. And yet it isn't that. Can't be. He has been in command for a good few years now. He doesn't do anything actually foolish, and gets his ship along all right without worrying anybody. I believe he hasn't brains enough to enjoy kicking up a row. I don't take advantage of him. I would scorn it. Outside the routine of duty he doesn't seem to understand more than half of what you tell him. We get a laugh out of this at times; but it is dull, too, to be with a man like this—in the long-run. Old Sol says he hasn't much conversation. Conversation! O Lord! He never talks. The other day I had been yarning under the bridge with one of the engineers, and he must have heard us. When I came up to take my watch, he steps out of the chart-room and has a good look all round, peeps over at the sidelights, glances at the compass, squints upwards at the stars. That's his regular performance. By-and-by he says: 'Was that you talking just now in the port alleyway?' 'Yes, sir.' 'With the third engineer?' 'Yes, sir.' He walks off to starboard, and sits under the dodger on a little camp-stool of his, and for half an hour perhaps he makes no sound, except that I heard him sneeze once. Then after a while I hear him getting up over there, and he strolls across to port, where I was. 'I can't understand what you can find to talk about,' says he. 'Two solid hours. I am not blaming you. I see people ashore at it all day long, and then in the evening they sit down and keep at it over the drinks. Must be saying the same things over and over again. I can't understand.'

"Did you ever hear anything like that? And he was so

patient about it. It made me quite sorry for him. But he is exasperating, too, sometimes. Of course one would not do anything to vex him even if it were worth while. But it isn't. He's so jolly innocent that if you were to put your thumb to your nose and wave your fingers at him he would only wonder gravely to himself what got into you. He told me once quite simply that he found it very difficult to make out what made people always act so queerly. He's too dense to trouble about, and that's the truth."

Thus wrote Mr. Jukes to his chum in the Western ocean trade, out of the fullness of his heart and the liveliness of his fancy.

He had expressed his honest opinion. It was not worth while trying to impress a man of that sort. If the world had been full of such men, life would have probably appeared to Jukes an unentertaining and unprofitable business. He was not alone in his opinion. The sea itself, as if sharing Mr. Jukes' good-natured forbearance, had never put itself out to startle the silent man, who seldom looked up, and wandered innocently over the waters with the only visible purpose of getting food, raiment, and house-room for three people ashore. Dirty weather he had known, of course. He had been made wet, uncomfortable, tired in the usual way, felt at the time and presently forgotten. So that upon the whole he had been justified in reporting fine weather at home. But he had never been given a glimpse of immeasurable strength and of immoderate wrath, the wrath that passes exhausted but never appeased—the wrath and fury of the passionate sea. He knew it existed, as we know that crime and abominations exist; he had heard of it as a peaceable citizen in a town hears of battles, famines, and floods, and yet knows nothing of what these things mean—though, indeed, he may have been mixed up in a street row, have gone without his dinner once, or been soaked to the skin in a shower. Captain MacWhirr had sailed over the surface of the oceans as some men go skimming over the years of existence to sink gently into a placid grave, ignorant of life to the last, without ever having been made to see all it may contain of perfidy, of violence, and of terror. There are on sea and land such men thus fortunate—or thus disdained by destiny or by the sea.

II

Observing the steady fall of the barometer, Captain Mac-Whirr thought, "There's some dirty weather knocking about." This is precisely what he thought. He had had an experience of moderately dirty weather—the term *dirty* as applied to the weather implying only moderate discomfort to the seaman. Had he been informed by an indisputable authority that the end of the world was to be finally accomplished by a catastrophic disturbance of the atmosphere, he would have assimilated the information under the simple idea of dirty weather, and no other, because he had no experience of cataclysms, and belief does not necessarily imply comprehension. The wisdom of his country had pronounced by means of an Act of Parliament that before he could be considered as fit to take charge of a ship he should be able to answer certain simple questions on the subject of circular storms such as hurricanes, cyclones, typhoons; and apparently he had answered them, since he was now in command of the *Nan-Shan* in the China seas during the season of typhoons. But if he had answered he remembered nothing of it. He was, however, conscious of being made uncomfortable by the clammy heat. He came out on the bridge, and found no relief to this oppression. The air seemed thick. He gasped like a fish, and began to believe himself greatly out of sorts.

The *Nan-Shan* was ploughing a vanishing furrow upon the circle of the sea that had the surface and the shimmer of an undulating piece of gray silk. The sun, pale and without rays, poured down leaden heat in a strangely indecisive light, and the Chinamen were lying prostrate about the decks. Their bloodless, pinched, yellow faces were like the faces of bilious invalids. Captain MacWhirr noticed two of them especially, stretched out on their backs below the bridge. As soon as they had closed their eyes they seemed dead. Three others, however, were quarreling barbarously away forward; and one big fellow, half naked, with herculean shoulders, was hanging limply over a winch; another, sitting on the deck, his knees up and his head drooping sideways in a girlish attitude, was plaiting his pigtail with infinite languor depicted in his whole person and in the very movement of his fingers. The smoke struggled with difficulty out of the funnel, and instead of streaming away spread itself out like an infernal sort of cloud, smelling of sulphur and raining soot all over the decks.

"What the devil are you doing there, Mr. Jukes?" asked Captain MacWhirr.

This unusual form of address, though mumbled rather than spoken, caused the body of Mr. Jukes to start as though it had been prodded under the fifth rib. He had had a low bench brought on the bridge, and sitting on it, with a length of rope curled about his feet and a piece of canvas stretched over his knees, was pushing a sail-needle vigorously. He looked up, and his surprise gave to his eyes an expression of innocence and candor.

"I am only roping some of that new set of bags we made last trip for whipping up coals," he remonstrated, gently. "We shall want them for the next coaling, sir."

"What became of the others?"

"Why, worn out, of course, sir."

Captain MacWhirr, after glaring down irresolutely at his chief mate, disclosed the gloomy and cynical conviction that more than half of them had been lost overboard, "if only the truth was known," and retired to the other end of the bridge. Jukes, exasperated by this unprovoked attack, broke the needle at the second stitch, and dropping his work got up and cursed the heat in a violent undertone.

The propeller thumped, the three Chinamen forward had given up squabbling very suddenly, and the one who had been plaiting his tail clasped his legs and stared dejectedly over his knees. The lurid sunshine cast faint and sickly shadows. The swell ran higher and swifter every moment, and the ship lurched heavily in the smooth, deep hollows of the sea.

"I wonder where that beastly swell comes from," said Jukes aloud, recovering himself after a stagger.

"Northeast," grunted the literal MacWhirr, from his side of the bridge. "There's some dirty weather knocking about. Go and look at the glass."

When Jukes came out of the chart-room, the cast of his countenance had changed to thoughtfulness and concern. He caught hold of the bridge-rail and stared ahead.

The temperature in the engine-room had gone up to a hundred and seventeen degrees. Irritated voices were ascending through the skylight and through the fiddle of the stokehold in a harsh and resonant uproar, mingled with angry clangs and scrapes of metal, as if men with limbs of iron and throats of bronze had been quarreling down there. The second engineer was falling foul of the stokers for letting the steam go down. He was a man with arms like a blacksmith, and generally feared; but that afternoon the stokers were answering him back recklessly, and slammed the furnace doors with the fury of despair. Then the noise ceased suddenly, and the second engineer appeared, emerging out of the stokehold streaked with grime and soaking wet like a chimney-sweep coming out of a well. As soon as his head was clear of the fiddle he began to scold Jukes for not trimming properly the stokehold ventilators; and in answer Jukes made with his hands deprecatory soothing signs meaning: "No wind—can't be helped—you can see for yourself."

But the other wouldn't hear reason. His teeth flashed angrily in his dirty face. He didn't mind, he said, the trouble of punching their blanked heads down there, blank his soul, but did the condemned sailors think you could keep steam up in the God-forsaken boilers simply by knocking the blanked stokers about? No, by George! You had to get some draught, too—may he be everlastingly blanked for a swab-headed deck-hand if you didn't! And the chief, too, rampaging before the steam-gauge and carrying on like a lunatic up and down the engine-room ever since noon. What did Jukes think he was stuck up there for, if he couldn't get one of his decayed, good-for-nothing deck-cripples to turn the ventilators to the wind?

The relations of the "engine-room" and the "deck" of the *Nan-Shan* were, as is known, of a brotherly nature; therefore Jukes leaned over and begged the other in a restrained tone not to make a disgusting ass of himself; the skipper was on the other side of the bridge. But the second declared mutinously that he didn't care a rap who was on the other side of the bridge, and Jukes, passing in a flash from lofty disapproval into a state of exaltation, invited him in unflattering terms to come up and twist the beastly things to please himself, and catch such wind as a donkey of his sort could find. The second rushed up to the fray. He flung himself at the port ventilator as though he meant to tear it out bodily and toss it overboard. All he did was to move the cowl round a few inches, with an enormous expenditure of force, and seemed spent in the effort. He leaned against the back of the wheelhouse, and Jukes walked up to him.

"Oh, Heavens!" ejaculated the engineer in a feeble voice. He lifted his eyes to the sky, and then let his glassy stare descend to meet the horizon that, tilting up to an angle of forty degrees, seemed to hang on a slant for a while and settled down slowly. "Heavens! Phew! What's up, anyhow?"

Jukes, straddling his long legs like a pair of compasses, put
on an air of superiority. "We're going to catch it this time,"
he said. "The barometer is tumbling down like anything,
Harry. And you trying to kick up that silly row. . . ."

The word "barometer" seemed to revive the second engineer's mad animosity. Collecting afresh all his energies, he
directed Jukes in a low and brutal tone to shove the unmentionable instrument down his gory throat. Who cared for
his crimson barometer? It was the steam—the steam—that
was going down; and what between the firemen going faint
and the chief going silly, it was worse than a dog's life for
him; he didn't care a tinker's curse how soon the whole show
was blown out of the water. He seemed on the point of
having a cry, but after regaining his breath he muttered
darkly, "I'll faint them," and dashed off. He stopped upon
the fiddle long enough to shake his fist at the unnatural daylight, and dropped into the dark hole with a whoop.

When Jukes turned, his eyes fell upon the rounded back
and the big red ears of Captain MacWhirr, who had come
across. He did not look at his chief officer, but said at once,
"That's a very violent man, that second engineer."

"Jolly good second, anyhow," grunted Jukes. "They
can't keep up steam," he added, rapidly, and made a grab at
the rail against the coming lurch.

Captain MacWhirr, unprepared, took a run and brought
himself up with a jerk by an awning stanchion.

"A profane man," he said, obstinately. "If this goes on,
I'll have to get rid of him the first chance."

"It's the heat," said Jukes. "The weather's awful. It
would make a saint swear. Even up here I feel exactly as if
I had my head tied up in a woollen blanket."

Captain MacWhirr looked up. "D'ye mean to say, Mr.
Jukes, you ever had your head tied up in a blanket? What
was that for?"

"It's a manner of speaking, sir," said Jukes, stolidly.

"Some of you fellows do go on! What's that about saints swearing? I wish you wouldn't talk so wild. What sort of saint would that be that would swear? No more saint than yourself, I expect. And what's a blanket got to do with it —or the weather either. . . . The heat does not make me swear—does it? It's filthy bad temper. That's what it is. And what's the good of your talking like this?"

Thus Captain MacWhirr expostulated against the use of images in speech, and at the end electrified Jukes by a contemptuous snort, followed by words of passion and resentment: "Damme! I'll fire him out of the ship if he don't look out."

And Jukes, incorrigible, thought: "Goodness me! Somebody's put a new inside to my old man. Here's temper, if you like. Of course it's the weather; what else? It would make an angel quarrelsome—let alone a saint."

All the Chinamen on deck appeared at their last gasp.

At its setting the sun had a diminished diameter and an expiring brown, rayless glow, as if millions of centuries elapsing since the morning had brought it near its end. A dense bank of cloud became visible to the northward; it had a sinister dark olive tint, and lay low and motionless upon the sea, resembling a solid obstacle in the path of the ship. She went floundering towards it like an exhausted creature driven to its death. The coppery twilight retired slowly, and the darkness brought out overhead a swarm of unsteady, big stars, that, as if blown upon, flickered exceedingly and seemed to hang very near the earth. At eight o'clock Jukes went into the chart-room to write up the ship's log.

He copied neatly out of the rough-book the number of miles, the course of the ship, and in the column for "wind" scrawled the word "calm" from top to bottom of the eight hours since noon. He was exasperated by the continuous, monotonous rolling of the ship. The heavy inkstand would slide away in a manner that suggested perverse intelligence

in dodging the pen. Having written in the large space
under the head of "Remarks" "Heat very oppressive," he
stuck the end of the pen-holder in his teeth, pipe fashion,
and mopped his face carefully.

"Ship rolling heavily in a high cross swell," he began again,
and commented to himself, "Heavily is no word for it."
Then he wrote: "Sunset threatening, with a low bank of
clouds to N. and E.   Sky clear overhead."

Sprawling over the table with arrested pen, he glanced
out of the door, and in that frame of his vision he saw all
the stars flying upwards between the teakwood jambs on a
black sky.   The whole lot took flight together and disappeared, leaving only a blackness flecked with white flashes,
for the sea was as black as the sky and speckled with foam
afar.   The stars that had flown to the roll came back on the
return swing of the ship, rushing downwards in their glittering multitude, not of fiery points, but enlarged to tiny discs
brilliant with a clear wet sheen.

Jukes watched the flying big stars for a moment, and then
wrote: 8 P. M.   Swell increasing.   Ship laboring and taking
water on her decks.   Battened down the coolies for the night.
Barometer still falling."   He paused, and thought to himself,
"Perhaps nothing whatever'll come of it."   And then he
closed resolutely his entries: "Every appearance of a typhoon
coming on."

On going out he had to stand aside, and Captain Mac-
Whirr strode over the doorstep without saying a word or
making a sign.

"Shut the door, Mr. Jukes, will you?" he cried from within.

Jukes turned back to do so, muttering ironically: "Afraid
to catch cold, I suppose."   It was his watch below, but he
yearned for communion with his kind; and he remarked
cheerily to the second mate: "Doesn't look so bad, after all
—does it?"

The second mate was marching to and fro on the bridge,

tripping down with small steps one moment, and the next climbing with difficulty the shifting slope of the deck. At the sound of Jukes' voice he stood still, facing forward, but made no reply.

"Hallo! That's a heavy one," said Jukes, swaying to meet the long roll till his lowered hand touched the planks. This time the second mate made in his throat a noise of an unfriendly nature.

He was an oldish, shabby little fellow, with bad teeth and no hair on his face. He had been shipped in a hurry in Shanghai, that trip when the second officer brought from home had delayed the ship three hours in port by contriving (in some manner Captain MacWhirr could never understand) to fall overboard into an empty coal-lighter lying alongside, and had to be sent ashore to the hospital with concussion of the brain and a broken limb or two.

Jukes was not discouraged by the unsympathetic sound. "The Chinamen must be having a lovely time of it down there," he said. "It's lucky for them the old girl has the easiest roll of any ship I've ever been in. There now! This one wasn't so bad."

"You wait," snarled the second mate.

With his sharp nose, red at the tip, and his thin pinched lips, he always looked as though he were raging inwardly; and he was concise in his speech to the point of rudeness. All his time off duty he spent in his cabin with the door shut, keeping so still in there that he was supposed to fall asleep as soon as he had disappeared; but the man who came in to wake him for his watch on deck would invariably find him with his eyes wide open, flat on his back in the bunk, and glaring irritably from a soiled pillow. He never wrote any letters, did not seem to hope for news from anywhere; and though he had been heard once to mention West Hartlepool, it was with extreme bitterness, and only in connection with the extortionate charges of a boarding-house. He was one of those men who are picked up at need in the ports of the world. They are competent enough, appear hopelessly hard up, show no evidence of any sort of vice, and carry about them all the signs of manifest failure. They come aboard on an emergency, care for no ship afloat, live in their own atmosphere of casual connection amongst their shipmates who know nothing of them, and make up their minds to leave at inconvenient times. They clear out with no words of leave-taking in some God-forsaken port other men would fear to be stranded in, and go ashore in company of a shabby sea-chest, corded like a treasure-box, and with an air of shaking the ship's dust off their feet.

"You wait," he repeated, balanced in great swings with his back to Jukes, motionless and implacable.

"Do you mean to say we are going to catch it hot?" asked Jukes with boyish interest.

"Say? . . . I say nothing. You don't catch me," snapped the little second mate, with a mixture of pride, scorn, and cunning, as if Jukes' question had been a trap cleverly detected. "Oh, no! None of you here shall make a fool of me if I know it," he mumbled to himself.

Jukes reflected rapidly that this second mate was a mean little beast, and in his heart he wished poor Jack Allen had never smashed himself up in the coal-lighter. The far-off blackness ahead of the ship was like another night seen through the starry night of the earth—the starless night of the immensities beyond the created universe, revealed in its appalling stillness through a low fissure in the glittering sphere of which the earth is the kernel.

"Whatever there might be about," said Jukes, "we are steaming straight into it."

"*You've* said it," caught up the second mate, always with his back to Jukes. "You've said it, mind—not I."

"Oh, go to Jericho!" said Jukes, frankly; and the other emitted a triumphant little chuckle.

"You've said it," he repeated.

"And what of that?"

"I've known some real good men get into trouble with their skippers for saying a dam' sight less," answered the second mate feverishly. "Oh, no! You don't catch me."

"You seem deucedly anxious not to give yourself away," said Jukes, completely soured by such absurdity. "I wouldn't be afraid to say what I think."

"Aye, to me! That's no great trick. I am nobody, and well I know it."

The ship, after a pause of comparative steadiness, started upon a series of rolls, one worse than the other, and for a time Jukes, preserving his equilibrium, was too busy to open his mouth. As soon as the violent swinging had quieted down somewhat, he said: "This is a bit too much of a good thing. Whether anything is coming or not I think she ought to be put head on to that swell. The old man is just gone in to lie down. Hang me if I don't speak to him."

But when he opened the door of the chart-room he saw his captain reading a book. Captain MacWhirr was not lying down: he was standing up with one hand grasping the edge of the bookshelf and the other holding open before his face a thick volume. The lamp wriggled in the gimbals, the loosened books toppled from side to side on the shelf, the long barometer swung in jerky circles, the table altered its slant every moment. In the midst of all this stir and movement Captain MacWhirr, holding on, showed his eyes above the upper edge, and asked, "What's the matter?"

"Swell getting worse, sir."

"Noticed that in here," muttered Captain MacWhirr. "Anything wrong?"

Jukes, inwardly disconcerted by the seriousness of the eyes looking at him over the top of the book, produced an embarrassed grin.

"Rolling like old boots," he said, sheepishly.

"Aye! Very heavy—very heavy. What do you want?"

At this Jukes lost his footing and began to flounder.

"I was thinking of our passengers," he said, in the manner of a man clutching at a straw.

"Passengers?" wondered the Captain gravely. "What passengers?"

"Why, the Chinamen, sir," explained Jukes, very sick of this conversation.

"The Chinamen! Why don't you speak plainly? Couldn't tell what you meant. Never heard a lot of coolies spoken of as passengers before. Passengers, indeed! What's come to you?"

Captain MacWhirr, closing the book on his forefinger, lowered his arm and looked completely mystified. "Why are you thinking of the Chinamen, Mr. Jukes?" he inquired.

Jukes took a plunge, like a man driven to it. "She's rolling her decks full of water, sir. Thought you might put her head on perhaps—for a while. Till this goes down a bit —very soon, I dare say. Head to the eastward. I never knew a ship roll like this."

He held on in the doorway, and Captain MacWhirr, feeling his grip on the shelf inadequate, made up his mind to let go in a hurry, and fell heavily on the couch.

"Head to the eastward?" he said, struggling to sit up. "That's more than four points off her course."

"Yes, sir. Fifty degrees. . . . Would just bring her head far enough round to meet this. . . ."

Captain MacWhirr was now sitting up. He had not dropped the book, and he had not lost his place.

"To the eastward?" he repeated, with dawning astonishment. "To the . . . Where do you think we are bound to? You want me to haul a full-powered steamship four points off her course to make the Chinamen comfortable! Now, I've heard more than enough of mad things done in the world —but this. . . . If I didn't know you, Jukes, I would think

you were in liquor.   Steer four points off. . . . And what
afterwards?   Steer four points over the other way, I suppose,
to make the course good.   What put it into your head that
I would start to tack a steamer as if she were a sailing-ship?"

"Jolly good thing she isn't," threw in Jukes, with bitter
readiness.   "She would have rolled every blessed stick out of
her this afternoon."

"Aye!   And you just would have had to stand and see
them go," said Captain MacWhirr, showing a certain anima-
tion.   "It's a dead calm, isn't it?"

"It is, sir.   But there's something out of the common coming, for sure."

"Maybe.   I suppose you have a notion I should be getting
out of the way of that dirt," said Captain MacWhirr, speaking with the utmost simplicity of manner and tone, and fixing the oilcloth on the floor with a heavy stare.   Thus he
noticed neither Jukes' discomfiture nor the mixture of vexation and astonished respect on his face.

"Now, here's this book," he continued with deliberation,
slapping his thigh with the closed volume.   "I've been reading the chapter on the storms there."

This was true.   He had been reading the chapter on the
storms.   When he had entered the chart-room, it was with
no intention of taking the book down.   Some influence in
the air—the same influence, probably, that caused the steward to bring without orders the Captain's sea-boots and oilskin coat up to the chart-room—had as it were guided his
hand to the shelf; and without taking the time to sit down
he had waded with a conscious effort into the terminology of
the subject.   He lost himself amongst advancing semi-circles,
left- and right-hand quadrants, the curves of the tracks, the
probable bearing of the center, the shifts of wind and the
readings of barometer.   He tried to bring all these things
into a definite relation to himself, and ended by becoming
contemptuously angry with such a lot of words and with so

much advice, all head-work and supposition, without a glimmer of certitude.

"It's the damnedest thing, Jukes," he said. "If a fellow was to believe all that's in there, he would be running most of his time all over the sea trying to get behind the weather."

Again he slapped his leg with the book; and Jukes opened his mouth, but said nothing.

"Running to get behind the weather! Do you understand that, Mr. Jukes? It's the maddest thing!" ejaculated Captain MacWhirr, with pauses, gazing at the floor profoundly. "You would think an old woman had been writing this. It passes me. If that thing means anything useful, then it means that I should at once alter the course away, away to the devil somewhere, and come booming down on Fu-chau from the northward at the tail of this dirty weather that's supposed to be knocking about in our way. From the north! Do you understand, Mr. Jukes? Three hundred extra miles to the distance, and a pretty coal bill to show. I couldn't bring myself to do that if every word in there was gospel truth, Mr. Jukes. Don't you expect me. . . ."

And Jukes, silent, marveled at this display of feeling and loquacity.

"But the truth is that you don't know if the fellow is right, anyhow. How can you tell what a gale is made of till you get it? He isn't aboard here, is he? Very well. Here he says that the center of them things bears eight points off the wind; but we haven't got any wind, for all the barometer falling. Where's his center now?"

"We will get the wind presently," mumbled Jukes.

"Let it come, then," said Captain MacWhirr, with dignified indignation. "It's only to let you see, Mr. Jukes, that you don't find everything in books. All these rules for dodging breezes and circumventing the winds of heaven, Mr. Jukes, seem to me the maddest thing, when you come to look at it sensibly."

He raised his eyes, saw Jukes gazing at him dubiously, and tried to illustrate his meaning.

"About as queer as your extraordinary notion of dodging the ship head to sea, for I don't know how long, to make the Chinamen comfortable; whereas all we've got to do is to take them to Fu-chau, being timed to get there before noon on Friday. If the weather delays me—very well. There's your log-book to talk straight about the weather. But suppose I went swinging off my course and came in two days late, and they asked me: 'Where have you been all that time, Captain?' What could I say to that? 'Went around to dodge the bad weather,' I would say. 'It must've been dam' bad,' they would say. 'Don't know,' I would have to say; 'I've dodged clear of it.' See that, Jukes? I have been thinking it all out this afternoon."

He looked up again in his unseeing, unimaginative way. No one had ever heard him say so much at one time. Jukes, with his arms open in the doorway, was like a man invited to behold a miracle. Unbounded wonder was the intellectual meaning of his eye, while incredulity was seated in his whole countenance.

"A gale is a gale, Mr. Jukes," resumed the Captain, "and a full-powered steam-ship has got to face it. There's just so much dirty weather knocking about the world, and the proper thing is to go through it with none of what old Captain Wilson of the *Melita* calls 'storm strategy.' The other day ashore I heard him hold forth about it to a lot of shipmasters who came in and sat at a table next to mine. It seemed to me the greatest nonsense. He was telling them how he out-maneuvered, I think he said, a terrific gale, so that it never came nearer than fifty miles to him. A neat piece of head-work he called it. How he knew there was a terrific gale fifty miles off beats me altogether. It was like listening to a crazy man. I would have thought Captain Wilson was old enough to know better."

Captain MacWhirr ceased for a moment, then said, "It's your watch below, Mr. Jukes?"

Jukes came to himself with a start. "Yes, sir."

"Leave orders to call me at the slightest change," said the Captain. He reached up to put the book away, and tucked his legs upon the couch. "Shut the door so that it don't fly open, will you? I can't stand a door banging. They've put a lot of rubbishy locks into this ship, I must say."

Captain MacWhirr closed his eyes.

He did so to rest himself. He was tired, and he experienced that state of mental vacuity which comes at the end of an exhaustive discussion that has liberated some belief matured in the course of meditative years. He had indeed been making his confession of faith, had he only known it; and its effect was to make Jukes, on the other side of the door, stand scratching his head for a good while.

Captain MacWhirr opened his eyes.

He thought he must have been asleep. What was that loud noise? Wind? Why had he not been called? The lamp wriggled in its gimbals, the barometer swung in circles, the table altered its slant every moment; a pair of limp sea-boots with collapsed tops went sliding past the couch. He put out his hand instantly, and captured one.

Jukes' face appeared in a crack of the door: only his face, very red, with staring eyes. The flame of the lamp leaped, a piece of paper flew up, a rush of air enveloped Captain Mac-Whirr. Beginning to draw on the boot, he directed an expectant gaze at Jukes' swollen, excited features.

"Came on like this," shouted Jukes, "five minutes ago . . . all of a sudden."

The head disappeared with a bang, and a heavy splash and patter of drops swept past the closed door as if a pailful of melted lead had been flung against the house. A whistling could be heard now upon the deep vibrating noise outside. The stuffy chart-room seemed as full of draughts as a shed.

Captain MacWhirr collared the other sea-boot on its violent
passage along the floor. He was not flustered, but he could
not find at once the opening for inserting his foot. The
shoes he had flung off were scurrying from end to end of the
cabin, gamboling playfully over each other like puppies. As
soon as he stood up he kicked at them viciously, but without
effect.

He threw himself into the attitude of a lunging fencer, to
reach after his oilskin coat; and afterwards he staggered all
over the confined space while he jerked himself into it. Very
grave, straddling his legs far apart, and stretching his neck,
he started to tie deliberately the strings of his sou'wester
under his chin, with thick fingers that trembled slightly. He
went through all the movements of a woman putting on her
bonnet before a glass, with a strained, listening attention, as
though he had expected every moment to hear the shout of
his name in the confused clamor that had suddenly beset his
ship. Its increase filled his ears while he was getting ready
to go out and confront whatever it might mean. It was
tumultuous and very loud—made up of the rush of the wind,
the crashes of the sea, with that prolonged deep vibration of
the air, like the roll of an immense and remote drum beating
the charge of the gale.

He stood for a moment in the light of the lamp, thick,
clumsy, shapeless in his panoply of combat, vigilant and red-
faced.

"There's a lot of weight in this," he muttered.

As soon as he attempted to open the door the wind caught
it. Clinging to the handle, he was dragged out over the
doorstep, and at once found himself engaged with the wind
in a sort of personal scuffle whose object was the shutting of
that door. At the last moment a tongue of air scurried in
and licked out the flame of the lamp.

Ahead of the ship he perceived a great darkness lying upon
a multitude of white flashes; on the starboard beam a few

amazing stars drooped, dim and fitful, above an immense waste of broken seas, as if seen through a mad drift of smoke.

On the bridge a knot of men, indistinct and toiling, were making great efforts in the light of the wheel-house windows that shone mistily on their heads and backs. Suddenly darkness closed upon one pane, then on another. The voices of the lost group reached him after the manner of men's voices in a gale, in shreds and fragments of forlorn shouting snatched past the ear. All at once Jukes appeared at his side, yelling, with his head down.

"Watch—put in—wheelhouse shutters—glass—afraid—blow in."

Jukes heard his commander upbraiding.

"This—come—anything—warning—call me."

He tried to explain, with the uproar pressing on his lips.

"Light—air—remained—bridge—sudden—north-east—could turn—thought—you—sure—hear."

They had gained the shelter of the weather-cloth, and could converse with raised voices, as people quarrel.

"I got the hands along to cover up all the ventilators. Good job I had remained on deck. I didn't think you would be asleep, and so . . . What did you say, sir? What?"

"Nothing," cried Captain MacWhirr. "I said—all right."

"By all the powers! We've got it this time," observed Jukes in a howl.

"You haven't altered her course?" inquired Captain MacWhirr, straining his voice.

"No, sir. Certainly not. Wind came out right ahead. And here comes the head sea."

A plunge of the ship ended in a shock as if she had landed her forefoot upon something solid. After a moment of stillness a lofty flight of sprays drove hard with the wind upon their faces.

"Keep her at it as long as we can," shouted Captain MacWhirr.

Before Jukes had squeezed the salt water out of his eyes all the stars had disappeared.

III

Jukes was as ready a man as any half-dozen young mates that may be caught by casting a net upon the waters; and though he had been somewhat taken aback by the startling viciousness of the first squall, he had pulled himself together on the instant, had called out the hands and had rushed them along to secure such openings about the deck as had not been already battened down earlier in the evening. Shouting in his fresh, stentorian voice, "Jump, boys, and bear a hand!" he led in the work, telling himself the while that he had "just expected this."

But at the same time he was growing aware that this was rather more than he had expected. From the first stir of the air felt on his cheek the gale seemed to take upon itself the accumulated impetus of an avalanche. Heavy sprays enveloped the *Nan-Shan* from stem to stern, and instantly, in the midst of her regular rolling, she began to jerk and plunge as though she had gone mad with fright.

Jukes thought, "This is no joke." While he was exchanging explanatory yells with his captain, a sudden lowering of the darkness came upon the night, falling before their vision like something palpable. It was as if the masked lights of the world had been turned down. Jukes was uncritically glad to have his captain at hand. It relieved him as though that man had, by simply coming on deck, taken most of the gale's weight upon his shoulders. Such is the prestige, the privilege, and the burden of command.

Captain MacWhirr could expect no relief of that sort from any one on earth. Such is the loneliness of command. He was trying to see, with that watchful manner of a seaman who stares into the wind's eye as if into the eye of an adversary, to penetrate the hidden intention and guess the aim and force of the thrust. The strong wind swept at him out of a vast obscurity; he felt under his feet the uneasiness of his ship, and he could not even discern the shadow of her shape. He wished it were not so; and very still he waited, feeling stricken by a blind man's helplessness.

To be silent was natural to him, dark or shine. Jukes, at his elbow, made himself heard yelling cheerily in the gusts, "We must have got the worst of it at once, sir." A faint burst of lightning quivered all round, as if flashed into a cavern—into a black and secret chamber of the sea, with a floor of foaming crests.

It unveiled for a sinister, fluttering moment a ragged mass of clouds hanging low, the lurch of the long outlines of the ship, the black figures of men caught on the bridge, heads forward, as if petrified in the act of butting. The darkness palpitated down upon all this, and then the real thing came at last.

It was something formidable and swift, like the sudden smashing of a vial of wrath. It seemed to explode all round the ship with an overpowering concussion and a rush of great waters, as if an immense dam had been blown up to windward. In an instant the men lost touch of each other. This is the disintegrating power of a great wind: it isolates one from one's kind. An earthquake, a landslip, an avalanche, overtake a man incidentally, as it were—without passion. A furious gale attacks him like a personal enemy, tries to grasp his limbs, fastens upon his mind, seeks to rout his very spirit out of him.

Jukes was driven away from his commander. He fancied himself whirled a great distance through the air. Everything disappeared—even, for a moment, his power of thinking; but his hand had found one of the rail-stanchions. His distress was by no means alleviated by an inclination to disbelieve the reality of this experience. Though young, he had seen some bad weather, and had never doubted his ability to imagine the worst; but this was so much beyond his powers of fancy that it appeared incompatible with the existence of any ship whatever. He would have been incredulous about himself in the same way, perhaps, had he not been so harassed by the necessity of exerting a wrestling effort against a force trying to tear him away from his hold. Moreover, the conviction of not being utterly destroyed returned to him through the sensations of being half-drowned, bestially shaken, and partly choked.

It seemed to him he remained there precariously alone with the stanchion for a long, long time. The rain poured on him, flowed, drove in sheets. He breathed in gasps; and sometimes the water he swallowed was fresh and sometimes it was salt. For the most part he kept his eyes shut tight, as if suspecting his sight might be destroyed in the immense flurry of the elements. When he ventured to blink hastily, he derived some moral support from the green gleam of the starboard light shining feebly upon the flight of rain and sprays. He was actually looking at it when its ray fell upon the uprearing sea which put it out. He saw the head of the wave topple over, adding the mite of its crash to the tremendous uproar raging around him, and almost at the same instant the stanchion was wrenched away from his embracing arms. After a crushing thump on his back he found himself suddenly afloat and borne upwards. His first irresistible notion was that the whole China Sea had climbed on the bridge. Then, more sanely, he concluded himself gone overboard. All the time he was being tossed, flung, and rolled in great volumes of water, he kept on repeating mentally, with the utmost precipitation, the words: "My God! My God! My God! My God!"

All at once, in a revolt of misery and despair, he formed the crazy resolution to get out of that. And he began to thresh about with his arms and legs. But as soon as he commenced his wretched struggles he discovered that he had become somehow mixed up with a face, an oilskin coat, somebody's boots. He clawed ferociously all these things in turn, lost them, found them again, lost them once more, and finally was himself caught in the firm clasp of a pair of stout arms. He returned the embrace closely round a thick solid body. He had found his captain.

They tumbled over and over, tightening their hug. Suddenly the water let them down with a brutal bang; and, stranded against the side of the wheelhouse, out of breath and bruised, they were left to stagger up in the wind and hold on where they could.

Jukes came out of it rather horrified, as though he had escaped some unparalleled outrage directed at his feelings. It weakened his faith in himself. He started shouting aimlessly to the man he could feel near him in that fiendish blackness, "Is it you, sir? Is it you, sir?" till his temples seemed ready to burst. And he heard in answer a voice, as if crying far away, as if screaming to him fretfully from a very great distance, the one word "Yes!" Other seas swept again over the bridge. He received them defencelessly right over his bare head, with both his hands engaged in holding.

The motion of the ship was extravagant. Her lurches had an appalling helplessness: she pitched as if taking a header into a void, and seemed to find a wall to hit every time. When she rolled she fell on her side headlong, and she would be righted back by such a demolishing blow that Jukes felt her reeling as a clubbed man reels before he collapses. The gale howled and scuffled about gigantically in the darkness, as though the entire world were one black gully. At certain moments the air streamed against the ship as if sucked through a tunnel with a concentrated solid force of impact that seemed to lift her clean out of the water and keep her up for an instant with only a quiver running through her from end to end. And then she would begin her tumbling again as if dropped back into a boiling caldron. Jukes tried hard to compose his mind and judge things coolly.

The sea, flattened down in the heavier gusts, would uprise and overwhelm both ends of the *Nan-Shan* in snowy rushes of foam, expanding wide, beyond both rails, into the night. And on this dazzling sheet, spread under the blackness of the clouds and emitting a bluish glow, Captain MacWhirr could catch a desolate glimpse of a few tiny specks black as ebony, the tops of the hatches, the battened companions, the heads of all the covered winches, the foot of a mast. This was all he could see of his ship. Her middle structure, covered by the bridge which bore him, his mate, the closed wheelhouse where a man was steering shut up with the fear of being swept overboard together with the whole thing in one great crash—her middle structure was like a half-tide rock awash upon a coast. It was like an outlying rock with the water boiling up, streaming over, pouring off, beating round—like a rock in the surf to which shipwrecked people cling before they let go—only it rose, it sank, it rolled continuously, without respite and rest, like a rock that should have miraculously struck adrift from a coast and gone wallowing upon the sea.

The *Nan-Shan* was being looted by the storm with a senseless, destructive fury: trysails torn out of the extra gaskets, double-lashed awnings blown away, bridge swept clean, weather-cloths burst, rails twisted, light-screens smashed—and two of the boats had gone already. They had gone unheard and unseen, melting, as it were, in the shock and smother of the wave. It was only later, when, upon the white flash of another high sea hurling itself amidships, Jukes had a vision of two pairs of davits leaping black and empty out of the solid blackness, with one overhauled fall flying and an iron-bound block capering in the air, that he became aware of what had happened within about three yards of his back.

He poked his head forward, groping for the ear of his commander. His lips touched it—big, fleshy, very wet. He cried in an agitated tone, "Our boats are going now, sir."

And again he heard that voice, forced and ringing feebly, but with a penetrating effect of quietness in the enormous discord of noises, as if sent out from some remote spot of peace beyond the black wastes of the gale; again he heard a man's voice—the frail and indomitable sound that can be made to carry an infinity of thought, resolution and purpose, that shall be pronouncing confident words on the last day, when heavens fall, and justice is done—again he heard it, and it was crying to him, as if from very, very far—"All right."

He thought he had not managed to make himself understood. "Our boats—I say boats—the boats, sir! Two gone!"

The same voice, within a foot of him and yet so remote, yelled sensibly, "Can't be helped."

Captain MacWhirr had never turned his face, but Jukes caught some more words on the wind.

"What can—expect—when hammering through—such —— Bound to leave—something behind—stands to reason."

Watchfully Jukes listened for more. No more came. This was all Captain MacWhirr had to say; and Jukes could picture to himself rather than see the broad squat back before him. An impenetrable obscurity pressed down upon the ghostly glimmers of the sea. A dull conviction seized upon Jukes that there was nothing to be done.

If the steering-gear did not give way, if the immense volumes of water did not burst the deck in or smash one of the hatches, if the engines did not give up, if way could be kept on the ship against this terrific wind, and she did not bury herself in one of these awful seas, of whose white crests alone, topping high above her bows, he could now and then get a sickening glimpse—then there was a chance of her coming

out of it.   Something within him seemed to turn over, bringing uppermost the feeling that the *Nan-Shan* was lost.

"She's done for," he said to himself, with a surprising mental agitation, as though he had discovered an unexpected
meaning in this thought.   One of these things was bound to
happen.   Nothing could be prevented now, and nothing
could be remedied.   The men on board did not count, and
the ship could not last.   This weather was too impossible.

Jukes felt an arm thrown heavily over his shoulders; and
to this overture he responded with great intelligence by
catching hold of his captain round the waist.

They stood clasped thus in the blind night, bracing each
other against the wind, cheek to cheek and lip to ear, in the
manner of two hulks lashed stem to stern together.

And Jukes heard the voice of his commander hardly any
louder than before, but nearer, as though, starting to march
athwart the prodigious rush of the hurricane, it had approached him, bearing that strange effect of quietness like
the serene glow of a halo.

"D'ye know where the hands got to?" it asked, vigorous
and evanescent at the same time, overcoming the strength of
the wind, and swept away from Jukes instantly.

Jukes didn't know.   They were all on the bridge when
the real force of the hurricane struck the ship.   He had no
idea where they had crawled to.   Under the circumstances
they were nowhere, for all the use that could be made of
them.   Somehow the Captain's wish to know distressed
Jukes.

"Want the hands, sir?" he cried, apprehensively.

"Ought to know," asserted Captain MacWhirr.   "Hold
hard."

They held hard.   An outburst of unchained fury, a vicious
rush of the wind absolutely steadied the ship; she rocked
only, quick and light like a child's cradle, for a terrific moment of suspense, while the whole atmosphere, as it seemed,

streamed furiously past her, roaring away from the tenebrous earth.

It suffocated them, and with eyes shut they tightened their grasp. What from the magnitude of the shock might have been a column of water running upright in the dark, butted against the ship, broke short, and fell on her bridge, crushingly, from on high, with a dead burying weight.

A flying fragment of that collapse, a mere splash, enveloped them in one swirl from their feet over their heads, filling violently their ears, mouths and nostrils with salt water. It knocked out their legs, wrenched in haste at their arms, seethed away swiftly under their chins; and opening their eyes, they saw the piled-up masses of foam dashing to and fro amongst what looked like the fragments of a ship. She had given way as if driven straight in. Their panting hearts yielded, too, before the tremendous blow; and all at once she sprang up again to her desperate plunging, as if trying to scramble out from under the ruins.

The seas in the dark seemed to rush from all sides to keep her back where she might perish. There was hate in the way she was handled, and a ferocity in the blows that fell. She was like a living creature thrown to the rage of a mob: hustled terribly, struck at, borne up, flung down, leaped upon. Captain MacWhirr and Jukes kept hold of each other, deafened by the noise, gagged by the wind; and the great physical tumult beating about their bodies, brought, like an unbridled display of passions, a profound trouble to their souls. One of those wild and appalling shrieks that are heard at times passing mysteriously overhead in the steady roar of a hurricane, swooped, as if borne on wings, upon the ship, and Jukes tried to outscream it.

"Will she live through this?"

The cry was wrenched out of his breast. It was as unintentional as the birth of a thought in the head, and he heard nothing of it himself. It all became extinct at once—

thought, intention, effort—and of his cry the inaudible vibration added to the tempest waves of the air.

He expected nothing from it. Nothing at all. For indeed what answer could be made? But after a while he heard with amazement the frail and resisting voice in his ear, the dwarf sound, unconquered in the giant tumult.

"She may!"

It was a dull yell, more difficult to seize than a whisper. And presently the voice returned again, half submerged in the vast crashes, like a ship battling against the waves of an ocean.

"Let's hope so!" it cried—small, lonely and unmoved, a stranger to the visions of hope or fear; and it flickered into disconnected words: "Ship. . . . This. . . . Never—Anyhow . . . for the best." Jukes gave it up.

Then, as if it had come suddenly upon the one thing fit to withstand the power of a storm, it seemed to gain force and firmness for the last broken shouts:

"Keep on hammering . . . builders . . . good men. . . . And chance it . . . engines. . . . Rout . . . good man."

Captain MacWhirr removed his arm from Jukes' shoulders, and thereby ceased to exist for his mate, so dark it was; Jukes, after a tense stiffening of every muscle, would let himself go limp all over. The gnawing of profound discomfort existed side by side with an incredible disposition to somnolence, as though he had been buffeted and worried into drowsiness. The wind would get hold of his head and try to shake it off his shoulders; his clothes, full of water, were as heavy as lead, cold and dripping like an armor of melting ice: he shivered —it lasted a long time; and with his hands closed hard on his hold, he was letting himself sink slowly into the depths of bodily misery. His mind became concentrated upon himself in an aimless, idle way, and when something pushed lightly at the back of his knees he nearly, as the saying is, jumped out of his skin.

In the start forward he bumped the back of Captain Mac-Whirr, who didn't move; and then a hand gripped his thigh. A lull had come, a menacing lull of the wind, the holding of a stormy breath—and he felt himself pawed all over. It was the boatswain. Jukes recognized these hands, so thick and enormous that they seemed to belong to some new species of man.

The boatswain had arrived on the bridge, crawling on all fours against the wind, and had found the chief mate's legs with the top of his head. Immediately he crouched and began to explore Jukes' person upwards with prudent, apologetic touches, as became an inferior.

He was an ill-favored, undersized, gruff sailor of fifty, coarsely hairy, short-legged, long-armed, resembling an elderly ape. His strength was immense; and in his great lumpy paws, bulging like brown boxing-gloves on the end of furry forearms, the heaviest objects were handled like playthings. Apart from the grizzled pelt on his chest, the menacing demeanor and the hoarse voice, he had none of the classical attributes of his rating. His good nature almost amounted to imbecility: the men did what they liked with him, and he had not an ounce of initiative in his character, which was easy-going and talkative. For these reasons Jukes disliked him; but Captain MacWhirr, to Jukes' scornful disgust, seemed to regard him as a first-rate petty officer.

He pulled himself up by Jukes' coat, taking that liberty with the greatest moderation, and only so far as it was forced upon him by the hurricane.

"What is it, bos'n, what is it?" yelled Jukes, impatiently. What could that fraud of a bos'n want on the bridge? The typhoon had got on Jukes' nerves. The husky bellowings of this other, though unintelligible, seemed to suggest a state of lively satisfaction.   There could be no mistake.   The old fool was pleased with something.

The boatswain's other hand had found some other body, for in a changed tone he began to inquire: "Is it you, sir? Is it you, sir?"   The wind strangled his howls.

"Yes!" cried Captain MacWhirr.

IV

All that the boatswain, out of a superabundance of yells, could make clear to Captain MacWhirr was the bizarre intelligence that "All them Chinamen in the fore 'tween deck have fetched away, sir."

Jukes to leeward could hear these two shouting within six inches of his face, as you may hear on a still night half a mile away two men conversing across a field.   He heard Captain MacWhirr's exasperated "What?   What?" and the strained pitch of the other's hoarseness.   "In a lump . . . seen them myself. . . . Awful sight, sir . . . thought . . . tell you."

Jukes remained indifferent, as if rendered irresponsible by the force of the hurricane, which made the very thought of action utterly vain.   Besides, being very young, he had found the occupation of keeping his heart completely steeled against the worst so engrossing that he had come to feel an overpowering dislike towards any other form of activity whatever.   He was not scared; he knew this because, firmly believing he would never see another sunrise, he remained calm in that belief.

These are the moments of do-nothing heroics to which even good men surrender at times.   Many officers of ships can no doubt recall a case in their experience when just such a trance of confounded stoicism would come all at once over a whole ship's company.   Jukes, however, had no wide experience of men or storms.   He conceived himself to be calm —inexorably calm; but as a matter of fact he was daunted;

not abjectly, but only so far as a decent man may, without becoming loathsome to himself.

It was rather like a forced-on numbness of spirit. The long, long stress of a gale does it; the suspense of the interminably culminating catastrophe; and there is a bodily fatigue in the mere holding on to existence within the excessive tumult; a searching and insidious fatigue that penetrates deep into a man's breast to cast down and sadden his heart, which is incorrigible, and of all the gifts of the earth —even before life itself—aspires to peace.

Jukes was benumbed much more than he supposed. He held on—very wet, very cold, stiff in every limb; and in a momentary hallucination of swift visions (it is said that a drowning man thus reviews all his life) he beheld all sorts of memories altogether unconnected with his present situation. He remembered his father, for instance: a worthy business man, who at an unfortunate crisis in his affairs went quietly to bed and died forthwith in a state of resignation. Jukes did not recall these circumstances, of course, but remaining otherwise unconcerned he seemed to see distinctly the poor man's face; a certain game of nap played when quite a boy in Table Bay on board a ship, since lost with all hands; the thick eyebrows of his first skipper; and without any emotion, as he might years ago have walked listlessly into her room and found her sitting there with a book, he remembered his mother—dead, too, now—the resolute woman, left badly off, who had been very firm in his bringing up.

It could not have lasted more than a second, perhaps not so much. A heavy arm had fallen about his shoulders; Captain MacWhirr's voice was speaking his name into his ear.

"Jukes!   Jukes!"

He detected the tone of deep concern. The wind had thrown its weight on the ship, trying to pin her down amongst the seas. They made a clean breach over her, as over a deep-swimming log; and the gathered weight of

crashes menaced monstrously from afar.   The breakers flung
out of the night with a ghostly light on their crests—the
light of sea foam that in a ferocious, boiling-up pale flash
showed upon the slender body of the ship the toppling rush,
the downfall, and the seething mad scurry of each wave.
Never for a moment could she shake herself clear of the
water; Jukes, rigid, perceived in her motion the ominous
sign of haphazard floundering.   She was no longer struggling
intelligently.   It was the beginning of the end; and the note
of busy concern in Captain MacWhirr's voice sickened him
like an exhibition of blind and pernicious folly.

The spell of the storm had fallen upon Jukes.   He was
penetrated by it, absorbed by it; he was rooted in it with a
rigor of dumb attention.   Captain MacWhirr persisted in his
cries, but the wind got between them like a solid wedge.   He
hung round Jukes' neck as heavy as a millstone, and suddenly the sides of their heads knocked together.

"Jukes!   Mr. Jukes, I say!"

He had to answer that voice that would not be silenced.
He answered in the customary manner: ". . . Yes, sir."

And directly, his heart, corrupted by the storm that breeds
a craving for peace, rebelled against the tyranny of training
and command.

Captain MacWhirr had his mate's head fixed firm in the
crook of his elbow, and pressed it to his yelling lips mysteriously.   Sometimes Jukes would break in, admonishing
hastily: "Look out, sir!" or Captain MacWhirr would bawl
an earnest exhortation to "Hold hard, there!" and the whole
black universe seemed to reel together with the ship.   They
paused.   She floated yet.   And Captain MacWhirr would
resume his shouts.   ". . . Says . . . whole lot . . . fetched
away. . . . Ought to see . . . what's the matter."

Directly the full force of the hurricane had struck the
ship, every part of her deck became untenable; and the
sailors, dazed and dismayed, took shelter in the port alleyway

under the bridge. It had a door aft, which they shut; it was very black, cold, and dismal. At each heavy fling of the ship they would groan all together in the dark, and tons of water could be heard scuttling about as if trying to get at them from above. The boatswain had been keeping up a gruff talk, but a more unreasonable lot of men, he said afterwards, he had never been with. They were snug enough there, out of harm's way, and not wanted to do anything, either; and yet they did nothing but grumble and complain peevishly like so many sick kids. Finally, one of them said that if there had been at least some light to see each other's noses by, it wouldn't be so bad. It was making him crazy, he declared, to lie there in the dark waiting for the blamed hooker to sink.

"Why don't you step outside, then, and be done with it at once?" the boatswain turned on him.

This called up a shout of execration. The boatswain found himself overwhelmed with reproaches of all sorts. They seemed to take it ill that a lamp was not instantly created for them out of nothing. They would whine after a light to get drowned by—anyhow! And though the unreason of their revilings was patent—since no one could hope to reach the lamp-room, which was forward—he became greatly distressed. He did not think it was decent of them to be nagging at him like this. He told them so, and was met by general contumely. He sought refuge, therefore, in an embittered silence. At the same time their grumbling and sighing and muttering worried him greatly, but by-and-by it occurred to him that there were six globe lamps hung in the 'tween-deck, and that there could be no harm in depriving the coolies of one of them.

The *Nan-Shan* had an athwartship coal-bunker, which, being at times used as cargo space, communicated by an iron door with the fore 'tween-deck. It was empty then, and its manhole was the foremost one in the alleyway. The boat-

swain could get in, therefore, without coming out on deck
at all; but to his great surprise he found he could induce no
one to help him in taking off the manhole cover. He groped
for it all the same, but one of the crew lying in his way refused to budge.

"Why, I only want to get you that blamed light you are
crying for," he expostulated, almost pitifully.

Somebody told him to go and put his head in a bag. He
regretted he could not recognize the voice, and that it was too
dark to see; otherwise, as he said, he would have put a head
on *that* son of a sea-cook, anyway, sink or swim. Nevertheless, he had made up his mind to show them he could get
a light, if he were to die for it.

Through the violence of the ship's rolling, every movement was dangerous. To be lying down seemed labor
enough. He nearly broke his neck dropping into the bunker.
He fell on his back, and was sent shooting helplessly from
side to side in the dangerous company of a heavy iron bar—
a coal-trimmer's slice, probably—left down there by somebody. This thing made him as nervous as though it had been
a wild beast. He could not see it, the inside of the bunker
coated with coal-dust being perfectly and impenetrably
black; but he heard it sliding and clattering, and striking
here and there, always in the neighborhood of his head. It
seemed to make an extraordinary noise, too—to give heavy
thumps as though it had been as big as a bridge girder. This
was remarkable enough for him to notice while he was flung
from port to starboard and back again, and clawing desperately the smooth sides of the bunker in the endeavor to stop
himself. The door into the 'tween-deck not fitting quite
true, he saw a thread of dim light at the bottom.

Being a sailor, and a still active man, he did not want much
of a chance to regain his feet; and as luck would have it, in
scrambling up he put his hand on the iron slice, picking it up
as he rose. Otherwise he would have been afraid of the thing

breaking his legs, or at least knocking him down again. At first he stood still. He felt unsafe in this darkness that seemed to make the ship's motion unfamiliar, unforeseen, and difficult to counteract. He felt so much shaken for a moment that he dared not move for fear of "taking charge again." He had no mind to get battered to pieces in that bunker.

He had struck his head twice; he was dazed a little. He seemed to hear yet so plainly the clatter and bangs of the iron slice flying about his ears that he tightened his grip to prove to himself he had it there safely in his hand. He was vaguely amazed at the plainness with which down there he could hear the gale raging. Its howls and shrieks seemed to take on, in the emptiness of the bunker, something of the human character, of human rage and pain—being not vast but infinitely poignant. And there were, with every roll, thumps, too—profound, ponderous thumps, as if a bulky object of five-ton weight or so had got play in the hold. But there was no such thing in the cargo. Something on deck? Impossible. Or alongside? Couldn't be.

He thought all this quickly, clearly, competently, like a seaman, and in the end remained puzzled. This noise, though, came deadened from outside, together with the washing and pouring of water on deck above his head. Was it the wind? Must be. It made down there a row like the shouting of a big lot of crazed men. And he discovered in himself a desire for a light, too—if only to get drowned by —and a nervous anxiety to get out of that bunker as quickly as possible.

He pulled back the bolt: the heavy iron plate turned on its hinges; and it was as though he had opened the door to the sounds of the tempest. A gust of hoarse yelling met him: the air was still, and the rushing of water overhead was covered by a tumult of strangled, throaty shrieks that produced an effect of desperate confusion. He straddled his legs the whole width of the doorway and stretched his neck. And at first he perceived only what he had come to seek: six small yellow flames swinging violently on the great body of the dusk.

It was stayed like the gallery of a mine, with a row of stanchions in the middle, and cross-beams overhead, penetrating into the gloom ahead—indefinitely. And to port there loomed, like the caving in of one of the sides, a bulky mass with a slanting outline. The whole place, with the shadows and the shapes, moved all the time. The boatswain glared: the ship lurched to starboard, and a great howl came from that mass that had the slant of fallen earth.

Pieces of wood whizzed past. Planks, he thought, inexpressibly startled, and flinging back his head. At his feet a man went sliding over, open-eyed, on his back, straining with uplifted arms for nothing; and another came bounding like a detached stone with his head between his legs and his hands clenched. His pigtail whipped in the air; he made a grab at the boatswain's legs, and from his opened hand a bright white disc rolled against the boatswain's foot. He recognized a silver dollar, and yelled at it with astonishment. With a precipitated sound of trampling and shuffling of bare feet, and with guttural cries, the mound of writhing bodies piled up to port detached itself from the ship's side and, sliding, inert and struggling, shifted to starboard, with a dull, brutal thump. The cries ceased. The boatswain heard a long moan through the roar and whistling of the wind; he saw an inextricable confusion of heads and shoulders, naked soles kicking upwards, fists raised, tumbling backs, legs, pigtails, faces.

"Good Lord!" he cried, horrified, and banged-to the iron door upon this vision.

This was what he had come on the bridge to tell. He could not keep it to himself; and on board ship there is only one man to whom it is worth while to unburden yourself.

On his passage back the hands in the alleyway swore at him for a fool. Why didn't he bring that lamp? What the devil did the coolies matter to anybody? And when he came out, the extremity of the ship made what went on inside of her appear of little moment.

At first he thought he had left the alleyway in the very moment of her sinking. The bridge ladders had been washed away, but an enormous sea filling the after-deck floated him up. After that he had to lie on his stomach for some time, holding to a ringbolt, getting his breath now and then, and swallowing salt water. He struggled farther on his hands and knees, too frightened and distracted to turn back. In this way he reached the after-part of the wheelhouse. In that comparatively sheltered spot he found the second mate. The boatswain was pleasantly surprised—his impression being that everybody on deck must have been washed away a long time ago. He asked eagerly where the Captain was.

The second mate was lying low, like a malignant little animal under a hedge.

"Captain? Gone overboard, after getting us into this mess." The mate, too, for all he knew or cared. Another fool. Didn't matter. Everybody was going by and by.

The boatswain crawled out again into the strength of the wind; not because he much expected to find anybody, he said, but just to get away from "that man." He crawled out as outcasts go to face an inclement world. Hence his great joy at finding Jukes and the Captain. But what was going on in the 'tween-deck was to him a minor matter by that time. Besides, it was difficult to make yourself heard. But he managed to convey the idea that the Chinamen had broken adrift together with their boxes, and that he had come up on purpose to report this. As to the hands, they were all right. Then, appeased, he subsided on the deck in a sitting posture, hugging with his arms and legs the stand of the engine-room telegraph—an iron casting as thick as a post. When that

went, why he expected he would go, too.   He gave no more
thought to the coolies.

Captain MacWhirr had made Jukes understand that he
wanted him to go down below—to see.

"What am I to do then, sir?"   And the trembling of his
whole wet body caused Jukes' voice to sound like bleating.

"See first . . . bos'n . . . says . . . adrift."

"That bos'n is a confounded fool," howled Jukes, shakily.
The absurdity of the demand made upon him revolted
Jukes.   He was as unwilling to go as if the moment he had
left the deck the ship were sure to sink.

"I must know . . . can't leave. . . ."

"They'll settle, sir."

"Fight . . . bos'n says they fight. . . . Why? Can't have
. . . fighting . . . board ship. . . . Much rather keep you
here . . . case . . . I should . . . washed overboard myself. . . . Stop it . . . some way.   You see and tell me
. . . through engine-room tube.   Don't want you . . .
come up here . . . too often.   Dangerous . . . moving
about . . . deck."

Jukes, held with his head in chancery, had to listen to what
seemed horrible suggestions.

"Don't want . . . you get lost . . . so long . . . ship
isn't. . . . Rout . . . Good man . . . Ship . . . may . . .
through this . . . all right yet."

All at once Jukes understood he would have to go.

"Do you think she may?" he screamed.

But the wind devoured the reply, out of which Jukes heard
only the one word, pronounced with great energy ". . . Always. . . ."

Captain MacWhirr released Jukes, and bending over the
boatswain, yelled, "Get back with the mate."   Jukes only
knew that the arm was gone off his shoulders.   He was dismissed with his orders—to do what?   He was exasperated

into letting go his hold carelessly, and on the instant was blown away. It seemed to him that nothing could stop him from being blown right over the stern. He flung himself down hastily, and the boatswain, who was following, fell on him.

"Don't you get up yet, sir," cried the boatswain. "No hurry!"

A sea swept over. Jukes understood the boatswain to splutter that the bridge ladders were gone. "I'll lower you down, sir, by your hands," he screamed. He shouted also something about the smokestack being as likely to go overboard as not. Jukes thought it very possible, and imagined the fires out, the ship helpless. . . . The boatswain by his side kept on yelling. "What? What is it?" Jukes cried distressfully; and the other repeated, "What would my old woman say if she saw me now?"

In the alleyway, where a lot of water had got in and splashed in the dark, the men were still as death, till Jukes stumbled against one of them and cursed him savagely for being in the way. Two or three voices then asked, eager and weak, "Any chance for us, sir?"

"What's the matter with you fools?" he said brutally. He felt as though he could throw himself down amongst them and never move any more. But they seemed cheered; and in the midst of obsequious warnings, "Look out! Mind that manhole lid, sir," they lowered him into the bunker. The boatswain tumbled down after him, and as soon as he had picked himself up he remarked, "She would say, 'Serve you right, you old fool, for going to sea.'"

The boatswain had some means, and made a point of alluding to them frequently. His wife—a fat woman—and two grown-up daughters kept a greengrocer's shop in the Eastend of London.

In the dark, Jukes, unsteady on his legs, listened to a faint thunderous patter. A deadened screaming went on steadily at his elbow, as it were; and from above the louder tumult of the storm descended upon these near sounds.   His head swam. To him, too, in that bunker, the motion of the ship seemed novel and menacing, sapping his resolution as though he had never been afloat before.

He had half a mind to scramble out again; but the remembrance of Captain MacWhirr's voice made this impossible. His orders were to go and see.   What was the good of it, he wanted to know.   Enraged, he told himself he would see— of course.   But the boatswain, staggering clumsily, warned him to be careful how he opened that door; there was a blamed fight going on.   And Jukes, as if in great bodily pain, desired irritably to know what the devil they were fighting for.

"Dollars!   Dollars, sir.   All their rotten chests got burst open.   Blamed money skipping all over the place, and they are tumbling after it head over heels—tearing and biting like anything.   A regular little hell in there."

Jukes convulsively opened the door.   The short boatswain peered under his arm.

One of the lamps had gone out, broken perhaps.   Rancorous, guttural cries burst out loudly on their ears, and a strange panting sound, the working of all these straining breasts.   A hard blow hit the side of the ship: water fell above with a stunning shock, and in the forefront of the gloom, where the air was reddish and thick, Jukes saw a head bang the deck violently, two thick calves waving on high, muscular arms twined round a naked body, a yellow face, open-mouthed and with a set wild stare, look up and slide away.   An empty chest clattered turning over; a man fell head first with a jump, as if lifted by a kick; and farther off, indistinct, others streamed like a mass of rolling stones down a bank, thumping the deck with their feet and flourishing their arms wildly. The hatchway ladder was loaded with coolies swarming on it like bees on a branch.   They hung on the steps in a crawl-ing, stirring cluster, beating madly with their fists the under-side of the battened hatch, and the headlong rush of the water above was heard in the intervals of their yelling.   The ship heeled over more, and they began to drop off: first one, then two, then all the rest went away together, falling straight off with a great cry.

Jukes was confounded.   The boatswain, with gruff anxi-ety, begged him, "Don't you go in there, sir."

The whole place seemed to twist upon itself, jumping in-cessantly the while; and when the ship rose to a sea Jukes fancied that all these men would be shot upon him in a body. He backed out, swung the door to, and with trembling hands pushed at the bolt. . . .

As soon as his mate had gone, Captain MacWhirr, left alone on the bridge, sidled and staggered as far as the wheel-house.   Its door being hinged forward, he had to fight the gale for admittance, and when at last he managed to enter, it was with an instantaneous clatter and a bang, as though he had been fired through the wood.   He stood within, holding on to the handle.

The steering-gear leaked steam, and in the confined space the glass of the binnacle made a shiny oval of light in a thin white fog.   The wind howled, hummed, whistled, with sud-den booming gusts that rattled the doors and shutters in the vicious patter of sprays.   Two coils of lead-line and a small canvas bag hung on a long lanyard, swung wide off, and came back clinging to the bulkheads.   The gratings under-foot were nearly afloat; with every sweeping blow of a sea, water squirted violently through the cracks all round the door, and the man at the helm had flung down his cap, his coat, and stood propped against the gear-casing in a striped cotton shirt open on his breast.   The little brass wheel in his hands had the appearance of a bright and fragile toy.   The cords of his neck stood hard and lean, a dark patch lay in the hollow of his throat, and his face was still and sunken as in death.

Captain MacWhirr wiped his eyes. The sea that had nearly taken him overboard had, to his great annoyance, washed his sou'-wester hat off his bald head. The fluffy, fair hair, soaked and darkened, resembled a mean skein of cotton threads festooned round his bare skull. His face, glistening with sea-water, had been made crimson with the wind, with the sting of sprays. He looked as though he had come off sweating from before a furnace.

"You here?" he muttered, heavily.

The second mate had found his way into the wheel-house some time before. He had fixed himself in a corner with his knees up, a fist pressed against each temple; and this attitude suggested rage, sorrow, resignation, surrender, with a sort of concentrated unforgiveness. He said mournfully and defiantly, "Well, it's my watch below now, ain't it?"

The steam gear clattered, stopped, clattered again; and the helmsman's eyeballs seemed to project out of a hungry face as if the compass card behind the binnacle glass had been meat. God knows how long he had been left there to steer, as if forgotten by all his shipmates. The bells had not been struck; there had been no reliefs; the ship's routine had gone down wind; but he was trying to keep her head north-north-east. The rudder might have been gone for all he knew, the fires out, the engines broken down, the ship ready to roll over like a corpse. He was anxious not to get muddled and lose control of her head, because the compass-card swung far both ways, wriggling on the pivot, and sometimes seemed to whirl right round. He suffered from mental stress. He was horribly afraid, also, of the wheelhouse going. Mountains of water kept on tumbling against it. When the ship took one of her desperate dives the corners of his lips twitched.

Captain MacWhirr looked up at the wheelhouse clock. Screwed to the bulk-head, it had a white face on which the black hands appeared to stand quite still. It was half-past one in the morning.

"Another day," he muttered to himself.

The second mate heard him, and lifting his head as one grieving amongst ruins, "You won't see it break," he exclaimed. His wrists and his knees could be seen to shake violently. "No, by God! You won't. . . ."

He took his face again between his fists.

The body of the helmsman had moved slightly, but his head didn't budge on his neck—like a stone head fixed to look one way from a column. During a roll that all but took his booted legs from under him, and in the very stagger to save himself, Captain MacWhirr said austerely, "Don't you pay any attention to what that man says." And then, with an indefinable change of tone, very grave, he added, "He isn't on duty."

The sailor said nothing.

The hurricane boomed, shaking the little place, which seemed air-tight; and the light of the binnacle flickered all the time.

"You haven't been relieved," Captain MacWhirr went on, looking down. "I want you to stick to the helm, though, as long as you can. You've got the hang of her. Another man coming here might make a mess of it. Wouldn't do. No child's play. And the hands are probably busy with a job down below. . . . Think you can?"

The steering-gear leaped into an abrupt short clatter, stopped smoldering like an ember; and the still man, with a motionless gaze, burst out, as if all the passion in him had gone into his lips: "By Heavens, sir! I can steer forever if nobody talks to me."

"Oh! aye! All right. . . ." The Captain lifted his eyes for the first time to the man, ". . . Hackett."

And he seemed to dismiss this matter from his mind. He stooped to the engine-room speaking-tube, blew in, and bent

his head.   Mr. Rout below answered, and at once Captain
MacWhirr put his lips to the mouthpiece.

With the uproar of the gale around him he applied alter-
nately his lips and his ear, and the engineer's voice mounted
to him, harsh and as if out of the heat of an engagement.
One of the stokers was disabled, the others had given in, the
second engineer and the donkey-man were firing up.   The
third engineer was standing by the steam valve.   The engines
were being tended by hand.   How was it above?

"Bad enough.   It mostly rests with you," said Captain
MacWhirr.   Was the mate down there yet?   No?   Well,
he would be presently.   Would Mr. Rout let him talk
through the speaking-tube?—through the deck speaking-
tube, because he—the Captain—was going out again on the
bridge directly.   There was some trouble amongst the Chinamen.   They were fighting, it seemed.   Couldn't allow fighting anyhow. . . .

Mr. Rout had gone away, and Captain MacWhirr could
feel against his ear the pulsation of the engines, like the beat
of the ship's heart.   Mr. Rout's voice down there shouted
something distantly.   The ship pitched headlong, the pulsation leaped with a hissing tumult, and stopped dead.   Captain MacWhirr's face was impassive, and his eyes were fixed
aimlessly on the crouching shape of the second mate.   Again
Mr. Rout's voice cried out in the depths, and the pulsating
beats recommenced, with slow strokes—growing swifter.

Mr. Rout had returned to the tube.   "It don't matter
much what they do," he said, hastily; and then, with irrita-
tion, "She takes these dives as if she never meant to come up
again."

"Awful sea," said the Captain's voice from above.

"Don't let me drive her under," barked Solomon Rout up
the pipe.

"Dark and rain.   Can't see what's coming," uttered the

voice. "Must—keep—her—moving—enough to steer—and chance it," it went on to state distinctly.

"I am doing as much as I dare."

"We are—getting—smashed up—a good deal up here," proceeded the voice mildly. "Doing—fairly well—though. Of course, if the wheelhouse should go. . . ."

Mr. Rout, bending an attentive ear, muttered peevishly something under his breath.

But the deliberate voice up there became animated to ask, "Jukes turned up yet?" Then, after a short wait, "I wish he would bear a hand. I want him to be done and come up here in case of anything. To look after the ship. I am all alone. The second mate's lost. . . ."

"What?" shouted Mr. Rout into the engine-room, taking his head away. Then up the tube he cried, "Gone overboard?" and clapped his ear to.

"Lost his nerve," the voice from above continued in a matter-of-fact tone. "Damned awkward circumstance."

Mr. Rout, listening with bowed neck, opened his eyes wide at this. However, he heard something like the sounds of a scuffle and broken exclamations coming down to him. He strained his hearing; and all the time Beale, the third engineer, with his arms uplifted, held between the palms of his hands the rim of a little black wheel projecting at the side of a big copper pipe. He seemed to be poising it above his head, as though it were a correct attitude in some sort of game.

To steady himself, he pressed his shoulder against the white bulkhead, one knee bent, and a sweat-rag tucked in his belt hanging on his hip. His smooth cheek was begrimed and flushed, and the coal dust on his eyelids, like the black penciling of a make-up, enhanced the liquid brilliance of the whites, giving to his youthful face something of a feminine, exotic, and fascinating aspect. When the ship pitched he would with hasty movements of his hands screw hard at the little wheel.

"Gone crazy," began the Captain's voice suddenly in the tube. "Rushed at me. . . . Just now. Had to knock him down. . . . This minute. You heard, Mr. Rout?"

"The devil!" muttered Mr. Rout. "Look out, Beale!"

His shout rang out like the blast of a warning trumpet, between the iron walls of the engine-room. Painted white, they rose high into the dusk of the skylight, sloping like a roof; and the whole lofty space resembled the interior of a monument, divided by floors of iron grating, with lights flickering at different levels, and a mass of gloom lingering in the middle, within the columnar stir of machinery under the motionless swelling of the cylinders. A loud and wild resonance, made up of all the noises of the hurricane, dwelt in the still warmth of the air. There was in it the smell of hot metal, of oil, and a slight mist of steam. The blows of the sea seemed to traverse it in an unringing, stunning shock, from side to side.

Gleams, like pale long flames, trembled upon the polish of metal; from the flooring below the enormous crank-heads emerged in their turns with a flash of brass and steel—going over; while the connecting-rods, big-jointed, like skeleton limbs, seemed to thrust them down and pull them up again with an irresistible precision. And deep in the half-light other rods dodged deliberately to and fro, crossheads nodded, discs of metal rubbed smoothly against each other, slow and gentle, in a commingling of shadows and gleams.

Sometimes all those powerful and unerring movements would slow down simultaneously, as if they had been the functions of a living organism, stricken suddenly by the blight of languor; and Mr. Rout's eyes would blaze darker in his long sallow face. He was fighting this fight in a pair of carpet slippers. A short shiny jacket barely covered his loins, and his white wrists protruded far out of the tight sleeves, as though the emergency had added to his stature, had lengthened his limbs, augmented his pallor, hollowed his eyes.

He moved, climbing high up, disappearing low down, with a restless, purposeful industry, and when he stood still, holding the guard rail in front of the starting-gear, he would keep glancing to the right at the steam gauge, at the water gauge, fixed upon the white wall in the light of a swaying lamp. The mouths of two speaking-tubes gaped stupidly at his elbow, and the dial of the engine-room telegraph resembled a clock of large diameter, bearing on its face curt words instead of figures. The grouped letters stood out heavily black, around the pivot-head of the indicator, emphatically symbolic of loud exclamations: AHEAD, ASTERN, SLOW, HALF, STAND BY; and the fat black hand pointed downwards to the word FULL, which, thus singled out, captured the eye as a sharp cry secures attention.

The wood-encased bulk of the low-pressure cylinder, frowning portly from above, emitted a faint wheeze at every thrust, and except for that low hiss the engines worked their steel limbs headlong or slow with a silent, determined smoothness. And all this, the white walls, the moving steel, the floor plates under Solomon Rout's feet, the floors of iron grating above his head, the dusk and the gleams, uprose and sank continuously, with one accord, upon the harsh wash of the waves against the ship's side. The whole loftiness of the place, booming hollow to the great voice of the wind, swayed at the top like a tree, would go over bodily, as if borne down this way and that by the tremendous blasts.

"You've got to hurry up," shouted Mr. Rout, as soon as he saw Jukes appear in the stokehold doorway.

Jukes' glance was wandering and tipsy; his red face was puffy, as though he had overslept himself. He had had an arduous road, and had traveled over it with immense vivacity, the agitation of his mind corresponding to the exertions of his body. He had rushed up out of the bunker, stumbling in the dark alleyway amongst a lot of bewildered men who, trod upon, asked "What's up, sir?" in awed mutters all round him;—down the stokehold ladder, missing many iron rungs in his hurry, down into a place deep as a well, black as Tophet, tipping over back and forth like a see-saw. The water in the bilges thundered at each roll, and lumps of coal skipped to and fro, from end to end, rattling like an avalanche of pebbles on a slope of iron.

Somebody in there moaned with pain, and somebody else could be seen crouching over what seemed the prone body of a dead man; a lusty voice blasphemed; and the glow under each fire-door was like a pool of flaming blood radiating quietly in a velvety blackness.

A gust of wind struck upon the nape of Jukes' neck and next moment he felt it streaming about his wet ankles. The stokehold ventilators hummed; in front of the six fire-doors two wild figures, stripped to the waist, staggered and stooped, wrestling with two shovels.

"Hallo! Plenty of draught now," yelled the second engineer at once, as though he had been all the time looking out for Jukes. The donkeyman, a dapper little chap with a dazzling fair skin and a tiny, gingery mustache, worked in a sort of mute transport. They were keeping a full head of steam, and a profound rumbling, as of an empty furniture van trotting over a bridge, made a sustained bass to all the other noises of the place.

"Blowing off all the time," went on yelling the second. With a sound as of a hundred scoured sauce-pans, the orifice of a ventilator spat upon his shoulder a sudden gush of salt water, and he volleyed a stream of curses upon all things on earth including his own soul, ripping and raving, and all the time attending to his business. With a sharp clash of metal the ardent pale glare of the fire opened upon his bullet head, showing his spluttering lips, his insolent face, and with another clang closed like the white-hot wink of an iron eye.

"Where's the blooming ship? Can you tell me? blast my eyes! Under water—or what? It's coming down here in tons. Are the condemned cowls gone to Hades? Hey? Don't you know anything—you jolly sailor-man you . . . ?"

Jukes, after a bewildered moment, had been helped by a roll to dart through; and as soon as his eyes took in the comparative vastness, peace and brilliance of the engine-room, the ship, setting her stern heavily in the water, sent him charging head down upon Mr. Rout.

The chief's arm, long like a tentacle, and straightening as if worked by a spring, went out to meet him, and deflected his rush into a spin towards the speaking-tubes. At the same time Mr. Rout repeated earnestly:

"You've got to hurry up, whatever it is."

Jukes yelled "Are you there, sir?" and listened. Nothing. Suddenly the roar of the wind fell straight into his ear, but presently a small voice shoved aside the shouting hurricane quietly.

"You, Jukes?—Well?"

Jukes was ready to talk: it was only time that seemed to be wanting. It was easy enough to account for everything. He could perfectly imagine the coolies battened down in the reeking 'tween-deck, lying sick and scared between the rows of chests. Then one of these chests—or perhaps several at once—breaking loose in a roll, knocking out others, sides splitting, lids flying open, and all these clumsy Chinamen rising up in a body to save their property. Afterwards every fling of the ship would hurl that tramping, yelling mob here and there, from side to side, in a whirl of smashed wood, torn clothing, rolling dollars. A struggle once started, they would be unable to stop themselves. Nothing could stop them now except main force. It was a disaster. He had seen it, and that was all he could say. Some of them must be dead, he believed. The rest would go on fighting. . . .

He sent up his words, tripping over each other, crowding

the narrow tube. They mounted as if into a silence of an enlightened comprehension dwelling alone up there with a storm. And Jukes wanted to be dismissed from the face of that odious trouble intruding on the great need of the ship.

V

He waited. Before his eyes the engines turned with slow labor, that in the moment of going off into a mad fling would stop dead at Mr. Rout's shout, "Look out, Beale!" They paused in an intelligent immobility, stilled in mid-stroke, a heavy crank arrested on the cant, as if conscious of danger and the passage of time. Then, with a "Now, then!" from the chief, and the sound of a breath expelled through clenched teeth, they would accomplish the interrupted revolution and begin another.

There was the prudent sagacity of wisdom and the deliberation of enormous strength in their movements. This was their work—this patient coaxing of a distracted ship over the fury of the waves and into the very eye of the wind. At times Mr. Rout's chin would sink on his breast, and he watched them with knitted eyebrows as if lost in thought.

The voice that kept the hurricane out of Jukes' ear began: "Take the hands with you . . . ," and left off unexpectedly.

"What could I do with them, sir?"

A harsh, abrupt, imperious clang exploded suddenly. The three pairs of eyes flew up to the telegraph dial to see the hand jump from FULL to STOP, as if snatched by a devil. And then these three men in the engine-room had the intimate sensation of a check upon the ship, of a strange shrinking, as if she had gathered herself for a desperate leap.

"Stop her!" bellowed Mr. Rout.

Nobody—not even Captain MacWhirr, who alone on deck had caught sight of a white line of foam coming on at such a height that he couldn't believe his eyes—nobody was to know the steepness of that sea and the awful depth of the hollow the hurricane had scooped out behind the running wall of water.

It raced to meet the ship, and, with a pause, as of girding the loins, the *Nan-Shan* lifted her bows and leaped. The flames in all the lamps sank, darkening the engine-room. One went out. With a tearing crash and a swirling, raving tumult, tons of water fell upon the deck, as though the ship had darted under the foot of a cataract.

Down there they looked at each other, stunned.

"Swept from end to end, by God!" bawled Jukes.

She dipped into the hollow straight down, as if going over the edge of the world. The engine-room toppled forward menacingly, like the inside of a tower nodding in an earthquake. An awful racket, of iron things falling, came from the stokehold. She hung on this appalling slant long enough for Beale to drop on his hands and knees and begin to crawl as if he meant to fly on all fours out of the engine-room, and for Mr. Rout to turn his head slowly, rigid, cavernous, with the lower jaw dropping. Jukes had shut his eyes, and his face in a moment became hopelessly blank and gentle, like the face of a blind man.

At last she rose slowly, staggering, as if she had to lift a mountain with her bows.

Mr. Rout shut his mouth; Jukes blinked; and little Beale stood up hastily.

"Another one like this, and that's the last of her," cried the chief.

He and Jukes looked at each other, and the same thought came into their heads. The Captain! Everything must have been swept away. Steering-gear gone—ship like a log. All over directly.

"Rush!" ejaculated Mr. Rout thickly, glaring with enlarged, doubtful eyes at Jukes, who answered him by an irresolute glance.

The clang of the telegraph gong soothed them instantly. The black hand dropped in a flash from STOP to FULL.

"Now then, Beale!" cried Mr. Rout.

The steam hissed low. The piston-rods slid in and out. Jukes put his ear to the tube. The voice was ready for him. It said: "Pick up all the money. Bear a hand now. I'll want you up here." And that was all.

"Sir?" called up Jukes. There was no answer.

He staggered away like a defeated man from the field of battle. He had got, in some way or other, a cut above his left eyebrow—a cut to the bone. He was not aware of it in the least: quantities of the China Sea, large enough to break his neck for him, had gone over his head, had cleaned, washed, and salted that wound. It did not bleed, but only gaped red; and this gash over the eye, his disheveled hair, the disorder of his clothes, gave him the aspect of a man worsted in a fight with fists.

"Got to pick up the dollars." He appealed to Mr. Rout, smiling pitifully at random.

"What's that?" asked Mr. Rout, wildly. "Pick up . . . ? I don't care. . . ." Then, quivering in every muscle, but with an exaggeration of paternal tone, "Go away now, for God's sake. You deck people'll drive me silly. There's that second mate been going for the old man. Don't you know? You fellows are going wrong for want of something to do. . . ."

At these words Jukes discovered in himself the beginnings of anger. Want of something to do—indeed. . . . Full of hot scorn against the chief, he turned to go the way he had come. In the stokehold the plump donkeyman toiled with his shovel mutely, as if his tongue had been cut out; but the second was carrying on like a noisy, undaunted maniac, who had preserved his skill in the art of stoking under a marine boiler.

"Hallo, you wandering officer! Hey! Can't you get

some of your slush-slingers to wind up a few of them ashes? I am getting choked with them here. Curse it! Hallo! Hey! Remember the articles: *Sailors and firemen to assist each other.* Hey! D'ye hear?"

Jukes was climbing out frantically, and the other, lifting up his face after him, howled, "Can't you speak? What are you poking about here for? What's your game, anyhow?"

A frenzy possessed Jukes. By the time he was back amongst the men in the darkness of the alleyway, he felt ready to wring all their necks at the slightest sign of hanging back. The very thought of it exasperated him. *He* couldn't hang back. They shouldn't.

The impetuosity with which he came amongst them carried them along. They had already been excited and startled at all his comings and goings—by the fierceness and rapidity of his movements; and more felt than seen in his rushes, he appeared formidable—busied with matters of life and death that brooked no delay. At his first word he heard them drop into the bunker one after another obediently, with heavy thumps.

They were not clear as to what would have to be done. "What is it? What is it?" they were asking each other. The boatswain tried to explain; the sounds of a great scuffle surprised them: and the mighty shocks, reverberating awfully in the black bunker, kept them in mind of their danger. When the boatswain threw open the door it seemed that an eddy of the hurricane, stealing through the iron sides of the ship, had set all these bodies whirling like dust: there came to them a confused uproar, a tempestuous tumult, a fierce mutter, gusts of screams dying away, and the tramping of feet mingling with the blows of the sea.

For a moment they glared amazed, blocking the doorway. Jukes pushed through them brutally. He said nothing, and simply darted in. Another lot of coolies on the ladder,

struggling suicidally to break through the battened hatch to
a swamped deck, fell off as before, and he disappeared under
them like a man overtaken by a landslide.

The boatswain yelled excitedly: "Come along. Get the
mate out. He'll be trampled to death. Come on."

They charged in, stamping on breasts, on fingers, on faces,
catching their feet in heaps of clothing, kicking broken
wood; but before they could get hold of him Jukes emerged
waist deep in a multitude of clawing hands. In the instant
he had been lost to view, all the buttons of his jacket had
gone, its back had got split up to the collar, his waistcoat
had been torn open. The central struggling mass of Chinamen went over to the roll, dark, indistinct, helpless, with a
wild gleam of many eyes in the dim light of the lamps.

"Leave me alone—damn you. I am all right," screeched
Jukes. "Drive them forward. Watch your chance when
she pitches. Forward with 'em. Drive them against the
bulkhead. Jam 'em up."

The rush of the sailors into the seething 'tween-deck was
like a splash of cold water into a boiling caldron. The commotion sank for a moment.

The bulk of Chinamen were locked in such a compact
scrimmage that, linking their arms and aided by an appalling
dive of the ship, the seamen sent it forward in one great
shove, like a solid block. Behind their backs small clusters
and loose bodies tumbled from side to side.

The boatswain performed prodigious feats of strength.
With his long arms open, and each great paw clutching at a
stanchion, he stopped the rush of seven entwined Chinamen
rolling like a boulder. His joints cracked; he said, "Ha!"
and they flew apart. But the carpenter showed the greater
intelligence. Without saying a word to anybody he went
back into the alleyway, to fetch several coils of cargo gear
he had seen there—chain and rope. With these life-lines
were rigged.

There was really no resistance. The struggle, however it began, had turned into a scramble of blind panic. If the coolies had started up after their scattered dollars they were by that time fighting only for their footing. They took each other by the throat merely to save themselves from being hurled about. Whoever got a hold anywhere would kick at the others who caught at his legs and hung on, till a roll sent them flying together across the deck.

The coming of the white devils was a terror. Had they come to kill? The individuals torn out of the ruck became very limp in the seamen's hands: some, dragged aside by the heels, were passive, like dead bodies, with open, fixed eyes. Here and there a coolie would fall on his knees as if begging for mercy; several, whom the excess of fear made unruly, were hit with hard fists between the eyes, and cowered; while those who were hurt submitted to rough handling, blinking rapidly without a plaint. Faces streamed with blood; there were raw places on the shaven heads, scratches, bruises, torn wounds, gashes. The broken porcelain out of the chests was mostly responsible for the latter. Here and there a Chinaman, wild-eyed, with his tail unplaited, nursed a bleeding sole.

They had been ranged closely, after having been shaken into submission, cuffed a little to allay excitement, addressed in gruff words of encouragement that sounded like promises of evil. They sat on the deck in ghastly, drooping rows, and at the end the carpenter, with two hands to help him, moved busily from place to place, setting taut and hitching the lifelines. The boatswain, with one leg and one arm embracing a stanchion, struggled with a lamp pressed to his breast, trying to get a light, and growling all the time like an industrious gorilla. The figures of seamen stooped repeatedly, with the movements of gleaners, and everything was being flung into the bunker: clothing, smashed wood, broken china, and the dollars, too, gathered up in men's jackets. Now and then a

sailor would stagger towards the doorway with his arms full
of rubbish; and dolorous, slanting eyes followed his movements.

With every roll of the ship the long rows of sitting Celes-
tials would sway forward brokenly, and her headlong dives
knocked together the line of shaven polls from end to end.
When the wash of water rolling on the deck died away for a
moment, it seemed to Jukes, yet quivering from his exertions,
that in his mad struggle down there he had overcome the
wind somehow: that a silence had fallen upon the ship, a
silence in which the sea struck thunderously at her sides.

Everything had been cleared out of the 'tween-deck—all
the wreckage, as the men said. They stood erect and tottering above the level of heads and drooping shoulders. Here
and there a coolie sobbed for his breath. Where the high
light fell, Jukes could see the salient ribs of one, the yellow,
wistful face of another; bowed necks; or would meet a dull
stare directed at his face. He was amazed that there had
been no corpses; but the lot of them seemed at their last
gasp, and they appeared to him more pitiful than if they had
been all dead.

Suddenly one of the coolies began to speak. The light
came and went on his lean, straining face; he threw his head
up like a baying hound. From the bunker came the sounds
of knocking and the tinkle of some dollars rolling loose; he
stretched out his arm, his mouth yawned black, and the incomprehensible guttural hooting sounds, that did not seem to
belong to a human language, penetrated Jukes with a strange
emotion as if a brute had tried to be eloquent.

Two more started mouthing what seemed to Jukes fierce
denunciations; the others stirred with grunts and growls.
Jukes ordered the hands out of the 'tween-decks hurriedly.
He left last himself, backing through the door, while the
grunts rose to a loud murmur and hands were extended after
him as after a malefactor. The boatswain shot the bolt, and

remarked uneasily, "Seems as if the wind had dropped, sir."

The seamen were glad to get back into the alleyway. Secretly each of them thought that at the last moment he could rush out on deck—and that was a comfort. There is something horribly repugnant in the idea of being drowned under a deck. Now they had done with the Chinamen, they again became conscious of the ship's position.

Jukes, on coming out of the alleyway, found himself up to the neck in the noisy water. He gained the bridge, and discovered he could detect obscure shapes as if his sight had become preternaturally acute. He saw faint outlines. They recalled not the familiar aspect of the *Nan-Shan,* but something remembered—an old dismantled steamer he had seen years ago rotting on a mudbank. She recalled that wreck.

There was no wind, not a breath, except the faint currents created by the lurches of the ship. The smoke tossed out of the funnel was settling down upon her deck. He breathed it as he passed forward. He felt the deliberate throb of the engines, and heard small sounds that seemed to have survived the great uproar: the knocking of broken fittings, the rapid tumbling of some piece of wreckage on the bridge. He perceived dimly the squat shape of his captain holding on to a twisted bridge-rail, motionless and swaying as if rooted to the planks. The unexpected stillness of the air oppressed Jukes.

"We have done it, sir," he gasped.

"Thought you would," said Captain MacWhirr.

"Did you?" murmured Jukes to himself.

"Wind fell all at once," went on the Captain.

Jukes burst out: "If you think it was an easy job——"

But his captain, clinging to the rail, paid no attention. "According to the books the worst is not over yet."

"If most of them hadn't been half dead with seasickness and fright, not one of us would have come out of that 'tween-deck alive," said Jukes.

"Had to do what's fair by them," mumbled MacWhirr, stolidly. "You don't find everything in books."

"Why, I believe they would have risen on us if I hadn't ordered the hands out of that pretty quick," continued Jukes with warmth.

After the whisper of their shouts, their ordinary tones, so distinct, rang out very loud to their ears in the amazing stillness of the air. It seemed to them they were talking in a dark and echoing vault.

Through a jagged aperture in the dome of clouds the light of a few stars fell upon the black sea, rising and falling confusedly. Sometimes the head of a watery cone would topple on board and mingle with the rolling flurry of foam on the swamped deck; and the *Nan-Shan* wallowed heavily at the bottom of a circular cistern of clouds. This ring of dense vapors, gyrating madly round the calm of the center, encompassed the ship like a motionless and unbroken wall of an aspect inconceivably sinister. Within, the sea, as if agitated by an internal commotion, leaped in peaked mounds that jostled each other, slapping heavily against her sides; and a low moaning sound, the infinite plaint of the storm's fury, came from beyond the limits of the menacing calm. Captain MacWhirr remained silent, and Jukes' ready ear caught suddenly the faint, long-drawn roar of some immense wave rushing unseen under that thick blackness which made the appalling boundary of his vision.

"Of course," he started resentfully, "they thought we had caught at the chance to plunder them. Of course! You said—pick up the money. Easier said than done. They couldn't tell what was in our heads. We came in, smash—right into the middle of them. Had to do it by a rush."

"As long as it's done . . . ," mumbled the Captain, without attempting to look at Jukes. "Had to do what's fair."

"We shall find yet there's the devil to pay when this is over," said Jukes, feeling very sore. "Let them only recover a bit, and you'll see. They will fly at our throats, sir. Don't forget, sir, she isn't a British ship now. These brutes know it well, too. The damned Siamese flag."

"We are on board, all the same," remarked Captain Mac-Whirr.

"The trouble's not over yet," insisted Jukes, prophetically, reeling and catching on. "She's a wreck," he added, faintly.

"The trouble's not over yet," assented Captain MacWhirr, half aloud. . . . "Look out for her a minute."

"Are you going off the deck, sir?" asked Jukes, hurriedly, as if the storm were sure to pounce upon him as soon as he had been left alone with the ship.

He watched her, battered and solitary, laboring heavily in a wild scene of mountainous black waters lit by the gleams of distant worlds. She moved slowly, breathing into the still core of the hurricane the excess of her strength in a white cloud of steam—and the deep-toned vibration of the escape was like the defiant trumpeting of a living creature of the sea impatient for the renewal of the contest. It ceased suddenly. The still air moaned. Above Jukes' head a few stars shone into a pit of black vapors. The inky edge of the cloud-disc frowned upon the ship under the patch of glittering sky. The stars, too, seemed to look at her intently, as if for the last time, and the cluster of their splendor sat like a diadem on a lowering brow.

Captain MacWhirr had gone into the chart-room. There was no light there; but he could feel the disorder of that place where he used to live tidily. His armchair was upset. The books had tumbled out on the floor: he scrunched a piece of glass under his boot. He groped for the matches, and found a box on a shelf with a deep ledge. He struck one, and puckering the corners of his eyes, held out the little flame towards the barometer whose glittering top of glass and metals nodded at him continuously.

It stood very low—incredibly low, so low that Captain

MacWhirr grunted.   The match went out, and hurriedly he
extracted another, with thick, stiff fingers.

Again a little flame flared up before the nodding glass and
metal of the top.   His eyes looked at it, narrowed with attention, as if expecting an imperceptible sign.   With his
grave face he resembled a booted and misshapen pagan burning incense before the oracle of a Joss.   There was no mistake.   It was the lowest reading he had ever seen in his life.

Captain MacWhirr emitted a low whistle.   He forgot
himself till the flame diminished to a blue spark, burnt his
fingers and vanished.   Perhaps something had gone wrong
with the thing!

There was an aneroid glass screwed above the couch.   He
turned that way, struck another match, and discovered the
white face of the other instrument looking at him from the
bulkhead, meaningly, not to be gainsaid, as though the wisdom of men were made unerring by the indifference of matter.   There was no room for doubt now.   Captain Mac-
Whirr pshawed at it, and threw the match down.

The worst was to come, then—and if the books were right,
this worst would be very bad.   The experience of the last
six hours had enlarged his conception of what heavy weather
could be like.   "It'll be terrific," he pronounced, mentally.
He had not consciously looked at anything by the light of
the matches except at the barometer; and yet somehow he
had seen that his water-bottle and the two tumblers had been
flung out of their stand.   It seemed to give him a more intimate knowledge of the tossing the ship had gone through.
"I wouldn't have believed it," he thought.   And his table
had been cleared, too; his rulers, his pencils, the inkstand—
all the things that had their safe appointed places—they were
gone, as if a mischievous hand had plucked them out one by
one and flung them on the wet floor.   The hurricane had
broken in upon the orderly arrangements of his privacy.

This had never happened before, and the feeling of dismay reached the very seat of his composure. And the worst was to come yet! He was glad the trouble in the 'tween-deck had been discovered in time. If the ship had to go after all, then, at least, she wouldn't be going to the bottom with a lot of people in her fighting teeth and claw. That would have been odious. And in that feeling there was a humane intention and a vague sense of the fitness of things.

These instantaneous thoughts were yet in their essence heavy and slow, partaking of the nature of the man. He extended his hand to put back the match box in its corner of the shelf. There were always matches there—by his order. The steward had his instructions impressed upon him long before. "A box . . . just there, see? Not so very full . . . where I can put my hand on it, steward. Might want a light in a hurry. Can't tell on board ship *what* you might want in a hurry. Mind, now."

And of course on his side he would be careful to put it back in its place scrupulously. He did so now, but before he removed his hand it occurred to him that perhaps he would never have occasion to use that box any more. The vividness of the thought checked him, and for an infinitesimal fraction of a second his fingers closed again on the small object as though it had been the symbol of all these little habits that chain us to the weary round of life. He released it at last, and letting himself fall on the settee, listened for the first sounds of returning wind.

Not yet. He heard only the wash of water, the heavy splashes, the dull shocks of the confused seas boarding his ship from all sides. She would never have a chance to clear her decks.

But the quietude of the air was startlingly tense and unsafe, like a slender hair holding a sword suspended over his head. By this awful pause the storm penetrated the de-

fences of the man and unsealed his lips. He spoke out in the
solitude and the pitch darkness of the cabin, as if addressing
another being awakened within his breast.

"I shouldn't like to lose her," he said half aloud.

He sat unseen, apart from the sea, from his ship, isolated,
as if withdrawn from the very current of his own existence,
where such freaks as talking to himself surely had no place.
His palms reposed on his knees, he bowed his short neck and
puffed heavily, surrendering to a strange sensation of weariness he was not enlightened enough to recognize for the
fatigue of mental stress.

From where he sat he could reach the door of a washstand
locker. There should have been a towel there. There was.
Good. . . . He took it out, wiped his face, and afterwards
went on rubbing his wet head. He toweled himself with
energy in the dark, and then remained motionless with the
towel on his knees. A moment passed, of a stillness so profound that no one could have guessed there was a man sitting
in that cabin. Then a murmur arose.

"She may come out of it yet."

When Captain MacWhirr came out on deck, which he did
brusquely, as though he had suddenly become conscious of
having stayed away too long, the calm had lasted already
more than fifteen minutes—long enough to make itself intolerable even to his imagination. Jukes, motionless on the
forepart of the bridge, began to speak at once. His voice,
blank and forced as though he were talking through hard-set
teeth, seemed to flow away on all sides into the darkness,
deepening again upon the sea.

"I had the wheel relieved. Hackett began to sing out that
he was done. He's lying in there alongside the steering-gear
with a face like death. At first I couldn't get anybody to
crawl out and relieve the poor devil. That bos'n's worse
than no good, I always said. Thought I would have had to
go myself and haul out one of them by the neck."

"Ah, well," muttered the Captain.   He stood watchful by Jukes' side.

"The second mate's in there, too, holding his head.   Is he hurt, sir?"

"No—crazy," said Captain MacWhirr, curtly.

"Looks as if he had a tumble, though."

"I had to give him a push," explained the Captain.

Jukes gave an impatient sigh.

"It will come very sudden," said Captain MacWhirr, "and from over there, I fancy.   God only knows, though.   These books are only good to muddle your head and make you jumpy.   It will be bad, and there's an end.   If we only can steam her round in time to meet it. . . ."

A minute passed.   Some of the stars winked rapidly and vanished.

"You left them pretty safe?" began the Captain abruptly, as though the silence were unbearable.

"Are you thinking of the coolies, sir?   I rigged life-lines all ways across that 'tween-deck."

"Did you?   Good idea, Mr. Jukes."

"I didn't . . . think you cared to . . . know," said Jukes—the lurching of the ship cut his speech as though somebody had been jerking him around while he talked— "how I got on with . . . that infernal job.   We did it. And it may not matter in the end."

"Had to do what's fair, for all—they are only Chinamen. Give them the same chance with ourselves—hang it all.   She isn't lost yet.   Bad enough to be shut up below in a gale——"

"That's what I thought when you gave me the job, sir," interjected Jukes, moodily.

"——without being battered to pieces," pursued Captain MacWhirr with rising vehemence.   "Couldn't let that go on in my ship, if I knew she hadn't five minutes to live. Couldn't bear it, Mr. Jukes."

A hollow echoing noise, like that of a shout rolling in a rocky chasm, approached the ship and went away again. The last star, blurred, enlarged, as if returning to the fiery mist of its beginning, struggled with the colossal depth of blackness hanging over the ship—and went out.

"Now for it!" muttered Captain MacWhirr. "Mr. Jukes."

"Here, sir."

The two men were growing indistinct to each other.

"We must trust her to go through it and come out on the other side. That's plain and straight. There's no room for Captain Wilson's storm-strategy here."

"No, sir."

"She will be smothered and swept again for hours," mumbled the Captain. "There's not much left by this time above deck for the sea to take away—unless you or me."

"Both, sir," whispered Jukes, breathlessly.

"You are always meeting trouble halfway, Jukes," Captain MacWhirr remonstrated quaintly. "Though it's a fact that the second mate is no good. D'ye hear, Mr. Jukes? You would be left alone if. . . ."

Captain MacWhirr interrupted himself, and Jukes, glancing on all sides, remained silent.

"Don't you be put out by anything," the Captain continued, mumbling rather fast. "Keep her facing it. They may say what they like, but the heaviest seas run with the wind. Facing it—always facing it—that's the way to get through. You are a young sailor. Face it. That's enough for any man. Keep a cool head."

"Yes, sir," said Jukes, with a flutter of the heart.

In the next few seconds the Captain spoke to the engine-room and got an answer.

For some reason Jukes experienced an access of confidence, a sensation that came from outside like a warm breath, and

made him feel equal to every demand. The distant muttering of the darkness stole into his ears. He noted it unmoved,
out of that sudden belief in himself, as a man safe in a shirt
of mail would watch a point.

The ship labored without intermission amongst the black
hills of water, paying with this hard tumbling the price of
her life. She rumbled in her depths, shaking a white plum-
met of steam into the night, and Jukes' thought skimmed like
a bird through the engine-room, where Mr. Rout—good man
—was ready. When the rumbling ceased it seemed to him
that there was a pause of every sound, a dead pause in which
Captain MacWhirr's voice rang out startlingly.

"What's that? A puff of wind?"—it spoke much louder
than Jukes had ever heard it before—"On the bow. That's
right. She may come out of it yet."

The mutter of the winds drew near apace. In the forefront could be distinguished a drowsy waking plaint passing
on, and far off the growth of a multiple clamor, marching
and expanding. There was the throb as of many drums in
it, a vicious rushing note, and like the chant of a tramping
multitude.

Jukes could no longer see his captain distinctly. The darkness was absolutely piling itself upon the ship. At most he
made out movements, a hint of elbows spread out, of a head
thrown up.

Captain MacWhirr was trying to do up the top button of
his oilskin coat with unwonted haste. The hurricane, with
its power to madden the seas, to sink ships, to uproot trees,
to overturn strong walls and dash the very birds of the air
to the ground, had found this taciturn man in its path, and,
doing its utmost, had managed to wring out a few words.
Before the renewed wrath of winds swooped on his ship,
Captain MacWhirr was moved to declare, in a tone of vexation, as it were: "I wouldn't like to lose her."

He was spared that annoyance.

VI

On a bright sunshiny day, with the breeze chasing her smoke far ahead, the *Nan-Shan* came into Fu-chau. Her arrival was at once noticed on shore, and the seamen in harbor said: "Look! Look at that steamer. What's that? Siamese—isn't she? Just look at her!"

She seemed, indeed, to have been used as a running target for the secondary batteries of a cruiser. A hail of minor shells could not have given her upper works a more broken, torn, and devastated aspect: and she had about her the worn, weary air of ships coming from the far ends of the world—and indeed with truth, for in her short passage she had been very far; sighting, verily, even the coast of the Great Beyond, whence no ship ever returns to give up her crew to the dust of the earth. She was incrusted and gray with salt to the trucks of her masts and to the top of her funnel; as though (as some facetious seaman said) "the crowd on board had fished her out somewhere from the bottom of the sea and brought her in here for salvage." And further, excited by the felicity of his own wit, he offered to give five pounds for her—"as she stands."

Before she had been quite an hour at rest, a meager little man, with a red-tipped nose and a face cast in an angry mould, landed from a sampan on the quay of the Foreign Concession, and incontinently turned to shake his fist at her.

A tall individual, with legs much too thin for a rotund stomach, and with watery eyes, strolled up and remarked, "Just left her—eh? Quick work."

He wore a soiled suit of blue flannel with a pair of dirty cricketing shoes; a dingy gray mustache drooped from his lip, and daylight could be seen in two places between the rim and the crown of his hat.

"Hallo! what are you doing here?" asked the ex-second mate of the *Nan-Shan*, shaking hands hurriedly.

"Standing by for a job—chance worth taking—got a quiet hint," explained the man with the broken hat, in jerky, apathetic wheezes.

The second shook his fist again at the *Nan-Shan*. "There's a fellow there that ain't fit to have the command of a scow," he declared, quivering with passion, while the other looked about listlessly.

"Is there?"

But he caught sight on the quay of a heavy seaman's chest, painted brown under a fringed sailcloth cover, and lashed with new manila line. He eyed it with awakened interest.

"I would talk and raise trouble if it wasn't for that damned Siamese flag. Nobody to go to—or I would make it hot for him. The fraud! Told his chief engineer—that's another fraud for you—I had lost my nerve. The greatest lot of ignorant fools that ever sailed the seas. No! You can't think . . ."

"Got your money all right?" inquired his seedy acquaintance suddenly.

"Yes. Paid me off on board," raged the second mate. " 'Get your breakfast on shore,' says he."

"Mean skunk!" commented the tall man, vaguely, and passed his tongue on his lips. "What about having a drink of some sort?"

"He struck me," hissed the second mate.

"No! Struck! You don't say?" The man in blue began to bustle about sympathetically. "Can't possibly talk here. I want to know all about it. Struck—eh? Let's get a fellow to carry your chest. I know a quiet place where they have some bottled beer. . . ."

Mr. Jukes, who had been scanning the shore through a pair of glasses, informed the chief engineer afterwards that "our late second mate hasn't been long in finding a friend. A chap looking uncommonly like a bummer. I saw them walk away together from the quay."

The hammering and banging of the needful repairs did not disturb Captain MacWhirr. The steward found in the letter he wrote, in a tidy chart-room, passages of such absorbing interest that twice he was nearly caught in the act. But Mrs. MacWhirr, in the drawing-room of the forty-pound house, stifled a yawn—perhaps out of self-respect—for she was alone.

She reclined in a plush-bottomed and gilt hammock-chair near a tiled fireplace, with Japanese fans on the mantel and a glow of coals in the grate. Lifting her hands, she glanced wearily here and there into the many pages. It was not her fault they were so prosy, so completely uninteresting—from "My darling wife" at the beginning, to "Your loving husband" at the end. She couldn't be really expected to understand all these ship affairs. She was glad, of course, to hear from him, but she had never asked herself why, precisely.

". . . They are called typhoons . . . The mate did not seem to like it . . . Not in books . . . Couldn't think of letting it go on. . . ."

The paper rustled sharply. ". . . A calm that lasted more than twenty minutes," she read perfunctorily; and the next words her thoughtless eyes caught, on the top of another page, were: "see you and the children again. . . ." She had a movement of impatience. He was always thinking of coming home. He had never had such a good salary before. What was the matter now?

It did not occur to her to turn back overleaf to look. She would have found it recorded there that between 4 and 6 A. M. on December 25th, Captain MacWhirr did actually think that his ship could not possibly live another hour in such a sea, and that he would never see his wife and children again. Nobody was to know this (his letters got mislaid so quickly)—nobody whatever but the steward, who had been greatly impressed by that disclosure. So much so, that he tried to give the cook some idea of the "narrow squeak we all had" by saying solemnly, "The old man himself had a dam' poor opinion of our chance."

"How do you know?" asked, contemptuously, the cook, an old soldier. "He hasn't told you, maybe?"

"Well, he did give me a hint to that effect," the steward brazened it out.

"Get along with you! He will be coming to tell *me* next," jeered the old cook, over his shoulder.

Mrs. MacWhirr glanced farther, on the alert. ". . . Do what's fair. . . . Miserable objects . . . Only three, with a broken leg each, and one . . . Thought had better keep the matter quiet . . . hope to have done the fair thing. . . ."

She let fall her hands. No: there was nothing more about coming home. Must have been merely expressing a pious wish. Mrs. MacWhirr's mind was set at ease, and a black marble clock, priced by the local jeweler at £3 18s. 6d., had a discreet stealthy tick.

The door flew open, and a girl in the long-legged, short-frocked period of existence flung into the room. A lot of colorless, rather lanky hair was scattered over her shoulders. Seeing her mother, she stood still, and directed her pale prying eyes upon the letter.

"From father," murmured Mrs. MacWhirr. "What have you done with your ribbon?"

The girl put her hands up to her head and pouted.

"He's well," continued Mrs. MacWhirr, languidly. "At least I think so. He never says." She had a little laugh. The girl's face expressed a wandering indifference, and Mrs. MacWhirr surveyed her with fond pride.

"Go and get your hat," she said after a while. "I am going out to do some shopping. There is a sale at Linom's."

"Oh, how jolly!" uttered the child, impressively, in unexpectedly grave, vibrating tones, and bounded out of the room.

It was a fine afternoon, with a gray sky and dry sidewalks. Outside the draper's Mrs. MacWhirr smiled upon a woman in a black mantle of generous proportions armored in jet and crowned with flowers blooming falsely above a bilious matronly countenance. They broke into a swift little babble of greetings and exclamations both together, very hurried, as if the street were ready to yawn open and swallow all that pleasure before it could be expressed.

Behind them the high glass doors were kept on the swing. People couldn't pass, men stood aside waiting patiently, and Lydia was absorbed in poking the end of her parasol between the stone flags. Mrs. MacWhirr talked rapidly.

"Thank you very much. He's not coming home yet. Of course it's very sad to have him away, but it's such a comfort to know he keeps so well." Mrs. MacWhirr drew breath. "The climate there agrees with him," she added, beamingly, as if poor MacWhirr had been away touring in China for the sake of his health.

Neither was the chief engineer coming home yet. Mr. Rout knew too well the value of a good billet.

"Solomon says wonders will never cease," cried Mrs. Rout joyously at the old lady in her armchair by the fire. Mr. Rout's mother moved slightly, her withered hands lying in black half-mittens on her lap.

The eyes of the engineer's wife fairly danced on the paper. "That captain of the ship he is in—a rather simple man, you remember, mother?—has done something rather clever, Solomon says."

"Yes, my dear," said the old woman meekly, sitting with bowed silvery head, and that air of inward stillness characteristic of very old people who seem lost in watching the last flickers of life. "I think I remember."

Solomon Rout, Old Sol, Father Sol, the Chief, "Rout, good man"—Mr. Rout, the condescending and paternal friend of youth, had been the baby of her many children—all dead by this time. And she remembered him best as a boy of ten—long before he went away to serve his apprenticeship in some great engineering works in the North. She had seen so little of him since, she had gone through so many years, that she had now to retrace her steps very far back to recognize him plainly in the mist of time. Sometimes it seemed that her daughter-in-law was talking of some strange man.

Mrs. Rout junior was disappointed. "H'm. H'm." She turned the page. "How provoking! He doesn't say what it is. Says I couldn't understand how much there was in it. Fancy! What could it be so very clever? What a wretched man not to tell us!"

She read on without further remark soberly, and at last sat looking into the fire. The chief wrote just a word or two of the typhoon; but something had moved him to express an increased longing for the companionship of the jolly woman. "If it hadn't been that mother must be looked after, I would send you your passage-money to-day. You could set up a small house out here. I would have a chance to see you sometimes then. We are not growing younger. . . ."

"He's well, mother," sighed Mrs. Rout, rousing herself.

"He always was a strong healthy boy," said the old woman, placidly.

But Mr. Jukes' account was really animated and very full. His friend in the Western Ocean trade imparted it freely to the other officers of his liner. "A chap I know writes to me about an extraordinary affair that happened on board his ship in that typhoon—you know—that we read of in the papers two months ago. It's the funniest thing! Just see for yourself what he says. I'll show you his letter."

There were phrases in it calculated to give the impression of light-hearted, indomitable resolution. Jukes had written them in good faith, for he felt thus when he wrote. He decribed with lurid effect the scenes in the 'tween-deck. " . . . It struck me in a flash that those confounded Chinamen couldn't tell we weren't a desperate kind of robbers. 'Tisn't good to part the Chinaman from his money if he is the stronger party. We need have been desperate indeed to go thieving in such weather, but what could these beggars know of us? So, without thinking of it twice, I got the hands away in a jiffy. Our work was done—that the old man had set his heart on. We cleared out without staying to inquire how they felt. I am convinced that if they had not been so unmercifully shaken, and afraid—each individual one of them—to stand up, we would have been torn to pieces. Oh! It was pretty complete, I can tell you; and you may run to and fro across the Pond to the end of time before you find yourself with such a job on your hands."

After this he alluded professionally to the damage done to the ship, and went on thus:

"It was when the weather quieted down that the situation became confoundedly delicate. It wasn't made any better by us having been lately transferred to the Siamese flag; though the skipper can't see that it makes any difference— 'as long as we are on board'—he says. There are feelings that this man simply hasn't got—and there's an end of it. You might just as well try to make a bedpost understand. But apart from this it is an infernally lonely state for a ship to be going about the China seas with no proper consuls, not even a gunboat of her own anywhere, nor a body to go to in case of some trouble.

"My notion was to keep these Johnnies under hatches for another fifteen hours or so; as we weren't much farther than that from Fu-chau. We would find there, most likely, some sort of a man-of-war, and once under her guns we were safe enough; for surely any skipper of a man-of-war—English, French, or Dutch—would see white men through as far as a row on board goes. We could get rid of them and their money afterwards by delivering them to their Mandarin or Taotai, or whatever they call these chaps in goggles you see being carried about in sedan-chairs through their stinking streets.

"The old man wouldn't see it somehow. He wanted to keep the matter quiet. He got that notion into his head, and a steam windlass couldn't drag it out of him. He wanted as little fuss made as possible, for the sake of the ship's name and for the sake of the owners—'for the sake of all concerned,' says he, looking at me very hard. It made me angry hot. Of course you couldn't keep a thing like that quiet; but the chests had been secured in the usual manner and were safe enough for any earthly gale, while this had been an altogether fiendish business I couldn't give you even an idea of.

"Meantime, I could hardly keep on my feet. None of us had a spell of any sort for nearly thirty hours, and there the old man sat rubbing his chin, rubbing the top of his head, and so bothered he didn't even think of pulling his long boots off.

" 'I hope, sir,' says I, 'you won't be letting them out on deck before we make ready for them in some shape or other.' Not, mind you, that I felt very sanguine about controlling these beggars if they meant to take charge. A trouble with a cargo of Chinamen is no child's play. I was dam' tired, too. 'I wish,' said I, 'you would let us throw the whole lot of these dollars down to them and leave them to fight it out amongst themselves, while we get a rest.'

" 'Now you talk wild, Jukes,' says he, looking up in his slow way that makes you ache all over, somehow. 'We must plan out something that would be fair to all parties.'

"I had no end of work on hand, as you may imagine, so I set the hands going, and then I thought I would turn in a bit. I hadn't been asleep in my bunk ten minutes when in rushes the steward and begins to pull at my leg.

" 'For God's sake, Mr. Jukes, come out! Come on deck quick, sir. Oh, do come out!'

"The fellow scared all the sense out of me. I didn't know what had happened: another hurricane—or what. Could hear no wind.

" 'The Captain's letting them out.   Oh, he is letting them out!   Jump on deck, sir, and save us.   The chief engineer has just run below for his revolver.'

"That's what I understood the fool to say.   However, Father Rout swears he went in there only to get a clean pocket-handkerchief.   Anyhow, I made one jump into my trousers and flew on deck aft.   There was certainly a good deal of noise going on forward of the bridge.   Four of the hands with the bos'n were at work abaft.   I passed up to them some of the rifles all the ships on the China coast carry in the cabin, and led them on the bridge.   On the way I ran against Old Sol, looking startled and sucking at an unlighted cigar.

" 'Come along,' I shouted to him.

"We charged, the seven of us, up to the chart-room.   All was over.   There stood the old man with his sea-boots still drawn up to the hips and in shirt-sleeves—got warm thinking it out, I suppose.   Bun Hin's dandy clerk at his elbow, as dirty as a sweep, was still green in the face.   I could see directly I was in for something.

" 'What the devil are these monkey tricks, Mr. Jukes?' asks the old man, as angry as ever he could be.   I tell you frankly it made me lose my tongue.   'For God's sake, Mr. Jukes,' says he, 'do take away these rifles from the men. Somebody's sure to get hurt before long if you don't. Damme, if this ship isn't worse than Bedlam!   Look sharp now.   I want you up here to help me and Bun Hin's China-man to count that money.   You wouldn't mind lending a hand, too, Mr. Rout, now you are here.   The more of us the better.'

"He had settled it all in his mind while I was having a snooze.   Had we been an English ship, or only going to land our cargo of coolies in an English port, like Hong-Kong, for instance, there would have been no end of inquiries and

bother, claims for damages and so on.   But these Chinamen
know their officials better than we do.

"The hatches had been taken off already, and they were all
on deck after a night and a day down below.   It made you
feel queer to see so many gaunt, wild faces together.   The
beggars stared about at the sky, at the sea, at the ship, as
though they had expected the whole thing to have been
blown to pieces.   And no wonder!   They had had a doing
that would have shaken the soul out of a white man.   But
then they say a Chinaman has no soul.   He has, though,
something about him that is deuced tough.   There was a
fellow (amongst others of the badly hurt) who had had his
eye all but knocked out.   It stood out of his head the size
of half a hen's egg.   This would have laid out a white man
on his back for a month: and yet there was that chap elbow-
ing here and there in the crowd and talking to the others as
if nothing had been the matter.   They made a great hub-
bub amongst themselves, and whenever the old man showed
his bald head on the foreside of the bridge, they would all
leave off jawing and look at him from below.

"It seems that after he had done his thinking he made that
Bun Hin's fellow go down and explain to them the only way
they could get their money back.   He told me afterwards
that, all the coolies having worked in the same place and for
the same length of time, he reckoned he would be doing the
fair thing by them as near as possible if he shared all the cash
we had picked up equally among the lot.   You couldn't tell
one man's dollars from another's, he said, and if you asked
each man how much money he brought on board he was
afraid they would lie, and he would find himself a long way
short.   I think he was right there.   As to giving up the
money to any Chinese official he could scare up in Fu-chau,
he said he might just as well put the lot in his own pocket at
once for all the good it would be to them.   I suppose they
thought so, too.

"We finished the distribution before dark.   It was rather
a sight: the sea running high, the ship a wreck to look at,
these Chinamen staggering up on the bridge one by one for
their share, and the old man still booted, and in his shirt-
sleeves, busy paying out at the chart-room door, perspiring
like anything, and now and then coming down sharp on myself or Father Rout about one thing or another not quite to
his mind.   He took the share of those who were disabled
himself to them on the No. 2 hatch.   There were three dollars left over, and these went to the three most damaged
coolies, one to each.   We turned to afterwards, and shoveled
out on deck heaps of wet rags, all sorts of fragments of things
without shape, and that you couldn't give a name to, and let
them settle the ownership themselves.

"This certainly is coming as near as can be to keeping the
thing quiet for the benefit of all concerned.   What's your
opinion, you pampered mail-boat swell?   The old chief says
that this was plainly the only thing that could be done.   The
skipper remarked to me the other day, 'There are things you
find nothing about in books.'   I think that he got out of it
very well for such a stupid man."

APPENDIX

FOR FURTHER STUDY

QUESTIONS AND TOPICS FOR DISCUSSION

1. Do you find any differences or changes in Conrad's personality and character as revealed in the several sections of this book? Compare (a) "The *Tremolino*," (b) "Initiation," (c) "*Youth*," (d) "First Command," (e) "The Writer Caught in the Exercise of His Craft," (f) "Verdicts and Rebuttals."

2. If "the child is father of the man," if "the boy is the man in miniature," in what respects does the Conrad who appears in "The Polish Heritage and Boyhood" foretell the Conrad who appears in the remainder of this book?

3. Genius was said by a French writer to be nothing but the power to live over one's childhood at will. What did he mean? If the term "childhood" may be broadly defined, had Conrad this power?

4. What specifically does Conrad learn from each experience related in "Ships and Shipmasters"? What parallel does he seem to find in the art of seamanship and the art of letters?

5. When Conrad finds himself unexpectedly in his important position as captain in "First Command," what qualities does he reveal? Can you find these same qualities in Conrad before this time? Compare and contrast the captain in the selection "First Command" and the captain in *The Secret Sharer*."

6. In the selection "The Congo," do you find anything new or different in Conrad's interests or attitude? What preparation was there in this experience for his later career as a novelist?

7. In the section on "The Writer," does Conrad seem to be the same person he appeared to be in the first two sections of this book? Do some of the same traits of character persist? What new traits appear?

8. If "even the most artful of writers," as Conrad says, "will give himself and his morality away in about every third sentence," what

does Conrad reveal about himself and his morality in *"The Secret Sharer"* and *"Typhoon"*? In what other works does he most unmistakably "give himself away"?

9. From your reading of Conrad, draw up a list of Conrad's (a) enthusiasms; (b) antipathies. What qualities in people does he seem spontaneously (a) to admire; (b) to dislike?

10. On the title-page to the volume *Youth*, Conrad placed this sentence from Grimm's Tales: "But the Dwarf answered: 'No; something human is dearer to me than the wealth of all the world.'" How does this quotation suggest the chief source of interest in his stories both for Conrad and his readers?

11. Compassion or pity is said to be Conrad's dominant characteristic. What evidence can you adduce to support or refute this judgment? Be specific.

12. What was Conrad's attitude toward the popular conception of him as, most of all, a writer of sea stories? What is probably the basis of that conception? Is it justified? Is it likely to continue?

13. Stevenson once said that he himself was fifty-five per cent artist and forty-five per cent adventurer. Make a similar analysis of Conrad.

14. William McFee wrote in an introduction to the volume *Youth* that men, except for "certain easily explained failures," react to the works of Conrad "in direct ratio to their integrity of character. The cunning, the avaricious, and the ignoble are not admirers of Conrad. There is something in the style and the spirit which reaches down into a man's moral resources and sounds them for him." Discuss the truth and justice of McFee's dictum. How is it with you?

CONTINUATION EXERCISES

I. WORDS

Ford Madox Ford, who was joint author with Conrad of three books, tells how Conrad would spend "nearly a whole day over one word."

Find additional examples in Conrad's works under each of the following headings:

A. Nouns that need no adjectives:
1. "The individuals torn out of the *ruck* became very limp."
2. "His face made crimson . . . with the *sting* of spray."
3. "They were no colonists; their administration was merely a *squeeze*."

B. Adjectives that help:
1. ". . . *incomprehensible, guttural, hooting* sounds———"
2. ". . . *dolorous, slanting* eyes followed his movements———"
3. ". . . that queer *twisted-about* appearance you see so often in men who work in the fields———"
4. ". . . a *flabby, pretending, weak-eyed* devil of a *rapacious* and *pitiless* folly."

C. Verbs adequate in themselves:
1. "Captain MacWhirr *sidled* and *staggered* as far as the wheelhouse."
2. "Jukes *blinked*."
3. ". . . in England where men and sea *interpenetrate*, so to speak."
4. "We could hear him *blubbering* somewhere in the shadows."
5. "The old barque *lumbered* on."

D. Abstract terms:
1. "Droll thing life is—that mysterious arrangement of merciless logic for a futile purpose."
2. "It was the stillness of an implacable force brooding over an inscrutable intention."
3. "It is the sea that gives it—the vastness, the loneliness surrounding their hard stolid souls."
4. Some titles of Conrad's works: *Victory, Chance, Suspense, Youth*.

II. FIGURES OF SPEECH

Conrad makes extraordinary use of similes to supplement or complete his meaning, and to add energy and beauty to his writing.

1. "Somebody in there moaned with pain, and somebody else could be seen crouching over what seemed to be the body of a dead man; a lusty voice blasphemed; and the glow under each fire-door was *like a pool of flaming blood* radiating quietly in a velvety blackness." Note how the simile in this passage from *Typhoon* accentuates the horror of the stokehold.
2. "It was as unintentional as the birth of a thought in the head."
3. "The pulsation of the engine like the beat of the ship's heart."

Make a collection of figures of speech from Conrad; note their origin and their effect. (Dr. Gustav Morf "counted as many as 279 similes introduced by *as if, as though, or like* in *Lord Jim* alone." Conrad, he says, likes to choose words and expressions "that have something magic, mystic, or enthralling about them"; that "have retained that primitive energy with which men's first words must have been charged.")

III. The Equivalent of Profanity

Although Conrad lived, as he said, "a rough, a very rough life" and presented many hard characters in his novels, yet, unlike some contemporary writers, he does not include profanity or coarseness in his dialogue. Find examples like the following, showing how he avoids doing so. What does he use as an equivalent? Is there gain or loss by his method?

1. ". . . began by calling me Pig, and from that went crescendo into unmentionable adjectives."
2. ". . . a lusty voice blasphemed."
3. "May he be everlastingly blanked for a swab-headed deck-hand."

IV. Sentence Effects

A. Short sentences:

a. For rapidity, excitement:

"He dropped behind the canoe. The prau was coming. She and I ran, and as we rushed along, I heard shots. My brother fired—once—twice, and the booming of the gong ceased. There was silence behind us."

b. For crispness, compactness:
   1. "We live as we dream—alone."
   2. "An ideal is often but a flaming vision of reality."

Find in Conrad's works additional sentences that illustrate each effect. Try to explain their structure and their effect. Then, playing what Stevenson called the "sedulous ape," try to imitate them in sentences of your own. Imagine a situation in which short sentences could be naturally used—for example, a fire, a rescue, or the last minute of a close game. After writing your sentences, read them aloud several times, and revise them for euphony if you can do so. Conrad, it is reported, would read a "sentence over and over to see how it sounded."

B. Long sentences following the leisurely course of the thought:
   1. "A wave of movement passed through the crowd from end to end, passed along the heads, swayed the bodies, ran along the jetty like a ripple on the water, like a breath of wind on a field—and all was still again."
   2. "Darkness oozed out from between the trees, through the tangled maze of the creepers, from behind the great fantastic and unstirring leaves; the darkness mysterious and invincible; the darkness scented and poisonous of impenetrable forests."
   3. "My relation with the sea, which, beginning mysteriously, like any great passion the inscrutable gods send to mortals, went on unreasoning and invincible, surviving the test of disillusion, defying the disenchantment that lurks in every day of a strenuous life; went on full of love's delight and love's anguish, facing them in open-eyed exultation; without bitterness and without repining, from the first hours to the last."
   4. "There was a completeness in it [the sailors' response] something like a principle, and masterful like an instinct—a disclosure of something secret—of that hidden some-

> thing, that gift of good or evil that makes racial differ-
> ence, that shapes the fate of nations."

Find other examples of this kind of sentence, and analyze them as
you did those in the previous group. Then try to place in one long
sentence an experience or reflection such as Conrad expressed in the
long sentences quoted above. Study and revise this sentence according to the directions given under A. *Suggestions:* the coming on of
the complete eclipse of the sun; the course of an illness; the growth
of our country; responsibilities of the time; the uses of adversity
(depression).

   C. Balanced sentences; parallel construction:

      1. "Wherever he stands, at the beginning or the end of
         things, a man has to sacrifice his gods to his passions or
         his passions to his gods."
      2. "It was our fate to pump in that ship—to pump out of
         her, to pump into her; and after keeping water out of
         her to save ourselves from being drowned, we frantically
         poured water into her to save ourselves from being
         burned."

Following the directions under A, find additional examples of
these two kinds of sentences, and write some original sentences
showing balanced or parallel construction. *Suggestions:* youth and
age; prohibition and temperance; two roads—two alternatives; two
types of authors or people.

   D. Cadence; harmony; rhythm:

      1. ". . . Truth, which like Beauty itself, floats elusive,
         obscure, half submerged, in the silent, still waters of
         mystery."
      2. "And I thought of men of old who, centuries ago, went
         that road in ships that sailed no better, to the land of
         palms, and spices, and yellow sands, and of brown nations
         ruled by kings more cruel than Nero the Roman, and
         more splendid than Solomon the Jew."
      3. "It is when we try to grapple with another's need that

> we perceive how incomprehensible, wavering, and misty
> are the beings that share with us the sight of the stars
> and the warmth of the sun."

The *vers-libre* (free-verse) movement was characterized, especially, by two devices: (1) The writers of this type of verse shook off the shackles of meter and rhyme; (2) they varied the length of lines, not in accordance with set rules, but at the will of the poet himself, in conformity with cadence, rhythm, and structural symmetry. Some of Conrad's sentences fit readily into the free-verse scheme. The following is an example:

> "Oh, the glamour of youth!
> Oh, the fire of it,
> more dazzling than the flames of the burning ship,
> throwing a magic light on the wide earth;
> leaping audaciously to the sky,
> presently to be quenched by time;
> more cruel, more pitiless, more bitter than the sea——
> and like the flames of the burning ship
> surrounded by an impenetrable night."

Compare the above with Carl Sandburg's "Fog," Edgar Lee Masters' "Anne Rutledge," or any other free-verse poem that you know. Divide some other passages of Conrad similarly. *Suggestions: Youth,* pp. 117, 118, 119, 122; *The Lagoon,* pp. 256, 261, 268.

FOR FURTHER STUDY OF CONRAD'S SHORT STORIES

Youth

1. Conrad originally published the story *Youth* with two other stories, *Heart of Darkness* and *The End of the Tether*—the three stories together forming, as he said, a trilogy of the three ages of man: youth, middle age, and old age. Each story is, however, complete in itself and independent of the others. Is it perhaps significant that he called the whole volume *Youth?*

2. In *Youth* he tells of buying in London a complete set of Byron's works, which he presumably read on the voyage. Could the theme of *Youth* be expressed in Byron's well-known line, "The days of our youth are the days of our glory"?

3. Conrad was interested in what people do in a crisis. To use the word he uses of Captain MacWhirr when confronted by a typhoon, a crisis is their "opportunity."—What did Captain Beard think most about when the *Judea* was in difficulty? What were his first words after the ship had blown up? Compare what Captain Beard says and does in this emergency with what Captain MacWhirr in *Typhoon* says and does in his crisis. How did the "crew of Liverpool hard cases" behave in the crisis? What is Conrad's explanation? Show young Marlow's—that is, young Conrad's—behavior and attitude throughout.

4. What does Conrad mean when he says that the incidents related in *Youth* might be taken to represent "the endeavor, the test, the trial of life,"—"a symbol of existence"? What other stories in literature are built up around situations that either disclose or make character? What experiences in our contemporary life might be considered as a sort of moral equivalent of the experiences related in *Youth*? Suggest situations that might be made into stories similar to *Youth*.

5. Why was the prolonged waiting for the ship to sail—i.e., unemployment—worse "morally," as Conrad says, than the hard work of pumping, etc.?

6. What gave the greatest thrill to Conrad,—"the sea itself," the East, the "old rattle-trap *Judea*," or "Youth alone"?

THE LAGOON

1. Conrad wrote thus about *The Lagoon* to a friend: "A Malay tells a story to a white man who is spending a night at his hut. It's a tricky thing with the usual forests, rivers, stars, wind, sunrise, and so on."—What are some of Conrad's "tricks"? Be specific. In the same letter, he uses the adjective *Conradese*. From what you know of Conrad, how should you define the adjective made up from his name? What specifically *Conradese* is there in *The Lagoon* in (a) subject matter; (b) style and manner?

2. What are the crises in Arsat's life? How does he behave in each? Is Arsat just a Malay or every man? What does Conrad seem to think of his qualities?

3. Contrast the manner and style of the two stories, *The Lagoon* and *The Secret Sharer*. Is *The Lagoon* Eastern, Malayan, in its imagery and tone? Is *The Secret Sharer*? Should it be?

The Secret Sharer

1. In bare statement, *The Secret Sharer* narrates the concealment, protection, and escape of a murderer.—Is the reader interested in the mere outcome, or in the amazing, profound situation? Is the escape the real triumph? What complication does the escape resolve? Do we sympathize with the murderer? Why? How does Conrad influence or determine the reader's attitude? (Hugh Walpole says: "*The Secret Sharer* is a most marvelous story . . . marvelous in the contrast between the confined limitations of its stage and the vast implications of its moral idea.")

2. What are the elements in the story that create suspense? Trace first the more obvious use of the steward for this purpose. Then show the more subtle fear inherent in the situation: that the honor of the ship is in jeopardy ("as if we would harbor a chap . . ."). Compare the situation in *The Secret Sharer* with that in "The Ship We Serve" (p. 79).

3. Conrad said of this story in a letter to a friend: "Every word fits, and there's not a single uncertain note. Luck, my boy! Pure Luck!"—What is meant by the expression, "Every word fits"? Was it all "luck"? In what ways is the setting vivid and appropriate? Do you think the calm increases the tenseness of the situation? Find examples of Conrad's use of the "right word." Test the details—the cigar, ladder, pretense of deafness, etc.—to see whether all are relevant. Draw a plan of the captain's cabin.

4. *The Secret Sharer* has been included in a collection of the twenty-five best stories in our language. What are some of the requirements of a supremely good short story in (a) setting; (b) plot; (c) character? Apply the requirements to *The Secret Sharer*.

Typhoon

1. From what you can gather from the story, describe the ship before and after the typhoon. Draw up a list of the crew.

2. Collect the evidence in the story on Captain MacWhirr's (a) appearance; (b) mentality; (c) character. Study his vocabulary, his sentences. What do you learn of his family? Trace the use that Conrad makes of the Siamese flag for disclosing MacWhirr's mind and temperament. Note MacWhirr's "you don't find everything in books" (p. 347) recurring as a sort of refrain in the story (pp. 390, 400, 408). What other devices does Conrad use to make the reader understand MacWhirr? What preparation is made for his action during the course of the typhoon? How does he act? What does he say?

3. Show how Jukes serves as a foil to MacWhirr. What comes out concerning both men in their conversation?

4. Study the letters of MacWhirr, Jukes, and Rout describing the incidents of the typhoon (pp. 400–408). In what way is each letter characteristic of the man who wrote it?

5. What is the fundamental characteristic of the coolies? What is their attitude towards the captain and the crew? Why? Why are "dollars" so essential a part in any incident in which they appear?

6. From the story and from what you can learn elsewhere, what are the principal characteristics of a typhoon? What was its course in the story? How long did it last?

7. It has been said that Conrad's description of the typhoon produces almost a "physical experience." Find those passages of description that seem to affect the reader most. How does Conrad produce his effects? How much comes indirectly from the description of the effects on the characters in the story?

8. How did the various characters act in the crisis? Who showed up most favorably?

SUGGESTIONS FOR FURTHER READING IN CONRAD

For additional autobiographical matter, one might read the remainder of *A Personal Record* and *The Mirror of the Sea,* which latter Conrad called "my book, the soul of my life." Much of both books is, of course, included in the first part of this volume. It is interesting to note, however, that Doctor Morf holds that a more "real Conrad" appears in the fiction than in the autobiographical pieces; that the exile, the outcast, the man without a country who is portrayed in one novel after another, is really a "repressed" Conrad, the Polish Conrad, who—it may be unconsciously—expresses thus his deepest self. However that may be, to know Conrad completely one must read his great works of fiction. The following suggested list of novels and stories is grouped in general according to their sureness of appeal and the ease with which they can be read. Not all his subject matter is equally interesting; and his art is sometimes rather subtle. Some guidance is really necessary if the uninitiated reader is not to be discouraged.

1. THE ROVER. An amazing, compact story, told in limpid, flawless style, of a retired buccaneer who in his last days becomes involved in a situation more surprising and dramatic than his adventures on the lawless Indian Ocean. The setting is the Giens peninsula near Toulon during Nelson's blockade and just before the battle of Trafalgar.

2. THE NIGGER OF THE "NARCISSUS." Based on the voyage of the sailing ship *Narcissus* from Bombay to Dunkirk, it is the portrayal of life in a merchant ship, the psychological study of one man's mind, the presentation of a human life in a microcosm. "It is the story," says Conrad, "by which, as a creative artist, I stand or fall." The storm scene is comparable to that in *Typhoon.* "You

will, I think, in the *Nigger* and in *Typhoon,* find my best effects in the description of moving water."

3. VICTORY. Put by Conrad, according to Richard Curle, "among his chief successes. It is interesting to remember that when he made his one public appearance in New York, it was from the last pages of *Victory* that he read aloud to his audience." Heyst, the hero, under the spell of the islands of the Malay Archipelago, is a profound mystery to all who encounter him: "enchanted Heyst," a "puffect g'n'lman but a ut-uto-utopist," "queer chap, that Swede" are some of their characterizations. Lena, the heroine, who makes the supreme sacrifice, supplies the title to the story (see page 236); hers, Conrad remarks, was a "tremendous victory, capturing the very sting of death in the service of love."

4. ALMAYER'S FOLLY. Something of the genesis of this novel is given on pages 211–220. It is Conrad's first work, and some consider it also his greatest. The only book, Conrad said, that he had "done light-heartedly—I was so surprised to find that I could do it." It is the story of the ambitions and disappointments of a Dutch trader far up a river in Borneo—of great trading schemes, subtle Malay intrigues, and the elopement of his beautiful half-caste daughter. The opinion of Mr. Jacques of the *Torrens,* its first reader, was that it is all "perfectly" clear.

5. AN OUTCAST OF THE ISLANDS. The answer to Edward Garnett's "Why not write another?" Although it was written after *Almayer's Folly* and in a way is a sequel, it covers an earlier period of time. Here appear Almayer again, but a younger and less disappointed man; Aïssa, the girl who assassinates Willems, the confidential clerk of Hudig and Co.; the one-eyed Babalatchi; and many other natives and Eurasians whom Conrad had seen during those years he spent in the Malay Archipelago. It is not so unmistakably a masterpiece as its predecessor.

6. *Shorter Stories*

THE BRUTE, from *A Set of Six.* The tale of the mad career of a perverse ship that seemed from the moment of launching to its sudden end to have a malicious spirit of destruction.

FREYA OF THE SEVEN ISLES, from *'Twixt Land and Sea.* Of this story Conrad said in a letter to a friend: "As to faking a

TABLE OF REFERENCES

Books Used in the Table

Conrad, Jessie: *Joseph Conrad as I Knew Him*. Doubleday, Doran & Company, Inc., 1927.

Conrad, Joseph:[1] *Almayer's Folly*, 1928; *Chance*, 1913; *Last Essays*, 1926; *Lord Jim*, 1899; *The Mirror of the Sea*, 1906; *The Nigger of the "Narcissus,"* 1897; *Nostromo*, 1904; *Notes on Life and Letters*, 1921; *An Outcast of the Islands*, 1896; *A Personal Record*, 1912; *The Shadow Line*, 1916; *Tales of Hearsay*, 1925; *Tales of Unrest*, 1898; *'Twixt Land and Sea*, 1912; *Typhoon*, 1902; *Victory*, 1915; *Youth*, 1903; *Within the Tides*, 1916.

Cross, Wilbur L.: *Your Contemporary Novelists*. The Macmillan Company, 1930.[2]

Curle, Richard: *The Last Twelve Years of Joseph Conrad*. Doubleday, Doran & Company, Inc., 1928.

Jean-Aubry, G.: *Joseph Conrad, Life and Letters*. Two Volumes. Doubleday, Doran & Company, Inc., 1927.

Keating, George B.: *A Conrad Memorial Library*. Doubleday, Doran & Company, Inc., 1929.

Mégroz, R. L.: *Joseph Conrad's Mind and Method*. Faber and Faber, 1931.[3]

Morf, Gustav: *The Polish Heritage of Joseph Conrad*. Ray Long and Richard R. Smith, Inc., 1930.[4]

Symons, Arthur: *Notes on Joseph Conrad, with Some Unpublished Letters*. Myers and Company, 1925.

---

[1] All references are to pages in the Uniform Edition of the Works of Joseph Conrad (J. M. Dent and Sons, Ltd., London) and the Concord Edition of the Works of Joseph Conrad (Doubleday, Doran & Company, Inc., New York).

[2] The passage on page 87 is reprinted by permission of The Macmillan Company, Publishers.

[3] The passages on pages 208, 209, and 228 are reprinted by permission of Faber and Faber, London.

[4] The passage on page 3 is reprinted by permission of Ray Long and Richard Smith, Publishers.

PAGE	REFERENCE
3 My full name ...	Jean-Aubry I, 290 (Letter to Edward Garnett, 1900)
3 Racially I belong ...	Jean-Aubry II, 289 (letter to George T. Keating, 1922)
3 My maternal uncle ...	Morf, 2 (letter quoted from *New Republic*, August 4, 19198)
4. My father Apollonius ...	Jean-Aubry I, 291–292 (Letter to Edward Garnett, 1900)
4 One of the most ...	*A Personal Record*, ix–xii
6 Since the age of five ...	*A Personal Record*, 70–73
8 Into this coldly ...	*Notes on Life and Letters*, 166–169
10 I remember my mother ...	*A Personal Record*, xii
11 I remember in my early years ...	*A Personal Record*, 23–24
12 I remember well the day...	*A Personal Record*, 64–65
13 Meeting with calm fortitude ...	*A Personal Record*, 29
13 EATING A DOG—PRO PATRIA.	*A Personal Record*, 32–35
16 PRINCE ROMAN'S VISIT	*Tales of Hearsay*, 31–36
20 MILITANT GEOGRAPHY	*Last Essays*, 11–13; 15–17
24 SUMMARY OF EDUCATION	Jean-Aubry II, 289 (Letter to George T. Keating, 1922)
25 It was the year ...	*A Personal Record*, 41–42
26 I don't mean to say ...	*A Personal Record*, 120–121
26 People wondered what ...	*A Personal Record*, 42–43
28 We sat down by ...	*A Personal Record*, 40–41
29 I tell you ...	*A Personal Record*, 41
29 The enthusiastic old ...	*A Personal Record*, 43–44
31 What I had in view ...	*A Personal Record*, 121–122
31 FIRST EXPERIENCES ON SALT WATER	*A Personal Record*, 123–124; 126–127; 130
34 THE "TREMOLINO"	*The Mirror of the Sea*, 155–183
61 SIGNING ON	*Notes on Life and Letters*, 155–156; 150–153
64 INITIATION	*The Miror of the Sea*, 137–148

PAGE   REFERENCE
 74 MERETRICIOUS GLORY   *The Mirror of the Sea*, 33–35
 77 A DEAF MAN VS. AN
      ANGRY ONE   *The Mirror of the Sea*, 38–41
 79 THE SHIP WE SERVE   *Notes on Life and Letters*, 185–
                                   189
 83 A SHIP IS NOT A SLAVE   *The Mirror of the Sea*, 52–56
 87 YOUTH   *Youth*, 3–42
124 THE ERA OF EXAMINA-
      TIONS   *A Personal Record*, 110–120
133 FIRST COMMAND   *The Shadow Line*, 3–6; 27–33;
                                   36–41; 43–57; 62; 65–75; 77–
                                   90; 93–95; 98–101; 121; 125;
                                   126; 127; 129–132
183 TORRES STRAIT   *Last Essays*, 18–21
187 THE CONGO   *Youth*, 92–94; 95–98; 101–105;
                                   107–113; 119–120; 145–146
201 THE "TORRENS"   *Last Essays*, 22–28
207 There are ships . . .   *A Personal Record*, 135–136
208 The North Sea had been. . . *Notes on Life and Letters*, 155
208 After hearing it spoken. . . Mégroz, 32–33 (authorized inter-
                                   view)
209 St. Anne's . . .   Mégroz, 28–29
209 The fact of my . . .   *A Personal Record*, v; vii
210 When I wrote . . .   Jean-Aubry II, 206 (Letter to
                                   Hugh Walpole, 1918)
211 THE MAN ALMAYER   *A Personal Record*, 74–76; 85–
                                   89
216 *Almayer's Folly* was never *A Personal Record*, 68–69
217 THE FIRST READER OF
      ALMAYER'S FOLLY   *A Personal Record*, 15–19
220 WHY NOT WRITE AN-
      OTHER?   *An Outcast of the Islands*, vi–viii
222 HENCEFORTH TO BE A
      WRITER   *The Nigger of the "Narcissus*,"
                                   ix–x
223 THE ARTIST'S CREED   *The Nigger of the "Narcissus*,"
                                   xi–xvi

PAGE		REFERENCE
228	Give me the right word...	*A Personal Record*, xvi
228	I am always worrying ...	Mégroz, 40
228	My Jim ...	*Lord Jim*, ix
229	The end of ...	Jean-Aubry I, 295 (Letter to John Galsworthy, 1900)
229	In 1875 or ...	*Nostromo*, vii–x
230	THE WRITER CAUGHT IN THE EXERCISE OF HIS CRAFT	*A Personal Record*, 97–102
236	THE ORIGIN OF A HEROINE	*Victory*, xv–xvii
238	A Note on *Victory*	Jessie Conrad, 143–144
239	I proceed to admit ...	*A Personal Record*, 108–109
240	Perhaps you won't find ...	Jean-Aubry II, 185 (Letter to Sir Sidney Colvin, 1917)
240	A reviewer observed ...	*Within the Tides*, vii–viii
242	You know yourself ...	Curle, 37
242	*Youth* has been called ...	Jean-Aubry II, 342 (Letter to Henry S. Canby, 1924)
242	As a matter of fact ...	*Last Essays*, 142–143
243	As for the writing ...	Symons, 16
243	I would not like ...	*A Personal Record*, xvii
243	I am content ...	*Almayer's Folly*, x
243	There are those ...	*Tales of Unrest*, 26
243	I think that ...	*A Personal Record*, xx
244	As in political ...	*A Personal Record*, xix–xx
244	I do not mean ...	*Chance*, xi–xii
244	The ethical view ...	*A Personal Record*, 92
244	Of him from whom ...	*Notes on Life and Letters*, 9–10
255	THE LAGOON	*Tales of Unrest*
271	THE SECRET SHARER	*'Twixt Land and Sea*
320	TYPHOON	*Typhoon*

GLOSSARY

OF FOREIGN WORDS AND PHRASES, AND NAUTICAL TERMS

A. B., able seaman.

able seaman, able-bodied seaman, a sailor who is practically conversant with, and able to perform, all the duties of a sailor, and who has a special rating and higher pay than the ordinary sailor.

à la Jean Jacques Rousseau, *Fr.,* in the manner of Jean Jacques Rousseau.

Américain, Catholique, et gentilhomme, Fr., American, Catholic, and gentleman.

anchor-watch, a small watch composed of one or two men appointed to look after the ship while at anchor or in port.

aneroid glass, a portable barometer, containing no liquid, which shows the atmospheric pressure less accurately than the mercurial barometer.

balancelle, a large coast boat with a single mast; used on the Mediterranean. This word is used interchangeably with *felucca* by some authorities; others make a distinction.

barocco, It., baroque.

barometer, an instrument for indicating the atmospheric pressure; used for forecasting the weather.

batten, a strip of light wood.

battened, fastened down with battens or wooden strips over tarpaulin.

beam, (1) the transverse pieces of timber or iron which support the deck and hold the ship's sides together; (2) the widest part of the ship's hull.

belaying pin, a strong pin around which ropes are wound to make them fast.

béret, Fr., a round soft cap.

bilge, the flat or nearly flat part of the ship's bottom.

binnacle, a case, box, or stand containing a ship's compass.

binnacle light, a lamp to illuminate the compass at night.

block, a mechanical contrivance fitted with grooved pulleys for raising heavy weights.

boat hook, an iron hook, fixed to a long pole, to pull or push into place a boat, raft, log, etc.

boatswain, a superior seaman in charge of operations in forward part of ship.

bolt-ropes, a superior kind of hemp cordage sewed on the edges of sails to strengthen them.

bonnes fortunes, Fr., amorous adventures.

bos'n, Corruption of boatswain, representing its common pronunciation.

bouillabaisse, Fr., Provençal fish-soup with garlic.

bowman, the man who rows the foremost oar in a boat.

bowsprit, a spar projecting forward

from the stem of a ship, to which forestays are fastened.

brace, a rope through a block at the end of a yard, by which the yard is swung and trimmed horizontally.

breach, the breaking of waves.

bridge, a raised platform extending from side to side of a ship above the rail, for the use and convenience of the officer in charge.

brig, a two-masted, square-rigged vessel.

bulkhead, any upright partition separating the various compartments of a ship.

bulwark, ship's side above the deck.

bunker, a large bin for holding coal.

burnous, Fr., burnoose—an Arabian cloak with a hood.

caban, *Fr.,* hooded outer garment.

calk, to fill the seams of a ship with oakum (the untwisted shreds of old rope), and then to seal them with melted pitch.

campo, It., countryside.

canaille, Fr., canallia, It., a term of opprobrium: Dog!

cargo, the lading of a ship or other vessel.

cast anchor, "Your journalist 'casts' his anchor. Now, an anchor is never cast. . . . It is let go. . . . The anchor ready for its work is already overboard, and is not thrown over, but simply allowed to fall."—Conrad.

cathead, a projecting piece of timber or iron near the bow of a vessel, to which the anchor is hoisted and secured.

ce métier de chien, Fr., this dog's life.

charogne, Fr., a term of opprobrium: carrion.

charter party, a written agreement by which a ship-owner lets a vessel to another person.

chart-room, room where maps and instruments are kept.

château, castle.

chevalier de la Légion d'Honneur, Fr., knight of the Legion of Honor.

Chi va piano va sano, It., who goes slowly goes safely; slow but sure.

chocks, blocks of wood, especially in wedge shape, for stopping the motion of any rolling object.

chronometer-box, a box containing a very accurate clock swung in gimbals.

cleat, a bar of wood or iron with protruding horns around which ropes are wound.

clipper, a sailing vessel with a sharp bow, built and rigged for fast sailing.

coal-lighter, an open barge used for loading and unloading coal from large ships.

coal-trimmer, one employed to stow and shift coal on a vessel.

coamings, raised pieces of wood or iron around a hatchway to prevent water from running below.

companion, a skylight to admit light to a cabin or lower deck.

compass-card, the circular card to which the needles of the compass are attached, and which pivots on a cone at its center.

Conway **boy,** a seaman trained in the cadet ship *Conway,* moored in the Mersey, Liverpool, where boys are prepared for the merchant marine.

counter, that portion of a vessel's stern from the water-line to its extreme outward swell, knuckle, or overhang.

cross swell, waves running in different directions, owing to a sudden change of wind, or to the crossing of winds and currents.

cuddy, the galley or pantry of a small vessel.

davits, curved arms extending over the ship's side, having tackle to carry, hoist, or lower boats.

de cape et d'épée, Fr., swashbuckling.

deep ship, a ship lying low in the water; one having a deep draught.

dégagé, Fr., free and easy.

departure, ". . . the last professional sight of land. . . . It is the technical as distinguished from the sentimental 'good-bye.' —It is not the ship's going away from her port."—Conrad.

derelict, an abandoned ship.

de visu Lat., visual.

dinghy, a small rowboat used for general service between ship and land.

donkey-man, one employed to run the donkey-engine, which is used to pump water into the boilers or from the hold.

draught, the depth a ship sinks into water, especially when laden.

dungaree trousers, a working garment made of a coarse kind of East Indian cotton stuff.

even keel, in a horizontal position with central line of the vessel level.

fathom, unit of measure containing six feet. Used chiefly for measuring rope and depth of water.

feather, to turn (the oar) horizontally on the backward stroke to cut the resistance of the wind.

felucca, a three-masted vessel, with provisions for rowing in an emergency. See **balancelle.**

fetch away, to get loose.

Flying Dutchman, a legendary Dutch captain who for some heinous offense was condemned to sail the sea, beating against head winds, till the Day of Judgment; used also as the name of his ship.

foc'sle, contraction of forecastle, the forward part of the ship where the sailors live.

forebits, posts of wood or iron to which cables or ropes are made fast.

fore-deck, the forward end of the upper deck of a vessel.

forepeak scuttle, an opening in the deck, leading down into the forepeak, or the space formed by the angle of the bow.

fore-rigging, the chains and ropes used to support and raise the foreyards.

foreyard, the lower yard on the foremast of a square-rigged vessel.

funnel, smokestack on a steamship.

gabelou, Fr., an opprobrious term for a government ship.

galley, the kitchen of a vessel.

gangway, a portable platform extending from the ship's side to the dock.

gaskets, narrow strips of canvas or small ropes used to bind the furled sail to the yard or mast.

gear, ropes, blocks, etc.

gimbals, a contrivance moving on pivots in which a lamp, compass, or barometer may swing freely to maintain its equilibrium regardless of the tilting of the ship.

gins, machines for raising or moving heavy weights.

glass, barometer.

gouvernante, Fr., housekeeper or nurse.

grande dame, *Fr.,* great lady; bluestocking.

gripes, lashings to hold the boats in their places either on the decks or on the davits of a ship.

guardacosta, *It.,* coast guard.

gunwales, the upper edge of the ship's side.

half-decked pilot-boat, a partly decked and partly open boat in which pilots cruise off shore to meet incoming vessels.

harbor-master, an officer charged with the duty of enforcing harbor regulations, especially as to berthing and mooring.

Hard alee! a command to put the tiller as far as possible to leeward; i. e., away from the wind.

hatches, a temporary covering of planks over any opening in the deck of a ship.

hatchway, an opening, usually square or oblong, in the deck of a ship.

head-rails, the rail around the bow of a ship.

helmsman, the man who steers the vessel.

Histoire des Treize, *Fr., Story of the Thirteen,* one of Balzac's most romantic works.

hooker, a sailor's contemptuous term for any antiquated or clumsy craft.

hulk, a heavy or clumsy ship.

hull, the body of a vessel exclusive of masts, sails, and rigging.

Il faut, cependant, faire attention à ne pas gâter sa vie. Fr. One must, however, take care not to spoil one's life.

Il faut la tuer. Fr. She must be killed.

Il y a toujours la manière. Fr. There are ways and ways of doing things.

jetty, a pier of wood or stone to serve either as a landing or as a breakwater to protect the harbor.

Je vous donne ma parole d'honneur. Fr. I give you my word of honor.

jib boom, a spar or boom which serves as an extension of the bowsprit, the spar projecting from the stem of the ship.

jury rig, temporary or makeshift arrangement for sailing a ship.

jury rudder, a temporary rudder rigged on a ship in case of an accident.

kedge, to change the position of a ship by winding in the hawser attached to a small anchor—i. e., the kedge anchor—at some distance.

kedge anchor, a small anchor.

keel, a timber running stem to stern along the bottom of a vessel.

keelson, a line of joined timbers lying along the keel, binding the floor timbers to the keel.

knightheads, timbers rising from the bow of a ship, to which are secured the end of the bowsprit.

knot, the unit by which the speed of a vessel is given; a nautical mile (6,080 ft.).

la belle Madame Delestang, Fr., the beautiful Madame Delestang.

lagoon, a shallow sound or lake connecting with the sea.

landfall, "A *landfall* is made and done with at the first cry of 'Land ho!'. . . . It is not a synonym of arrival."—Conrad.

landlubber, a term applied contemptuously by sailors to those who are clumsy and ignorant on shipboard.

lateen sail, a triangular sail used in the Mediterranean and adjacent waters.

launch, an open power-boat used for transporting passengers for short distances.

la vache enragée, Fr., "the mad cow"—to eat which is the idiom for suffering extreme privation.

lazarette, a space between decks, usually near the stem, used as a storeroom.

lee rail, the rail on that side of the ship away from the wind.

lee shore, a shore on the lee side of the vessel, i. e., opposite to that against which the wind blows, or farthest from the point from which the wind blows; a source of danger in stormy weather.

le jeune homme, Fr., the young man.

lepero, It., lowest sort of man.

le petit ami de Baptistin, Fr., the little friend of Baptistin.

lift, a rope leading from the masthead to the extremity of a yard below,—used for raising, supporting, or squaring the yard.

list, a careening or leaning of a ship to one side.

log book, a book in which is entered the daily progress of a ship at sea; a sea journal or diary—usually called simply log.

lookout man, a sailor who keeps watch at the post of external observation, as on a ship's mast.

loom, that part of an oar which is inboard from the rowlock.

luff up, to bring the head of a vessel up into the wind.

main brace, the rope attached to the lower yard on the mainmast.

main hatch, the principal opening of a vessel; usually the one just forward of the mainmast.

Mais en vérité c'est les valeurs idéales des faits et gestes humains qui se sont imposés à mon activité artistique. Fr. What I have been concerned with as an artist has been the ideal values of human conduct.

Mais il est parfait, cet homme. Fr. But he is perfect, that man.

maquis, rank growth of underbrush.

maroon, to put ashore and leave on a desolate island or coast.

master mariner, the master, or captain, of a merchant vessel, certified to be competent to command.

master, the commander of a merchant vessel; colloquially called captain.

mate, an officer in a merchant vessel ranking next below the captain. If there are more than one they are called respectively, first or chief mate, second mate, etc.

merci, monsieur. Fr. Thank you, sir.

mess, to eat with others.

mizzen, the mast nearest the stern on a vessel.

mizzen-shrouds, ropes leading from the mizzen to give lateral support to the masts.

mooring hawser, a large rope for securing a ship at a dock, etc.

N'oublie pas ton français, mon chéri. Fr. Don't forget your French, my dear.

off-shore tack, a course of the vessel in the direction from the shore, when close-hauled—i. e., going to windward.

ormolu frame, a frame made of ground bronze or brass, gilded, to imitate gold.

padrone, It., skipper.

painter, a rope, usually at the bow for fastening a boat.

par la Madonne, Fr., by our Lady.

patron, Fr., skipper.

petty officers, on vessels corresponding in rank roughly to non-commissioned officers in the army.

Place de la Comédie, Fr., a public square in Paris.

pole-mast, a mast composed of a single piece.

poop, a deck above the ordinary deck in the rear part of a ship.

por el Rey, Sp., in the name of the king.

port, (1) an opening in a ship's side for any purpose, as to admit light and air; (2) that side of a vessel on the left hand of a person who stands on board facing the bow (formerly larboard)—opposed to starboard; (3) a harbor.

pour prendre congé, Fr., to bid good-bye.

Prenez la barre, monsieur. Fr. Take hold of the tiller, sir.

pro patria, Lat., for country.

punt, a long, narrow, flat-bottomed boat, usual'y propelled with a pole.

qua, Lat., as.

quarter-deck, that part of the spar, or upper, deck abaft the main-mast, reserved for officers, etc.

ratlines, series of small ropes forming a ladder up the shrouds, the ropes attached to the sides of the ship to support the masts.

ready about, order to a crew to prepare for tacking.

reefed, reduced (the sail) in size by rolling or folding in a certain portion.

Rey netto, Sp., genuine or real king.

riding-light, a white light visible from all directions, shown by a vessel at anchor.

ringbolt, a metal bolt with an eye to which is fitted a ring.

roadstead, a place, less protected than a harbor, where ships may ride at anchor.

rope-becket, a short piece of rope, with a knot at one end and an eye at the other.

royal, a small sail on the royal mast above the top-gallant sail. Usually the highest sail, though at times topped by a light skysail.

rudder-casing, a casing of wood in which the shaft of the rudder pivots.

rudder-chains, strong chains attached to each side of the rudder by which the ship can be steered if something goes wrong with the rudder-head.

rudder-head, the upper end of the rudder shaft to which the tiller, or steering handle, is attached.

run, the hollow curve of the ship near the rudder.

saloon, one of the main cabins of a vessel.

salvage, property saved at sea by other than the owner.

sampan, a skiff, used on the coasts of China, Japan, and neighboring islands.

sarong, the chief article of dress worn by both sexes in the Malay Archipelago.

scuppers, openings cut through the side of the ship above the deck to allow the water to run off the deck.

scuttle, to make a hole in the side of the ship, especially for purpose of sinking.

sea-chest, large box of wood or other material with a lid, in which a sailor keeps personal belongings.

sextant, an instrument for observing altitudes so as to ascertain latitude.

Shift the helm! the order to put the helm from starboard to port, or the reverse.

shore-fast, a rope or chain by which a vessel is moored to a wharf or pier.

signorino, It., young gentleman, young sir; diminutive of *signore.*

skipper, colloquial term for the master of a vessel.

slice, a long iron bar for removing clinkers from a furnace grate.

slush-slinger, water-slinger—a derisive term for sailor.

sounding-rod, a graduated piece of iron used to tell the depth of water in a ship's pump-well, and consequently in the hold.

sou'-wester, contraction of southwester. A waterproof hat made broad behind to protect the neck from water.

spanker, a fore-and-aft sail set on the after side of the mizzen of a ship.

spanker boom, a long pole or spar used to extend the foot or bottom of the spanker.

spar, any mast, yard, boom, gaff, or the like.

square the yards, to lay the yards at right angles with the keel and mast.

square-rigged, having the principal sails extend on yards suspended

horizontally at the middle, and always setting almost equally on each side of the keel.

stanchion, an upright support on a deck used as a support for an awning, etc.

stand by, to be, or get, ready.

starboard, that side of the vessel on the right hand of a person who stands on board facing the bow—opposed to port (formerly larboard).

steam pinnace, a light vessel used as a tender for a larger ship.

stern sheets, the space in an open boat abaft not occupied by the seats.

stick, mast.

stokehold, the space in front of the boilers of a ship from which the furnaces are fed; called also fire-room.

stream cable, a light hawser or chain used on a small anchor when the ship is riding in sheltered water.

stunsail, contraction of studding sail, a light sail set at the side of a principal square sail of a vessel in free winds to increase her speed.

sumpitan, a blow-gun used by the Malays.

tack, to bring the ship's head around, so that the wind catches the sails from the other side.

taffrail, the upper part of a ship's stern, which is sometimes flat and ornamented with carved work.

tartane, tartan—a coasting vessel with one mast used in the Mediterranean.

thwart, a seat across a boat on which the oarsman sits.

tiffin, a luncheon, especially at midday,

tiller, a lever of wood or metal

fitted to the rudder head and used for turning the rudder from side to side.

top-gallant, the mast or sail above the topmast and below the royal mast.

traditore, It., traitor.

trepang, a sea-slug, or worm, from six to twenty-four inches in length, inhabiting Far-Eastern waters.

trident, a three-pronged spear, Neptune's symbol of authority.

trim, an adjustment of the cargo so that the ship rides evenly in the water.

truck, a small wooden cap at the summit of a masthead having holes in it to hold flag or signal ropes.

trysail, a fore-and-aft sail connected to a lower mast and used chiefly as a storm sail.

'tween-decks, colloquial for between-decks, the space between any two decks of the ship.

typhoon, a violent cyclonic storm occurring in the North Pacific, and corresponding to the West Indian hurricanes.

union jack, the upper inner corner of a nation's flag used as its national emblem.

virtuti militari, Lat., for military valor.

vieux amis, Fr., old friends.

Vieux Port, Fr., Old Harbor as distinguished from New Harbor.

Vous êtes bête, mon cher. Voyons! Ça n'a aucune conséquence. Fr. You are foolish, my dear. Come, that's of no consequence.

water-butt, a large open-headed cask used as a reservoir for water.

weather-cloth, a tarpaulin, or water-proofed canvas, rigged up as a shelter for officers and the men on watch.

wheel, on a sailing vessel, a large wheel with handles controlling the rudder by ropes attached to the tiller.

wheelhouse, a small house on or above deck, containing the steering wheel.

whipping, hoisting.

winch, a machine having a barrel or drum on which to coil a rope, etc., more or less like a windlass.

windlass, a cylindrical drum around which rope or chain is wound, shortening the length of rope when turned—used for raising heavy weights or to draw the ship to dock.

windward, in the direction from which the wind blows.

yard, a long cylindrical spar having a rounded taper toward each end, slung crosswise to a mast.

KEY TO THE MAP

1. ROMANCE: Cuba and Jamaica.
2. NOSTROMO.
3. Course of the *Brute*.
4. Course of the *Narcissus* from Bombay to Dunkirk.
5. HEART OF DARKNESS voyage ("The Congo").
6. THE SECRET AGENT and CHANCE, laid partly in London.
7. THE ROVER: southern France and Peninsula of Giens. THE "TREMOLINO" and THE ARROW OF GOLD: Marseilles and the Mediterranean.
8. UNDER WESTERN EYES: in Petrograd, then in Geneva.
9. LORD JIM: scene of shipwreck.
10. Course taken by the *Judea* in YOUTH. The *Torrens* took a similar course from Plymouth to Adelaide, Australia, calling on return voyage at Cape Town.
11. END OF THE TETHER.
12. FALK, THE SECRET SHARER, THE SHADOW LINE: the Gulf of Siam.
13. THE LAGOON, FREYA OF THE SEVEN ISLES.
14. ALMAYER'S FOLLY and AN OUTCAST OF THE ISLANDS: Bulungan (called Sambir in the story). THE RESCUE: southern coast of Borneo and Carimata Island.
15. VICTORY: island setting off south coast of Celebes.
16. TYPHOON: the storm encountered by the *Nan-Shan* en route from Formosa to Fu-Chau.
17. KARAIN: laid partly in Mindanao.
18. Torres Strait, between northern Australia and New Guinea.

GREENLAND

ICE

BRITISH
ISLES

Azores

Canary Is.

Cape
Verde Is.

MEXICO

Gulf of Mexico

CUBA

WEST
INDIES

CENTRAL
AMERICA

Jamaica

①

Pacific

Bogota

Quito

②

SOUTH
AMERICA

Atlant

③

St. Hele

Oce

N.

W.   E.

S.

③

Falkland Is.

Cape Horn

Ocean